THE CAMBRIDGE COMPANION TO LITERATURE AND PSYCHOANALYSIS

The Cambridge Companion to Literature and Psychoanalysis explains the link between literature and psychoanalysis for students, critics, and teachers. It offers a twenty-first-century resource for defining and analyzing the psychoanalytic dimensions of human creativity in contemporary society. Essays provide critical perspectives on selected canonical authors, such as William Shakespeare, Jane Austen, Virginia Woolf, Toni Morrison, and James Baldwin. It also offers analysis of contemporary literature of social, sexual, and political turmoil, as well as of newer forms such as film, graphic narrative, and autofiction. Divided into four sections, each offering the reader different subject areas to explore, this volume shows how psychoanalytic approaches to literature can provide valuable methods of interpretation. It will be a key resource for students, teachers, and researchers in the field of literature and psychoanalysis as well as literary theory.

Vera J. Camden is Professor of English at Kent State University and Clinical Assistant Professor of Psychiatry at Case Western Reserve University. She is also Training and Supervising Analyst at the Cleveland Psychoanalytic Center and Geographic Rule Supervising Analyst for the Institute for Psychoanalytic Education of the NYU Medical School. She is Associate Editor of *American Imago* and American Editor of the *Journal of Graphic Novels and Comics*.

D0782125

THE CAMBRIDGE COMPANION
TO
LITERATURE AND PSYCHOANALYSIS

EDITED BY
VERA J. CAMDEN
Kent State University

CAMBRIDGE
UNIVERSITY PRESS

CAMBRIDGE
UNIVERSITY PRESS

University Printing House, Cambridge CB2 8BS, United Kingdom

One Liberty Plaza, 20th Floor, New York, NY 10006, USA

477 Williamstown Road, Port Melbourne, VIC 3207, Australia

314–321, 3rd Floor, Plot 3, Splendor Forum, Jasola District Centre,
New Delhi – 110025, India

103 Penang Road, #05–06/06, Visioncrest Commercial, Singapore 238467

Cambridge University Press is part of the University of Cambridge.

It furthers the University's mission by disseminating knowledge in the pursuit of
education, learning, and research at the highest international levels of excellence.

www.cambridge.org
Information on this title: www.cambridge.org/9781108477482
DOI: 10.1017/9781108763691

© Cambridge University Press 2022

First published 2022

A catalogue record for this publication is available from the British Library.

ISBN 978-1-108-47748-2 Hardback
ISBN 978-1-108-73288-8 Paperback

CONTENTS

CONTENTS

FIGURES

ABBREVIATIONS

SE Sigmund Freud, *The Standard Edition of the Complete Psychological Works of Sigmund Freud*, ed. and trans. James Strachey, 24 vols. (London: Hogarth Press, 1953–1974).

CONTRIBUTORS

CATHERINE BATES is Research Professor at the Centre for the Study of the Renaissance at the University of Warwick. She is author of *The Rhetoric of Courtship in Elizabethan Language and Literature* (Cambridge, 1992); *Play in a Godless World: The Theory and Practice of Play in Shakespeare, Nietzsche, and Freud* (London, 1999); *Masculinity, Gender and Identity in the English Renaissance Lyric* (Cambridge, 2007); *Masculinity and the Hunt: Wyatt to Spenser* (Oxford, 2013), winner of the British Academy Rose Mary Crawshay Prize 2015; and *On Not Defending Poetry: Defence and Indefensibility in Sidney's Defence of Poesy* (Oxford, 2017), winner of the *Studies in English Literature, 1500–1900* Elizabeth Dietz award 2019. She is also editor of *The Cambridge Companion to the Epic* (Cambridge, 2010); *The Blackwell Companion to Renaissance Poetry* (Chichester, 2018); is currently editing *The Oxford Handbook of Philip Sidney*; and, with Patrick Cheney, co-editing *Sixteenth-Century British Poetry*, volume 4 of the *Oxford History of Poetry in English*.

JOSIE BILLINGTON is Professor in English Literature at the University of Liverpool, UK. She has published widely, as editor and critic, on Victorian fiction and poetry (Charlotte Brontë, Elizabeth Barrett Browning, George Eliot, Elizabeth Gaskell, Margaret Oliphant, Leo Tolstoy). She has led interdisciplinary studies on the value of literary reading in relation to depression, dementia, chronic pain, prisoner and community health and has published extensively on the power of literary reading to influence mental health and wellbeing (*Is Literature Healthy?*, Oxford University Press, 2016; *Reading and Mental Health*, Palgrave, 2019). She is a member of the UK Arts and Humanities Research Council (AHRC) Peer Review College, a UK Higher Education Academy National Teaching Fellow, and Vice President of the International Society for the Empirical Study of Literature (IGEL).

BEATRIZ L. BOTERO holds a PhD in psychology from Universidad Autónoma de Madrid, Spain. She also holds a PhD in Spanish literature from the University of Wisconsin-Madison, where she also teaches. She is the author of *Identidad imaginada: novelística colombiana del siglo XXI* (Pliegos Editores, 2020) and editor of *Women in Contemporary Latin American Novels: Psychoanalysis and Gendered Violence* (Palgrave Macmillan, 2018).

VERA J. CAMDEN is Professor of English at Kent State University and Clinical Assistant Professor of Psychiatry at Case Western Reserve University. She is Training and Supervising Analyst at the Cleveland Psychoanalytic Center and Geographic Rule Supervising Analyst for the Institute for Psychoanalytic Education of the New York University Medical School. She is co-editor of *American Imago* and American editor for *the Journal of Graphic Novels and Comics*. She specializes in seventeenth-century British literature, psychoanalysis, and comics.

KATHERINE DALSIMER is on the faculty of the Columbia University Center for Psychoanalytic Training and Research and is Clinical Professor of Psychology in the Department of Psychiatry, Weill Medical College, Cornell University. She is the author of *Female Adolescence: Psychoanalytic Reflections on Literature* and *Virginia Woolf: Becoming a Writer*, both published by Yale University Press.

CARLA FRECCERO is Distinguished Professor of Literature and History of Consciousness, and Affiliated Faculty in Feminist Studies at UCSC, where she has taught since 1991. Her books include *Father Figures* (Cornell,1991); *Popular Culture* (NYU, 1999); and *Queer/Early/Modern* (Duke, 2006). She co-edited *Premodern Sexualities* (Routledge, 1996); *Species/Race/Sex*, a special issue of *American Quarterly* 65.3 (2013); and *Animots*, a special issue of *Yale French Studies* 127 (2015). Her current book project, on nonhuman animals and figuration, is *Animate Figures*. In 2010 she won the Critical Animal Studies Faculty Paper of the Year. Her fields include early modern European literature and history; critical theory; feminist and queer theories; popular culture and cultural studies; psychoanalysis; and animal studies.

MARGARET ANN FITZPATRICK HANLY, PhD, is a Training and Supervising psychoanalyst, in the Canadian Institute of Psychoanalysis, in private practice in Toronto, Canada. She is a past-director of the Toronto Institute of Psychoanalysis; Chair, International Psychoanalytic Association Committee on Clinical Observation; Treasurer, Executive Editorial Board, *Psychoanalytic Quarterly*; and member of the editorial boards of the *International Journal of Psychoanalysis* and the *Canadian Journal of Psychoanalysis*.

VICKY LEBEAU is Professor of English at the University of Sussex. She has published widely in the field of psychoanalysis and culture and is a Scholar of the British Psychoanalytic Council.

ZEHRA MEHDI is a doctoral candidate in the Department of Religion, Columbia University. Her doctoral thesis studies Muslim responses to Hindu nationalism by examining the psychoanalytic role of religion in working through trauma and forging resistance against state persecution. Her research interests are political psychology, , religious minorities and nationalism, trauma and violence, gender theory, psychoanalytic anthropology, and Partition literature. She is a practicing psychoanalytic psychotherapist from India. She is currently co-editing an edited volume, *Remembering, Repeating and Working Through Selfhood: Essays by Katherine P. Ewing*, Columbia University Press (2023).

LISA RUDDICK is an Associate Professor Emerita in the Department of English at the University of Chicago. She is the author of *Reading Gertrude Stein: Body, Text, Gnosis* (Cornell, 1990), and of recent pieces describing the ways in which professionalization in the academic humanities can cut individuals off from their moral resources and their intuitive awareness. An excerpt from her book-in-progress on this subject appeared in a widely read article of 2015 titled "When Nothing Is Cool."

MARI RUTI is Distinguished Professor of Critical Theory and of Gender and Sexuality Studies at the University of Toronto. She is the author of thirteen books, including *The Singularity of Being: Lacan and the Immortal Within* (2012); *The Call of Character* (2013); *The Ethics of Opting Out: Queer Theory's Defiant Subjects* (2017); *Distillations: Theory, Ethics, Affect* (2018); and *Penis Envy and Other Bad Feelings: The Emotional Costs of Everyday Life* (2018).

ELLEN HANDLER SPITZ writes interpretively on the arts, psychology, and the aesthetic lives of children. Her books include: *Art and Psyche, Image and Insight, Museums of the Mind, Inside Picture Books, The Brightening Glance: Imagination and Childhood, Illuminating Childhood*, and *Magritte's Labyrinth*. She has published on children's books in *The New Republic, The New York Times*, and *The Psychoanalytic Study of the Child*. Her works have been translated into Italian, Japanese, Serbian, and Chinese. She teaches currently at Yale University.

MADELON SPRENGNETHER is Regents Professor Emerita of the University of Minnesota. She has published extensively on Shakespeare, Freud, feminism, and psychoanalysis. Her book publications include *The (M)other Tongue: Essays in Feminist Psychoanalytic Interpretation* (1985), *The Spectral Mother: Freud, Feminism and Psychoanalysis* (1990), *Shakespearean Tragedy and Gender* (1996), and *Mourning Freud* (2018).

JEREMY TAMBLING was formerly Professor of Literature at Manchester University and before that, Professor of Comparative Literature at the University of Hong Kong. He is author of several books, three of them on Dickens: *Dickens, Violence and the Modern State: Dreams of the Scaffold* (Macmillan 1995), *Going Astray: Dickens and*

London (Longman, 2008), and *Dickens' Novels as Poetry: Allegory and the Literature of the City* (Routledge 2014). He edited *David Copperfield* for Penguin (2004) and has written numerous articles on early modern and nineteenth-century literature, and critical and cultural theory. His most recent book was *Histories of the Devil: Marlowe to Mann, and the Manichees* (Macmillan, 2017).

ADELE TUTTER, MD, PhD, teaches at Columbia University, where she is Associate Clinical Professor of Psychiatry; Director, the Psychoanalytic Studies Program of the Graduate School of Arts and Sciences; and Faculty, the Center for Psychoanalytic Training and Research. She also teaches at the New York Psychoanalytic Institute. Her interdisciplinary scholarship has earned the American Psychoanalytic Association Menninger, CORST, and Ticho prizes, among others. Tutter is co-editor (with Leon Wurmser) of *Grief and Its Transcendence: Memory, Identity, Creativity* (Routledge, 2015); editor, *The Muse: Psychoanalytic Explorations of Creative Inspiration* (Routledge, 2016); and author, *Dream House: An Intimate Portrait of the Philip Johnson Glass House* (University of Virginia Press, 2016). She sits on the editorial boards of *The International Journal of Psychoanalysis*, *Psychoanalytic Quarterly*, and *American Imago*, and maintains a private practice of psychoanalysis in Manhattan.

EMMY WALDMAN received her PhD in English from Harvard University, where she studied and taught subjects ranging from poetry to pedagogy in the digital environment. Her research, poised at the intersection between the visual and the verbal, focuses on contemporary comics as a medium for self-expression and filial witness. She has long been interested in psychoanalysis, which informs her writing and thinking.

JEAN WYATT'S latest book is *Love and Narrative Form in Toni Morrison's Later Novels* (2017), which was awarded the Toni Morrison Book Prize for the Best Single-Authored book on Toni Morrison (2018). Her latest essay is "Freud, Laplanche, Leonardo: Sustaining Enigma," in *American Imago* (2019). She is co-editor, with Sheldon George, of a collection of essays, *Reading Contemporary African American and Black British Women Writers: Race, Ethics, Narrative Structure*, published by Routledge (2020). She is Professor of English at Occidental College, where she teaches courses in British modernism and contemporary African American and Native American writers.

VALENTINO L. ZULLO is the Ohio Center for the Book Scholar-in-Residence at Cleveland Public Library where he co-leads the Get Graphic program and is a licensed social worker practicing as a maternal depression therapist at OhioGuidestone. He is American editor of the *Journal of Graphic Novels and Comics*. He has published on the history of comics and psychoanalysis in his article "Keeping Horror in Mind: Psychoanalysis and the 'New Direction' of EC Comics" published in the *Journal of Popular Culture*.

ACKNOWLEDGMENTS

This volume reflects my two professional identities of English professor and psychoanalyst, fostered over thirty years ago by the Academic Challenge Grant from the State of Ohio to inaugurate the Center for Literature and Psychoanalysis at Kent State University, in conjunction with the Cleveland Psychoanalytic Center. This linkage of two great Northeast Ohio institutions of higher learning deepened my dedication to what I have, in this volume, called the "companionate" marriage of Literature and Psychoanalysis. I thank both institutions for their support over the years. I am especially grateful to the Kent State University Research Council for granting an Academic Research Leave to allow me to complete *The Cambridge Companion to Literature and Psychoanalysis*.

For unflagging help with all the details that go into the production of an edited collection, I thank Valentino Zullo for his editorial and research acumen, as well as clinical insights. I also thank Katherine Loughry, Summer Corson, and Faith King for research assistance. Peter Rudnytsky's body of work on the consilience of literature and psychoanalysis has lighted my way for many years. Adele Tutter not only generously contributed her own work to this collection but also has been immensely helpful with editorial interventions. Through the many fluctuations of this pandemic year, Ray Ryan has affirmed that our collection matters to students – and to all readers – who care deeply about what Freud called the "sciences" of human civilization. I am grateful for his dedication. Thanks are also due to Edgar Mendez for his patience and courtesy. Most of all, I thank the volume's contributors themselves, who have exhibited all that is best about literary scholarship as well as the healing arts.

CHRONOLOGY

COMPILED BY
VERA J. CAMDEN AND VALENTINO L. ZULLO

This volume places literature before psychoanalysis, foregrounding the work of poets, novelists, playwrights, film-makers, comics artists, and other creators as foundational to psychoanalysis past and present. So, while this timeline begins with Sigmund Freud himself, and the familiar touchstones of his discovery of psychoanalysis in theory and practice, it takes as one of the principal ideas, advocated by this volume, that Freud not only derived clinical concepts from literature, but also that he wrote literature himself. We recall Freud won the Goethe Prize in 1930. He is, indisputably, one of the great prose stylists of modern literature. Freud's major case studies remain classics of literature even as they inaugurated the clinical form of the case report. By the same token many of the most influential theorists and practitioners of psychoanalysis have been saturated in literature and have themselves been gifted writers. Thus, we have selected representative psychoanalytic authors such as Wilfred Bion, Christopher Bollas, Sándor Ferenczi, Melanie Klein, Julia Kristeva, Jacques Lacan, Adam Phillips, Donald Winnicott, and others.

While no timeline can claim to be comprehensive, we hope it will accurately reflect important trends. The early analysts, including those who were close to Freud, such as Otto Rank and Ernest Jones, quite often turned to literature to formulate their ideas. Thus, we have provided examples which reflect the expansion of psychoanalysis as a field, recognizing those theorists who relied upon literature, or themselves wrote what we consider literary as well as clinical classics. But as psychoanalysis increasingly became a subfield of medical psychiatry in the United States, the influence of literature on clinical practice receded. At the same time, however, academic applications of psychoanalysis in literary theory and criticism, and in the humanities in general, increased dramatically. Indeed, the impactful studies of race, gender, sexuality, and culture were conceived within the academy at this time, each in their own way springing from the marriage of literature and psychoanalysis.

For further discussion of such trends, the reader can consult the Introduction to this volume, as well as the suggestions for Further Reading.

Chronology

1885–1886	Sigmund Freud studies with Jean-Martin Charcot at La Salpêtrière Hospital
1891	Freud, *On Aphasia*
1895	Freud and Josef Breuer, *Studies on Hysteria*
1899/1900	Freud, *The Interpretation of Dreams*
1902	Establishment of the Wednesday Psychological Society, later the Vienna Psychoanalytic Society (1908)
1905	Freud, *Fragment of an Analysis of a Case of Hysteria* (Dora)
1907	Freud, "Delusions and Dreams in Jensen's *Gradiva*" Otto Rank, *Der Künstler* (*The Artist*)
1908	Freud, "Creative Writers and Day-Dreaming"
1909	Freud, *Analysis of a Phobia in a Five-year-old Boy* (Little Hans) Freud, *Notes Upon A Case of Obsessional Neurosis* (Rat Man) Freud travels with Carl Jung and Sándor Ferenczi to the United States and gives lectures at Clark University
1910	Founding of the International Psychoanalytical Association (formerly International Psychoanalytical Congress) Freud, "Leonardo da Vinci, A Memory of His Childhood"
1911	Founding of the American Psychoanalytic Association Freud, *Psycho-Analytic Notes on an Autobiographical Account of a Case of Paranoia (Dementia Paranoides)* (Daniel Paul Schreber case)
1912	Alfred Adler establishes The Society for Free Psychoanalysis, later The Society for Individual Psychology Freud founds *Imago,* inaugurated with the four essays that would become *Totem and Taboo*
1913	Ernest Jones establishes the London Psychoanalytical Society (later British Psychoanalytical Society) Ferenczi establishes the Hungarian Psychoanalytic Association in Budapest
1917	Freud, "Mourning and Melancholia" Virginia and Leonard Woolf found the Hogarth Press, which publishes Freud in English

1918   Frankfurt School established at Institute for Social Research, at Goethe University Frankfurt
        Freud, *From the History of an Infantile Neurosis* (The Wolf Man)

1920   Establishment of *The International Journal of Psychoanalysis*
        Freud, *Beyond the Pleasure Principle*
        Tavistock Clinic founded in London

1923   Ernest Jones, *Essays in Applied Psycho-analysis*

1926   Freud, *The Question of Lay Analysis*

1930   Freud awarded the Goethe Prize
        Freud, *Civilization and Its Discontents*

1932   Melanie Klein, *The Psychoanalysis of Children*

1933   Wilhelm Reich, *Character Analysis*

1936   Anna Freud, *The Ego and the Mechanisms of Defense*
        Lacan presents "Mirror Stage" at the International Psychoanalytical Congress in Marienbad

1937   Ella Freeman Sharpe, *Dream Analysis: A Practical Handbook for Psycho-Analysts*
        Melanie Klein and Joan Riviere, *Love, Hate, and Reparation*

1939   W. H. Auden, "In Memory of Sigmund Freud"
        Freud and Hanns Sachs establish *American Imago*
        Freud, *Moses and Monotheism*

1941   Erich Fromm, *Escape from Freedom*
        Karen Horney establishes the American Institute for Psychoanalysis
        Edmund Wilson, *The Wound and the Bow: Seven Studies in Literature*

1942   Hanns Sachs, *The Creative Unconscious: Studies in the Psychoanalysis of Art*

1943   Géza Roheim, *The Origin and Function of Culture*

1945   Founding of *The Psychoanalytic Study of the Child*

1949   Simone de Beauvoir, *The Second Sex* (English translation, 1952)
        Marie Bonaparte, *The Life and Works of Edgar Allan Poe: A Psycho-analytic Interpretation*
        Sándor Ferenczi, "Confusion of the Tongues Between the Adults and the Child – (The Language of Tenderness and of Passion)" (delivered in 1932 at the Wiesbaden Congress)
        Ernest Jones, *Hamlet and Oedipus*

1950   Erik Erikson, *Childhood and Society*

1985   Jeffrey Berman, *The Talking Cure: Literary Representations of Psychoanalysis*

Charles Bernheimer and Claire Kahane, eds. *In Dora's Case: Freud – Hysteria – Feminism*

Didier Anzieu, *The Skin Ego* (English translation, 1989)

Jane Gallop, *Reading Lacan*

Juliet Mitchell and Jacqueline Rose, *Feminine Sexuality: Jacques Lacan and the École Freudienne*

1986   Freud Museum opens in London

The Center for Literature and Psychoanalysis established at Kent State University

1987   Nicolas Abraham and Mária Török, *The Shell and the Kernel: Renewals of Psychoanalysis*

Christopher Bollas, *The Shadow of the Object: Psychoanalysis of the Unthought Known*

Stanley Cavell, *Disowning Knowledge in Seven Plays of Shakespeare*

Toril Moi, ed., *French Feminist Thought: A Reader*

Peter Rudnytsky, *Freud and Oedipus*

1988   Peter Gay, *Freud: A Life for Our Times*

Donald Meltzer and Meg Harris Williams, *The Apprehension of Beauty: the Role of Aesthetic Conflict in Development, Art and Violence*

Stephen Mitchell, *Relational Concepts in Psychoanalysis: An Integration*

Elisabeth Young-Bruehl, *Anna Freud: A Biography*

1989   American Psychoanalytic Association lifts policy prohibiting non-medical candidates.

Vera J. Camden, ed., *Compromise Formations: Current Directions in Psychoanalytic Criticism*

Slavoj Žižek, *The Sublime Object of Ideology*

1990   Judith Butler, *Gender Trouble: Feminism and the Subversion of Identity*

Eve Kosofsky Sedgwick, *Epistemology of the Closet*

Madelon Sprengnether, *The Spectral Mother: Freud, Feminism, and Psychoanalysis*

1991   Peter Rudnytsky, ed., *Transitional Objects and Potential Spaces: Literary Uses of D. W. Winnicott*

Ellie Ragland-Sullivan and Mark Bracher, eds. *Lacan and the Subject of Language*

Introduction

VERA J. CAMDEN

Reading to Recover
Literature and Psychoanalysis

Conceived within the cultural matrix of nineteenth-century Vienna, psychoanalysis was fostered by the European intellectual and social movements vanguard of the first part of the twentieth century.[1] In the second half of the twentieth century, psychoanalysis went on to flourish in the American and European academies, first in medicine and then in the humanities.[2] Indeed, in the post–World War II medical establishment of the 1950s and 1960s, psychoanalysis dominated the theory and practice of psychiatry, especially in the United States, and entered the cultural and clinical mainstream as a prestigious and pervasive model of the mind. This was to change. By the 1970s, psychoanalysis would be banished from the prominent place it had once held in medicine, clinically employed by a remnant of followers by the end of the decade, and dwindling through the next decade.[3] Retreating under the increasing dominance of biological psychiatry and behavioral health models,[4] this once-queen of psychiatry departments, changed into different regalia, and was now coronated across campus from the medical schools in humanities departments.

In departments of philosophy, English, history, cultural studies, and modern languages for the next several decades, psychoanalysis held court in conferences, classrooms, and academic presses, presiding over a postmodern "turn to theory."[5] The variety of psychoanalysis prevailing in this period was defined by the theories of French psychoanalyst, Jacques Lacan who assumed the position of linguistic legate of Sigmund Freud. Shoshana Felman introduced English-speaking readers to Lacan's theory that the "unconscious is structured like a language."[6] And the "texts" of language, literature, and culture all came to reveal unconscious, unsettling, and unstable truths that fragment the "autonomous ego."[7] For Felman, reading "otherwise" meant reading against the grain of conventional American literary criticism, resisting confidence in authorial intention and textual stability, and initiating the reader and critic into a new relation between literature and psychoanalysis. Freud had already pervaded popular culture, but for about three transformative decades at the end of the twentieth century, psychoanalysis as reinvented by Jacques Lacan became a tool to study culture – still a queen, but this time exiled from psychiatric practice and enthroned in humanities departments.[8]

Now, in the twenty-first century, things have, again, changed. There has been a swing in the pendulum of the academy, veering away from theory in general and psychoanalysis in particular. This, according to Marjorie Garber, may be a sign of "success": psychoanalytic "concepts have naturalized, become adopted or adapted into the ordinary language and practice of our world. ...This is what happens to 'theory' when it succeeds. It disappears, transmuted into the light of common day."[9] However true this interesting notion may be regarding the naturalization of psychoanalytic concepts, it may also be that, to quote Jane Austen's Mr. Knightley, success "should not, perhaps, have come so soon."[10] Forty years after her landmark volume, Felman herself is hardly so sanguine as to the success of theory, especially as we confront the "barbarians at the gate of democracy".[11] She writes,

> In 1977 I proposed that we had to learn how to "read otherwise" psychoanalysis, and primarily how to "read otherwise" *through* psychoanalysis. In 2017 I am suggesting that, in our neoliberal age, what we must "read otherwise" – what I feel today it has become *most urgent to read otherwise* – is literature.[12]

The Cambridge Companion to Literature and Psychoanalysis takes up such urgent advice, avowing that psychoanalysis *itself* derives life and purpose from literature. If medical psychoanalysis repudiated Freud's literary roots, the same can also be said for the dominion of postmodern critical theory[13] in "academia" – that it, too, neglects the literature Felman is now imploring us to read, and to read "closely."

Christopher Bollas, both a literary scholar and a practicing psychoanalyst, shares the imperative to bring "meaning in our lives and in our societies, by making use of psychological insight, within the experience of democracy."[14] To make his point he draws from E. M. Forster's *Howard's End*, which dramatizes how, at the turn of the twentieth century, the market-driven mentality that defined the emerging modern era separated words from feeling. Bollas offers an important correction to the conventional interpretation of Forster's well-known phrase, "only connect":

> Forster's intention is not always grasped. He does not mean that people should connect with one another – this is not an early step toward early relationalism – but that we need to connect our speech with our feelings. . . . "Live in fragments

no longer" alludes to a psychological catastrophe in selves who no longer feel internally integrated.[15]

Such disconnection and dissociation indeed has become naturalized, culminating in the abandonment of insight and truth in our "fake news" era.[16] We have entered a different and dire moment in this strange new millennium.

The essays included in *The Cambridge Companion to Literature and Psychoanalysis* were gathered together in a period of quarantine for contributors and editors alike – what we are now calling "Covid Time."[17] Our correspondence coincided with losses, spoken and unspoken, with grief and uncertainty both professionally and personally. These realities bring gravity and grace to the chapters that unfold, in which one might suggest feeling is reconnected with words as each author reads literature and psychoanalysis through this shared crisis. Along with the pandemic, we have witnessed environmental disasters amidst social, political, and cultural upheaval across the globe. The psychological toll on the world's population from this concatenation may be incalculable. In such troubled times, what can a companion volume on literature and psychoanalysis offer us?

The answer, one hopes, is that it can propose what the Anglo-American Puritans called a companionate marriage,[18] in this case, not between two minds, but between two mentalities, two languages of human meaning. Literature and psychoanalysis draw from the heart of each other and in doing so foster new creations. For if psychoanalysis is a practice that offers amelioration of human suffering, literature is the source of that practice. Retrieving that source offers us a way to connect language not only with feeling, but also with action. As Felman asks,

> Can we rekindle the torch of literature and revitalize its dialogue with psychoanalysis, in rejuvenating and renewing both our search for, and our contact with, their common truth, as a perpetual reminder of what can never be forgotten, and simultaneously, as an act that is yet to come?[19]

Freud, of course, depended upon literature for the defining "paradigm" of the prototypical event in the psychic life of the human subject. Writing to Wilhelm Fliess in 1897, he identifies the "gripping power" of the Oedipus complex discovered in his readings of Sophocles (and later confirmed in his reading of Shakespeare's *Hamlet*): "the Greek legend seizes upon a compulsion of which everyone recognizes because he senses its existence within himself."[20] In the power of literature to "seize" upon our humanity, and bring *anagnorisis*, or the recognition of truth in us and in our world, Freud recovered a tool for self-analysis from which he derived insights that led to scientific discoveries and clinical methods.

Literature remains the generative core and repository of the creativity that makes us human. For it was, after all, Freud who admitted, "Before the problem of the creative artist, analysis must, alas, lay down its arms."[21] Such surrender strengthens practitioners of all stripes. Adam Phillips summarizes the situation:

> Indeed, so remarkable is [psychoanalysts' transference to literature] . . . that it is perhaps the one thing that could be said to unite the increasingly disparate schools of psychoanalysis. Freud, Jung, Lacan, Winnicott, Bion, Meltzer, Milner, Segal, among many others, all agree in their privileging of the poetic.[22]

The significance of this bond has often been elided in academic as well as clinical discussions of psychoanalytic theory. Pierre Bayard puts it this way: "As it is often practiced, the psychoanalytical approach to texts places knowledge on the side of psychoanalysis and not on that of literature. In doing so, it risks diminishing literature and underestimating literature's own ability to produce knowledge."[23] Against this trend, *The Cambridge Companion to Literature and Psychoanalysis* places literature at the center of psychoanalytic thought. The authors who have written for this volume are literary critics and clinical practitioners, each of whom in their own way, pays respect to the creativity of mutual recognition, and in literature's ability to produce knowledge.

Freud himself wrote great and lasting literature. His cases brought him admiration, but also notoriety as a storyteller.[24] Somewhat to his chagrin, he won the Goethe Prize for literature in 1930. He may have denied his pleasure in being called a novelist, yet he was the first to admit his reverence for the narrative method; his tendency to let his discoveries unfold, scene by scene, as in a detective story, has often linked him to Sherlock Holmes.[25] While contemporary psychoanalytic thinkers may not share Freud's erudition any more than they share his genius, they are heirs to his psychology of the mind and to his technique of treatment. That psychology and that technique were shaped by an intellectual legacy imbued with a humanistic as well as scientific view of human experience. The consilience between literature and psychoanalysis predicated Freud's discoveries of the unconscious. This same family bond can foster revelatory and revolutionary truths for the next generation.[26]

***

As a psychoanalyst and professor, I stay "awake to the uses of fictions"[27] to learn how literary knowledge can impact, inform, and advance the psychoanalytic process as a treatment for the individual *and* the society. The historical imbrication of psychoanalytic theory and practice within the full matrix of cultural knowledge should not be relegated to history or to the inspiration of its early founder and his followers. It should instead inspire continued theoretical innovation and application as a method of research and practice. Such alertness to culture will take us into public places and creative spaces. And it will teach us how to "connect" language to feeling. What would it mean, Adam Phillips asks, for an analyst to be more like a poet in her practice? "[W]hat would be the cure for a poet-analyst?"[28] Freud answers this question in his idea of a "psychoanalytic university," offering a model curriculum for such a "poet-analyst." He writes,

> [A]nalytic instruction would include branches of knowledge which are remote from medicine [such as] ... the history of civilization, the psychology of religion, and the science of literature – unless he is well at home in these subjects, an analyst cannot make anything of a large amount of his material.[29]

He made this rarely cited appeal in the face of the "medicalization" of psychoanalysis in the United States, as noted above.[30] Though a devoted physician and rigorous scientist, Freud nevertheless depended upon the cultural knowledge stored in myth, literature, religion, and philosophy for the strength of his healing techniques and the depths of his research in the past of the individual as well as human civilization. He is adamant that his method should allow for an analysis of the very foundations of civilization, as well as the cutting-edge research of scientists and physicians who grapple with myriad dimensions of the human condition.

For the purposes of this collection, it is important to note that Freud's admiration and utilization of the truths of creative writing did not exclusively cluster around the "greats." Words will "travel hither and thither," says Virginia Woolf, who with her husband, Leonard, first published Freud in the Hogarth Press they ran out of their London living room. Words will go "a-roving," and will "gad" about.[31] Somewhat of a gad-about reader himself, Freud often drew upon popular literature and culture to make his points.[32] For instance, in his analysis of Jensen's *Gradiva* (a book Stanley Hyman unfairly calls "an absurd little novel"[33]), Freud identifies creative writing as his source and ally:

> But creative writers are valuable allies and their evidence is to be prized highly, for they are apt to know a whole host of things between heaven and earth of which our philosophy has not yet let us dream. In their knowledge of the mind they are far in advance of us everyday people, for they draw upon sources which we have not yet opened up for science.[34]

In accord, *The Cambridge Companion to Literature and Psychoanalysis* offers readings that are rooted in literary history but also branch out into contemporary literacies, media, and mentalities, recognizing that creative forms are produced daily of which we can hardly dream.

***

The alliance of storytelling with psychoanalysis has produced powerful testimonials from creative writers themselves. As an opening for the reader into this companion volume, I thus offer a brief discussion of the American poet, Hilda Doolittle's (H. D.) record of her analysis with Freud during the cataclysmic years of the 1930s in Vienna before the War. Her *Tribute to Freud* was proclaimed by Freud's first biographer, Ernest Jones, as "the most delightful and precious appreciation of Freud's personality that is ever likely to be written."[35] Here, H. D. reveals that Freud regarded her – the renowned poet – as much a student as a patient. Perhaps for this reason, he wanted her to know the sheer value of his discoveries to human history and human thought. She writes,

> One day he said, "I struck oil. It was I who struck oil. But the contents of the oil wells have only just been sampled. There is oil enough, material enough for research and exploitation to last fifty years, to last one hundred years, or longer. ... You [H. D.] discovered for yourself what I discovered for the [human] race."[36]

She does not take up this claim at this moment because, she said, she had been "shattered" by the intensity of his challenges to her ("My bat-like thought-wings would beat painfully in that sudden searchlight"). But she returns to his "struck oil" metaphor at some length later in her *Tribute*, in reflections that sustain the link between literature and psychoanalysis. For what she pursues in her examination of the meaning, as well as the impact of this oil metaphor upon her own imagination and her own treatment, deepens one's sense of Freud's debt to culture in his discoveries and the prospect of its impact on future generations. At first H. D. objects to the crude and mechanical image of the oil strike to capture the discoveries of psychoanalysis. As a poet, she prefers the metaphor of water – the ancient wellspring of life, the living waters of biblical mythology – to Freud's modern "Texas gold." Her objections to Freud's repeated comparison of his discoveries to the oil boom reveal the poet's conviction that the sources of psychoanalysis lay deep in cultural repositories, as she remarks:

> They called it "a well of living water" in the old days, or simply "the still waters". The Professor spoke of this source of inspiration in terms of oil. It focused the abstraction, made it concrete, a modern business symbol. ... He used the idiom or slang of the counting-house, of Wall Street .... We visualize stark uprights and skeleton-like steel cages ....

She finds his analogy crude and unexpected, and in her initial disparagement sounds like the Texas rancher who, when he happened upon oil while digging for water for his cattle, was downright mad: "I wanted water, and they got me oil. I tell you I was mad, mad clean through. We needed water for ourselves and for our cattle to drink."[37] Despite her distaste for the mechanical and materialistic image of the oil well, H. D. accepts the resilience and utility of Freud's metaphor of modernity. Psychoanalysis gushes from below the rocks, sediment, and shale of thousands of years of "casual, slack or even wrong or evil thinking."[38] And she admits "it is difficult to imagine the Professor saying solemnly, 'I drew by right of inheritance from the great source of inspiration of Israel and the Psalmist–. .. I stumbled upon a well of living water, the river of life ...' But no, that was not the Professor's way of talking." Freud announces to H. D. that she is a student of "the greatest mind of this, and perhaps succeeding generations." She, however, emphasizes his debt to human history: "the point is that for all of [Freud's] ... amazing originality," he was drawing from a deep well of human consciousness that "others – long ago – had dipped into," placing him in the pantheon of the Psalmist, Socrates, and Sophocles.[39]

H. D.'s contribution to literature and psychoanalysis, the *Tribute* to her professor that links her to him for posterity, owes its original conception to Freud's late-life resignation to being misunderstood. She captures an intriguing moment in her treatment in the following scene:

> He does not lay down the law, only this once – this one law. He says, "Please never – I mean never, at any time, in any circumstance, endeavor to defend me, if and when you hear about abusive remarks made about me and my work."

> He explained it carefully. He might have been giving me a lesson in geometry or demonstrating the inevitable course of a disease once the virus has entered the system. At this point, he seemed to indicate (as if there were a chart of a fever patient, pinned on the wall before us), at the least suggestion that you may be about to being a counter-argument in my defense, the anger or the frustration of the assailant will be driven deeper. You will do no good to the detractor by mistakenly beginning a logical defense. You will drive the hatred or the fear or the prejudice deeper. You will do no good to yourself, for you will only expose your own feelings – I take for granted that you have deep feelings about my discoveries, or you would not be here ... .[40]

Freud warns his patient, the poet, of the tribulations of defending psychoanalysis: a defense will only further distance his critics from the theories and practice of psychoanalysis. They will be distanced, and she exposed. As if he is charting a diagnosis of "fever patients" who argue against his discoveries, Freud cautions against robust apology for psychoanalysis. Thus, we are to understand, rather than expose herself by writing a defense, H. D. writes a *Tribute to Freud*. This companion volume, in its turn, aspires to pay tribute to the powerful synergy of literature and psychoanalysis.

***

Students are deeply interested in the psychological underpinnings, implications, and interpretations of literary texts of all sorts and often take literature courses in search of personal identity. Literary and cultural encounters from diverse contexts deepen students' access to their own inner resources within the context of their *communitas*. Psychoanalytic paradigms, when unself-consciously introduced to students hungry for a way to speak about their search for meaning, allow for a frank exploration of human experience that helps make sense of their world. Anxious about what is true and what is false in received knowledge, students are preoccupied with personal identity in a constantly changing world dominated by social media and an endangered political, economic, and environmental future. As Bollas points out, "Since the 1980s, neoliberalism[41] had progressively abandoned the notion that human beings could guide their future, transferring society's collective ambition to 'market forces' that came to determine the nature, value, and outcome of the world in which we live."[42] In such a world, art and literature are at risk of becoming at best commodities, at worst irrelevant. We risk the loss of our culture and fall into melancholia. "Even though youth will try to find the bright side of life, our melancholia seeps into their veins."[43]

The Cambridge Companion to Literature and Psychoanalysis holds as self-evident that a young person might want and even need to read Shakespeare, Toni Morrison, Art Speigelman, or Sa'adat Hasan Manto – to name a few of the authors represented in the pages that follow – to ameliorate the melancholia that seeps into their veins. In a recent piece in the *New Yorker*, Alexandra Schwartz writes her own tribute to the critic Vivian Gornick in a wide ranging, largely biographical essay whose narrative flow pivots on its main question: how might one "use" literature to live? Schwartz writes,

> I asked Gornick how she knew that literature was something worthy of study. She looked at me as if I had asked how she knew that clean water was good to drink. I felt ashamed. . . . I was thinking in terms of the market, and she in terms of the soul.
>
> "Because it was so thrilling. Because it made me feel alive," she said. "And as if I was in the presence of exciting and absorbing realities. The way people feel when they get religious."

Gornick identifies the wellspring that H. D. felt resonated with Freud's metaphor of the riches beneath the earth's surface: "I felt that there was a story beneath the surface of ordinary, everyday life. And the books that contain that story. And, if I can get to it, life will be rich."[44]

Psychoanalyst, D. W. Winnicott, in one of his most influential papers, "The Fear of Breakdown," posits a mode of diagnosing and treating traumatic memory by witnessing its living remnants in patients who fear psychic collapse. He ends up describing in his "lapidary"[45] prose, the natural companionship of literature and psychoanalysis. Winnicott says that what he is about to describe has already been "dealt with" by the poets: "Naturally, if what I say has truth in it, this will already have been dealt with by the world's poets, but the flashes of insight that come in poetry cannot absolve us from our painful task of getting step by step away from ignorance towards our goal."[46] For the poets may have found, and indeed dealt with the truth of unknown or unspoken things – giving them "a local habitation and a name,"[47] but the psychoanalyst, by dint of often long and laborious discovery and formulation, can enlist those truths to offer a way out of ignorance, and toward psychological and even social transformation. Therefore, Winnicott is not as modest as he may sound in assigning the psychoanalyst the step-by-step work of uncovering in his analysis and the unspoken truths that the poet may already have found. T. S. Eliot's claims, in "Virgil and the Christian World" that the poet may well "know," but may not understand the ways that the reader (analyst) may utilize his gripping truths:

> ... if the word "inspiration" is to have any meaning, it must mean just this, that the speaker or writer is uttering something which he does not wholly understand – or which he may even misinterpret when the inspiration has departed from him. ... A poet may believe that he is expressing only his private experience ... yet for his readers what he has written may come to be the expression both of their own secret feelings and of the exultation or despair of a generation. He need not know what his poetry will come to mean to others.[48]

Exceeding the author's expression, intention, or even knowledge, literature offers transformation in the midst of suffering and oppression. James Baldwin, for instance, witnesses the power of literature in his own development, but also offers a social dimension of literary transformation:

> You think your pain and your heartbreak are unprecedented in the history of the world, but then you read. It was Dostoevsky and Dickens who taught me that the things that tormented me most were the very things that connected me with all the people who were alive, or who ever had been alive. Only if we face

these open wounds in ourselves can we understand them in other people. An artist is a sort of emotional or spiritual historian. His role is to make you realize the doom and glory of knowing who you are and what you are. He has to tell, because nobody else in the world *can* tell what it is like to be alive.[49]

The Cambridge Companion to Literature and Psychoanalysis avers that psychoanalysis, like literature, needs no defense, nor should it wield its powers in offense. Here H. D., once again, identifies another, final characteristic of this volume. She reflects:

> This was the gist of the matter. In our talks together he rarely used any of the now rather overworked technical terms, invented by himself and elaborated on by the growing body of doctors, psychologists, and nerve specialists who form the somewhat formidable body of the International Psycho-Analytical Association.[50]

Her association to Freud's refraining from use of the language of psychoanalysis here is intriguing, stressing how he refuses to encapsulate orthodoxies in special terms. She rather offers us a Freud who speaks directly: authoritative, yes, but accessible. By the time he was treating H. D., it might be suggested that Freud was himself tired of the very nomenclature he himself had coined. It must be admitted that there is a large body of jargon-filled work by psychoanalytic literary critics who have long "elaborated upon" the "overworked technical terms" of psychoanalysis. I need not review this vast literature here. For any reader of psychoanalytic criticism will find many such examples of psychoanalytic interpretations of literature that strain to contain or even reduce creativity within theories of mental disorders. Such essays in psychoanalytic orthodoxies do not appear in this collection. Rather, contributors to this volume avoid using psychoanalysis to excavate literature of its life or of its power to startle. Nor do they use an overwrought model of psychoanalysis that speaks over literature, putting it in its place. Rather, as readers will see, their pairing of literature and psychoanalysis works collaboratively to plumb energy from the wells Freud struck long ago, guided as he was by the poets and philosophers who had gone before him.

****

The essays in *The Cambridge Companion to Literature and Psychoanalysis* offer critical and personal perspectives on selected canonical authors, followed by analysis of contemporary literature of social, sexual, and political turmoil, as well as of newer forms such as film, graphic narrative, and autofiction. The volume divides into four sections, each offering the reader different entry points and subject areas to explore. Yet the collection requires no particular order of reading. Each chapter may fruitfully be read as a freestanding piece on various and timely topics. Taken a whole this volume can be seen as a testament to the the truth found in Freud's writing that literature produces psychoanalytic knowledge, as it draws from the wellspring of human culture, and nature. The volume exemplifies how creative, critical, and clinical writing engenders psychoanalytic insight into history, while at the same time yielding fresh truths regarding what it means to be human within the contemporary moment. Indeed, one of the distinctions of this volume, I hope, is its practicality. Even when it is at its most theoretical, its over-arching claim is that we read to recover.

The Cambridge Companion to Literature and Psychoanalysis is divided into sections which historicize the link between literature and psychoanalysis, while acknowledging current trends in the field. Madelon Sprengnether opens **In History** with a discussion of Freud's analysis of "Dora," an early psychoanalytic case study, which in many ways reads as a Victorian novella. The inaugural chapter in this volume thus shows how early psychoanalytic practice rests on literary structures of narrative interpretation, in effect, foreordaining the varieties of psychoanalytic experiences. The ensuing chapters of this section thus unfold as pendants to the fundamental linkage of literature and psychoanalysis soldered by this opening piece. Drawing upon William Shakespeare's play *Hamlet* as a Ur text in psychoanalytic theory, Catherine Bates shapes her reading of *Hamlet* around Freud's essay on the "Uncanny," modeling the persistent productivity of this pairing. The family resemblance that characterizes Freud's epiphanic relation to Shakespeare, among other literary greats, is tinged with the inevitable "sibling rivalry" of such relation. Margaret Ann Fitzpatrick Hanly – uncannily – also uncovers sibling rivalry in the novels of Jane Austen. Perhaps the most recognized figure in English literary history next only to Shakespeare, Jane Austen, the "lady novelist," suffered pathologizing phrases like "regulated hatred"[51] during the mid-twentieth-century salad days of Freudian criticism. Margaret Ann Fitzpatrick Hanly reparatively shows how psychoanalysis can indeed discern the fine brush strokes of Austen's prose, rather than blur them. Fitzpatrick Hanly's simple yet profound recognition that love and hate define all sibling relationships allows the reader to share in Jane Austen's unashamed delight in the young lives of the sisters and brothers who inhabit her comic universe. If Austen's comedies end happily and resist psychoanalysis, Virginia Woolf's writings, by contrast, have invited more than their share of psychoanalytic sleuthing. Katherine Dalsimer's chapter highlights Woolf's conflicted identification with her mother, Julia Duckworth Stephen's creativity, reproducing for this volume two of Vanessa Bell's water-color paintings, sewn into the pages of an unpublished collection of her mother's little known children's stories. A tragically different sort of children's stories closes this first section of the volume, as Jean Wyatt analyzes the narratives of enslaved children that throb through the novels of Toni Morrison. Drawing on Jean Laplanche's concept of *après-coup*, Wyatt shows how Morrison's revelations of family history extracted from the archives of slaveholders presages current psychoanalytic descriptions of the transmission of trauma across time and continents. A belated reckoning with race in America was forecast by Morrison's prophetic novels and critical essays, offering the perfect opening to the next section of this volume.

In Society considers how literature and psychoanalysis address political as well as personal testimonies and the intergenerational transmission of trauma. Zehra Mehdi questions communal conflict in South Asia, using the work of Melanie Klein to analyze how private citizens internalize the political partition of India and Pakistan into a dynamic of self-destruction. Beatriz Botero similarly looks to psychoanalytic drive theory to illustrate how violence in Latin American violence novels enacts the tensions between Eros and Thanatos, the battle between love and death. Readers bear witness to urban decay and desperation, using psychoanalytic theories of sadomasochistic dynamics to understand how the internalization of violence can take hold of a national identity. Both of these essays reckon with the oppressive origins of colonialism which continues to perpetuate the suffering – and provoke the rage – of peoples around the world. War torn European culture and the lingering aftermath of the Holocaust are examined by Adele Tutter, who takes up Bruce Chatwin's elegant and elegiac novel, *Utz*. Dramatizing the psychic hunger of the art collector who adventures in search of endangered, precious Meissen sculptures in shattered Czechoslovakia, Tutter integrates contemporary "thing theory"[52] with conventional psychoanalytic notions of the fetish. Aesthetic ambition survives the horrors of the Holocaust, as the pursuit of beautiful objects belies a longing for human love. Taking such timeless quests into communities outside of the classroom, in a surprising turn Josie Billington introduces us to literary reading groups. She makes an important contribution and concession to the power of literature to change lives in the most directly social space. Her final chapter in this section shows how the consolations of literature can serve the betterment and health of participants in therapeutic reading groups.[53] The pairing of literature and psychoanalysis in such environments offers a fulfillment of Freud's late-life mission, as mentioned above, to bring psychoanalysis into society – including but not limited to educational institutions.

The next section, In Sight, takes its cue from Didier Anzieu, who beckons the reader into the twenty-first century through the *image*. He proclaims, "psychoanalysis has a greater need of people who think in images than of scholars, scholiasts, abstract or formalistic thinkers."[54] The visual media that reconfigures contemporary culture may be best understood from a psychoanalytic perspective. Comics and graphic narratives today are more popular than ever and are used to tell stories once considered unpresentable in other media forms. Thus, Emmy Waldman's chapter considers the evolution of storytelling and how psychoanalysis contends with the emergence of new experiences of selfhood in comics, a form that has been associated with childhood because of its access to an affective range that mere print eludes. Sounding a similar sense of changing subjectivities in the face of new media, Ellen Handler Spitz's psychoanalytic study of children's literature in the context of psychosexual development addresses the fearful prospect of a cultural childhood's "end" in our world turned upside down by the iPhone screen, made all the more urgent by the forced isolation of a pandemic and screen-based learning. Handler Spitz offers cautious optimism about the resilience of children as readers when she considers the endless endurance of the children's book, exemplified in Elena Ferrante's lushly illustrated *The Beach at Night*. Her depiction of a child's doll caught up a nightmare of abandonment provokes an affective state in the viewing subject, that resonates with the dream-like medium of film. Vicky Lebeau's analysis of contemporary film maker Andrea Arnold's 2003 film *Wasp* puts deprivation in dialogue with Winnicott's theories regarding "the good enough mother."[55] Film and psychoanalysis coupled as narrative forces bear witness to and document traumatic histories of class and wealth disparity and its effect on creative capacity amidst desperate poverty. Her perspective on class is made all the more topical now as we witness class contrasts under a global crisis of healthcare, education, and economic endurance.

The concluding section of this volume, **In Theory**, affirms the place of theory as foundational to psychoanalytic paradigms of interpretation, whether in literary criticism, pedagogy, or clinical practice. The influence of literature on the evolution of psychoanalytic theory is surveyed in Jeremy Tambling's history of the connection between literature and psychoanalysis throughout modern intellectual history, that had reached its apogee with the dominance of the Lacanian psychoanalysis within the academy at the end of the twentieth century. For Tambling, psychoanalysis teaches that dreams ultimately resist interpretation, even as literary texts, like human beings, are not fully interpretable; the instability of all human identity is endemic to psychoanalysis itself. Resisting such postmodern theories of the human subject, literary theorist Lisa Ruddick takes us "Beyond the Fragmented Subject" of human identity implied in such postmodern varieties of psychoanalytic experience to offer an alternative model. For Ruddick, contemporary relational psychoanalysis offers more amenable models for literary criticism. Her chapter decries the ways that theories of instability and "shattered identities" become literalized in the lives of students, offering relational psychoanalysis as a preferred pathway to critical insight and indeed self-knowledge. Taking up a similar urgency regarding the ways that theoretical assumptions define and even dictate everyday experience – including increasing reliance upon data and diagnostic models – philosopher Mari Ruti explains how the emergence of "queer theory" as a liberatory framework draws from psychoanalytic discourse, especially methodology. Rather than simply recreate antinormativity as a new norm, Mari Ruti's chapter features the ways that a fresh application of psychoanalysis can be used to explore human existence itself as "queer" within James Baldwin's *Giovanni's Room*. Very much in sync with such newer visions of theory informed by literary instruction and, indeed, activism, Carla Freccero considers the "place" of the animal on planet earth. Her turn to the hybrid philosophical essay and short story, "The Name of the Dog, or Natural Right" by philosopher, Emmanuel Levinas inspires what she calls "figural logics." Her chapter concludes the volume, offering as it does a "Talmudic" rather than conventionally humanistic reading of literature. In her imagined consilience between theory and practice, one might well recognize Freud's idea of a psychoanalytic university: capacious and active, integrated and diverse, lighted by the wisdom of the ages – and literature.

****

American novelist Marilynne Robinson has described the power of literature in this way: "I believe that all literature is acknowledgment. . . . Literature says, this is what sadness feels like and this is what holiness feels like and people feel acknowledged in what they already feel."[56] *The Cambridge Companion to Literature and Psychoanalysis* as a collection attempts such an acknowledgment. Though it may lay down its arms before the creative writer, it must, in turn, take up arms against the sea of troubles we face in our time. Forces far more powerful than academic fashion have assumed frightening indifference to the truths of both fact and fiction, destabilizing not just the individual but society itself. H. D. hoped that the wellspring of art and literature that fed Freud's genius would help stave off the threats to human freedom they both faced between two world wars. *The Cambridge Companion to Literature and Psychoanalysis* will have done its job if it returns the reader to that same endless resource.

Notes

1. Louis Rose, *The Freudian Calling: Early Viennese Psychoanalysis and the Pursuit of Cultural Science* (Detroit: Wayne State University Press, 1998). As Michal Shapira writes, "After World War I, psychoanalysis in Germany and Austria was tied to social reformist movements. Once analysis left the European continent

for Britain, they tied their future and faith to social democracy and joined the efforts of their native colleagues in fighting against fascism," *The War Inside: Psychoanalysis, Total War, and the Making of the Democratic Self in Postwar Britain* (Cambridge: Cambridge University Press, 2013), 85. George Makari similarly claims, "psychoanalysis in Germany and Austria rode the tide of social reformist movements and made its way into schools, clinics, and courts," *Revolution in Mind: The Creation of Psychoanalysis* (New York, NY: Harper, 2008), 404.

2. Freud himself lamented the enshrinement of psychoanalysis in medicine, *The Question of Lay Analysis* (1926), *SE* 20: 177–258.

3. On the history of psychoanalysis' populist rise and its fading into a specialist discipline in the United States, see Dagmar Herzog, *Cold War Freud: Psychoanalysis in an Age of Catastrophes* (Cambridge: Cambridge University Press, 2017).

4. Anne Harrington describes the rise of biological psychiatry in *Mind Fixers: Psychiatry's Troubled Search for the Biology of Mental Illness* (New York: W. W. Norton & Company, 2019).

5. See Terry Eagleton, *The Significance of Theory* (Oxford: Wiley-Blackwell, 1991) on the pivotal turn to theory in literary criticism.

6. See Shoshana Felman, ed., *Literature and Psychoanalysis: The Question of Reading: Otherwise* (Baltimore, MD: Johns Hopkins University Press, 1982). First published as *Yale French Studies* 55/56 (1977).

7. Felman, for instance, assails the "ego of the analyst" who "must not be taken as the clinical criterion for reality, normality, or health...," *Jacques Lacan and the Adventure of Insight: Psychoanalysis in Contemporary Culture* (Cambridge, MA: Harvard University Press, 1987), 12.

8. Lawrence Samuel documents the popular history of psychoanalysis in *Shrink: A Cultural History of Psychoanalysis in America* (Lincoln: University of Nebraska Press, 2013).

9. Marjorie Garber, "Identity Theft," *International Forum of Psychoanalysis* 27, no. 2 (2018): 80.

10. Jane Austen, *Emma*, eds., Richard Cronin and Dorothy McMillan (Cambridge: Cambridge University Press, 2013), 523.

11. See Felman, "Preface (To Reopen the Question)," *Paragraph* 40, no. 3 (2017): iii–xxiii.

12. Ibid., xi–xii.

13. For the history of the turn to theory in the humanities, see Eagleton, *After Theory* (New York: Basic Books, 2004).

14. Christopher Bollas, *Meaning and Melancholia: Life in the Age of Bewilderment* (New York: Routledge, 2018), 129.

15. Bollas, *Meaning and Melancholia*, 24.

16. Ibid., Chapter 4, "Human Character Changes" on *Howard's End* and Chapter 12, "I hear that . . ." on "fake news." See also Michiko Kakutani, *The Death of Truth: Notes on Falsehood in the Age of Trump* (New York, Tim Duggan Books, 2018).

17. See Vera J. Camden, "Psychoanalysis and the Pandemic," *Fifteen Eighty Four*, May 21, 2020, www.cambridgeblog.org/2020/05/psychoanalysis-and-the-pandemic/

18. On the companionate marriage, see Ulrike Tancke, "Bethinke Thy Selfe" in *Early Modern England: Writing Women's Identities* (New York: Rodopi, 2010).
19. Felman, "Preface (To Reopen the Question)," xviii.
20. Sigmund Freud, Letter from Freud to Fliess, October 15, 1897, *The Complete Letters of Sigmund Freud to Wilhelm Fliess, 1887–1904* (Cambridge, MA: Belknap Press, 1986), 272.
21. Freud, "Dostoevsky and Parricide" (1928), *SE* 21: 177.
22. Adam Phillips, *Promises, Promises: Essays on Literature and Psychoanalysis* (New York: Basic Books, 2002), 4.
23. Pierre Bayard and Rachel Bourgeois, trans, "Is It Possible to Apply Literature to Psychoanalysis?," *American Imago* 56, no. 3 (1999): 207.
24. In his case of Dora, one of the greatest examples of his storytelling, Freud disparages those readers who are titillated by his record of his young patient's sexuality. See Freud, "A Fragment of an Analysis of a Case of Hysteria," *SE* 7:8. See also, Adele Tutter, "Sex, Subtext, Ur-Text: Freud, Dora and the Suggestive Text," *The International Journal of Psychoanalysis* 101, no. 3 (2020): 523–48.
25. See Carlo Ginzburg and Anna Davin, "Morelli, Freud and Sherlock Holmes: Clues and Scientific Method," *History Workshop* 9 (Spring 1980), 5–36.
26. See Riccardo Steiner's essay, "In Vienna Veritas …?," *International Journal of Psycho-Analysis* 75 (1994): 511–83, for further elaboration on myth and literature in Freud's education and its impact on his defining early theories.
27. Adam Phillips, *Terrors and Experts* (Cambridge, MA: Harvard University Press, 1995), 35.
28. Phillips, *Promises, Promises*, 6.
29. Freud, *The Question of Lay Analysis*, 246.
30. Ibid., 229–34.
31. Virginia Woolf, *BBC Radio*, April 29, 1937.
32. For a discussion of psychoanalysis and popular comics, see Vera J. Camden and Valentino L. Zullo, "Comics on the Couch: Introduction," *American Imago* 77, no. 3 (Fall 2020), 443–58.
33. Stanley Hyman, *The Tangled Bank* (Cambridge, MA: Athenaeum Press, 1962), 351.
34. Freud, "Delusions and Dreams in Jensen's *Gradiva*" (1907), *SE* 9: 8.
35. Ernest Jones, "Review of *Tribute to Freud*," *International Journal of Psycho-Analysis*, 38 (1957): 126.
36. H. D., *Tribute to Freud* (Boston: Norman Holmes Pearson, 1974), 18.
37. Diana Davids Hinton, and Roger M. Olien, *Oil in Texas: The Gusher Age, 1895–1945* (Austin, Texas: University of Texas Press, 2002), 75–76. William Thomas Waggoner (1852–1934) struck oil and struck it rich while drilling for water in 1902. Freud's oil image seems oddly innocent, for how could he know that the very fossil fuel he finds so enriching and energizing, derived from the hidden layers of the earth will become a plague that threatens the future of the planet? As Timothy Morton reflects: "Agrologistics was a disaster early on, yet it was repeated across Earth. There is a good Freudian term for the blind thrashing (and threshing) of this destructive machination: *death drive*." *Dark Ecology: For a Logic of Future Existence* (New York: Columbia University Press, 2016), 53.
38. H. D., *Tribute to Freud*, 82–83.
39. Ibid.,18.

40. Ibid., 87.
41. On "neoliberalism," see Simon Springer, Kean Birch, and Julie MacLeavy, eds. *The Handbook of Neoliberalism* (New York: Routledge, 2016).
42. Bollas, *Meaning and Melancholia*, xxiii.
43. Ibid., 128.
44. Alexandra Schwartz, "Look Again: Vivian Gornick revisits the books she's read – and the lives she's lived," *The New Yorker* (February 10, 2020): 19.
45. Alison Bechdel, *Are You My Mother?: A Comic Drama* (New York: Houghton Mifflin Harcourt, 2012), 131.
46. D. W. Winnicott, "Fear of Breakdown," *International Review of Psycho-Analysis* 1 (1974): 103.
47. William Shakespeare, *A Midsummer Night's Dream*, ed. R. A. Foakes (Cambridge: Cambridge University Press, 2003), V.i.12–17.
48. T. S. Eliot, "Virgil and the Christian World," in *On Poetry and Poets* (London: Faber and Faber, 1957), 122–23.
49. James Baldwin, "Telling Talk from a Negro Writer," *Life*, May 24, 1963. Thanks are due to Danielle French for pointing me to this powerful passage.
50. H. D., *Tribute to Freud*, 87.
51. D. W. Harding, *Regulated Hatred: An Aspect of the Work of Jane Austen* (Cambridge: Deighton, Bell & Co., 1940).
52. Bill Brown, A *Sense of Things: The Object Matter of American Literature* (Chicago: University of Chicago Press, 2003).
53. See ReLIT, the bibliotherapy program directed by Paula Byrne: www.relitfoundation.org/about
54. Didier Anzieu, *The Skin Ego: A Psychoanalytic Approach to the Self*, trans. Chris Turner (New Haven: Yale University Press, 1989), 6.
55. D. W. Winnicott, *Playing and Reality* (London: Tavistock Publications, 1971).
56. Casey Cep, "Book of Revelation: Marilynne Robinson's Novels of Redemption," *The New Yorker* (October 5, 2020): 53.

PART I

In History

I

MADELON SPRENGNETHER

Varieties of Psychoanalytic Experience

"Psychoanalysis is inherently literary."[1]

Mark Doty

Let us imagine, for a moment, that it is 1900.

You are a doctor of nervous diseases, specializing in the treatment of hysteria, who has recently published a monumental study of the interpretation of dreams.[2] You are married to the sweetheart of your youth and occupy a spacious apartment in a respectable quarter of Vienna, where you are raising a family of six – nicely balanced between boys and girls.

Your wife manages the household, leaving you free to read, write, and receive patients whose ailments you hope to relieve through a new form of treatment based on principles you have developed through an arduous process of introspection. You believe that you have discovered the essence of psychic life, as expressed in classic Greek tragedy.

At forty-four, you are in the prime of life, and you expect to make a name for yourself – one that will transcend the narrow circumstances of your origins and lead to world renown.

Now imagine that you are a young woman, eighteen years of age, who is seriously unhappy. You suffer from headaches, depression, a slight limp, shortness of breath, an intermittent cough, and a vaginal discharge. You dislike your mother, who spends her time in obsessive housecleaning, and you have taken to criticizing your once beloved father in the sharpest terms. You are highly intelligent, but unlike your older brother, you do not attend university.

At the height of your discontent, you have contemplated suicide. Alarmed, your father decides to have you examined by his friend, the doctor of nervous diseases, who also once treated him for syphilis. Your name will become famous, but not in a way that you imagine or desire.

Your physician is Sigmund Freud, and you are Ida Bauer, known to the world as "Dora."

Why begin with Dora? The title of this essay, "Varieties of Psychoanalytic Experience," prompts another question. Why varieties? Had Freud established the discipline of psychoanalysis once and for all, would there be any need for variation? Freud thought not. Yet his texts read otherwise. Like great works of literature, they open themselves to ever-new forms of interpretation.

The narrative strategies of "Fragment of an Analysis of a Case of Hysteria," as Freud titled his treatment of Ida Bauer, are such that they invite continuing inquiry.[3] This chapter takes the Dora case history as exemplary of how psychoanalysis has developed and mutated over time; it offers an entrance into and a means of addressing a vast, and potentially uncontainable, subject. Psychoanalysis, like literature (as I have argued elsewhere)[4] is not a fixed entity, but rather a mobile, evolutionary system, responding to new developments in theory and practice as well as in culture and society. The Dora case history serves, in this respect, as a key text, enabling and precipitating the varieties of psychoanalytic experience that ensue from Freud's early (and subsequent) formulations.

Freud as a Literary Writer

Steven Marcus famously compared Freud's analysis of Dora to a "modern experimental novel." Expanding on this thesis, he claimed:

> Its narrative and expository course, for example, is neither linear nor rectilinear, instead its organization is plastic, involuted, and heterogeneous and follows spontaneously an inner logic that seems frequently to be at odds with itself; it often loops back around itself and is multidimensional in its representation of both its material and itself.

Pursuing this analogy, he maintains that "what Freud has written is in parts rather like a play by Ibsen, or more precisely like a series of Ibsen's plays."[5] In addition, Freud himself plays a role in this drama; he is "not only Ibsen the creator and playwright, he is also and directly one of the characters in the action and in the end suffers in a way that is comparable to the suffering of the others."[6] Lastly, Freud (in his self-construction as a character within his own narrative) resembles the "unreliable narrator" of the fiction of the early twentieth century. Whether or not one agrees with this characterization, Marcus' essay authorized an endless series of re-interpretations of this most fascinating and problematic of case histories.

What is it about this piece of writing that encourages readers to second-guess its author? Interestingly, Freud himself raised this issue when he observed in *Studies on Hysteria* that his case histories often read like fiction:

> I have not always been a psychotherapist. Like other neuropathologists, I was trained to employ local diagnoses and electro-prognosis, and it will strike me myself as strange that the case histories I write should read like short stories and that, as one might say, they lack the serious stamp of science.[7]

To make matters more complex, Freud was not above writing fiction in the guise of nonfiction, as evident in his essay "Screen Memories," published shortly before his treatment of Ida Bauer. Here, he invents the character of the young man with whom he discusses memory as a reconstruction. The young man in question is a disguised version of himself. At the end of this essay, he declares that memory itself is an unreliable narrator. "It may indeed be questioned," he states,

> whether we have any memories at all *from* our childhood: memories *relating* to our childhood may be all that we possess. Our childhood memories show us our earliest years not as they were but as they appeared at the later periods when the memories were aroused.[8]

Freud's method of dream interpretation[9] assumes that appearances are deceiving, requiring an understanding of the workings of symbol, metaphor, condensation, and displacement – strategies he also employs in his dissection of a childhood memory in "Screen Memories." But if memory is a reconstruction, requiring an elaborate labor of analysis, what does that make a case history, especially one that involves a single (and self-interested) narrator?

Transference/Countertransference/Intersubjectivity

Leaving aside the issue of Freud's self-representation in the Dora case history, let us turn to the lesson he drew from it, which focuses less on the content of his interpretation than on the dynamic of the doctor/patient relationship. Having failed to persuade Dora of her repressed desire for Herr K. (the husband of her father's lover), Freud reflects on what went wrong. He concludes that he missed a crucial element: Dora's feelings toward him, which he describes as "transference." "Transferences," he explains, "are new editions or facsimiles of the tendencies or phantasies, which are aroused and made conscious during the progress of the analysis; but they have this peculiarity, which is characteristic for their species, that they replace some earlier person by the person of the physician."[10] He concludes that from the beginning of his analysis with Dora "I was replacing her father in her imagination, which was not unlikely, in view of the difference between our ages."[11] Regarding him as a stand-in for the disappointing men in her life, Dora "transferred" onto him the full force of her love, anger, and ambivalence. Had Freud understood this sooner, he believes, he might have been able to dissolve her resistance by recognizing its source. While many have found fault with the specifics of Freud's interpretation of Dora's dilemma, no one has questioned his concept of transference. Rather, it resides at the heart of psychoanalytic theory and practice.

For Freud and his immediate followers, psychoanalysis was largely a one-way street, meaning that the analyst functioned as a blank or neutral screen onto which the patient projected his or her phantasies and emotions. By interpreting patients' responses within the treatment space, the analyst gained insight into the problems they were struggling with. This is the so-called "one-person" model of treatment. Such a view, however, depended on a questionable assumption: that analysts are sufficiently self-aware as to preclude irrelevant assumptions or associations of their own.

Freud's preeminent biographers, Ernest Jones[12] and Peter Gay,[13] both assume that he achieved the seemingly impossible goal of complete self-understanding. In Jones' words: "In the summer of 1897, Freud undertook his most heroic feat – a psychoanalysis of his own unconscious ... Once done, it is done forever. For no one again can be the first to explore those depths."[14] While less hyperbolic in his praise, Peter Gay concurs: "What matters to the student of psychoanalysis," he states, "is not whether Freud had (or imagined) an Oedipus complex, but whether his claim that it is the complex through which everyone must pass can be substantiated by independent observation or ingenious experiments."[15] The truth-value of Freud's self-analysis, as a result, may not be questioned.

Ironically, Freud himself called attention to the incompleteness, if not the fallibility, of the analyst's labor of self-scrutiny. In "Recommendations to Physicians Practicing Psycho-Analysis," he established the rule "that anyone who wishes to carry out analyses on other people shall first himself undergo an analysis by someone with expert knowledge."[16] At the same time, such analysis "will, as may be imagined, remain incomplete," necessitating an ongoing process of self-examination. Late in life, Freud expressed new doubts about the possibility of achieving an end to analysis. In "Analysis Terminable and Interminable," he recommends that,

> every analyst should periodically – at intervals of five years or so – subject
> himself to analysis once more, [with the result that] not only the therapeutic

analysis of patients but his own analysis would change from a terminable into an interminable task.[17]

The effectiveness of psychoanalytic treatment appears to rest on unstable criteria, beginning with the trainee's analysis at the hands of a senior physician, whose own analysis depends on the expertise of his superior – in an infinite regress, going all the way back to Freud. It would only be a matter of time for someone to question the authority and supposed neutrality of analysts other than the founder himself. What happens, for instance, when the analyst brings a part of his or her own unconscious history or habit of emotional response into the treatment? The result is the phenomenon of countertransference, now perceived as an essential aspect of the analyst's awareness and self-inquiry.

There is a parallel development in the field of literary criticism over the course of the twentieth century; from certitude to instability, from an emphasis on the authority of the interpreter to his or her subjective position; and from a set of agreed-upon tenets to a multitude of conflicting points of view, depending on one's theoretical allegiance, as inflected by individual response.

If as I have suggested, the Dora case offers a window into Freud's own process of thinking, including his openness to revision of his original theories and assumptions, it also helps us to view this process as fundamental to the evolution of psychoanalysis itself. Viewing the Dora case history through the lens of countertransference, for instance, we may observe Freud's own biases: his assumption that Herr K. (whose wife is involved in an adulterous affair with a man who is impotent) is a virile male; his assurance that Dora would have been excited by the advances of a man old enough to be her father; his conclusion that Dora is "in love" with Herr K., as she is in love with her father, and even Freud himself, and that the repression of this desire is the cause of her hysteria.

At this distance in time, it is hard to defend Freud from charges of insensitivity. Although he does not doubt Dora's interpretation of her status as a pawn in the relationship between her father and Herr K, he seems oddly in league with the adults who ignore her distress. Rather, he appears to urge Dora to submit to the deal that would deliver her to Herr K. as the price of her silence about her father's affair with Frau K.

In his eagerness to demonstrate his new understanding of human sexuality, reaching all of the way back to the polymorphous aims and objects of infancy,[18] Freud seems overly invested in his interpretation of Dora's discontent as evidence of her repressed desire. In the grip of this need or obsession, he ignores the inappropriateness of his responses to her expressions of anger and disgust. Given that Freud was in the throes of inventing the theory and practice of psychoanalysis, one should not judge him harshly. At the same time, a thoughtful reading of the Dora case history appears to corroborate the concept of countertransference. From this point of view, Freud was more interested in demonstrating the validity of his own ideas than he was in the intricate dynamics of the treatment relationship.

Countertransference assumes that treatment involves two individuals, each bringing his or her own history into analysis.[19] While one has undergone a lengthy process of training and supervision, the other is seeking help for problems that appear baffling, overwhelming, or simply intractable. Yet the closeness of their connection impacts both – hence the shift from a "one-person" to a "two-person" model of treatment.

Moving beyond the back-and-forth dynamics of transference and countertransference, intersubjectivity examines the space of relationship between the analytic pair, a co-creation resulting from the treatment process.[20] The narrative construction of the patient's life-history that results is a product of their mutual interaction. A refinement of this theory seeks to define the special nature of this relationship, which involves a suspension of conscious thought resembling that of a waking dream.

Oedipal/Preoedipal Dynamics

Freud's concept of transference, as developed in the aftermath of his treatment of Dora and amplified by subsequent developments in the theory of countertransference and intersubjectivity, intersect with other, fast-moving changes in the field of psychoanalysis. Chief among these is the shift in emphasis from the dynamics of the Oedipus complex to those of the preoedipal period, as evidenced by developments in the field of object relations theory and attachment theory, among others.

These bodies of theory assume that the very earliest stages of life exert a shaping influence on the evolution of our personalities and the challenges we face throughout our lives. Even more importantly, they displace Freud's emphasis on the Oedipus complex as the crucible of psychic development. This seismic shift has further implications in terms of social and political theory.

The groundwork for object relations theory was laid by Freud. Although he did not explore the preoedipal period, he acknowledged its existence – consigning it to the period of individual prehistory analogous to the "Minoan-Mycenean civilization behind the civilization of Greece."[21] The earliest stage of development, he acknowledged, revolves around the mother-infant relationship, which he declined to investigate, much less to theorize.[22] Yet his own daughter Anna Freud chose to focus on the field of child development, which involves mothers, early care-givers, and nannies. Her case studies, like her father's, set the stage for a body of literature in child development that sustained the importance of narrative in demonstrating analytic concepts as well as treatment modalities.

Anna Freud, who founded the Hampstead War Nurseries to treat children separated from their parents in wartime London, also introduced direct observation into the analysis of children's development and behavior.[23] Others, like John Bowlby, who noted the effects of emotional neglect on children in orphanages, extended this field to include research into early childhood development.[24] Both might be viewed as precursors of present-day attachment theory, which focuses on real-time interactions between mothers and children as a basis for its observations and conclusions.

The British School of object relations is wide and deep, including such figures as W. R. D. Fairbairn, Harry Guntrip, Margaret Mahler, and D. W. Winnicott.[25] Among these, Winnicott enjoys the most prominence today. He specialized in the treatment of children too young to lie on a couch, free associate, or even find words to express their thoughts and feelings. He developed a method of play therapy with such children, which allowed him to enter into a mixed form of verbal and nonverbal communication. He called this the "squiggle" game.

Winnicott would begin by drawing a line on a piece of paper and invite his patient to add one of his or her own. They would continue in this way, as a joint drawing began to emerge. In its most successful form, the child would begin to talk about the emerging design, which Winnicott would interpret. Winnicott entered, through this game, into a unique form of two-person treatment, with the important difference that he was analyzing a child.

In shifting their focus from the oedipal to the preoedipal period, child analysts faced multiple challenges, including their small patients' restless-ness, lack of comprehension of complex terminology, and corresponding paucity of words to give expression to their wishes, dreams, and fantasies. Play therapy, involving the use of dolls, toys, and the therapist's willingness to meet their clients on their own level (including sitting on the floor), offered not only a new means of treatment but also new methods of interpretation. Melanie Klein, who disagreed with Anna Freud on the primacy of ego development, was nevertheless a critical figure in the establishment of child analysis. Klein, who considered herself a faithful follower of Freud, created a body of theory that tests some of his most cherished concepts.

For Freud, psychoanalytic theory begins with his formulation of the Oedipus complex, which rests on the assumption of the father's prohibition of his son's incestuous desire for his mother through the threat of castration. The son, in turn, renounces his wish to eliminate his father and marry his mother in favor of assuming the position of the father, over time. So wedded was Freud to this idea that he extended it into a theory of civilization. In *Totem and Taboo*, Freud proposed that there once existed a primal horde, in which the all-powerful father kept the available women to himself. His jealous sons rose up against him, killed him, and ate him – memorializing this act in a ritual feast. Succumbing at last to guilt for this deed, the sons instituted a prohibition against incest, hence deferring the satisfaction of their own desires in recognition of the father's preeminent authority.[26]

In Freud's account, only fathers and sons matter. It is difficult, if not impossible, to fit mothers and daughters into this scheme. Klein performed such a feat, by reversing Freud's focus on a commanding father to that of an awesome mother. Whereas Freud imagines the inner conflicts of a male child threatened by the power of his father, Klein constructs the fantasy life of an infant dependent on the giving and withholding functions of its mother's breast. Both create a myth of origins – but from radically different assumptions and points of departure.[27] However one might weigh Klein's views against those of Freud, one clear difference stands out. In Klein's conceptual framework, as in that of the field of object relations as a whole, mothers precede fathers in the drama of psychological development. The significance of this displacement cannot be underestimated, as it intersects with changes in the social and political worlds that are still in process.

Object Relations Theory/American Feminism/Lacan

For proponents of object relations, the journey of human development begins (metaphorically if not actually) at the breast. We do not enter the world as self-contained individuals but rather as helpless and unformed creatures radically in need of care, the quality and sensitivity of which set the course of our future lives. Most assume that the infant's first caregiver is a nurturing female figure, ideally its mother. Many others posit an initial stage of mother/infant fusion, necessitating a titrated process of separation and individuation. If all goes well, the neonate will begin to differentiate itself from its original source of nurture and to tolerate greater and greater degrees of autonomous functioning.

None of the originators of these ideas considered themselves as defecting from Freud. Rather, they assumed that the preoedipal period provides a missing piece in the psychoanalytic puzzle. The drama of the preoedipal period, they presumed, yields in time to the Oedipus complex. Yet the implications of "thinking through the mother," as opposed to "thinking through the father" are more de-centering than they may appear.[28] To return to Freud's analysis of Ida Bauer, what might have he have concluded had he examined more closely the women in her life, beginning with her mother, whom he dismisses as neurotically obsessed with housecleaning? What might he have discovered had he psychoanalyzed the "variety" of the mother's perspective? Given that her husband had suffered from syphilis before their marriage (and gonorrhea after) would not her actions make sense? Freud focuses instead on Dora's Oedipal desire to be penetrated by her father and Herr K. At the same time, he reveals a deeper (and unanalyzed), interest in what I would call the "scene of nursing." The scene of nursing precedes and displaces the fantasy of parental coitus, which Freud termed the "primal scene."

Both Dora and Frau K nurse Dora's father in his periods of illness, an activity that intensifies their feelings of attachment. In Frau K's case, this intimate form of care leads to adultery. Freud's reconstruction of this piece of family history makes sense; what is curious about it is the way that he describes sexual engagement between the amorous pair. Assuming that Dora's father is impotent, he alleges that Frau K must gratify him by performing fellatio. Having stated this as a fact, he concludes that Dora herself fantasizes this kind of activity, by drawing a questionable series of analogies between the penis, the nipple, and thumb-sucking. To his conjectured fantasy, Freud attributes Dora's childhood habit of sucking her thumb to her present-day fantasy of fellatio.

> It then needs very little creative power to substitute the sexual object of the moment (the penis) for the original object (the nipple) or for the finger which does duty for it, and to place the current sexual object in the situation in which gratification was originally obtained. So we see that this excessively repulsive and perverted phantasy of sucking at a penis has the most innocent origin. It is a new version of what may be described as a prehistoric impression of sucking at the mother's or a nurse's breast – an impression which has usually been revived by contact with children who are being nursed. In most instances, a cow's udder has aptly played the part of an image intermediate between a nipple and a penis.[29]

In this elaborate reconstruction of Dora's desire, Freud imagines a kind of merger between the nurse and the object of her care. At first, she offers service to an invalid rendered childlike in his need; next she sucks at his penis, as if it were a nipple and she an infant drawing sustenance from her charge. If Herr Bauer's penis becomes a nipple, however, what does that make him but a mother? Having dismissed Dora's actual mother from his range of concern, Freud seems unable to tease out the implications of the maternal functions and desires of Dora and Frau K., turning instead to the virile Herr K. and his proposal that Dora become his lover. In doing so he utterly misses the intensity of Dora's maternal longings as epitomized in her hours staring at images of the Madonna and child in museums and her eager attendance at early feminist gatherings.[30] While contemporary followers of Freud did not challenge his analysis, the tide of opinion turned away from such phallocentric interpretations with the advent of object relations and other preoedipal theories in combination with the rise of second wave feminism in the United States and abroad.

Early second-wave feminists mounted attacks on Freud's theories of female castration and penis envy. For these activists, Freud and psychoanalysis as a way of thinking about social problems were simply irrelevant. A different form of engagement between feminism and psychoanalysis emerged in the work of women analysts and social critics such as Dorothy Dinnerstein and Nancy Chodorow.[31] Chodorow's analysis of how women raise daughters who replicate their mothers' social functions, according to the psychological script described and prescribed by object relations theory, had a revolutionary impact on literary as well as psychoanalytic thinking about women. Viewing object relations theory in the light of her training in Sociology and Anthropology, Chodorow argued that social arrangements that rely on (nearly) exclusive female mothering lead not only to the stereotyped gender positions characteristic of patriarchy but also to the female psychological conditioning that results in women's disposition to mother and to raise daughters who replicate this role. Mothers, Chodorow proposed, regard female children as more similar to themselves than other, prolonging the period of their attachment to girls, while encouraging boys to perceive themselves as different. Girls, as a result, remain closer to their mothers throughout their lives, while boys strive to distance themselves from the maternal matrix. This set of assumptions, she argued, is so deeply embedded in patriarchy as to appear both natural and inevitable. Yet if social structures are humanly constructed, rather than timeless and universal, how might psychological theories change under altered social conditions?

Chodorow's analysis of gender relations in the light of object relations theory inspired an outpouring of responses among American feminists whose long-term effects remain undetermined. The simplest way to describe the impact of her work would be to say that it elevated the subject of mothers and daughters to the status of legitimate social, literary, and psychoanalytic concerns.

While object relations theory occupied the field in Great Britain and the United States, Jacques Lacan began to transform psychoanalytic thinking on the continent.[32] Lacan, who presented his work as a "return" to Freud, created a body of theory of his own, which rivals that of his master. For

Lacan, who was influenced by the field of structural linguistics, language is not only key to human development but also to the mysteries of the unconscious. Reconceiving (and renaming) the preoedipal period as the Imaginary, he constructed a two-tier system of development in which the infant moves from a condition of nonverbal connection to the body of the mother to the father's Symbolic world of language and culture.

By shifting the terms preoedipal and oedipal to the Imaginary and Symbolic, Lacan created a structural paradigm that focuses on the "name" of the father, as opposed to his possession of a penis. Instead of threatening his sons with literal castration, he imposes his "nom" (name) or "non" (no) on the child as a means of separating it from its mother. The father, in Lacan's theory, stands for a cultural, rather than a personal, imperative – the demand that each child renounce the polymorphous pleasures of the preoedipal period for the necessity of engaging in the social networks created by language and culture. Lacan's scheme does not fundamentally alter the patriarchal structure of society, but it does offer room for feminists seeking more flexible possibilities for female voices and writing practices. French feminists rose to this challenge, by articulating an interim location in language and writing termed "l'écriture féminine." The theory and practice of "feminine writing" derives from the supposed maternal space of speech and writing on the borderline of patriarchal control. Hélène Cixous, Cathérine Clément, Luce Irigaray, Julia Kristeva, and others explored this uncharted territory by expanding Lacan's definition of the Imaginary and by offering their own examples of this kind of writing.[33]

In these, and other, ways, British, American, and French feminists wrestled with the patriarchal underpinnings of psychoanalysis, which appear to promise liberation from Victorian attitudes toward sexuality and the expression of desire, while failing to alter the status of women. In a very general sense, however, one may say that the movement from oedipal to preoedipal areas of investigation and theory has displaced Freud's focus on the drama of masculine development as key to the evolution of Western civilization. If mothers, for whatever reason, have become as significant as fathers in each child's experience of coming-into-being, nothing less than a paradigm shift has occurred.

Trauma/Mourning/History/Culture

In addition to having been taken to task for his phallocentrism, Freud has also been criticized for his emphasis on intrapsychic processes, at the expense of interpsychic ones. Psychoanalysis, as a result, has been rebuked for its focus on individuals in isolation from the social and cultural forces that set the parameters of their real and imagined lives. There is some truth to this assertion, but a more fruitful approach to this issue lies in tracing the gradual movement toward the inclusion of material and historical perspectives into psychoanalytic thinking. Juliet Mitchell (along with Nancy Chodorow) anticipated such an effort from the point of view of second-wave feminism. In *Psychoanalysis and Feminism*, Mitchell argued that Freud's constructions of femininity and female desire underpin the social structure of patriarchy.[34] As such, they *describe* rather than *prescribe* the gender roles within this social system. Although Mitchell did not foresee the kinds of gender diversity that have emerged since, she offered a means of locating psychoanalysis within the parameters of history and culture, which have led, over time, to new developments in psychoanalytic theory and practice. Another significant move in this direction stems from trauma theory as it has evolved over the course of the twentieth century. Freud provided a starting point for this line of thinking. Reflecting, in *Beyond the Pleasure Principle* on the phenomenon of "shell shock" among soldiers returning from the Front, he articulated the concept of "repetition compulsion" to describe their state of psychic arrest and inability to move forward in their lives.[35] Trauma theory was slow, however, to develop as a field of inquiry. It was not until the late 1970s that psychologists, psychoanalysts, and clinical social workers began to attend to the symptoms reported by veterans returning from the Vietnam War.[36] While some were able to re-enter their former lives, others suffered from recurring nightmares, fight or flight responses to external stimuli, depression, and other debilitating emotional conditions. The concept of Post-Traumatic Stress Disorder (PTSD) evolved from these observations. As the understanding of PTSD gained acceptance, it expanded to include other forms of traumatic response, such as those reported by battered women, victims of sexual assault, incest, and survivors of the Holocaust. The convergence of trauma studies in the above areas spoke to many simultaneously developing fields of social inquiry. Freud's initial observations concerning the problems of soldiers devastated by their experiences of modern warfare became newly relevant to researchers attempting to understand and treat those afflicted by other forms of trauma deriving from the conditions of both private and public life.

Several forces from within and outside of psychoanalysis have combined, over time, to transform the field of psychoanalytic theory from one that focuses on the individual's inner life to the ways in which that life is filtered through, experienced, and comprehended in terms of history and culture. For instance, the movement from a one-person to a two-person and even three-person view of psychoanalysis altered the concept of analytic neutrality by recognizing analysts' needs to interrogate their personal history and motives and hence the contingency of their interpretations as well as to acknowledge the nonverbal aspects of their interactions with patients. In addition, the shift from oedipal to preoedipal concerns opened research into mother/infant relationships and the influence of the child's early environment on its development. Finally, trauma theory rests on the assumption that external factors, such as physical or emotional abuse, can inflict lasting emotional damage. The field of Holocaust Studies, which makes use of trauma theory to elucidate the responses of survivors and their descendants, has made a major contribution to this evolving body of theory.[37] Holocaust Studies, in turn, have contributed to the efforts of those seeking to comprehend the long-term aftereffects of political abuses such as colonial occupation, slavery, and genocide.

These developments intersect with contemporary theories of mourning, including the work of Julia Kristeva[38] on the preoedipal dynamics of depression, that of Nicolas Abraham and Maria Torok[39] on the concept of the "crypt," and the groundbreaking study of Alexander and Margarete Mitscherlich[40] on the failure of post-war Germany to acknowledge its complicity with Hitler's rise to power and to confront the damage to the nation that ensued. For Kristeva, Lacan's concept of the Imaginary offers not only a position from which to challenge the order of the Symbolic but also as a means of exploring the depths of clinical depression or melancholia. Melancholia, for her, is a languageless condition, locked into form of mute despair. This state mimics the infant's initial state of oneness with its mother, which requires a process of mourning in order to dissolve. Kristeva's account, which depends on the subject's ability to renounce the illusion of fusion with the body of the all-fulfilling mother, reads:

> From the analyst's point of view, the possibility of concatenating signifiers (words or actions) appears to depend upon going through mourning for an archaic and indispensable object – and on the related emotions as well. Mourning for The Thing – such a possibility comes out of transposing, beyond loss and on an imaginary or symbolic level, the imprints of an interchange with the other articulated according to a certain order.[41]

Kristeva theorizes that our first task as individuals is to encounter and absorb the experience of loss. Her thinking about melancholia owes much to the work of Nicolas Abraham and Maria Torok on the concept of the crypt. In *The Shell and the Kernel*, Abraham and Torok draw a distinction between the process of "introjection" and "incorporation" of loss. While introjection involves a gradual metabolism or internalization of the lost object, incorporation attempts to swallow it whole, creating an inner space that resembles a tomb, isolated from the individual's conscious awareness and haunting it from within. Abraham and Torok's description of this process is metaphorically powerful.

> Reconstituted from the memories of words, scenes, and affects, the objectal correlative of the loss is buried alive in the crypt as a full-fledged person, complete with its own topography. The crypt includes the actual or supposed traumas that made introjection impossible. ... Sometimes in the dead of night, when libidinal fulfillments have their way, the ghost of the crypt comes back to haunt the cemetery guard, giving him strange and incomprehensible signals, making him perform bizarre acts, or subjecting him to unexpected sensations.[42]

The crypt gives rise to the phenomenon of haunting, the creation of a phantom memory whose source or point of origin becomes virtually untraceable. This concept is useful in analyzing how families transmit their unresolved traumas to future generations. In this way, psychoanalysis opens out into history.

Alexander and Margarete Mitscherlich applied trauma and mourning theory to culture in their study of the post-war German response to the moral, social, and economic collapse of their country. Ordinary German citizens, they claim, turned their backs on the past in a frantic attempt to reconstruct their broken world. A first level of response, they maintain, included the denial of feelings such as responsibility or guilt, leading to a kind of psychic numbness in relation to the past. Their description of this process is compelling.

> In the first place, a striking emotional rigidity was evidenced in response to the piles of corpses in the concentration camps, to the disappearance into captivity of entire German armies, to the news of the slaughter of millions of Jews, Poles, and Russians, and the murder of political opponents in one's own ranks. ... This quasi-stoical attitude ... also made it possible, in the second step, for Germans to identify with the victors easily and without any sign of wounded pride. This shift of identification also helped ward off the sense of being implicated and prepared the way for the third phase: the manic undoing of the past, the huge collective effort of reconstruction.[43]

For the Mitscherlichs, the post-war German failure to mourn fostered a manic effort of self-reinvention. While delaying a reckoning with the past, it also created a legacy of haunting. The extent to which a society is able to confront its ghost history, they suggest, it may also achieve an integration of the past and a degree of psychic health.

The field of Holocaust Studies, while following its own path of development, benefited from trauma theory in several ways. Key to the concept of PTSD is the sudden and overwhelming nature of emotional or external stimuli, which blocks the normal processes of memory and narrative formation. In the neurobiological view, traumatic shock releases a surge of the stress hormone cortisol, which bypasses the hippocampus (the seat of memory), registering itself instead in physiological forms of disturbance, such as recurring nightmares, fight, flight, or freeze responses to seemingly innocuous stimuli, and ultimately the inability to create an integrated personal narrative. Many Holocaust survivors, in this view, could not connect their new lives in altered circumstances to what had happened in the recent and more distant past. Unable to find words for their experiences, they simply did not speak of them – hoping also to spare their children and grandchildren the experiences they had undergone. The movement to recover and record the memories of survivors as they aged brought this phenomenon to light. It also helped to make sense of the phantom effects of survivors' experiences on their descendants. What is not spoken by one generation may be communicated to the next, as Abraham and Torok have described. The silent movement across families and cultures of such phantom histories may be understood, in the language of Holocaust Studies, as "the intergenerational transmission of loss."

Concepts such as the crypt, phantom memory, and the intergenerational transmission of trauma have proved useful to literary and cultural critics, historians, sociologists, and political scientists as well as to psychologists, psychiatrists, and psychoanalysts. If, as many now believe, traumatic histories can be conveyed across generations, then we may begin to speculate more deeply about the interactions between our inner and external psychic lives. This field, which includes psychoanalytic explorations of gender, racial, class, and political forms of oppression, has developed rapidly in recent decades. These areas of investigation are dynamic and inter-involved, leading to changes in social practices and theory once regarded as fixed and immutable.

Given Freud's emphasis on narrative construction (and reconstruction) in psychoanalysis, one may argue that he anticipated such profound alterations in psychoanalytic theory and practice that have transpired since. Yet he did not foresee the specific nature of these changes nor their social and political impact. In this sense, his writing of the Dora case history initiated a way of thinking and writing that authorized the continuing development of psychoanalysis, without dictating its content. While I do not mean to suggest that Freud would have approved of the shift from oedipal to preoedipal studies nor that he would have endorsed the innovations of such thinkers as Lacan, I do believe that his literary manner of writing (including a reliance on symbol, metaphor, narrative voice, and a highly convoluted manner of presentation) encouraged his followers to exercise their own insight and creativity. Among major changes in psychoanalytic theory post-Freud, I would include the following: homosexuality is no longer listed in the Diagnostic and Statistical Manual (DSM) as a psychological disorder; the concept of penis envy as the cornerstone of female development has fallen by the wayside; and acceptance of gender diversity as expressed in LGBTQ identities and behaviors is widespread, as is the legalization of same-sex marriage. None of these developments, which began in the second half of the twentieth century, are ones that Freud conceived of or imagined.

While Freud altered the ways that we understand and interpret our individual lives, including our frustrations, conflicts, obsessions, and unwelcome states of mind, such as uncontrolled aggression, self-abnegation, or depression, he did not seek to change the social order he inherited and sought to analyze. He never abandoned, for instance, his adherence to the Oedipus complex as the key to individual development as well as to the evolution of civilization itself. With the benefit of hindsight, we can see how Freud's sociocultural background and experience obscured his capacity to respond fully to his patient Dora's dilemma. A consideration of her status as a young woman in a prosperous, fin-de-siècle, Viennese family may illustrate the difficulty of her (and Freud's) situation.

In his zeal to demonstrate his theories of hysteria and dream interpretation as dependent on unconscious wishes, rooted in the repression of sexual desire, Freud urged Dora to accept the bargain presented to her by her father and Herr K. While agreeing with her interpretation of their complicity in deciding her fate, he also appears to have suggested that Dora acquiesce. In the absence of evidence that Herr K.'s advances involved anything more than a sexual liaison with a girl young enough to be his daughter, Freud offered a fantasy of his own – that Herr K. planned to divorce his wife to marry Dora. He appears to have presented this interpretation to Dora in one of their final meetings:

> May you not have thought that he wanted to get divorced from his wife so as to marry you? . . . I imagine that this was a perfectly serious plan for the future in your eyes. You have not even got the right to assert that it was out of the question for Herr K. to have had any such intention; you have told me enough about him that points directly towards him having such an intention. Nor does his behavior at L– contradict this view. After all, you did not let him finish his speech and do not know what he meant to say to you.[44]

If Herr K. did not finish his speech, how would anyone know what he had meant to say? Freud's solution to Dora's dilemma acknowledges her intelligence and perspicacity in comprehending the situation she has been presented with. But instead of helping her to find a way out, he urges her further into it. "Incidentally," he concludes, in the reported speech above: "if your temptation at L. had a different upshot, this would have been the only possible solution for all parties concerned."[45] How would Dora's acceptance of Herr K.'s offer to become his mistress have presented a solution for "all parties concerned?" While it would have satisfied Dora's father in his desire to continue his affair with Frau K., and may also have offered Herr K. the sexual satisfaction that he craved, how would it have served Dora?

Here, the class-based aspect of this case begins to emerge. What if Dora had acceded to Herr K.'s advances in the absence of a divorce and marriage proposal? Even supposing that she was attracted to him as a lover, she would have sacrificed her market value for any future marriage prospects. With a keen eye to such matters, Dora observed how both her father and Herr K. had sought to seduce the lower-class women employed as governesses in their households. Both men had pressed their claims by saying that they could "get nothing" out of their wives. Dora's governess left her employment as a result. The governess in Herr K.'s household suffered a more problematic fate. She was dismissed, after succumbing to Herr K.'s advances. Surely, Dora could perceive her own possible future should she offer herself to Herr K. Philip Rieff in his introduction to the Collier Books translation of the Dora case history, summarized Dora's quandary as follows:

> The sick daughter has a sick father, who has a sick mistress, who has a sick husband, who proposes himself to the sick daughter as her lover. Dora does not want to hold hands in this charmless circle – although Freud does, at one point, indicate that she should.[46]

Dora came to her own decision. She confronted her father, Herr K. and Frau K. with her assessment of their relations and received confirmation from them. She then reported the result of this encounter to Freud as a prelude to terminating treatment. Given the limited choices available to her and lacking the education and resources to establish economic security for herself, she held out for a socially sanctioned marriage.

Freud's Enduring Legacy

We do not know what Dora thought and felt, as she left no record of her own. Yet her story, as transmitted through Freud's case history, continues to engage us, not only because of its literary construction but also because it appears to contain within it the seeds of psychoanalytic theories that have unfolded over time. These include Freud's speculations about transference, which led to the theories of countertransference and intersubjectivity; his acknowledgment (however muted) of the preoedipal underpinnings of desire circulating among Frau K., Dora's father, and Dora; and his implicit recognition of the restriction of Dora's options as a woman in a rigidly patriarchal society.

Emphasis has shifted, moreover, in the postmodern era, from the assumption of universal truth, rooted in a fixed set of theories and social structures, to more contingent approaches to such complex issues as gender identity, female and maternal subjectivity, and the role of trauma (transmitted across generations) to affect individual and social realities. Finally, the field of psychoanalysis as a whole has moved away from the purely verbal realm of interpretation toward the realm of the inarticulate, in terms of the analyst's states of reverie, as well as the patient's pre-symbolic and hence unrepresented states of being.[47] Freud's ideas have permeated Western consciousness and culture. He established a lexicon for describing psychic life, including (but not limited to): the unconscious; infantile sexuality; the Oedipus complex; the ego, superego, and the id; trauma; melancholia; the pleasure principle; and the death instinct. Yet he has no pure disciples today. Rather, contemporary analysts find inspiration in his writings to develop theories and practices of their own. What Freud shares with literary authors, then, is his focus on human subjectivity in its full range of complexity and variety of manifestations. Like great literary writers, moreover, Freud bequeathed a body of work that opens itself to ever-new insights and possibilities of interpretation.

Notes

1. Mark Doty, Presentation ("Memory, Memoir and Meaning." Weekend Workshop of "New Directions: Writing with a Psychoanalytic Edge," February 2016).
2. See Sigmund Freud, *The Interpretation of Dreams* (1900), SE 4: 1–338.
3. Freud, "Fragment of an Analysis of a Case of Hysteria" (1905), SE 7: 1–122.
4. Madelon Sprengnether, "Literature and Psychoanalysis," in *The Routledge Handbook of Psychoanalysis in the Social Sciences and the Humanities*, eds. Anthony Elliott and Jeffrey Prager (London: Routledge, 2016), 300–13.
5. Steven Marcus, "Freud and Dora: Story, History, Case History," in *In Dora's Case: Freud-Hysteria-Feminism*, eds. Charles Bernheimer and Claire Kahane (New York: Columbia University Press), 64.
6. Marcus, "Freud and Dora," 65.
7. Freud, *Studies on Hysteria* (1895), SE 2: 160–61.
8. Freud, "Screen Memories" (1899), SE 3: 3–22.
9. Freud, *The Interpretation of Dreams*, SE 4:1–338.
10. Freud, "Fragment," 116.
11. Ibid., 118.
12. See Ernest Jones, *The Life and Work of Sigmund Freud*, 3 vols. (New York: Basic Books: 1953, 1955, 1957).

13. See Peter Gay, *Freud: A Life for Our Time* (New York: W. W. Norton, 1988).

14. Jones, *Life and Work of Sigmund Freud*, 1:319.

15. Gay, *Freud*, 90.

16. Freud, "Recommendations to Physicians Practicing Psycho-Analysis" (1912), *SE* 12: 116.

17. Freud, "Analysis Terminable and Interminable" (1937), *SE* 23: 248–49.

18. See "Infantile Sexuality" (1905), *SE* 7: 173–206.

19. For a comprehensive overview of the concept of countertransference, see Theodore Jacobs, "Countertransference Past and Present: A Review of the Concept," *International Journal of Psychoanalysis* 80, no. 3 (1999): 575–94.

20. Intersubjectivity may be viewed as a refinement of object relations theory, as it relies on the assumption that the individual psyche evolves not in isolation but in the context of the early child-caring relationship. Absent this premise, the kind of inter-involvement between analyst and patient described by Ogden and others would not be possible.

21. Freud, "Female Sexuality," *SE* 21:225–26.

22. I have discussed this issue at length in *The Spectral Mother: Freud, Feminism, and Psychoanalysis* (Ithaca, NY: Cornell University Press, 1990).

23. See Anna Freud, *Introduction to Psychoanalysis: Lectures for Child Analysts and Teachers*, *The Writings of Anna Freud*, vol. 1 (Madison, CT: International Universities Press, 1974).

24. See John Bowlby, *Attachment and Loss* (London: Hogarth Press, 1969).

25. For representative examples of the British school, see W. R. D. Fairbairn, *An Object Relations Theory of the Personality* (New York: Basic Books, 1952); Harry Guntrip, *Schizoid Phenomena, Object Relations and the Self* (London: Hogarth Press, 1968); Margaret Mahler, *On Human Symbiosis and the Vicissitudes of Individuation* (New York: International Universities Press, 1968); D. W. Winnicott, *Therapeutic Consultations in Child Psychiatry* (London: Hogarth, 1971).

26. Freud, *Totem and Taboo* (1913), *SE* 13: 1–161.

27. For Klein, the infant's inner world is split in ways that feel intolerable. Love and gratitude for the fulfilling breast war with hate and destructive impulses toward the breast that is absent or unavailable. Lacking a means to contain such overwhelming emotions, the infant projects them outwards – into fantasy constructions of the "good" and "bad" breast. Under optimal conditions, the developing child will integrate its interior world in a way that allows it to accept both love and hate toward the same indispensable object. At this point in time, it will move from what Klein calls the "paranoid-schizoid phase" to the "depressive position." The depressive position involves the capacity to feel guilt as well as the need and desire for reparation. Both Freud and Klein offer theories of psychic evolution that account for guilt and renunciation, but only Klein includes the concept of reparation or making amends. Melanie Klein, *Love, Guilt and Reparation & Other Works 1921–1945* (New York: Delacorte, 1975).

28. The phrase "thinking through the mother" is adapted from Virginia Woolf's famous quote "For we think back through our mothers if we are women," Virginia Woolf, *A Room of One's Own* (London: Hogarth Press, 1929).

29. Freud, "Fragment," 51.

30. Freud, "Fragment," 96.

31. Dorothy Dinnerstein, *The Mermaid and the Minotaur: Sexual Arrangements and Human Malaise* (New York: Harper and Row, 1976) and Nancy Chodorow, *The Reproduction of Mothering: Psychoanalysis and the Sociology of Gender* (Berkeley: University of California Press, 1978).

32. See Jacques Lacan, *Écrits: A Selection*, trans. Alan Sheridan (London: Tavistock, 1977).

33. As an introduction, see Hélène Cixous, and Cathérine Clément, *The Newly Born Woman*, trans. Betsy Wing (Minneapolis: University of Minnesota Press, 1986); Luce Irigaray, "And the One Doesn't Stir Without the Other," trans. Helene Vivienne Wenzel, *Signs* 7 (1985): 60–67 and Julia Kristeva, *Black Sun: Depression and Melancholia*, trans. Leon Roudiez (New York: Columbia University Press, 1989).

34. Juliet Mitchell, *Psychoanalysis and Feminism* (New York: Pantheon, 1974).

35. See Freud, *Beyond the Pleasure Principle* (1920), *SE* 18: 1–64.

36. For an excellent history of the development of trauma theory, see Bessel Van der Kolk, Lars Weisaeth, and Onno van der Hart, "History of Trauma in Psychiatry," in *Traumatic Stress: The Effects of Overwhelming Stress on Mind, Body, and Society* (New York; Guilford Press, 1996), 47–74. See also Dagmar Herzog's account in of the role of Holocaust studies in the evolution of Post Traumatic Stress Disorder as a psychoanalytic concept, *Cold War Freud* (Cambridge: Cambridge University Press, 2017).

37. The field of Holocaust studies is too vast to document here. As a starting point, I recommend Cathy Caruth, ed. "Psychoanalysis, Culture and Trauma," *American Imago* 48, no. 1 (1991): 1–175.

38. See Kristeva, *Black Sun*.

39. Nicolas Abraham and Maria Torok, *The Shell and the Kernel*, Vol. 1, ed., trans. Nicolas T. Rand (Chicago: University of Chicago Press, 1994).

40. Alexander Mitscherlich and Margarete Mitscherlich, *The Inability to Mourn*, trans. Beverly R. Placzek (New York: Grove Press, 1975).

41. Kristeva, *Black Sun*, 40.

42. Abraham and Torok, *Shell and the Kernel*, 130.

43. Mitscherlich and Mitscherlich, *The Inability to Mourn*, 28.

44. Freud, "Fragment," 99.

45. Ibid, 100.

46. Philip Rieff, "Introduction," in *Dora: An Analysis of a Case of Hysteria* (New York: Macmillan, 1963), x.

47. Intersubjectivity, for instance, posits an intuitive and almost unconscious connection that arises from the analytic process. Wilfred Bion, who emphasized the need for the analyst to attend to the patient's confused and inarticulate states of mind (which he termed "beta" elements), was an influential figure in this field. For Bion, the task of the analyst was to recognize and engage with the patient's wordless and disorganized mental processes in order to bring them into the realm of "alpha" awareness and articulation, *Learning from Experience* (New York: Basic Books, 1962). See also Thomas Ogden's concept of the "intersubjective analytic third," *Reverie and Interpretation* (Northvale, NJ: Jason Aronson, 1997).

2

CATHERINE BATES

Recognitions
Shakespeare, Freud, and the Story of Psychoanalysis

Literature – drama especially, tragedy in particular, and Shakespeare above all – plays an integral part in the story of psychoanalysis.[1] When, in the months following his father's death, Freud abandoned the seduction theory – no longer attributing neurosis to the experience of external childhood trauma, as his early work on hysteria had led him to do, but rather to the internal dramas of infantile sexuality (the foundation of what would become classic psychoanalytic theory) – it was through the medium of tragic drama that he announced the change. As he confided (privately, in the first instance, to his friend Wilhelm Fliess), in the course of his own self-analysis "[a] single idea of general value dawned on me. I have found, in my own case too, [the phenomenon of] being in love with my mother and jealous of my father, and I now consider it a universal event in early childhood." Freud justified this startling leap from the particular to the general by making a direct appeal to the Western literary canon: "If this is so, we can understand the gripping power of *Oedipus Rex* [...] the Greek legend seizes upon a compulsion which everyone recognizes because he senses its existence within himself. Everyone in the audience was once a budding Oedipus in fantasy." "Fleetingly," he goes on, "the thought passed through my head that the same thing might be at the bottom of *Hamlet* as well [...] How does he explain his irresolution in avenging his father by the murder of his uncle [...] How better than through the torment he suffers from the obscure memory that he himself had contemplated the same deed against his father out of passion for his mother [...] His conscience is his unconscious sense of guilt."[2]

When Freud first went public with the new theory in *The Interpretation of Dreams,* he nuanced the difference between the two plays by noting that, where the Oedipal fantasy is acted out in Sophocles' play, it remains repressed in Shakespeare's: a difference he attributed to "the secular advance of repression in the emotional life of mankind," and used to explain why *Hamlet* had such a powerful effect on modern audiences.[3] It also became clear that Freud's particular take on Shakespeare's play had emerged from his situation as a recently bereaved son, and that it was this that had motivated his identification with both Shakespeare – who wrote *Hamlet* in the months following his own father's death – and, of course, with Hamlet himself.[4] The effect, as one critic notes, is to open up "a sudden sense of infinite regress, with layers upon layers of identification and loss."[5] Whether Freud found the Oedipus complex within the play (as he claimed) or the play guided him toward finding it in himself is, ultimately, undecidable, for the theory and the literary text exist in a mutually reinforcing relation.[6] Among critics, this is a common theme. "Is Shakespeare Freudian or is Freud Shakespearean?," asks one; the "double impact" of Shakespeare on Freud and of Freud on how we read Shakespeare is the theme of another.[7] "Nowhere is this chiasmatic bond tighter," writes a third, "than in Freud's attachment to *Hamlet*."[8] It is for this reason that, like this critic and many others, I will focus here on this particular play as the most apt of illustrative examples.

What happens when Freud peers into the text and sees something looking back at him is, as he notes in his letter to Fliess, essentially an act of recognition: an encounter, a facing, a meeting of minds.[9] Across the centuries, stretching to the Renaissance and beyond, as far back even as ancient Greece – from millennia of cultural and historical difference – a basic pattern emerges: a discernible structure of desire that links past to present in a continuity of human experience that can be scientifically identified, classified, and named. At some level, a sense of relief and joy characterizes this moment, as if it were a kind of family reunion (the classic plot-resolution of Shakespearean comedy and romance): fathers are recognized in these literary greats, and brothers in the experiences they and their characters share. The fundamental likeness of those long-lost relatives – recognized at last – is what allows Freud to lay claim to universal validity and bestows on him the confidence of a triumphant discoverer and pioneer. It puts his theory on a whole new footing – secured and grounded in the greatest literary works of Western civilization – and allows him to bask in their reflected glory. All the jubilation of the classic mirror-relation is here, as Freud sees himself reflected in his most venerated writers and their heroes, and they in him. Paired because alike in a crucial respect, they exist in a specular relation that is typically narcissistic and idealizing: a "kind of identificatory correspondence, vividly illustrating an identity both with and of the *same*."[10]

This is only half the story, however, for while they share important characteristics, these bereaved, Oedipal sons are not entirely alike. As they relate to one another – both backwards and forwards in time – Freud, Hamlet, Shakespeare, and Oedipus might very well be similar, but for all that they are not self-same: to identify is not to be identical because it entails an encounter with things both like and unlike. Their relation is less that of a mirror-image, therefore, than of a metaphor, in which selected elements are singled out as similar against a great many that are not (my mistress' eyes are like the sun insofar as they are bright and round, but, in being neither large, hot, distant, singular, and so on, nothing like it in every other respect). If Freud's joyous hailing of Oedipus and Hamlet feels a bit like a family reunion, it is because the affinity he finds with them is indeed that of a family resemblance: certain features are recognizably there, but identity depends on difference. To that extent, since they are of the same kin but a different kind – *heimlich* and *unheimlich* in equal measure – their relation could best be described as "uncanny," and to say this is to foreground the dissonance which no such relation is without.[11] For the look-alike, twin, or brother, of course, evokes not only the gratifications of fellow-feeling, but also resentment, hostility, and aggression, as the jealousy of the father which they share gets turned against one another in filial competition and rivalry. In Freud's case, his veneration for Shakespeare as "the greatest of poets" came to be matched by his bizarre attachment to the theory that the true author of Shakespeare's works was not the lowly actor from Stratford but the noble Earl of Oxford (a view in which he persisted from 1921 to his death): "this is the ancient story of literary influence and its anxieties," writes Harold Bloom, "the threatening precursor had to be exposed, dismissed, disgraced."[12] As joy gives way to suspicion, and denouncement replaces hail-fellow-well-met, we might trace a passage away from the mirror – the jubilatory delusions of the Imaginary – to the chronic alienations of the Symbolic: "a poetics of a double tongue rather than a poetics of a unified and unifying eye," as one critic writes.[13] Or, to put it another way, we might see here a passage from comedy to tragedy, much as Shakespeare himself moved, at the time of writing *Hamlet*, from a comedic world of double-plots, siblings, and twins – in which sameness and incestuous desire is benign and unthreatening, and ultimately promotes equality, community, and harmony (as in *Twelfth Night* or *As You Like It*) – to a tragic world in which the same phenomena are sinister and malign, provoke horror, disgust, and revenge, and result in polluted or unfulfilled marriages, and the isolation (not to mention death) of the hero.[14]

Behind these diverging impulses toward love and hate – the classic material of ambivalence – we might also make out the competing commands of the Oedipus complex: namely, that the son must be both like his father in some respects (strong, brave, masculine, heterosexual, and so on) but unlike him in others (forbidden sexual possession of the mother). Within the field of tragic drama, in turn, these contradictory commands might well translate – in good

Aristotelian fashion – into pity, in the first instance (a relation of sameness), and fear, in the second (a relation of difference).[15] It will, therefore, be on this doubled, troubled relation between like and unlike – rather than on the specific dynamics of a triangulated desire ("being in love with my mother and jealous of my father") – that I focus in the discussion that follows. For, as we shall see, this will tell us more not only about Shakespeare and Freud, literature and psychoanalysis, and the relation between the two, but also about the way in which, as readers and writers ourselves, we are implicated in that relation as well.

○○

The complications of Freud's Oedipal relation with father/brother Shakespeare, of course, are refracted and repeated many times over within *Hamlet* itself. In Hamlet's relation with, Laertes, for example, another bereaved and avenging son who – as his "more handsome double" and "a rival his own size" – serves as his foil: the idol or ideal ego of the mirror-stage that engenders in the hero both fascination and revenge.[16] But Hamlet's identifications with such "brother" figures proliferate well beyond Laertes, to include Horatio, Fortinbras, the grave-digger, and even Aeneas, whose famous speech retelling the fall of Troy and the death of his father, Priam, is rehearsed, at Hamlet's request, by the First Player.[17] The relative likeness and unlikeness of brothers, furthermore, is a problem the play puts center stage in the relation between Old Hamlet and Claudius. Hamlet's insistence on the absolute difference between them – "Hyperion to a satyr,"[18] graphically repeated when he holds their respective portraits before Gertrude to dramatize the contrast between the two – protests the sameness to which her incestuous marriage, in rendering them both indifferently "your husband,"[19] has reduced them. It is precisely because brotherhood is "the least differentiated relationship in most kinship systems" that, in myth and legend, it has anciently served as a narrative mechanism for establishing the differentials upon which society, civilization, law, even language, depend, and, conversely, for depicting the chaos or cultural suicide that ensues when those differentials are dispensed with.[20] The formal combat that took place in the play's prehistory between Old Hamlet and Old Fortinbras – equal in status and thus effectively "brother" kings – served the former function, decisively establishing the difference between victor and vanquished, and with it the just distribution of women and land. Claudius' furtive murder of his brother, by contrast, effectively undoes this work, and produces a world in which sexual, social, familial, and generational distinctions are lost, and weddings indistinguishable from funerals. As for Hamlet's identification with his father, while Shakespeare makes a point of giving them the same name (in a notable departure from his source), this seems only to exaggerate how different, almost unrecognizable they are. "Ironically, the two Hamlets meet as if the Edda were encountering Montaigne: the Archaic Age faces the High Renaissance."[21] Not only that, but the play proliferates with any number of different father-figures and father-surrogates (Old Hamlet, Old Fortinbras, Priam, Polonius, Yorick), although – also ironically – these seem nevertheless to have a great deal in common: dead in every case, their ghosts, memories, bodies, and skulls loom over the play with a distinctly undead presence.[22]

What Marjorie Garber describes as the "peculiar characteristic of ghostliness – that the ghost is a copy, somehow both nominally identical to and numinously different from a vanished or unavailable original," could be applied to these memories and corpses as well.[23] And this, in turn, opens up the whole question of the way art relates to life, the stage to the world it represents. For, on the one hand, as Hamlet extols, playing holds "the mirror up to nature"[24] – a model of ideal transparency which promises all the satisfactions of the mirror-relation with its lures of sameness and identity – while, on the other, theater is nothing but a second-hand simulacrum, a poor copy, a shadow, a ghost, forever different and alienated from the life it represents:

> Representation, stressing and registering itself *as* representation, calls up and evokes as something absent the truthful presentation it confesses truly it is not. There is therefore, as Shakespeare develops it, a structural pathos built into representation. The "re-" of representation effects the loss of presentation; it is responsible for that loss because representation is not only achieved over the dead body of the presence it repeats, but, more actively, this very repetition is what transforms such ideal presence into something of the past.[25]

Shakespeare explores this ambiguous, doubled, tragical-comical, similar-but-different relation of art to life throughout his work, but in *Hamlet* he seems intent on *re*doubling it. Versions of the death of king and father, for example, are re-presented twice, first in the Player's speech about Priam, and second in the play-within-a-play. The latter, in turn, has two titles (*The Murder of Gonzago* and "The Mouse-trap"), and it re-presents the scene of the murder twice, in dumb-show and in dialogue. The scene it replays doubles the murder of Old Hamlet by Claudius in the past with the would-be murder of Claudius by Hamlet in the future. It also serves the dual purpose of testing the veracity of the Ghost's account of that murder (being poisoned in the ear) and of Claudius' concomitant guilt. Every performance of Shakespeare's play, of course, goes on to redouble these duplications, not only re-playing the same drama in a different time or place with different actors, a different audience, and quite possibly a different script, but – with each re-playing – multiplying these already multiple points of comparison and contrast: these moments of recognition that entail both identification and alienation, these tensions between original and copy, between life and its ghostly counterpart, art.

"Whenever something can be doubled, it is," writes Frank Kermode, "revenges and revengers, lawful espials, ghostly visitations [...] These compulsive duplications occur everywhere," and they appear even in miniature, at the very linguistic level of the text which is characterized, to an extraordinary degree, by tropes that use two words to mean one thing (hendiadys) or one word to mean two (puns).[26] Then there is the question of how *Hamlet* relates to its own literary precursors: admiring and imitating them, on the one hand, ruthlessly exploiting and over-going them, on the other. One might start with the *Ur-Hamlet*, generally attributed to Thomas Kyd but conceivably by Shakespeare himself, in which case the ghost of that first, early *Hamlet* – thoroughly killed off, stifled, and suppressed in the process – is one of the many ghosts that haunts the play we have, making it a curious example of literary self-murder in the interests of literary self-determination.[27] If one of the antecedents of Shakespeare's play is *Oedipus Rex*, moreover, how fitting that Sophocles' drama should itself overflow with such doublings, including the hero's punning name (both "Swell-foot" and "Know-foot"); his suffering at the hands of the "double-lashing" curse that begins with the wounding of his ankles and ends with the blinding of his eyes, is set in motion when Laius strikes him with a twin-pronged goad, and leads to the double crime of parricide and incest which he unknowingly breeds in the "double mother-field" that is Jocasta, as a result of which he is fated to endure "double griefs and double evils" for the rest of his life.[28] The many doublings within *Hamlet* may find their similar-yet-different family relations here.[29] How fitting, too, that the Oedipus story should itself bifurcate into two potential sources, not only its rendition by Sophocles but its subsequent retelling by Seneca (with its own symptomatic imitations and deviations, of course), the version Shakespeare is most likely to have encountered at school. It was certainly a debased and parodic version of Seneca that went by the name of popular revenge tragedy on the sixteenth-century London stage, and in *Hamlet* such "Senecan" excess appears as a clear import – set apart in the "passionate speech"[30] about Priam and in the play-within-a-play – evidently Hamlet's idea of revenge drama rather than Shakespeare's. It is often remarked that, in writing *Hamlet*, Shakespeare acts out own his refusal to perpetuate a genre that had become manifestly *weary, stale, flat, and unprofitable* by 1601, this being as mindless and predictable as allowing oneself to get caught up in the repetitive and self-perpetuating cycles of revenge itself. "What the hero feels in regard to the act of revenge," writes one critic, "the creator feels in regard to revenge as theater."[31]

Hamlet's relations with a whole slew of father- and brother-figures, in other words, might also be seen to reflect Shakespeare's own ambivalent relations with the literary fore-fathers and "brother" dramatists whom he both followed and left behind. For, according to the humanist theory of the time, the sincerest form of imitation was not a slavish copy or impersonation but rather the relation "of a son to his father," with all that that entails. There is resemblance, of course – "seeing the son's face we are reminded of the father's" – but also difference – "if it came to measurement, the features would all be different" – so that, when imitating other writers, it was necessary to ensure "that if there is something similar, there is also a great deal that is dissimilar."[32] As a child of the Tudor grammar school that inculcated the practice of such humanist *imitatio*, Shakespeare would have been familiar with a system that "engages the aggressivity that always inheres in a mimetic relation in order to produce a style that both follows and modifies its model."[33] Here, as elsewhere, this Oedipal relation involved a split regime. On the one hand, there were the securities of sameness: the system was specifically designed to reproduce paternal authority, to turn out good, acculturated citizens (fathers, magistrates, gentlemen) – masters who were modelled on their masters (whether the giants of the classical canon or the schoolmasters themselves) – and so to produce the consolidated male egos supposedly reflected in the ideal ego of that mirrored relation. On the other, there were the determinations of difference: the self-alienations that necessarily arose from identifying with an Other from the outset – the shattering of that ideal-but-illusory reflection as surely as in Narcissus' pool – the identification not only with the schoolmaster and the master authors he taught but also with their characters (often passionate women, like Hecuba, whom the Player if not Hamlet effectively becomes) that did nothing to consolidate the male ego, and the destructive-creative energies that modified, mutilated, and murdered the inherited models in order to make new ones, and not only *dramatis personae* but a distinct "persona" or "character" of the writer's own: one which, as the words suggest, was no less acted or scripted.[34]

CR

I discuss these various aspects of *Hamlet* to make the point that, when Freud did a double take – looked into the play and recognized the Oedipus complex – it was not only the content of that complex (the family romance) that he saw, but also the very nature of that recognition scene itself. Its registering of sameness and difference was reflected there at every level: in

Shakespeare's relations with his literary fore-fathers and fellow playwrights (and they with their own); in the relations of his (and their) characters to one another; in the very language of his (and their) fictions; in the relation of one performance to another (whether theatrical or meta-theatrical); in the relation of the artistic representation to any original, initiating action, whether some reality or "life" inferred behind it or merely an infinite series of such ghostly representations stretching back without end. To focus on this aspect of the play – and Freud's reaction to it – is to show how Shakespeare's importance for psychoanalysis extends well beyond the Oedipus complex to include such defining ideas and categories as identification and desire; mourning and melancholia; aggression and defense; the uncanny; the return of the repressed; the compulsion to repeat; the death drive; narcissism; the mirror-stage; the Imaginary and the Symbolic; the constitution of the subject in and by language, the vicissitudes of the signifier, not to mention recognition itself.[35] Emerging from a recognition scene quite as consequential for Western culture as anything in *Hamlet* or *Oedipus Rex*, psychoanalysis was a literary genre from the beginning; and never more so than in its very determination to be different – to be verifiable and "scientific" – for in that drama itself (what else but a battle for mastery?), psychoanalytic theory merely repeated a version of the same struggle to differentiate that had been played out so many times between writers and within their works.[36] In the relation between psychoanalysis and literature neither is the master discourse, for both expose the illusoriness – the folly – of such supremacy even as they strive for it.[37]

The academic and clinical literature of psychoanalysis provides a spectacle of such familial battles no less illuminating: from Ernest Jones, the most faithful of sons, who nevertheless made his own modest contributions to Freud's reading of *Hamlet*, if only for his own self-respect; to Jacques Lacan, the apostate, schismatic, and *enfant terrible* of the psychoanalytic establishment, who sowed dissension within its ranks yet as a faithful son who was merely returning to the father a flock that had strayed; to Jean Laplanche who, correcting Freud's own tendencies to go astray, proved in his admonitions more faithful to the father's teaching than the father himself.[38] And the same struggles for individuation are played out within literary criticism, too (this chapter not excepted): venerating our admired authors while feeding off them, joining the collegial conversation while making sure to see or say something new. As Marjorie Garber rightly says, "there needs no ghost come from the grave to suggest that literary scholarship – and textual editing – are themselves a species of revenge."[39] But the last word will elude us as surely as closure will elude any avenger caught up in the cycle of revenge, for if the literary and psychoanalytic texts teach us anything it is that criticism is but "a *ghost effect*" of the texts we read.⁴⁰ We can, however (like Hamlet), become more self-aware, and if we are as committed to revenge as to an analysis interminable, we will at least keep on reading his story. That story, as Frank Kermode writes, is

> a fiction, a dream of passion, in which there are dreams within dreams, and mirror on mirror mirrored is all the show [...] the conversations of interpreters are shadows or images, fat or thin, and not matters of substance, except that where there is shadow there must be substance, and a light on it; so the end of all this shadowy talk is after all to keep a real and valued object in being.⁴¹

Notes

1. On the theater having "a special significance for Freud," see André Green, *The Tragic Effect: The Oedipus Complex in Tragedy*, trans. Alan Sheridan (Cambridge: Cambridge University Press, 1979), 1. For early surveys of Freud's extensive references to Shakespeare throughout his works, see Norman N. Holland, "Freud on Shakespeare," *PMLA* 75, no. 3 (1960): 163–73; and *Psychoanalysis and Shakespeare* (New York: Octagon Books, 1964).
2. Letter dated 15 October 1897, in Jeffrey Moussaieff Masson, ed., *The Complete Letters of Sigmund Freud to Wilhelm Fliess, 1887–1904* (Cambridge, MA: Harvard University Press, 1985), 272–73. In a letter dated 5 November 1897, Freud confirms that "I have not told it to anyone else," Masson, *Complete Letters of Sigmund Freud*, 277.
3. Sigmund Freud, *The Interpretation of Dreams* (1900), *SE* 4: 264.
4. Shakespeare wrote the play "under the immediate impact of his bereavement," Freud notes, "and, as we may well assume, while his childhood feelings about his father had been freshly revived," *SE* 4:265. In the Preface to the second edition of *Dreams* (1908), Freud acknowledges the personal significance of the book for him, "which I only grasped after I had completed it," namely, that it was "a portion of my own self-analysis, my reaction to my father's death – that is to say, to the most important event, the most poignant loss, of a man's life," *SE* 4: xxvi. One can see from a note enclosed with an earlier letter to Fliess, written only seven months after that loss, how Freud's analysis of his own bereavement might have led to his thinking about *Hamlet*: "Hostile impulses against parents (a wish that they should die) [...] are repressed at periods when compassion for the parents is aroused – at times of their illness or death. On such occasions it is a manifestation of mourning to reproach oneself for their death (so-called melancholia) or to punish oneself in a hysterical fashion, through the medium of the idea of retribution" Letter dated May 31, 1897, Masson, *Complete Letters of Sigmund Freud*, 250.
5. David Hillman, *Marx and Freud: Great Shakespeareans Volume X*, eds. Crystal Bartolovich, Jean E. Howard, David Hillman, and Adrian Poole (New York: Continuum, 2012), 118. For a similar analysis, see also Julia Reinhard Lupton and Kenneth Reinhard, *After Oedipus: Shakespeare in Psychoanalysis* (Ithaca, NY: Cornell University Press, 1993), 3–20.

6. See Freud's comment that "the conflict in *Hamlet* is so effectively concealed that it was left to me to unearth it," "Psychopathic Characters on the Stage" (written 1905 or 1906; published 1942), *SE* 7: 310.
7. Joel Fineman, *Shakespeare's Perjured Eye: The Invention of Poetic Subjectivity in the Sonnets* (Berkeley: University of California Press, 1986), 46; Hillman, *Marx and Freud*, 100, quoting the "Prospectus for Contributors" for the entire *Great Shakespeareans* series.
8. Philip Armstrong, *Shakespeare in Psychoanalysis* (London: Routledge, 2001), 21. For other recent book-length studies of *Hamlet* and psychoanalysis, see: James E. Groves, *Hamlet on the Couch: What Shakespeare Taught Freud* (London: Routledge, 2018); Simon Critchley and Jamieson Webster, *Stay, Illusion! The Hamlet Doctrine* (New York: Pantheon Books, 2013); and Marjorie Garber, *Shakespeare's Ghost Writers: Literature as Uncanny Causality* (New York: Routledge, 2nd ed., 2010).
9. In *Dreams* he adds that *Oedipus Rex* "makes a voice within us ready to recognize [*anzuerkennen*] the compelling force of destiny" in the play, and that the poet compels us "to recognize our own inner minds [*zur Erkenntnis unseres eigenen Innern*]," *SE* 4: 262, 263. Recognition, of course, is a crucial component in dramatic plots, as Aristotle pointed out in the *Poetics*. For a fascinating discussion of this theme in Sophocles, Aristotle, Shakespeare, and Freud (among others), see Terence Cave, *Recognitions: A Study in Poetics* (Oxford: Clarendon Press, 1988), 33. For Cave, Freud's "promotion of *Oedipus*, Oedipus and, by extension, recognition is second only to Aristotle's own in the history of poetics," Cave, 162.
10. Fineman, *Shakespeare's Perjured Eye*, 20 (italics original). Although Fineman is here discussing the relation between the poet and the young man in the Sonnets, his insights are applicable to Shakespeare's oeuvre as a whole.
11. See Freud, "The Uncanny" (1919), *SE* 17: 217–55.
12. Harold Bloom, *The Western Canon: The Books and School of the Ages* (New York: Riverhead Books, 1994), 349. For discussions of Freud's adherence to the Oxford hypothesis, see Holland, "Freud on Shakespeare," 164; Holland, *Psychoanalysis and Shakespeare*, 56–59; Bloom, *Western Canon*, 347–49; Garber, *Shakespeare's Ghost Writers*, 1–10; and Hillman, *Marx and Freud*, 131–35. On Shakespeare as "the greatest of poets," see "Some Character-Types Met with in Psycho-Analytic Work" (1916), *SE* 14: 313.
13. Fineman, *Shakespeare's Perjured Eye*, 15, comparing the sonnets addressed to the ideal young man with those addressed to the far from ideal dark lady.
14. See Joel Fineman, "Fratricide and Cuckoldry: Shakespeare's Doubles," in *Representing Shakespeare: New Psychoanalytic Essays*, ed. Murray M Schwartz and Coppélia Kahn (Baltimore: Johns Hopkins University Press, 1980), 70–109.
15. See the discussion in Green, *Tragic Effect*, 26–27.
16. Jacques Lacan emphasizes this aspect of the play in "Desire and the Interpretation of Desire in Hamlet," in *Literature and Psychoanalysis – The Question of Reading: Otherwise*, ed. Shoshana Felman (Baltimore: Johns Hopkins University Press, 1982), 11–52 (34). See also Philip Armstrong, *Shakespeare in Psychoanalysis*, 64–68, and *Shakespeare's Visual Regime: Tragedy, Psychoanalysis, and the Gaze* (London: Routledge, 2000), 14.

17. As Elizabeth J. Bellamy notes, Freud harbored his own identification with Aeneas: "in Freud's dreams, [Rome becomes] the city where he was destined to confront the burdens of being a son [...] the 'neurotic' site of a complex, and indeed overdetermined, interplay of filial piety, Oedipal anxieties, and imperial (or professional) ambition," *Translations of Power: Narcissism and the Unconscious in Epic History* (Ithaca: Cornell University Press, 1992), 43. On Hamlet's relation with such "brothers," see also Groves, *Hamlet on the Couch*, 164–76.

18. Shakespeare, *Hamlet*, I.ii.140. Citations from *The Riverside Shakespeare*, ed. G. Blakemore Evans et al. (Boston: Houghton Mifflin, 2nd ed., 1997).

19. Ibid., III.iv.63, 64.

20. René Girard, *A Theater of Envy: William Shakespeare* (New York: Oxford University Press, 1991), 274. See also the discussion in Fineman, "Fratricide and Cuckoldry." The archetypal tale of fratricidal enmity is the Biblical story of Cain and Abel, in which the elder brother (Cain) murders the younger out of spite because his offering was more pleasing to God; see Genesis 4: 1–16.

21. Harold Bloom, *Shakespeare: The Invention of the Human* (London: Fourth Estate, 1999), 387.

22. The other paternal surrogate, Claudius, who styles himself "Thy loving father, Hamlet" (IV.iii.50), is the exception to this rule. That his marriage to Gertrude represents the forbidden aspect of Oedipal identification manifests in Hamlet's desire to murder him and inability to do so: a contradiction summed up in the figure of Lucianus – the murderous "nephew to the king" (III.ii.244) in "The Mousetrap" – in whom Hamlet's identification with Claudius and disavowal of it is combined. If Hamlet relates to brother-figures along one axis, and father-figures along another, then Claudius – being his father's brother – marks the point at which those two axes meet and where the contradictory relations of sameness and difference effectively collide.

23. Garber, *Shakespeare's Ghost Writers*, 21.

24. III.ii.22.

25. Fineman, *Shakespeare's Perjured Eye*, 297 (italics original). For a discussion of the Platonic principles behind this distinction, see also Robert Weimann, "Mimesis in *Hamlet*," in *Shakespeare and the Question of Theory*, ed. Patricia Parker and Geoffrey Hartman (New York: Routledge, 1985), 275–91.

26. Frank Kermode, "Cornelius and Voltemand: Doubles in *Hamlet*," in *Forms of Attention* (Chicago: University of Chicago Press, 1985), 35–63 (51, 52), drawing on George T. Wright, "Hendiadys and *Hamlet*," *PMLA* 96, no. 2 (1981): 168–93. "One of Hamlet's functions," notes Lacan, "is to engage in constant punning, word-play, double-entendre – to play on ambiguity" like the typical Shakespearean fool, jester, and clown, "Desire and the Interpretation of Desire in *Hamlet*," 33.

27. Harold Bloom explores this hypothesis in *Shakespeare*, 383–431, reviving the work of Peter Alexander, *Hamlet: Father and Son* (Oxford: Clarendon Press, 1955).

28. Sophocles, *Oedipus the King*, ed. and trans. Thomas Gould (Englewood Cliffs, NJ: Prentice Hall, 1970), lines 417, 1257, 1320. As Gould notes, this doubleness is reflected in the language of the play as much as in its plot: "the word 'double,' *diplos*, appears again and again" (47). As examples of Sophoclean irony, Gould

also includes "grim puns, unintended *double entendres*, statements that are the very reverse of the truth, statements that are more true than the speaker knows," as well as word- or image-clusters "that recur again and again, either with dramatically changed meanings or echoing earlier passages in such a way as to give us a truer account of the events than is understood by the participants" (174). See also Jean-Pierre Vernant, "Ambiguity and Reversal: On the Enigmatic Structure of *Oedipus Rex*," trans. Page DuBois, *New Literary History* 9, no. 3 (1978): 475–501: "No literary genre in antiquity, in fact, uses so abundantly as tragedy expressions of double meaning, and *Oedipus Rex* includes more than twice as many ambiguous forms as the other plays of Sophocles" (475). This aspect of the play, and its psychoanalytic significance, is discussed by Cynthia Chase, "Oedipal Textuality: Reading Freud's Reading of *Oedipus*," in *Psychoanalytic Literary Criticism*, ed. Maud Ellmann (London: Longman, 1994), 56–75; and John Fletcher, *Freud and the Scene of Trauma* (New York: Fordham University Press, 2013), 136–52.

29. For Lupton and Reinhard, "[i]f *Hamlet* is the 'translation' of *Oedipus,* it is also a *translatio* in the sense of metaphor," *After Oedipus*, 6.

30. II.ii.432.

31. Girard, *Theater of Envy*, 274; Harold Bloom also calls *Hamlet* Shakespeare's "revenge upon revenge tragedy," *Hamlet: Poem Unlimited* (New York: Riverhead Books, 2003), 3. See also the lengthy discussion in Lupton and Reinhard, *After Oedipus*, 67–90: "in distinguishing itself from 'the Senecan,' Shakespeare's play melancholically identifies with that very difference. The difference *between* 'Shakespeare' and 'Seneca' becomes *Hamlet*'s own self-difference, as inscribed by the reflexive, permeable, reversible boundaries of the play's metatheatrical scenes" (68, italics original).

32. From a letter by Francis Petrarch to Giovanni Boccaccio (1366), in *Letters on Familiar Matters: XVII–XXV*, trans. Aldo S. Bernardo (Baltimore: Johns Hopkins University Press, 1985), letter 23.19 (301–02). As Thomas M. Greene notes in *The Light in Troy: Imitation and Discovery in Renaissance Poetry* (New Haven: Yale University Press, 1982), Petrarch's advice here "bears just this resemblance to a much briefer simile in Seneca" (96), namely that "[e]ven if there shall appear in you a likeness to him who, by reason of your admiration, has left a deep impress upon you, I would have you resemble him as a child resembles his father," Epistle 84.8, in Seneca, *Epistles, 66–92*, trans. Richard M. Gummere (Cambridge, MA: Harvard University Press, 1920), 281. This was a commonplace in the period. In *Ciceronianus* (1528), Erasmus similarly mocks "those ridiculous apes" who copy Cicero slavishly, as opposed to those "who are eager to be known as his true and worthy sons," trans. Betty I. Knott, in *The Collected Works of Erasmus* (Toronto: University of Toronto Press, 1986), 28.374. In *On Romances* (1554), Giraldi Cinthio remarks that imitation ought to be like the relation of "the son of the father, the brother of the other," trans. Henry L. Snuggs (Lexington, KY: University of Kentucky Press, 1968), 131.

33. Richard Halpern, *The Poetics of Primitive Accumulation: English Renaissance Culture and the Genealogy of Capital* (Ithaca: Cornell University Press, 1991), 38, with a note to Jacques Lacan, "Aggressivity in Psychoanalysis," in *Écrits: A Selection*, trans. Alan Sheridan (London: Routledge, 1977), 8–29.

34. As Thomas Hobbes famously wrote, "*Persona* in latine signifies the *disguise*, or *outward appearance* of a man, counterfeited on the Stage," *Leviathan* (1651), ed. C. B. Macpherson (London: Penguin, 1968), 217 italics original. Meanings of the word "character" extend to include: a distinctive mark, sign, emblem, an element of a writing system such as an alphabet, handwriting, a distinguishing feature, a distinctive nature, style, manner, or quality, a person portrayed in fiction or acted on the stage; see *OED* "character" *n*. On the Oedipal imaginary of Renaissance *imitatio*, see also: William Kerrigan, "The Articulation of the Ego in the English Renaissance," in *The Literary Freud: Mechanisms of Defense and the Poetic Will*, ed. Joseph H. Smith (New Haven: Yale University Press, 1980), 261–308; and Lynn Enterline, *Shakespeare's Schoolroom: Rhetoric, Discipline, Emotion* (Philadelphia: University of Pennsylvania Press, 2012), esp. 139–52.

35. As Shoshana Felman notes, for both Freud and Lacan "the reference of the clinical practice of psychoanalysis to the literary drama of the Oedipus hinges on the central question of the *recognition*," recognition being "the crucial *psychoanalytic stake* both of the clinical and of the literary work," "Beyond Oedipus: The Specimen Story of Psychoanalysis," in *Psychoanalytic Literary Criticism*, ed. Ellmann, 76–102 (82, italics original).

36. On the tension between the empirical scientist and the creative writer within Freud, see Hillman, *Marx and Freud*, 148–50: "Here, as so often in Freud, a doubleness emerges" (148).

37. See Shoshana Felman's now classic move to "displace the whole pattern of the relationship between literature and psychoanalysis from a structure of rival claims to authority and to priority to the scene of this structure's deconstruction," "To Open the Question," in *Literature and Psychoanalysis*, ed. Felman, 5–10 (8).

38. See Ernest Jones, *Hamlet and Oedipus* (London: Victor Gollancz, 1949). For variants on Freud's reading of *Hamlet* by Jones and other early analysts, see Holland, *Psychoanalysis and Shakespeare*, 163–206; and Armstrong, *Shakespeare in Psychoanalysis*, 26–39. For an introductory survey of the various splits, divisions, developments, and movements within psychoanalytic theory to the present day, especially as they relate to interpretations of Shakespeare, see Carolyn E. Brown, *Shakespeare and Psychoanalytic Theory* (London: Bloomsbury, 2015).

39. Garber, *Shakespeare's Ghost Writers*, 257.

40. Felman, "Turning the Screw of Interpretation," in *Literature and Psychoanalysis*, ed. Felman, 98 (italics original).

41. Kermode, "Cornelius and Voltemand," 63.

3

MARGARET ANN FITZPATRICK HANLY

Rivalry and the Favorite Child in Jane Austen's Pride and Prejudice and Persuasion

Jane Austen's famous comment on the scene which is "the delight of [her] life" presents the core subject matter that Austen shares with psychoanalysis: the dynamic interplay of family lives. She writes to her young niece, Anna, who is composing her first novel in 1814: "You are now collecting your People Delightfully, getting them exactly in such a spot as is the delight of my life; – 3 or 4 Families in a Country Village."[1] Austen brings three or four "families" to life in her novels: the sisters, brothers, mothers, fathers, cousins, aunts, and uncles of girls getting married. Her plots turn on the conflicting desires and aggressions of sister and brother rivals in the family, and with other families in the "village." She dramatizes conflicts within her characters, in the repressed fantasies and impulses generated in childhood, many of the same ideas, which psychoanalysis was infamous in its early days for identifying – the envy, jealousy, and rivalry that permeated childhood psychosexuality in the family, and were universal.[2] Freud said it was the poets who had discovered the unconscious, and literary theorists say it is Freud who clarified the dynamics of plot and character in fiction.[3]

Austen's dramatization of rivalry in *Pride and Prejudice*[4] and in *Persuasion*[5] is further illuminated by psychoanalytic understanding of the storied fantasies of early childhood rivalry, aggression, guilt, and childhood narcissism. Unconscious wishful fantasies of entitlement to preference by a parent influences attitudes in later life stages and derivatives of these repressed fantasies are a central subject of psychoanalysis.[6] The fantasies and attendant psychological capacities in and liabilities for the favorite child penetrate the surface expressions and shape Austen's characterizations in *Pride and Prejudice* and, with interesting variations, in *Persuasion*. In *Pride and Prejudice*, Elizabeth Bennet is her father's favorite; her sister Lydia is her mother's favorite. In *Persuasion*, Elizabeth Elliot is her father's favorite; her sister Anne is most like the mother who died when she was fourteen, and most valued by her mother's best friend, Lady Russell. What connects, and what differentiates, the characters and the fates of these sisters, the preferred children, in relation to pride, prejudice, and persuasion?

Rivalry and the Favorite Child in *Pride and Prejudice*

The famous opening lines of *Pride and Prejudice* announce, as inevitable, a rivalry among the neighboring families:

> It is a truth universally acknowledged, that a single man in possession of a good fortune, must be in want of a wife. However little known the feelings or views of such a man may be on his first entering a neighbourhood, this truth is so well fixed in the minds of the surrounding families, that he is considered the rightful property of some one or other of their daughters.[7]

Only one daughter will get the "property," the man of "good fortune," whom all the families consider to be rightfully theirs. Rivalry opens the novel and informs the actions of the plot.

Pride and Prejudice centers on the Bennet family, the five sisters, their mother and father. The family estate is to be inherited by William Collins when Mr. Bennet dies. After his death, survival of the family depends on the sisters' marrying well enough. By the second page of *Pride and Prejudice*, Mr. Bennet declares his preference for Elizabeth, "his little Lizzy," while Mrs. Bennet protests and names *her* favorites, Jane and Lydia. Mr. Bingley, the "single man in possession of a good fortune," has arrived in the neighborhood. Mrs. Bennet pleads with Mr. Bennet to visit him: "Indeed you must go, for it will be impossible for us to visit him if you do not." He refuses, teasing her:

> You are over-scrupulous, surely. I dare say Mr. Bingley will be very glad to see you; and I will send a few lines by you to assure him of my hearty consent to his marrying whichever he chooses of the girls, though I must throw in a good word for my little Lizzy.

Mrs. Bennet protests: "I desire you will do no such thing. Lizzy is not a bit better than the others; and I am sure she is not half so handsome as Jane, nor half so good-humored as Lydia. But you are always giving *her* the preference."[8] Austen's parents thus exacerbate the rivalry of the sisters.

Rivalry over the "need for acquisition and possession"[9] of love and admiration, of good husbands, of properties, informs the love triangles of *Pride and Prejudice*. Elizabeth competes with her mother for her father's love and approval. Mrs. Bennet competes with her nearest neighbor, Lady Lucas, to get a daughter married to Mr. Collins, who will inherit the Bennet estate. Mr. Darcy and Wickham were rivals for Darcy's father's favor, and Darcy competes with Wickham for Elizabeth. Caroline Bingley cannot conceal her intense jealousy of Elizabeth when she sees Darcy falling in love with her. Lydia runs off with Wickham, whom Elizabeth had found so pleasing that she told her aunt that it would be better if Wickham did not really fall in love with her and ask her to marry him. The rivalries are intense between "favorite children" in the novel.

By Chapter 3, at the Meryton ball, Bingley has fallen in love with handsome Jane, the eldest Bennet daughter, "the most beautiful creature I ever beheld." The proud Mr. Darcy has dismissed Elizabeth with faint praise: "tolerable but not handsome enough to tempt *me*."[10] Elizabeth is more wounded in her sense of self and angrier than she knows, for she has always been preferred by her father to her sisters and to her mother. George Wickham, a military officer, comes to town with his regiment. Elizabeth is attracted to his "soft" pleasing manners and "seductive" ways. All the girls in town have fallen in love with him. "Mr. Wickham was the happy man towards whom almost every female eye was turned, and Elizabeth was the happy woman by whom he finally seated himself."[11] Wickham quickly confides to Elizabeth that he was the godson of Darcy's father, son of his steward, had grown up with Darcy, and had been the "uncommon attachment" of Darcy's father. He brazenly lies to her, saying that Darcy was full of "jealousy," so he had refused to give Wickham the "living" (position and income) he had been promised in Mr. Darcy's will.[12] Elizabeth believes this slander against Darcy (who had dismissed her) without question. The main love plot of *Pride and Prejudice* is constructed on Elizabeth's misjudgments of Darcy and Wickham. Her prejudice against Darcy is rooted in wounded pride (a blow to her narcissism), and her prejudice in favor of Wickham is rooted in gratification; again, she is preferred to her sisters.

The negative effects on Mrs. Bennet's favorite child, the wild and willful Lydia (youngest sister), are easy to see. As Lydia leaves for Brighton to spend her time with the officers, at age fifteen, "Mrs. Bennet was diffuse in her good wishes for the felicity of her daughter, and impressive in her injunctions that she should not miss the opportunity of enjoying herself as much as possible."[13] A few weeks later, Lydia had run off with Wickham to London, unmarried, and, given the mores of the time, had ruined her sisters' chances to marry well-until Wickham was bribed into marrying her.

Elizabeth, Lydia: Contempt in Preferred Children

Austen gives Elizabeth, the beloved heroine of her novel and her father's favorite, a tendency to disdain. Elizabeth is angry and contemptuous of Bingley for his lack of resolution in loving and proposing to the sister she loves: "She could not think without anger, hardly without contempt, on that easiness of temper, that want of proper resolution, which now made him the slave of his designing friends."[14]

Elizabeth warns her father not to let Lydia go to Brighton with the officers, fearing that Lydia would disdain all restraint:

> Our importance, our respectability in the world must be affected by the wild volatility, the assurance and disdain of all restraint which mark Lydia's character. Excuse me, for I must speak plainly. If you, my dear father, will not take the trouble of checking her exuberant spirits ... she will, at sixteen, be the most determined flirt that ever made herself or her family ridiculous. ... [15]

Lydia arrives home, married to Wickham (because Darcy has paid off his substantial debts and provided Lydia with a dowry). For Lydia,

> nothing of the past was recollected with pain. ... Jane was distressed. Elizabeth looked expressively at Lydia; but she, who never heard nor saw anything of which she chose to be insensible, gaily continued. ... Elizabeth could bear it no longer. She got up, and ran out of the room.

Elizabeth returns to the room in time to see Lydia "walk up to her mother's right hand, and hear her say to her eldest sister, 'Ah! Jane, I take your place now, and you must go lower, because I am a married woman.'" Lydia's childish rivalrous impulses and contempt are dramatically expressed. Her infantile entitlement, unchecked in the youngest child, to possess first place as the mother's favorite is powerfully and simply expressed. Lydia gloats in taking over Jane's place, "I take your place now," with the protocol of the day, as the family goes in to dinner.[16] Austen's language stirs an unconscious depth perception as siblings vie for first "place" with the parents, the gods of early childhood. Lydia's characterization provides Austen with a wide canvass for her portrait of a reckless, cruel, rivalrous action and expression in a child preferred by the mother. Lydia says complacently to her mother in front of her sisters the next day, "my sisters must all envy me."[17]

Narcissistic Attributes in Austen's Characters

Mr. Bennet's possessive love for his favorite "Lizzy" contributes to her lively intelligence and strength of character, but also induces the guilt of the favorite child. When the tall, heavy, pompous Mr. Collins (who is to inherit the Bennet estate) arrives at Longbourn holding out an "olive branch," ready to marry one of the Bennet daughters, Mr. Bennet enjoys mocking his foolish ways, but Austen's main revelation in the passage concerns his relationship with Elizabeth. "Mr. Bennet's expectations were fully answered. His cousin was as absurd as he had hoped, and he listened to him with the keenest enjoyment, maintaining at the same time the most resolute composure of countenance, and except in an occasional glance at Elizabeth, requiring no partner in his pleasure."[18]

The father's fantasy remains pre-conscious as he shares his satiric pleasures with Elizabeth: "Except in an occasional glance at Elizabeth," her father requires "no partner in his pleasure."[19] The negation makes the positive signifiers all the more resonant: Elizabeth *is* the "partner in his pleasure." These "narrative fragments" will stir up old possessive longings in the reader to have first place with a parent.[20] Elizabeth knows she is the preferred daughter to the father among the sibling rivals and preferred over her mother. In "Stages in the Development of the Sense of Reality," Sándor Ferenczi writes, "All children live in the happy delusion of omnipotence," but "those who never get reconciled to the renunciation of their irrational wishes" will, with the "slightest provocation," "feel themselves insulted or slighted," because they cannot remain "the *only* or *favorite* children" of fate.[21] The persistence of the wish to be first in the parent's sexual love leads to "narcissistic regression" "after every disappointment in the object of love."[22] Austen's novel dramatizes the intensity with which Elizabeth felt insulted when Darcy refused to dance with her at the ball when she begins "abusing him"[23] as he proposes to her. Elizabeth is "the clear moral centre of the book, and her judgements of character are good in almost every case; this makes her two failures of judgment – about Darcy and about Wickham – surprising enough to provide the pivot on which the plot can turn."[24] Austen juxtaposes Elizabeth's lapse in judgment with her father's exacerbation of her natural but irrational wish to be his favorite through the recurring metaphor of blindness.

Later in the novel, Austen's narrator enters Elizabeth's thoughts as she thinks about the father on whose affection she depends: "To his wife he was very little otherwise indebted, than as her ignorance and folly had contributed to his amusement." Austen's language is strong when describing Mr. Bennet's "continual breach of conjugal obligation" in "exposing his wife to the contempt of her own children." And the narrator reveals a crucial effect of this "breach" in the couple on Elizabeth's psychic conflicts. The narrative expresses Elizabeth's thoughts (with no authorial overview) as she seems to think she can fully assess the effect on her of her father's behavior:

> Elizabeth, however, had never been blind to the impropriety of her father's behaviour as a husband. She has always seen it with pain, but ... she

endeavoured to forget what she could not overlook, and to banish from her thoughts that continual breach of conjugal obligation.[25]

However, Austen shapes the plot precisely to show that this narrative assertion is unreliable, that Elizabeth's habit of banishing negative thoughts (as preferred child to an affectionate father) does leave her "blind,"[26] with an unconscious guilt-ridden wishful triumph over the mother. Elizabeth joins in the "village" gossip against Darcy (who had disdained to dance with her) and believes Wickham, though she prides herself on her "discernment"[27] of character. Her blindness could have ruined her life.[28] Her subtle entitlement to being preferred colors her perception of both Wickham and Darcy, acting precisely as the precondition for her irrational belief in Wickham. Leonard Shengold describes a "fixed conviction," which has the power of a "narcissistic delusion," "involving self and parent" in "being the favorite of the parent."[29]

The negative effects on Elizabeth of Mr. Bennet's making her his preferred child require more attention to details in the language and plot, as they are harder to decipher than the effects on Lydia. When Darcy proposes to Elizabeth after her stay for some weeks near his aunt's estate, she refuses him in anger, accusing him both of spoiling Jane's marriage with Bingley and of cruelty to Wickham. She is very angry when Darcy talks of her "inferiority" while proposing. She refuses him, asking why he speaks "with so evident a design of offending and insulting" her and accuses him of treating Wickham's "misfortunes with contempt."[30] Darcy writes a long letter defending himself, making it clear that Wickham has "vicious propensities,"[31] having tried to seduce his fifteen-year-old sister, and slandering Darcy. Elizabeth's narcissism suffers a serious blow in recognizing her blindness, but she uses the correction to engage in change.

The strength and resilience of Elizabeth's character, partly rooted in her father's love and admiration and in her mother's loyal wish for good marriages for all her daughters, gives her a capacity for depressive self-understanding and growth, which is brilliantly depicted:

> She perfectly remembered everything that had passed in conversation between Wickham and herself. . . . She was now struck with the impropriety of such communications to a stranger.[32]
>
> . . .
>
> She grew absolutely ashamed of herself. – Of neither Darcy nor Wickham could she think, without feeling that she had been blind, partial, prejudiced, absurd.[33]

Elizabeth goes through a painful change of heart and mind, which brings about an internal separation from her family, even from her father and the "impropriety" of his "conduct." She "felt depressed beyond anything she had ever known before."[34] Austen's language conveys the chastening of the narcissism of the preferred child, always clever in the father's eyes, but now able to appreciate her mistakes and the strengths of Darcy's character.[35] Preferred children are prone to contempt for others and disdain for unflattering realities, showing residues of infantile wishes and expectations, which undermine the perception of realities unflattering to the sense of self. Darcy feels how much he owes Elizabeth for teaching him to give up his contempt: "What do I not owe you! You taught me a lesson, hard indeed at first. ... By you, I was properly humbled."[36] Austen dramatizes how pride in "an only son, (for many years an only *child*)" creates prejudice, entailing a failure to perceive reality, when reality testing was essential. Austen's characterization of Darcy's maternal aunt, Lady Catherine De Bourgh, reveals his aristocratic family's lack of psychic capacities to tolerate disappointment: "I have not been used to submit to any person's whims. I have not been in the habit of brooking disappointment."[37] Austen's famous irony shapes the plot, such that Lady Catherine's "perverseness and assurance" made her repeat Elizabeth's words, which had an "effect," "exactly contrariwise" to her intention; "it taught" Darcy "to hope"[38] and to propose again.

Rivalry and the Favorite Daughters in *Persuasion*

Austen opens *Persuasion* with characters who share something of Darcy's situation and character: his inherited wealth, his arrogance, his interest in "none beyond [his] own family circle," but they lack Darcy's knowledge of books and the world, his generous love for his sister, his capacity for friendship, his father who had been "benevolent and amiable."[39] Austen portrays Sir Walter Elliot and his favorite daughter, Elizabeth, almost as caricatures of vanity. "Sir Walter Elliot, of Kellynch-hall ... never took up any book but the Baronetage; there he found occupation for an idle hour and consolation in a distressed one; there his faculties were roused into admiration and respect ... there any unwelcome sensations, arising from domestic affairs, changed naturally into pity and contempt."[40]

A psychoanalytic viewpoint reveals that Austen characterizes Sir Walter and Elizabeth Elliot in more complex ways than caricature describes. The harshness of the satire is countered by words that suggest a sad absence of emotional contact: "Sir Walter had improved [the Baronetage] ... by inserting most accurately the day of the month on which he had lost his wife."[41] In a failed mourning, the death of his wife had only increased Sir Walter's "pity and contempt" for those of lesser rank, for the men in the navy whose looks are ravaged by the weather, or for the poor widow Mrs. Smith. Disdain and contempt for others serve as defensive attitudes against painful depressive feelings and a sense of helplessness. The idea that Sir Walter "improved' his favorite book by inserting "most accurately" the date of Lady Elliot's death tells the tale of an inability to tolerate the pain of loss or even anger at being left, the tale of a regression to early childhood narcissism.[42] Sir Walter's vanity is central in the opening passage of *Persuasion*, but Austen has signaled the importance to her story of the death of the mother of three daughters.

Anne Elliot, Favorite Child of Lady Russell

Sir Walter Elliot and his favorite Elizabeth are extreme instances of what is lost in lives carried on in a narcissistic bubble. Elizabeth Elliot's story, as we will see, is a tragic story of a loveless inner and outer life, though often treated with irony and satire in the narrative.[43] Anne's is a story of a renewed mourning for the mother who died when she was fourteen, and a renewed ability to claim the man she has loved intensely for many years. Anne has "an elegance of mind and sweetness of character, which must have placed her high with any people of real understanding." Anne's inner reflections, losses, attachments, perceptions of human frailty and strengths, capacity for human warmth and love, and intelligence form the central perspective of the novel. Austen dramatizes the benefits of not being the favorite, over-esteemed daughter, of a self-centered father: Anne "was nobody with either father or sister; her word had no weight; her convenience was always to give way; – she was only Anne."[44]

The love story and the engagement of Anne Elliot and Frederick Wentworth is briefly told in a narrative retrospective:

> Frederick Wentworth . . . was, at that time, a remarkably fine young man, with a great deal of intelligence, spirit, and brilliancy; and Anne an extremely pretty girl, with gentleness, modesty, taste, and feeling. . . .They were gradually acquainted and when acquainted, rapidly and deeply in love.[45]

Anne breaks off the engagement, persuaded by her mother's best friend, her godmother, Lady Russell, in advice Anne learns to regret.[46] She was persuaded to believe the engagement a wrong thing: indiscreet, improper, hardly capable of success, and not deserving it.[47] Austen's heroine, dismissed by her father and sister, obeys the tender mother figure whom she "had always loved and relied on." Anne continues to rely on Lady Russell, reflecting, even at twenty-seven, that if her father were to marry, she "would always have a home with Lady Russell." The growth in Anne's character depends on her ability to separate from this overly prudent mother.

If, in *Pride and Prejudice*, Elizabeth's misjudgment of Darcy and Wickham is the hinge on which the main plot turns, then in *Persuasion*, Lady Russell's misjudgment of Anne, Wentworth, and Mr. Elliot, organizes the main plot. In a psychoanalytic reading we can explore the unconscious motivations that Austen reveals in her language. Anne had to live with her mistake: "She had been forced into prudence in her youth, she learned romance as she grew older – the natural sequel of an unnatural beginning."[48] Anne continues to the end to defend her decision to follow Lady Russell's advice, though she thinks it was the wrong advice. However, Austen's text introduces complexities in Anne's mind and heart and in Lady Russell's that ask for further consideration. The favorite child will have a binding a loyalty to, a strong identification with, and a difficulty in separating from, the external and internal parent whose preference is significant in the child's sense of self.

When Anne and Wentworth become engaged again at the end of the novel, the narrator blithely comments, "Who can be in doubt of what followed? When any two young people take it into their heads to marry, they are pretty sure by perseverance to carry their point."[49] The "perseverance" of young lovers, "be they ever so poor or imprudent," presents a "truth" that illuminates Anne's particular character:

> Had [Anne] not imagined herself consulting his [Wentworth's] good, even more than her own, she could hardly have given him up. – The belief of being prudent, and self-denying principally for his advantage was her chief consolation, under the misery of a parting – a final parting.[50]

The perseverance of lovers is pronounced to be a stronger motivation than duty to a parent (Anne's conscience) or an urge to be "prudent, and self-denying." Where was Anne's perseverance when she was "young" and passionately in love, longing for Wentworth through eight years of separation? Austen poses an implicit question about another motivational force. Psychoanalysis answers that the force is unconscious guilt, reinforcing Anne's prudence and self-denial, guilt typically belonging to an unfinished mourning for a mother in a fourteen-year-old. Anne's unconscious regression to a guilt over the fantasy/wish of her childhood to be rid of the rival mother and take her place creates an unconscious need for punishment. Unconscious anger and disappointment at being left leads to aggression being turned against the self.[51] Oedipal longing and the projection of unsettling anger are depicted clearly in *Persuasion*. Austen constructs a plot that allows Anne to retrace the developmental steps, to replay the old rivalrous impulses stirred up in the regression in order to move on and to claim love. Freud theorizes the meaning of such a replay in his discussion of anxiety, and the reproduction of threatening situations in an effort to actively repeat and master them.[52]

The plot does facilitate the reworking of the rivalries for love and for possession of the parent. The second section of the novel is set at Uppercross, the home of the third Elliot sister married into the Musgrove family. Frederick Wentworth has returned to England, the war ended, a wealthy and accomplished man. His sister and brother-in-law admiral and Mrs. Croft have rented Kellynch Hall, since Sir Walter and Elizabeth have overspent and must move to Bath to "retrench." Kellynch is the next village to Uppercross, where Anne goes to stay with her sister Mary and her husband Charles Musgrove, in Uppercross cottage. Mr. and Mrs. Musgrove, senior, in Uppercross Great House, have several children. Their two eldest daughters have returned from school, and they and their cousins are "in love" with Captain Wentworth:

> The Miss Hayters, the females of the family of cousins already mentioned, were apparently admitted to the honour of being in love with him; and as for Henrietta and Louisa, they both seemed so entirely occupied by him, that nothing but the continued appearance of the most perfect good-will between themselves could have made it credible that they were not decided rivals.[53]

Wentworth bows; Anne curtseys; he is cool; and Mary passes on his comment that Anne is "altered beyond his knowledge." Why, the critics have asked, does Anne make no effort in the rivalry, to regain Wentworth's love? A psychoanalytic reading shows that a complex mourning must be renewed for Anne to work through her self-denials and to find her voice. Her depressive thoughts and self-sacrificing acts reveal an unfinished mourning, repressed unconscious anger toward the mother who left her, and a regression to Oedipal guilt.[54] For Moses Laufer,

> The developmental task of adolescence ... may interfere with the work of mourning the lost object and result in such well-known pathological solutions as depression; flattening of affect ... and disturbances of sexuality due to the guilt feelings attached to the death of the object.[55]

Austen's plot makes sense if we understand the subtle interactions between Anne and Wentworth as a renewed mourning. Wentworth enters Anne's neighborhood staying with his sister and brother-in-law, Admiral and Mrs. Croft, and spending his time with Charles Musgrove and his pretty sisters. Wentworth takes revenge on Anne for her rejection of him, without being conscious of what he is doing. Wentworth's disappointed and angry feelings toward Anne for allowing Lady Russell to persuade her to break their engagement are clear in his words to Louisa: "It is the worst evil in too yielding and indecisive a character, that no influence over it can be depended upon."[56] Mary told her that Captain Wentworth said she was "so altered he should not have known [her] again," and Anne "fully submitted, in silent, deep mortification."[57] Identified with a depressed mother who lost a baby when Anne was two,[58] and unconsciously guilty about the mother who died,[59] Anne's active desires for herself were held back.

During the autumn at Uppercross, Wentworth often refers, in Anne's presence, to the year of their engagement and Anne knows he remembers their love and engagement: "Once so much to each other! Now nothing! There had been a time when of all the large party now filling the drawing room at Uppercross, they would have found it most difficult not to speak to one another." "Now they were as strangers; nay, worse than strangers, for they never could become acquainted. It was a perpetual estrangement."[60] "His cold politeness, his ceremonious grace, were worse than anything."[61] Anne's internal suffering during this period of "estrangement" has been called strangely bitter and passive.[62] However, a psychoanalytic lens also picks up evidence of renewed mourning for the mother who died, half projected onto Wentworth, half experienced by Anne. She is grieving and mortified; he is angry, vengeful at being left.[63] Anne lives out a second mourning in her grieving his loss during these weeks they share at Uppercross, and in living through him, attending to the feelings she provokes in him.

Separation from the Possessive Parent in Anne Elliot

Anne has kept the full extent of the regret she suffers over Wentworth hidden from Lady Russell for seven years. Anne and Lady Russell meet after Louisa Musgrove has an accident at Lyme, and Anne tells her what seems to be "the attachment between Wentworth and Louisa."[64] Austen now gives surprisingly raw feelings to the usually calm, intellectual Lady Russell:

> Lady Russell had only to listen composedly, and wish them happy; but internally her heart reveled in angry pleasure, in pleased contempt, that the man who at twenty-three had seemed to understand somewhat of the value of an Anne Elliot should, eight years afterwards, be charmed by a Louisa Musgrove.[65]

Lady Russell, who is in "the place of a parent" for Anne, has "almost a mother's love," revels "in angry pleasure, in pleased contempt" because Wentworth shows himself as unworthy of Anne. Lady Russell is a mother who is jealous and possessive and unhappy about the idea of Anne's marrying a man of no rank. She is narcissistically invested in being "right," more than in Anne's wellbeing. Lady Russell reveals a maternal possessiveness in this contempt for her goddaughter's beloved. She is narcissistically invested in dismissing Wentworth and in fostering Anne's engagement to Sir Walter's heir, Mr. Walter Elliot. But Anne is gradually gaining independence from the woman who replaced her mother.

Near the end Anne herself is tempted to marry Mr. Elliot, thereby becoming a rival to her sister Elizabeth, who had always intended to marry him. Anne imagines accepting Mr. Elliot, despite her doubts about his past. And Lady Russell tries to persuade her that it would be a "very happy" marriage. Anne is "bewitched" by the idea that she would take her mother's place as Lady Elliot, restored to her childhood home:

> For a few minutes her heart and her imagination were bewitched. The idea of becoming what her mother had been, of having the precious name of 'Lady Elliot' first revived in herself; of being restored to Kellynch, calling it home again, her home forever, was a charm she could not immediately resist.[66]

Austen's language is clear: Anne's imagination is "bewitched." The idea of "becoming" what her mother had been is a "charm." The five-year-old imagination, which had become an unconscious fantasy, penetrates the surface of Anne's mind, returning from the unconscious fairy-tale world.[67] Anne is "bewitched" by the child's magical wish fulfillment: Kellynch will be her "home forever," a phrase suggesting the denial of death and passage of time. However, the elaboration of this fantasy is the sign of Anne's renewed capacity to tolerate robust desires belonging both to "the Oedipus and the sibling complex of the first sexual period."[68] This capacity to desire her mother's place, which belongs to the earlier incestuous period, had sunk under the guilt evoked on the occasion of a mother's death[69] but is now revived and worked through.

Anne Elliot, like Elizabeth Bennet, must learn to separate from a possessive parent, though "bewitched" as favorite child to feel her influence. Anne gives up her dependency on Lady Russell, who was limited in her judgment of character. Wentworth (only recognizing it later) acts out his anger through half the novel, finally working through his resentment at Anne's betrayal,[70] insisting, "Unjust I may have been, weak and resentful I have been, but never inconstant."[71] Wentworth despises her "weakness" but rediscovers his love for Anne, in part stirred up by jealousy of Mr. Elliot.

Elizabeth Elliot, Favorite of the Father

Austen's central love story belongs to her heroine Anne Elliot, but her characterization of Sir Walter's favorite daughter, Elizabeth, also deserves attention. Elizabeth is portrayed as utterly identified with her father, lacking the emotional capacity to mourn her mother's death, with an inner life "not sufficiently developed to bear the strain of the work of mourning," therefore utilizing "some mechanism of narcissistic self-protection to circumvent the process."[72] The dominant tone is a satire of Elizabeth's vanity, but Austen's language reveals more complex dynamics. Elizabeth Elliot has features also given to Elizabeth Bennet: "Elizabeth had succeeded, at sixteen, to all that was possible, of her mother's rights and consequence; and being very handsome, and very like himself, her influence had always been great, and they had gone on together most happily."[73]

Elizabeth "very like" Sir Walter has great "influence" over him. The phrase "succeeded . . . to all that was possible of her mother's rights and consequence" hints at an incestuous fantasy shared by Elizabeth and Sir Walter. Like Elizabeth Bennet, she was a "partner" in her father's "pleasure." However, Austen's narrative depicts a deeper regression in Elizabeth Elliot, to a child's narcissism, driven by a failed mourning. Her identification with a limited, self-centered father adds to her problems, for she fails to perceive reality even when her interests and safety are at stake. She has poor signal anxiety[74] and fails to perceive how she is in danger of being manipulated, blinded by a desperate hunger for admiration.

Elizabeth Bennet and Elizabeth Elliot, preferred by their fathers, are both prey to dangers that are exacerbated by the blind spots in their judgments. However, Austen differentiates Elizabeth Elliot's unquestioning admiration of her father and her clear "rights" to her (dead) mother's place from Elizabeth Bennet's observation of the flaws in Mr. Bennet, and ways of respecting her mother, flawed though she is. Elizabeth Bennet suffers the painful recognition that her poor judgment was generated by her vanity. Austen's language describing Elizabeth's change of heart is striking: "She grew absolutely ashamed of herself. – Of neither Darcy nor Wickham could she think, without feeling that she had been blind, partial, prejudiced, absurd."[75] Elizabeth Bennet gives up an exaggerated idea of her power to discern character, a child's bright wit overestimated by a father, in order to love another.

Elizabeth Elliot remains a child in her self-interested misperceptions. The story of her intention to marry the cousin who is her father's heir gives away the narrow workings of her mind: "She had, while a very young girl meant to marry" Mr. Walter Elliot, the "future Baronet." Mr. Elliot "had been forced into the introduction,"[76] but he "had purchased independence by uniting himself to a rich woman of inferior birth." Austen continues to describe Elizabeth Elliots's self-interested misperceptions:

This very awkward history of Mr. Elliot was still, after an interval of several years, felt with anger by Elizabeth, who had liked the man for himself, and still more for being her father's heir, and whose strong family pride could see only in him a proper match for Sir Walter Elliot's eldest daughter. . . . Yet so miserably had he conducted himself, that though she was at this present time (the summer of 1814) wearing black ribbons for his wife, she could not admit him to be worth thinking of again.[77]

Austen conveys Elizabeth's entitlement to anger and her self-deceptive thinking. While focused on the death of his wife, she "could not admit" that she was still determined to marry the heir to the family estate. Elizabeth is so identified with her mother, in her right *to be* Lady Elliot, that she cannot admit to any rivalry; for the identification is acting as a defense against loss.[78] She is stuck as her father's partner and cannot move on to love another. The narrator has some sympathy for Elizabeth's lot, mixed with satiric judgment: "Such were Elizabeth Elliot's sentiments and sensations; such the cares to alloy, the agitations to vary, the sameness and the elegance, the prosperity and the nothingness of her scene of life; such the feelings to give interest to a long, uneventful residence in one country circle, to fill the vacancies which there were no habits of utility abroad, no talents or accomplishments for home, to occupy."[79]

Persuasion opens with Sir Walter and Elizabeth having overspent and needing to "retrench." Elizabeth's best idea "to cut off some unnecessary charities" proves insufficient and she "felt herself ill-used and unfortunate." They found no way to lessen their expenses "without compromising their dignity . . . in a way not to be borne." Austen conveys the favorite child's tone in "not to be borne": the entitlement to have exactly what she wants.

Sir Walter and Elizabeth move to Bath to "retrench" and take with them the assiduously pleasing, divorced Mrs. Clay, who has set her sights on Sir Walter. Anne arrives weeks later in Bath, and Elizabeth boasts of their "superior" situation: "Their acquaintance was exceedingly sought after. Everybody was wanting to visit them. They had drawn back from many introductions, and still were perpetually having cards left by people of whom they knew nothing. Here were funds of enjoyment."[80]

The narrator mimics Elizabeth's voice and "mocks" the "funds of enjoyment" she finds in and being sought after and drawing back.[81] There is a biting satire as Elizabeth's empty pleasures are compared to Anne's ardent love: "but it would be an insult to the nature of Anne's felicity, to draw any comparison between it and her sister's; the origin of one all selfish vanity, of the other all generous attachment."[82] Anne is very happy in loving Wentworth, in knowing he returns her love, while Elizabeth can take pleasure only in appearances and rank, believing Mr. Elliot is "within her reach." The favorite daughter is trapped in narcissistic defenses that leave her blind to the realties that run counter to her wishes. She misjudges the dangerous Mr. Elliot and Mrs. Clay certain they are at her beck and call. Austen depicts the limitations in psychological capacities, which accrue after a failed mourning in adolescence: the regression to infantile wishful fantasies[83] and hunger for praise: "Sir Walter and Elizabeth were walking Mary into the other drawing-room ... regaling themselves with her admiration."[84] "Regaling" vividly evokes a child's insatiable need for attention.

Poor Reality Testing and Impoverished Judgment

Elizabeth's impoverished judgment and poor reality testing are dramatized in detail in *Persuasion*. Elizabeth is much more persuadable than her younger sister, Anne, for she is susceptible to the influence of those who would deceive and harm her. She "had not a fault to find in [Mr. Elliot]. He had explained away all the appearance of neglect on his own side. It had originated in misapprehension entirely." Anne is more cautious. "Allowances, large allowances, she knew, must be made for the ideas of those who spoke [her father and sister]. She heard it all under embellishment. All that sounded extravagant or irrational in the progress of the reconciliation might have no origin but in the language of the relators."[85]

Anne sees the "extravagant and irrational" in her father and sister. She had warned Elizabeth that the "assiduously pleasing" Mrs. Clay might be persuading Sir Walter to marry her. But Elizabeth has swallowed Mrs. Clay's false claim that she "reprobates all inequality of condition."[86] Elizabeth points to Mrs. Clay's "freckles" as an insurmountable "personal misfortune," concluding "an agreeable manner may set off handsome features, but can never alter plain ones." Finally, she dismisses Anne: "I think it rather unnecessary in *you* to be advising *me*."[87]

Mrs. Clay and Mr. Elliot play out their deceptive games and Elizabeth remains blind inside her narcissistic bubble. Anne has learned (from her old school friend, Mrs. Smith) that Mr. Elliot has contempt for her father and sister, while Mrs. Clay encourages Elizabeth to believe that he intends to marry her: "I never saw anybody in my life spell harder for an invitation. Poor man! I was really in pain for him; for your hard-hearted sister, Miss Anne, seems bent on cruelty." Elizabeth comments that Mr. Elliot looks up "with so much respect" to her father, and Mrs. Clay exclaims, "Exactly like father and son! Dear Miss Elliot, may I not say father and son?"[88] Anne is concerned for Elizabeth, deceived by those who flatter her: "It was so humiliating to reflect on the constant deception practised on her father and Elizabeth; to consider the various sources of mortification preparing for them!"[89] Mr. Elliot feigns admiration for Sir Walter, and Elizabeth seems to feel the admiration as hers. Austen places the favorite child and her father together in the text, as if they are almost one, with Elizabeth so absorbed in her father, that she scarcely has an independent identity.

Austen's ideas on the loss of human contact and warmth when vanity dominates the personality is conveyed vividly when Sir Walter and Miss Elliot enter the White Hart Inn to invite their son-in-law's family, the warm-hearted Musgroves, to an evening party. Anne "felt an instant oppression, and wherever she looked saw symptoms of the same. The comfort, the freedom, the gaiety of the room was over, hushed into cold composure, determined silence, or insipid talk, to meet the heartless elegance of her father and sister. How mortifying to feel that it was so!"[90]

Conclusion

Virginia Woolf extols Austen's work for its "surface animation" and "likeness to life" and beyond these for "an exquisite discrimination of human values."[91] The fates of the favorite children of Austen's *Pride and Prejudice* and *Persuasion* are rendered with Shakespearean observation and dramatic genius. Austen's universal appeal is rooted in the dramatization of the rivalries in "3 or 4 Families in a country Village," as the sisters and brothers struggle to make claims on the goods of life and love. As Ernst Kris writes,

> The fact that certain themes of human experience and conflict are recurrent wherever men live or where, at least, certain cultural conditions prevail – the fact that from Sophocles to Proust the struggle against incestuous impulses, dependency, guilt, and aggression, has remained a topic of Western literature – seems after almost half a century, as well established as any thesis in the social sciences.[92]

Austen's heroines, Elizabeth Bennet and Anne Elliot, face challenges in separating from their parents and rival sisters, in their flawed humanity, in order to develop a greater capacity for inner dialogue and love.

Notes

1. Deirdre Le Faye, ed., *Jane Austen's Letters*, 3rd ed. (Oxford: Oxford University Press, 1995), 287.
2. "New Introductory Lectures on Psycho-Analysis" (1933), SE 22: 123.
3. Lionell Trilling, "Freud and Literature," *in The Liberal Imagination: Essays on Literature and Society* (London: Martin Secker and Warburg, 1951), 34–57; Kenneth Burke, "Freud – and the Analysis of Poetry," *American Journal of Sociology* 45, no. 3 (1939): 391–417; Peter Brooks, *Reading for the Plot* (Cambridge, MA: Harvard University Press, 1984); Mary Jacobus, *The Poetics of Psychoanalysis: In the Wake of Klein* (Oxford: Oxford University Press, 2005).

4. Jane Austen, *Pride and Prejudice*, ed. James Kinsley (1813; repr. Oxford: Oxford University Press, 1990).

5. Jane Austen, *Persuasion*, ed. D. W. Harding (1818; repr. London: Penguin, 1965).

6. Freud, "Some Neurotic Mechanisms in Jealousy, Paranoia and Homosexuality," *SE* 17: 221–32. Peter B. Neubauer, "The Importance of the Sibling Experience," *The Psychoanalytic Study of the Child* 38 (1983): 325–36; Juliet Mitchell, *Siblings* (Cambridge: Polity, 2003); René Kaës, *Le Complex Fraternel* (Paris: Dunod, 2008); Hanly, "Sibling Rivalry, Separation, and Change in Austen's Sense and Sensibility," *International Journal of Psycho-Analysis* 97, no. 4 (2016): 1057–75.

7. Austen, *Pride and Prejudice*, 1.

8. Ibid., 2.

9. Neubauer, "Importance of the Sibling Experience," 333.

10. Austen, *Pride and Prejudice*, 7.

11. Ibid., 57.

12. Ibid., 60.

13. Ibid., 180.

14. Ibid., 103.

15. Ibid., 176–77.

16. Ibid., 240.

17. Ibid., 241.

18. Ibid., 51.

19. Ibid., 51.

20. Pinchas Noy, "A Theory of Art and Aesthetic Experience," *Psychoanalytic Review* 55 (1969): 640.

21. Sandor Ferenczi, *First Contributions to Psychoanalysis* (1913; repr. New York: Bruner Mazel, 1952), 232.

22. Ferenczi, *First Contributions to Psychoanalysis*, 233.

23. Austen, *Pride and Prejudice*, 281.

24. Claire Tomalin, *Jane Austen: A Life* (London: Penguin Books, 1997), 163.

25. Austen, *Pride and Prejudice*, 180–81.

26. Ibid., 159.

27. James Kinsley, "Introduction," in *Pride and Prejudice* by Jane Austen (Oxford: Oxford University Press, 1995), xxiii.

28. See Leonard Shengold, *The Delusions of Everyday Life* (New Haven, CT: Yale University Press, 1995).

29. Shengold, "Envy and Malignant Envy," *Psychoanalytic Quarterly* 63, no. 4 (1994): 615–40.

30. Austen, *Pride and Prejudice*, 145–47.

31. Ibid., 153.

32. Ibid., 158.

33. Ibid., 159.

34. Ibid., 160.

35. See Hanly, "Sibling Jealousy and Aesthetic Ambiguity in Austen's Pride and Prejudice," *Psychoanalytic Quarterly* 78, no. 2 (2009): 445–68.

36. Austen, *Pride and Prejudice*, 282.

37. Ibid., 272.

38. Ibid., 280.
39. Ibid., 282.
40. Austen, *Persuasion*, 35.
41. Ibid., 35.
42. See Hans Loewald, "Internalization, Separation, Mourning, and the Superego," *Psychoanalytic Quarterly* 31, no.4 (1962): 487.
43. See Marvin Mudrick, *Jane Austen: Irony as Defense and Discovery* (Princeton: Princeton University Press, 1952).
44. Austen, *Persuasion*, 37.
45. Ibid., 55.
46. Clara Tuite, *Romantic Austen: Sexual Politics and the Literary Canon* (Cambridge: Cambridge University Press, 2002).
47. Austen, *Persuasion*, 56.
48. Ibid., 58.
49. Ibid., 250.
50. Ibid., 58.
51. Freud, "'A Child Is Being Beaten': A Contribution to the Study of the Origin of Sexual Perversions" (1919), *SE* 17: 175–204; Rudolph M. Loewenstein, "A Contribution to the Psychoanalytic Theory of Masochism," *Journal of the American Psychoanalytic Association* 5 (1957): 197–234; Loewald, "Internalization, Separation, Mourning, and the Superego"; Moses Laufer, "Object Loss and Mourning during Adolescence," *The Psychoanalytic Study of the Child* 21 (1966): 269–93.
52. "Anxiety is the original reaction to helplessness in the trauma and is reproduced later on in the danger-situation as a signal for help. The ego, which experienced the trauma passively, now repeats it actively in a weakened version, in the hope of being able itself to direct its course." Freud, "Inhibitions, Symptoms and Anxiety" (1926), *SE* 20: 166–67.
53. Austen, *Persuasion*, 95–96.
54. Katherine Dalsimer, *Female Adolescence: Psychoanalytic Reflections on Literature* (New Haven: Yale University Press, 1986), 124; Hanly, "Object Loss, Renewed Mourning, and Psychic Change in Jane Austen's Persuasion," *International Journal of Psycho-Analysis* 88, no. 4 (2007): 1001–17.
55. Laufer, "Object Loss and Mourning," 291.
56. Austen, *Persuasion*, 110.
57. Ibid., 85.
58. Ibid., 35.
59. Harold Blum, "On Identification and Its Vicissitudes," *International Journal of Psycho-Analysis* 67 (1986): 267–76; Marie Bonaparte, "L'Identification d'une fille a sa mère Morte," *Revue Française de Psychanalyse* 2 (1928): 541–65; Laufer, "Object Loss and Mourning."
60. Austen, *Persuasion*, 88.
61. Austen, *Persuasion*, 96.
62. A. Walton Litz, "'Persuasion': Forms of Estrangement," in *Jane Austen: Bicentenary Essays*, ed. John Halperin (Cambridge: Cambridge University Press, 1975), 221–32.
63. Martha Wolfenstein, "How Is Mourning Possible?," *The Psychoanalytic Study of the Child* 21 (1966): 93–123.
64. Austen, *Persuasion*, 140.
65. Ibid., 40.

66. Ibid., 172.
67. Jacob Arlow, "Unconscious Fantasy and Disturbances of Conscious Experience," *Psychoanalytic Quarterly* 38, no. 1 (1969): 1–27.
68. Freud, "Some Neurotic Mechanisms."
69. Glenda A. Hudson, *Sibling Love and Incest in Jane Austen's Fiction* (London: Macmillan, 1992).
70. Hanly, "Object Loss, Renewed Mourning, and Psychic Change."
71. Austen, *Persuasion*, 240.
72. Helene Deutsch, "Absence of Grief," *Psychoanalytic Quarterly* 6, no. 1 (1937): 13.
73. Austen, *Persuasion*, 37.
74. "There are two reactions to real danger. One is an affective reaction, an outbreak of anxiety. The other is a protective action. The same will presumably be true of instinctual danger. We know how the two reactions can co-operate in an expedient way, the one giving the signal for the other to appear." Freud, "Inhibitions, Symptoms and Anxiety" (1926), *SE* 20: 165.
75. Austen, *Persuasion*, 159.
76. Ibid., 39.
77. Ibid., 39–40.
78. George R. Krupp, "Identification as a Defence against Anxiety in Coping with Loss," *International Journal of Psycho-Analysis* 46 (1965): 303–14.
79. Austen, *Persuasion*, 40.
80. Ibid., 151.
81. Harding, "Regulated Hatred: An Aspect of the Work of Jane Austen," in *Regulated Hatred and Other Essays on Jane Austen*, ed. M. Lawlor, 5–26 (1940; repr. London: Athlone, 1998).
82. Austen, *Persuasion*, 194.
83. Laufer, "Object Loss and Mourning."
84. Austen, *Persuasion*, 222.
85. Ibid., 154.
86. Ibid., 62.
87. Austen, *Persuasion*, 63.
88. Ibid., 219.
89. Ibid., 220.
90. Ibid., 230.
91. Virginia Woolf, "Jane Austen at Sixty," in *A Truth Universally Acknowledged: 33 Great Writers on Why We Read Jane Austen*, ed. Susannah Carson (1923; repr. New York: Random House, 2009), 265.
92. Ernst Kris, "Approaches to Art," in *Psychoanalytic Explorations in Art* (1942; repr. New York: International Universities Press, 1952), 17.

4

KATHERINE DALSIMER

Encountering Invisible Presence
Virginia Woolf and Julia Duckworth Stephen

"We think back through our mothers if we are women," Virginia Woolf famously declared in *A Room of One's Own* – a declaration that has leapt off the page and come to have a life of its own. She was speaking of women writers, longing for female progenitors but "looking about on shelves for books that were not there."[1] In this chapter, I explore the contradictions and complexities of Woolf's "thinking back through" her own mother, Julia Duckworth Stephen – her lifelong, evolving relationship with what she called the "invisible presence" of the mother who had died when she was thirteen years old. Woolf felt that in writing her great autobiographical novel *To the Lighthouse* she had profoundly altered that relationship – that she had done for herself, she asserted, "what psychoanalysts do for their patients." Her intriguing statement, rich in implications, invites further reflection.

Psychoanalysis was in the air Virginia Woolf breathed. Members of her circle, both friends and family, were instrumental in importing psychoanalysis from Vienna to London. And the Hogarth Press, which she founded with her husband Leonard Woolf in 1917, would be crucial in the dissemination of psychoanalytic writings in the English-speaking world. From the small hand-printing press they set up on their dining room table – and the 16-page pamphlet of instructions that accompanied it – would evolve the publishing house that introduced many important works of modernist poetry and fiction. In 1924 the Hogarth Press published the first two volumes of Freud's *Collected Papers*; over the next decades it would publish the whole of the International Psycho-analytical Library. Leonard Woolf's own interest in Freud dated to at least ten years earlier. He had written the first essay on Freud for a non-specialist readership, a review of "The Psychopathology of Everyday Life" that appeared in 1914 in *The New Weekly*. In his autobiography, some fifty years later, he takes pride in having "recognized and understood the greatness of Freud and the importance of what he was doing when this was by no means common" and quotes from that 1914 review:

Whether one believes in his theories or not, one is forced to admit that he writes with great subtlety of mind, a broad and sweeping imagination more characteristic of the poet than the scientist or medical practitioner ... his works are often a series of brilliant and suggestive hints.[2]

When the third volume of Freud's *Collected Papers* was published in 1925 – the case studies – the review in *The Nation & the Athenaeum* provoked such intense ongoing controversy in the Letters section that after four months the editor decreed: "This correspondence must now cease." In London, in the first part of the twentieth century, among the intelligentsia (the "ignorantsia," as Virginia Woolf would say) psychoanalysis filled the air – and would become, in W. H. Auden's words, "a whole climate of opinion."[3]

Though she suffered greatly, beginning in adolescence, from depression and episodes of psychosis, Woolf did not turn to psychoanalysis as a treatment. And wisely so. She had an illness for which there was no effective treatment in her lifetime: her diaries and letters leave no doubt in my mind that today she would be diagnosed as having bipolar disorder.[4] The medical specialists the Woolfs consulted over the years prescribed rest – in a darkened room, rest with no reading, no writing. Thus, when she was ill Virginia Woolf was deprived of precisely what was most sustaining to her. The ignorance of experts is scathingly portrayed in *Mrs. Dalloway* in the figures of Dr. Holmes and Sir William Bradshaw. In her diary it is epitomized by the advice of one of the Harley Street specialists they consulted, a Dr. Sainsbury: "Equanimity–practise equanimity Mrs Woolf."[5]

In contrast to the ignorance of experts, Virginia Woolf herself understood that what she had was an illness. Moreover, she recognized, long before its mechanism would be understood, that this illness has a hereditary component:

> My nervous system ... being a second hand one, used by my father and his father to dictate dispatches and write books with – how I wish they had hunted and fished instead! – I have to treat it like a pampered pug dog, and lie still directly my head aches.[6]

She intuited that a treatment would eventually be developed, but not for many years:

> [I] was almost submerged by headache – only mine aren't headaches, but enraged rats gnawing at the nape of my neck. I went to a doctor, at length; but all the comfort I got was that in 20 years, when I'm dead, and don't want a head, they will be able to cure them.[7]

But for all the suffering she endured, Woolf was not altogether sure that she would want to be free of her symptoms – even if that were possible. As she and Leonard were leaving their home in Richmond, a move she had long desired, she wrote in her diary, "I've had some very curious visions in this room too, lying in bed, mad, & seeing the sunlight quivering like gold water, on the wall. I've heard the voices of the dead here. And felt, through it all, exquisitely happy."[8] After a period when she was paralyzed by depression, withdrawn from human contact, when the horror and terror of her experience made her long for death, she reflected,

> But it is always a question whether I wish to avoid these glooms ... These 9 weeks give one a plunge into deep waters; which is a little alarming, but full of interest ... One goes down into the well & nothing protects one from the assault of truth.[9]

At times she railed against her illness, felt frustrated and impeded by it, and at other times she felt that it was essential to her art. In diaries and letters over the course of a lifetime, Woolf returns to the question again and again, without coming to a resolution: Was her illness a terrible obstacle to her art, or the necessary condition for it?

What she knew, from adolescence on, was that writing was a necessity for her.[10] "The only way I keep afloat is by working ... Directly I stop working I feel that I am sinking down, down. And as usual, I feel that if I sink further I shall reach the truth." To sink underwater was her metaphor for succumbing to depression and psychosis – and also for discovering "sea pearls" of truth. The metaphor strikes with chilling force because we read it knowing that ultimately this is the way Woolf would seek her death. At the age of fifty-nine, in 1941, Woolf committed suicide by walking into the River Ouse with a large stone in her pocket. She left notes to be found by her husband and sister.

****

Woolf had "merely glanced at the proof,"[11] she said, as the Hogarth Press began publishing Freud in 1924; her knowledge of psychoanalysis, she insisted, was just from "superficial talk." But when she began reading, it was voraciously: "I'm gulping up Freud." "Began reading Freud last night," she wrote in her diary on 2 December 1939, "to enlarge the circumference: to give my brain a wider scope: to make it objective, to get outside. Thus defeat the shrinkage of age. Always take on new things." And a week later: "Freud is upsetting: reducing one to whirlpool; & I daresay truly. If we're all instinct, the unconscious, what's all this about civilization, the whole man, freedom &c?"[12] These diary entries, from 1939, were written three months after Britain and France declared war on Germany. As World

War II began, Woolf was grappling with Freud's dark view of the human condition.

As a writer, Virginia Woolf had always had deep affinities with psychoanalysis – with its interests, its questions, even its methods. In an essay on "Modern Novels," she describes the life of the mind as envisaged by the contemporary writer. It is a description a psychoanalyst could fully endorse:

> The mind, exposed to the ordinary course of life, receives upon its surface a myriad impressions – trivial, fantastic, evanescent, or engraved with the sharpness of steel ... Let us record the atoms as they fall upon the mind in the order in which they fall, let us trace the pattern, however disconnected and incoherent in appearance, which each sight or incident scores upon the consciousness. Let us not take it for granted that life exists more in what is commonly thought big than in what is commonly thought small.[13]

The point of interest, she asserts, is very different than it had been in the past. The modern novelist

> has to have the courage to say that what interests him is no longer "this" but "that": out of "that" alone must he construct his work. For the moderns "that", the point of interest, lies very likely in the dark places of psychology. At once, therefore, the accent falls a little differently; the emphasis is upon something hitherto ignored; at once a different outline of form becomes necessary, difficult for us to grasp, incomprehensible to our predecessors.[14]

To explore these "dark places of psychology" Virginia Woolf developed, as a writer, a process very like the exploration that unfolds over time in analysis: "It took me a year's groping to discover what I call my tunnelling process, by which I tell the past by installments, as I have need of it. This is my prime discovery so far."[15] Suspending the deliberate directing of her thoughts, as the psychoanalytic patient is asked to do, Woolf found that the past does not reveal itself as a continuous, coherent, chronological narrative, but rises to consciousness piecemeal – by "installments" as she felicitously puts it.

Virginia Woolf was fascinated by memory, as Freud had been. "Why," she asks – posing a question that arises in any psychoanalytic treatment –

> have I forgotten so many things that must have been, one would have thought, more memorable than what I do remember? Why remember the hum of bees in the garden going down to the beach, and forget completely being thrown naked by father into the sea? (Mrs Swanwick says she saw that happen).[16]

This reflection on memory is *itself* an example of the unreliability of memory. Mrs. Swanwick, in a memoir, warmly recalled seeing Leslie Stephen and his family on the beach at St. Ives: "We watched with delight his naked babies running about the beach or being towed into the sea between his legs, and their beautiful mother." But Woolf's memory of this passage alters it, aligning it with her own present view of her father, endangering his young daughter by throwing her naked into the sea.

The past, she recognized, "is much affected by the present moment. What I write today I should not write in a year's time." Memories may be altered by knowledge of what has happened between the "remembered" *then* and the remembering present. Thinking about her older brother Thoby, who had died of typhoid fever when he was twenty-six, she tries "to recover the picture of a schoolboy." She remembers a scene of Thoby home from school on holiday, telling her tales of the Greeks and of Shakespeare, and she goes on to wonder what Thoby might have become, had he lived. And then she stops herself:

> The knell of those words affects my memory of a time when in fact they were not heard at all. We had no kind of foreboding that he was to die when he was twenty-six and I was twenty-four. That is one of the falsifications – that knell I always find myself hearing and transmitting – that one cannot guard against, save by noting it. Then I never saw him as I see him now, with all his promise ended. Then I thought only of the moment; him there in the room; just back from Clifton; or from Cambridge; dropping in to argue with me. It was, whatever date I give it, an exciting moment; in which we both pushed out from the mists of childhood.[17]

"Scene making," Woolf wrote, "is my natural way of marking the past. A scene always comes to the top; arranged; representative ... Is this liability of mine to scene receiving the origin of my writing impulse?"[18] But this way of marking the past is not reserved to writers: in remembering the past, we are *all* writers. From the continuous flow of time we select a particular scene. Or we alter a scene. Or we invent a scene. Is the process more accurately called "scene *making*" or "scene *receiving*"? Woolf uses first one verb, then the other – and both are apposite. The subjective experience is a passive one of receiving something that is there, waiting to be retrieved. "A scene comes to the top," she writes, capturing that conscious experience. But "scene *making*" points to the complex creative processes underlying the subjective experience.

Freud, in his 1899 paper "Screen Memories," had also addressed the curious selectivity of memory: "I feel surprised at forgetting something important, and I feel even more surprised, perhaps, at remembering something apparently indifferent." He suggests that the conscious experience of memories *emerging* is deceptive. Rather, memories are *created*:

> Our childhood memories show us our earliest years not as they were but as they appeared at the later periods when the memories were aroused. In these periods

of arousal, the childhood memories did not, as people are accustomed to say, *emerge*; they were *formed* at that time.[19]

Memories that appear to be indifferent or unimportant can be understood as "screens" for childhood fantasies, wishes, or experiences that are charged with conflict. A fantasy that remains unconscious, Freud wrote, "must be content to find its way allusively . . . into a childhood scene." Through these scenes, we create the past.

Woolf's childhood memories are the setting of her great novel *To the Lighthouse*. As she began to envisage it, she wrote in her diary that she intended it to be autobiographical: "This is going to be fairly short: to have father's character done complete in it; & mothers; & St. Ives; & childhood; & all the usual things I try to put in – life, death, &c. But the centre is father's character."[20] In the book she wrote, however, the center is unquestionably not father's character, but mother's: "The portrait of mother . . . is more like her to me than anything I would ever have conceived of as possible" her sister wrote to her after she read it.

> It is almost painful to see her so raised up from the dead. It was like meeting her again with oneself grown up and on equal terms and it seems to me the most astonishing feat of creation to have been able to see her in such a way.[21]

And Woolf herself mused that the book was less a novel than an "elegy."[22]

In the memoir she began at fifty-seven, Woolf looks back to writing *To the Lighthouse*, and the extraordinary effect it had on her:

> Until I was in the 40's . . . the presence of my mother obsessed me. I could hear her voice, see her, imagine what she would do or say as I went about my day's doings. She was one of the invisible presences who after all play so important a part in every life . . . It is perfectly true that she obsessed me, in spite of the fact that she died when I was thirteen, until I was forty-four. Then one day I made up, as I sometimes make up my books, *To the Lighthouse*; in a great, apparently involuntary, rush. One thing burst into another. Blowing bubbles out of a pipe gives the feeling of the rapid crowd of ideas and scene which blew out of my mind, so that my lips seem syllabling of their own accord.

An "invisible presence" – her phrase captures a continuing relationship, constant to the writer herself, unseen by others. "I wrote the book very quickly; and when it was written, I ceased to be obsessed by my mother. I no longer hear her voice; I do not see her. I suppose that I did for myself what psychoanalysts do for their patients. I expressed some very long felt and deeply felt emotion. And in expressing it I explained it and laid it to rest."[23]

She asks herself, "What is the meaning of 'explained' it? Why, because I described her and my feeling for her in that book, should my vision of her and my feeling for her become so much dimmer and weaker?" I would like to explore further the questions Woolf raises.

Some biographical background: Virginia Woolf was born, in 1882, into a large and very accomplished family – born, she wrote, "not of rich parents, but of well-to-do parents, born into a very communicative, literate, letter-writing, articulate late 19th century world." Her father was the eminent Victorian man of letters Sir Leslie Stephen, author of *The History of English Thought in the Eighteenth Century* and *The Science of Ethics*, among many books, and editor of the vast *Dictionary of National Biography*. Her mother, Julia Duckworth Stephen, was renowned for her beauty, and her striking looks are evident in the portrait by her aunt, the photographer Julia Margaret Cameron. Friends and relatives of the large extended family included many leading figures of the intellectual, literary, and artistic worlds of the late Victorian era.

Both her parents had previously been married, and both had been widowed. With the death of Leslie Stephen's first wife he was left with a five-year-old daughter. When Julia Duckworth was widowed at twenty-four, she was left with two young children, and a third was born six weeks later. When she and Leslie Stephen married, he was forty-six and she was thirty-two. There were four more children born of this marriage in four-and-a-half years: Vanessa, Thoby, Virginia, and Adrian. Thus there were eight children all together, of different ages, with different needs; in addition there were relatives and visitors. Julia Stephen, besides managing this crowded household, took on other responsibilities, visiting the needy and the sick. Years later her daughter would reach back toward her mother in memory and find there was little she could hold onto:

> Can I remember ever being alone with her for more than a few minutes? Someone was always interrupting. When I think of her spontaneously she is always in a room full of people ... What a jumble of things I can remember, if I let my mind run, about my mother; but they are all of her in company; of her surrounded; of her generalised; dispersed.[24]

There clung to her mother what Woolf called "an enduring melancholy." Was it the effect of her lifelong devotion to caring for her own invalid mother? Was it the sudden loss of her first husband, with whom "she had been happy as few people are happy"? Woolf adds bitterly, "It is notable that she never spoke of her first love; and in treasuring it changed it perhaps to something far fairer than it could have been, had life allowed it to endure."[25] Whatever the reason, her mother seemed always to be elsewhere. Virginia Woolf's earliest memory of her mother was "of her lap; the scratch of some beads on her dress comes back to me as I pressed my cheek against it." This sense memory distills into a single moment a poignant theme: beads on a mother's dress seem glittering and glamorous to a young girl, but are best admired from a distance.

Woolf does describe one moment of having her mother's full attention. Significantly, she won it with her writing: "How excited I used to be when the 'Hyde Park Gate News' was laid on her plate on Monday morning, and she liked something I had written! Never shall I forget my extremity of pleasure – it was like being a violin and being played upon." From the age of nine, Virginia collaborated with Thoby, Vanessa, and Adrian on "The Hyde Park Gate News," a paper that appeared every week, penned in a childish hand. High-spirited and humorous, it records the life of the Stephen family before the cruel losses that followed, which would darken the memory of those years. Their exuberant chronicle of family life stopped abruptly when Virginia was thirteen years old and their mother died.

The death of Julia Stephen, who died of rheumatic fever after an eight-week illness, was shattering. Soon afterward Virginia had her first breakdown, and heard for the first time what she was later to call "those horrible voices." The death of her mother, devastating in itself, was the first in a series of losses. Two years later, her half-sister Stella, age twenty-five, died of peritonitis soon after coming back from her honeymoon. Virginia was now fifteen. Stella's was "the second blow of death," she wrote, and others would follow. Her father died of cancer when she was twenty-two, and her brother Thoby of typhoid fever when she was twenty-four. Virginia Woolf was early acquainted with grief: and grief is at the heart of her autobiographical novel.

This sketch of the Stephen family – beautiful wife and mother, intellectual husband, eight children, household crowded with guests, family life brought to a sudden end by the death of the mother – will seem familiar to readers of *To the Lighthouse*. In writing it, I believe, Woolf was "thinking back through" the fictional Mrs. Ramsay to her own mother, and for this reason she came to command the center of the imaginative world of the novel – for the other characters, for readers and critics, and for Woolf herself.[26] It is noteworthy that unlike all the other characters – Lily Briscoe, Charles Tansley, William Bankes – Mr. and Mrs. Ramsay are given no first names: the reader is positioned to look up at them, as a child does.

Mrs. Ramsay's is the first voice we hear: "Yes, of course, if it's fine tomorrow," she assures her six-year-old son James. Then Mr. Ramsay appears:

"But," said his father, stopping in front of the drawing-room window, "it won't be fine." Had there been an axe handy, or a poker, any weapon that would have gashed a hole in his father's breast and killed him, there and then, James would have seized it.

Mrs. Ramsay tries to soothe James's feelings: "But it may be fine – I expect it will be fine."

Her only expression of irritation is an impatient twist of the stocking she is knitting, to bring to the lighthouse keeper for his son. She conjures up the dreariness and loneliness of the lighthouse keeper's life, the worry he must have about his wife and son, from whom he is obliged to live apart. Woolf places Mrs. Ramsay in that female tradition in which looking after the needs of others constitutes a life's work.

Like Julia Stephen, Mrs. Ramsay is beautiful, a woman, men fall in love with. Her husband's student, Charles Tansley (whose dissertation, she recalls, was about the influence of something upon somebody) walking into town with her, felt "for the first time in his life an extraordinary pride." The botanist William Bankes; the young Paul Rayley; Mr. Ramsay himself, who could not help noticing her beauty: the novel is filled with men who are in one way or another in love with Mrs. Ramsay. And it is not only men who feel her power. The artist Lily Briscoe gropes in her mind for words that would describe her feeling for Mrs. Ramsay. She

> had much ado to control her impulse to fling herself (thank Heaven she had always resisted so far) at Mrs. Ramsay's knee and say to her – but what could one say to her? – 'I'm in love with you'? No, that was not true. 'I'm in love with this all,' waving her hand at the hedge, at the house, at the children. It was absurd, it was impossible. One could not say what one meant.[27]

Ten years after the death of Mrs. Ramsay, the surviving characters gather at the house that has stood empty all this time. Andrew, the most promising of the sons, has died in the Great War; Prue, the daughter whose beauty took one's breath away, has died in childbirth. James and Cam, acquiescing to their father's wish, have agreed now to complete with him the trip to the lighthouse that had been under discussion in the opening scene. Both were children then, and they have been altered by grief. James, the six-year-old contentedly cutting out pictures in the scene of intimacy with his mother, at sixteen has become sullen. Silently watching as his sister is tempted to break their pact of resistance to their father, James expects her to give way "as he watched a look come upon her face, a look he remembered." His memory from the age of six is of course impressionistic: "They look down, he thought, at their knitting or something. Then suddenly they look up. There was a flash of blue, he remembered, and then somebody sitting with him laughed, surrendered, and he was very angry."[28] The memory that the reader knows to be particular, singular, has become, in his inner life, plural: "she" has become "they" as his memory of the scene with his mother has become an emblem for the perfidy of *all* women. The language of James' meditation is equivocal, encompassing the momentary loss we witnessed, that of his mother's attention when his father broke in on their intimacy, and the permanent abandonment of her death.

Cam, too, is altered by grief, but differently. As a child, she was the little girl who would *not* hand the gentleman the flower, as her nursemaid directed. She clenched her fist and stamped. In the years since their mother's death, Cam's wildness has been subdued. Brother and sister appear to Lily Briscoe "a melancholy couple" as they come lagging after their father, "with a pallor in their eyes" that makes her feel that "they suffered something beyond their years in silence."

Over the first part of the novel, the narrative circles around the figure at its center, Mrs. Ramsay. And suddenly, with the turn of a page, she is gone, without explanation. The world that was densely peopled is suddenly empty; there is only the desolate house with the wind blowing through it, a visual image of abandonment. The movement of the narrative, that had been shifting from the consciousness of one character to that of another, comes to an abrupt halt. No human voices are heard, only the impersonal voice of a disembodied narrator. The sudden change is confusing, disorienting. Woolf does more, here, than simply to show the ways grief has left its stamp on a young son and daughter. What she does is to *induce* grief, to *inflict* it on the reader.

The death of Mrs. Ramsay is noted only in a single sentence in brackets – indeed, in a subordinate clause within that bracketed sentence: "[Mr. Ramsay, stumbling along a passage one dark morning, stretched his arms out, but Mrs. Ramsay having died rather suddenly the night before, his arms, though stretched out, remained empty.]"[29] That is all we are to learn about the death of Mrs. Ramsay. The image of arms stretched out, but empty, is remembered from the early morning of May 5, 1895, after Julia Stephen died: "My father staggered from the bedroom as we came. I stretched out my arms to stop him, but he brushed past me, crying out something I could not catch, distraught."[30] By enclosing the death of Mrs. Ramsay between brackets, by referring to it only in passing, the author responds to the reader's engagement by ignoring it completely. It is a hard look into the heart of a child's grief.

Mrs. Ramsay's death, which is hidden from view, is in fact the central event of the novel. When the surviving characters return, ten years later, to complete the expedition to the lighthouse, her absence is everywhere felt. Nancy's question, "What does one send to the lighthouse?" declares this absence without naming it: Mrs. Ramsay knew exactly what to send to the lighthouse. There would be some magazines for the lighthouse keeper, to relieve the boredom of his watch; there would be the socks she was knitting for the lighthouse keeper's son, poor boy, with his tuberculous hip. Mrs. Ramsay is the Victorian ideal of a woman, spending herself in serving the needs of others.

This ideal was personified as "The Angel in the House" in the poem by Coventry Patmore; Julia Stephen's copy was signed by the poet himself, who was a close friend of her own mother.[31] And the Angel in the House looms large in a talk Woolf gave, "Professions for Women" – not as an ideal, but as an adversary. Woolf looks back to the start of her career as a writer, which she began at twenty-two by reviewing books. How could she review books by men when she had been taught to cajole and to flatter the opposite sex? In order to write, she would have to "do battle with a certain phantom" – a phantom she called the Angel in House:

> She was immensely charming. She was utterly unselfish. She excelled in the difficult arts of family life. She sacrificed herself daily. If there was chicken, she took the leg; if there was a draught, she sat in it – in short, she was so constituted that she never had a mind or a wish of her own, but preferred to sympathize always with the minds and wishes of others.

If she were to write, Woolf had to free herself from this phantom:

> I now record the one act for which I take some credit to myself . . . I turned upon her and caught her by the throat. I did my best to kill her . . . Had I not killed her she would have killed me. She would have plucked the heart out of my writing . . . Whenever I felt the shadow of her wing or the radiance of her halo upon my page, I took up the inkpot and flung it at her. She died hard. Her fictitious nature was of great assistance to her. It is far harder to kill a phantom than a reality. She was always creeping back when I thought I had despatched her. Though I flatter myself that I killed her in the end, the struggle was severe.[32]

The writer finds that she must kill – again, and again, and again – a presence she describes variously as angel, phantom, ghost. Returning from the essay to her autobiographical novel, I am suggesting that in writing *To the Lighthouse*, in killing the Angel in the House, Woolf was able finally to silence the "invisible presence" of her mother and give voice to her own rage – rage that she both inscribed and enacted in the novel.

There is another important sense in which Virginia Woolf silenced her mother. Throughout her life Woolf wrote mournfully about the difficulty she had in remembering her. Her attempts are always punctuated by questions and uncertainties: "She was born, I think, in 1848 [actually it was 1846];

I think in India ... An old governess – was she Mademoiselle Rose? did she give her the picture of Beatrice that hung in the dining room?" All that she has is conjecture; any family anecdote is a scrap of evidence she turns over and over in her hands, looking for clues, trying to draw inferences. "If I turn to my mother how difficult it is to single her out as she really was; to imagine what she was thinking, to put a single sentence into her mouth."

"What would one not give," she wrote at twenty-five, "to recapture a single phrase even! or the tone of the clear round voice."[33] And again at fifty-seven,

> For what reality can remain real of a person who died forty-four years ago at the age of forty-nine, without leaving a book, or a picture, or any piece of work – apart from the three children who now survive and the memory of her that remains in their minds? There is the memory; but there is nothing to check that memory by.[34]

In fact, Julia Duckworth Stephen's *Notes from Sick Rooms* was published by Smith, Elder, & Co. of London in 1883. In its fifty-two pages, gracefully written, thoughtful, and detailed, she gives advice about caring for patients drawn from her own experience. She covers a range of subjects – from bathing the patient, to positioning a candle shade at night so the patient will not be disturbed by light, to responding to the patient's anxieties, whether "real or fancied." And in discussing one seemingly trivial problem of the sick room, her voice sounds delightfully familiar:

> Among the number of small evils which haunt illness, the greatest, in the misery which it can cause, though the smallest in size, is crumbs. The origin of most things has been decided on, but the origin of crumbs in bed has never excited sufficient attention among the scientific world, though it is a problem which has tormented many a weary sufferer ... The torment of crumbs should be stamped out of the sick bed as if it were the Colorado beetle in a potato field.[35]

Even as she gets down to the minutiae of patient care, Julia Stephen shows her flair as a writer. The nurse, she says, must "wet her fingers and get the crumbs to stick to them. The patient's night-clothes must be searched; crumbs lurk in each tiny fold or frill." Crumbs *"lurk"*! This passage might almost have been written by Virginia Woolf herself.

In addition to *Notes from Sick Rooms*, Julia Stephen also wrote children's stories. Nine of these survive and the manuscripts are substantial in length, each between twenty and fifty pages long. Alex Zwerdling[36] describes them as easily readable fair copies; sometimes there is more than one version of a story, suggesting that Julia Stephen worked at revising her stories and perhaps wanted to circulate them. He cites two extant letters of Leslie

Stephen which indicate that he was negotiating with Routledge (unsuccessfully) to publish at least some of her stories. Did Virginia Woolf know about her mother's children's stories? She did. At one point the Hogarth Press was considering publishing one of them. The project did not come to fruition, but it got far enough along that her sister, the artist Vanessa Bell, did a series of watercolor illustrations for the story[37] which she stitched into appropriate places in the twenty-four-page typescript of the story. So Woolf's mournful statement that her mother did not leave a book, or any piece of work, is curious.

The picture Woolf gives of her mother is so self-consistent that it has convinced generations of readers and scholars. Julia Duckworth Stephen, we all know, was the model for the Virgin in Burne-Jones's 1879 painting of

Figure 4.1 Vanessa Bell, unpublished watercolor. Reprinted by permission of Washington State University Libraries Manuscripts, Archives, and Special Collections.

Figure 4.2 Vanessa Bell, unpublished watercolor. Reprinted by permission of Washington State University Libraries Manuscripts, Archives, and Special Collections.

the Annunciation. She was one of the signators of the "Appeal Against Women Suffrage" that was published in the June 1889 issue of *Nineteenth Century*. But there was more to Julia Stephen. Characterizing her mother as she consistently did, as a woman who left no book, no work by which to remember her, Virginia Woolf denied the grounds she did have for finding in her mother's interests some antecedent for her own. "We think back through our mothers if we are women," she asserted. Yet she seemed to regard herself as being without maternal precedent – sprung full-blown from her own imagination. Virginia Woolf yearned to hear her mother's voice, she writes repeatedly; and yet, in her pain and her rage at the mother who had died when she was thirteen – a mother whose attention, she felt, had always been elsewhere – perhaps she also wished to silence her.

To return, now, to Woolf's statement that in writing *To the Lighthouse* she had done for herself "what psychoanalysts do for their patients." We read these words, written toward the end of her life, and of course we must demur. She was able to find some relief, evidently, in silencing the voice of her mother. She "ceased to be obsessed" by her. She no longer imagined what her mother would do or say as she went about her daily life: "I no longer hear her voice." But what Virginia Woolf could not envisage, far less achieve, was a continuing relationship with the invisible presence of her mother, one in which her own voice could be heard as well as her mother's in ongoing counterpoint – a relationship of depth and complexity that would continue to evolve throughout her life, as girl and woman.

Notes

1. Virginia Woolf, *A Room of One's Own* (New York: Harcourt, Brace & World, 1929), 47.
2. Leonard Woolf, *Beginning Again* (New York: Harcourt Brace Jovanovich, 1963), 167–68.
3. W. H. Auden, "In Memory of Sigmund Freud," 1939. https://poets.org/poem/memory-sigmund-freud
4. Diaries and letters document her extremes of mood, which were episodic, and they also document – quietly, movingly – her capacity for ordinary human happiness: "We sit over the first waiting for the post – the cream of the day," she wrote on January 7, 1920, in Sussex. "Yet every part of the day here has its merits." She walks to her writing studio "over grass rough with frost & ground hard as brick"; at the end of the day "we tend our fire, cook coffee, read, I find, luxuriously, peacefully, at length." *The Diary of Virginia Woolf*, vol. II, ed. Anne Olivier Bell (London: Hogarth Press, 1978), 3. Kay Redfield Jamison, in the biography *Robert Lowell, Setting the River on Fire: A Study of Genius, Mania, and Character* (New York: Knopf, 2017) discusses the history of the diagnosis and treatment of bipolar disorder in relation to another brilliant writer.
5. *Diary* II, 189. August 16, 1922.
6. Virginia Woolf, *The Letters of Virginia Woolf*, vol. IV, ed. Nigel Nicolson (London: Hogarth Press, 1978), 144–45. February 27, 1930.
7. Virginia Woolf, *The Letters of Virginia Woolf*, vol. V, ed. Nigel Nicholson (London: Hogarth Press, 1979), 76. October 9, 1936.
8. *Diary* II, 283. January 9, 1924.
9. Virginia Woolf, *The Diary of Virginia Woolf*, vol. III, ed. Anne Olivier Bell (London: Hogarth Press, 1980), 111. September 28, 1926.
10. In *Virginia Woolf: Becoming a Writer* (New Haven: Yale University Press, 2001) I explored the multiple ways that writing served her, from adolescence on, in relation to what she called life's "sledge-hammer blows."
11. Virginia Woolf, *The Letters of Virginia Woolf*, vol. III, ed. Nigel Nicholson (London: Hogarth Press, 1977), 134. October 2, 1924.

12. Virginia Woolf, *The Diary of Virginia Woolf*, vol. V, ed. Anne Olivier Bell (London: Hogarth Press, 1984), 250.

13. Virginia Woolf, "Modern Novels," in *The Essays of Virginia Woolf*, vol. III, ed. Andrew McNeillie (1919; repr. London: Hogarth Press, 1988), 33–34.

14. Virginia Woolf, "Modern Fiction," in *The Essays of Virginia Woolf*, vol. IV, ed. Andrew McNeillie (1925; repr. London: Hogarth Press, 1994), 162.

15. *Diary* II, 272. October 15, 1923.

16. Virginia Woolf : *Moments of Being*, 2nd edition, ed. Jeanne Schulkind (New York: Harcourt Brace Jovanovich, 1985), 70.

17. *Moments of Being*, 140.

18. *Moments of Being*, 142.

19. Sigmund Freud, "Screen Memories," *SE* 3: 322.

20. *Diary* III, 18. May 14, 1925.

21. Vanessa Bell, *Selected Letters of Vanessa Bell*, ed. Regina Marler (New York: Pantheon, 1993), 317.

22. *Diary* III, 34. June 27, 1925.

23. *Moments of Being*, 80–81.

24. Ibid., 83–84.

25. Ibid., 32–33.

26. Mark Hussey, in his introduction to *To the Lighthouse* (New York: Harcourt, 2005) discusses critics' differing views of the relation between the Ramsays and Woolf's parents. The mother/daughter relationship in Woolf's writing has been explored by biographers and literary scholars, notably in Hermione Lee's monumental, richly detailed *Virginia Woolf* (New York: Knopf, 1997). For readings specifically on this subject, see Jane Lillienfeld, "The Deceptiveness of Beauty': Mother Love and Mother Hate *To the Lighthouse*," *Twentieth Century*, XXIII (1977), 345–76; Jane Marcus, "Virginia Woolf and Her Violin: Mothering, Madness, and Music," in *Virginia Woolf and the Languages of Patriarchy* (Bloomington, Indiana University Press, 1987), 96–114; Ellen Bayuk Rosenman, *The Invisible Presence: Virginia Woolf and the Mother-Daughter Relationship* (Baton Rouge: Louisiana State University Press, 1989). Another important contribution is Elizabeth Abel's *Virginia Woolf and the Fictions of Psychoanalysis* (Chicago: University of Chicago Press, 1989).

27. *To the Lighthouse* (1927; repr. New York: Penguin, 1992), 24. Page references throughout are to this edition.

28. Ibid., 183–84.

29. Ibid., 140.

30. *Moments of Being*, 91.

31. Julia Duckworth Stephen, *Stories for Children, Essays for Adults*, ed. Diane F. Gillespie and Elizabeth Steele (Syracuse University Press, 1987), 11.

32. This talk, which she gave in 1931 to the London branch of the National Society for Women's Service (four years after the publication of *To the Lighthouse*), was published posthumously as an essay. *The Essays of Virginia Woolf*, vol. VI, ed. Stuart N. Clarke (London: Hogarth Press, 2011), 480–81.

33. *Moments of Being*, 36.

34. *Moments of Being*, 85.

35. *Stories for Children, Essays for Adults*, 219.

36. Alex Zwerdling, *Virginia Woolf and the Real World* (Berkeley: University of California Press, 1986), 190. Julia Stephen's stories were published for the first time in 1987 in *Stories for Children, Essays for Adults*, which also brought back into print *Notes from Sick Rooms*, with generous introductions by the editors, Diane F. Gillespie and Elizabeth Steele. Kimberly Coates argues that Woolf's essay "On Being Ill" is a response to *Notes from Sick Rooms*: "Phantoms, Fancy (And) Symptoms: Virginia Woolf and The Art of Being Ill," *Woolf Studies Annual* 18 (2012): 1–28.

37. I wish to thank Greg Matthews of the Washington State University Library, Manuscript, Archives, and Special Collections, for having generously provided access to these illustrations.

5

JEAN WYATT

Dislocating the Reader
Slave Motherhood and The Disrupted Temporality of Trauma in Toni Morrison's Beloved

Psychoanalytic theory works most fruitfully on literary texts that, through their psychological sophistication or through the complex dynamics of their interactions with readers, require an account of unconscious processes taking place both in characters and in readers. Then the task of a literary critic is not to apply a psychoanalytic theory to a fictional text wholesale, using it as a key to unlock the text's mysteries, but rather to treat the affinities between a literary work and a particular psychoanalytic theory as a dialogue – a dialogue in which the fiction illuminates or even revises the psychoanalytic theory as effectively as the psychoanalytic paradigm illuminates the fiction. Toni Morrison's *Beloved* is such a novel.

In this chapter, I place into dialogue *Beloved* and Jean Laplanche's psychoanalytic theory of *Nachträglichkeit* (afterwardsness) in order to think about the effects of *Beloved's* nonlinear narrative structure on readers.[1] Morrison's novel and Laplanche's theory find common ground in the notion of temporal distortion as a marker of trauma and an expression of psychic suffering. Throughout *Beloved*, contorted understandings of time express the psychic disturbances of characters traumatized by slavery. And, at the level of narrative structure, Morrison uses temporal discontinuity to surprise readers into thinking differently about ethical issues.

In *Beloved* Morrison withholds key information, deferring an early scene (the pivotal event of the novel) until very late in the narration. Only after she has read over half the novel does a reader learn that nineteen years before the fictional present, Sethe killed her baby. Morrison uses chronological displacement to bring readers to perceive the infanticide from an enlarged ethical perspective.

Jean Laplanche's psychoanalytic theory of *Nachträglichkeit* offers a complicated temporal paradigm that I use to reveal the intricacies of reader response to *Beloved's* narrative form. *Nachträglichkeit* (translated as "afterwardsness" and "après-coup") is a concept recently developed by Jean Laplanche from Freud's early model of traumatic time. *Nachträglichkeit* names a lag in time characteristic of trauma.[2] An event of traumatic force that occurs at an early stage in life evokes intense emotion not at the moment of its occurrence, but only at a later stage of life, when the meaning of the earlier event is belatedly understood. Then, the delayed realization of what the act meant triggers emotional responses that would have been appropriate to the original violation, but are not appropriate to the present benign moment.

In a reader surprised after long readerly acquaintance with Sethe's mothering by the belated news that she murdered her baby, there is a similar dialectic of meaning between the present moment of discovery and the past reading – and then a movement in the other direction, as the feelings attached to the past narrative of Sethe's devoted mothering fill the reader's present moment with disbelief, surprise, and horror. A reader retrospectively understands the first half of the novel differently in the light of Sethe's act of infanticide. But at the same time she is led to perceive the fact of infanticide differently, for she has already witnessed, through the first half of the novel, the sustained, unflagging dedication of Sethe to her children. As in Laplanche's notion of *Nachträglichkeit*, both meaning and affect ricochet from the present moment of reading to the memory of past reading and back again. As a result of these structural gymnastics, a reader may learn to think differently about the ethics of maternal love and learn to judge even acts of maternal violence within the personal and historical context of the subject's life.

Temporal dislocation also characterizes the characters' processing of the traumas they experienced in slavery. As in current trauma theory – for example the theories of Cathy Caruth, Dori Laub, and Bessel Van der Kolk – characters in *Beloved* are invaded by images of a traumatic event that they cannot recall as a whole episode: trauma revisits them in the present in literal and fragmented form, so that they live again a meaningless violence that cannot be placed within a chronological narrative that might give the intrusive images some meaning.[3]

Dialogue between literary text and psychoanalytic theory goes both ways. If a Morrison novel, through its nuanced presentation of psychological complexity or through its formal effects on a reader, invites dialogue with a psychoanalytic model that can enrich understanding of the text, the stories of psychoanalysis in turn attract Toni Morrison, for reasons she suggests in the introduction to *Playing in the Dark*: "The narrative into which life seems to cast itself surfaces most forcefully in certain kinds of psychoanalysis."[4] Implying that she finds in psychoanalysis a parallel with her own narrative art, Morrison voices her admiration for psychoanalytic theory's ability to tell a story that captures a basic truth of human life and condenses it into a narrative form powerful in its impact.

The Difficulties of Writing *Beloved*

Beloved tells the story not of one slave mother, but of two slave mothers. The narrative centers on the slave mother Sethe, who killed her child. A second slave mother emerges only sporadically from the shadows of Sethe's deepest memories: the distant mother of Sethe's own childhood.

Most readers, despite their varying degrees of ambivalence toward their own mothers, retain from very early childhood the image of a nurturing, protective mother that functions as an anchor of security. For example, Erik Erikson describes a turning point in a baby's development when a baby can allow the mother to go out of its sight without experiencing overwhelming anxiety – because the baby has internalized the image of its mother. The internalized mother remains as a "feeling of inner goodness."[5] The internal good mother, Erikson says, founds a basic sense of security and safety in the world – or "basic trust," in Erikson's vocabulary. Similarly, contemporary trauma theorists Dori Laub and Nanette Auerhahn say that the "link between self and empathic other" is represented by the internalized mother figure, and that maternal image acts as the linchpin holding together "the very fabric of psychic life."[6] In confronting a reader with the figure of a mother who kills her child, an author risks creating in her reader intense affective discomfort: the internal image of the good mother that is the source of security stands in contradiction to the figure of a murdering mother who violates her bond with her child and annihilates all safety and security. A reader may well be inclined to find the nearest exit (i.e., close the book). The two powerful stories of slave motherhood, one of murder and the other of maternal deprivation, must be told, but the telling presents formidable challenges.

In an essay, Morrison herself acknowledges the seemingly insuperable difficulties that writing *Beloved* posed:

> [From writing the earlier novels] I learned a lot about how to do certain things. For *Beloved* though, there was almost nothing that I knew that I seemed sure of, nothing I could really use ... *Beloved* was like I'd never written a book before. It was brand new ... I thought, more than I've thought about any book, "I cannot do this." I thought that a lot. And I stopped for long, long, long periods of time and said, "I know I've never read a book like this because who can write it?"[7]

None of the literary techniques that Morrison had honed through writing her first three novels helped in the writing of *Beloved*. Her narrative resources disabled by the subject matter of *Beloved* (slavery), Morrison needed to invent a new narrative language and form. What she wanted, Morrison says in an essay, was a language that would "show the reader what slavery *felt* like," and even make the reader herself "experience what [slavery] felt like."[8] Morrison's characters are ex-slaves, living in Ohio in 1873. So it is the memories of the traumas inflicted by slavery that Morrison needed to represent. Yet trauma is uniquely resistant to narrative. Trauma overwhelms and dismantles a subject's mechanisms for making sense of what is happening, so it cannot be registered in the form of narrative memory. To convey to her reader directly the ways that traumatic memory distorts time, returning in fragmented images from the past to disrupt the present time of trauma survivors, Morrison created a language of temporal dislocation. The discontinuous narration of *Beloved* is full of unexplained leaps into different time periods, in a readerly imitation of the ways that Morrison's ex-slave characters were thrown off balance by intrusive memory fragments of past trauma. In one central episode,[9] readers are subjected to grammatical and temporal distortions of language that mimic the disorientation of Africans captured and thrown without explanation onto the slave ships of the Middle Passage.

Telling the story of a mother who murdered her child posed other challenges. How could Morrison contrive to circumvent a reader's rush to judgment on a mother who kills her own child? Philip Page, James Phelan, and Maggie Sale have persuasively argued that the author's presentation of the infanticide from the perspectives of several different narrators, each with a different interpretation, serves the purpose of complicating judgment on Sethe.[10] I want to add to this conversation two more narrative strategies. First, Morrison develops the several dimensions of slave mothering, historical and psychological, that put pressure on Sethe's mothering practices: she provides a historical background for the excesses of Sethe's mothering by providing glimpses of Sethe's own childhood, impoverished by a plantation system whose demands for her slave mother's labor in the fields left no time to attend to her baby daughter's needs. Second, she devises a narrative structure that delays the news of the infanticide for 148 pages, till a reader has become familiar with Sethe's absolute dedication to her children.

Narrative Structure and Reader Ethics: *Nachträglichkeit*

Morrison's experiments with narrative and psychological complexity invite the kind of dialogue between literary text and psychoanalytic theory that enriches the text while suggesting new ways of using, extending, or even contesting the psychoanalytic paradigm. I align the narrative structure of *Beloved* with Laplanche's revisionary model of Freud's notion of *Nachträglichkeit*, a psychological structure of belated response to trauma. This temporal structure, which Freud observed in many of his hysterical patients, is composed of two scenes widely separated by time and by a barrier of memory that prevents their conscious association.

Jean Laplanche often cites the example of "Emma" from Freud's *Project for a Scientific Psychology* to explain the structure of *Nachträglichkeit*.[11] At the age of eight, Emma goes into a shop to buy candy, and the shopkeeper gropes her through her clothes while grinning; Emma, not yet inducted into the world of adult sexuality, does not understand what he is doing and so has little or no emotional response. Several years later, after passing puberty, the now adolescent Emma goes into a clothing shop, sees two shop clerks laughing together, feels attracted to one, is assailed by overwhelming feelings of sexual excitation and horror, and rushes out of the shop. Emma develops a phobia against shopping, which is her presenting symptom when she comes to Freud's clinic. Through analysis it becomes clear that the perfectly banal details of the second scene – the shopboys laughing and handling clothing – reminded her suddenly of the shopkeeper's grin while he was touching her through her clothes. Only now, after the advent of puberty, does Emma have the knowledge and the psychosexual development necessary to comprehend the meaning of the initial incident: it was sexual, a sexual assault. She then represses the memory of the first event, but the affects aroused by the memory remain, attached now to the benign second episode of shopping.

In this example of the dislocated temporality of *Nachträglichkeit*, the subject's extreme emotional disturbance would have been appropriate to the first scene, but it was impossible for her to experience it then. Now, because she has the information requisite for understanding, she grasps the meaning of the first scene and responds to it, but her response is inappropriate to the present moment. In this paradigm of the missed encounter, the readiness of the subject always fails to coincide with the offerings of the moment: she comes to the event either "too early" or "too late."

The distinctive feature of *Nachträglichkeit* for my purposes here is that it structures a dialectic of meaning. On the one hand, meaning is projected backward from the present onto the past, as Emma realizes what the first scene signified; on the other hand, the content of the first scene is projected forward from the past to fill, inappropriately, the present scene. Like Freud's Emma, a reader of *Beloved* moves across two different scenes, which are also two different spheres of meaning.

Through the first half of the novel a reader knows some things but is ignorant of the root cause of Sethe's family's suffering: she knows that Sethe, her mother-in-law Baby Suggs, and Denver, Sethe's only living daughter, live in a house haunted by a baby ghost which they identify as Sethe's dead baby daughter.[12] When Paul D, an ex-slave from the same plantation as Sethe, finds her again after a separation of some nineteen years, he knocks the baby ghost out of the house in order to make some room for himself in the family home. The ghost returns in the body of an eighteen-year-old named Beloved. For some time Sethe's teen-aged daughter Denver, Beloved, Sethe and Paul D live together in an uneasy approximation of a nuclear family. It is only after reading 148 pages of the novel that a reader discovers the event that precipitated the events of the story she has just processed. Nineteen years before, when the slavecatchers came to take Sethe and her four children back to slavery, Sethe killed her baby girl rather than allow the slave-catcher to return her to slavery.

Throughout the first scene of reading (pp. 3–148), the reader learns about Sethe's extraordinary maternal devotion: she "wouldn't draw breath without her children," she says, and means it: her own life means far less to her than her children's lives. Her escape from slavery became urgent for her only because she "had to get her milk to her baby girl";[13] and despite enormous obstacles she delivered her mother's milk to that baby girl in faraway Ohio and promised never to leave her child again.

A multitude of details have shown us that Sethe is all-giving, selflessly devoted to her children, ever-present to their every need: she embodies, indeed, the impossible cultural ideal of "good mother." Because the new signifier, "infanticide," does not just give us a new vision of Sethe, but instead institutes a play of meaning between the first scene of reading and the second scene of reading, a reader is pressured to forego a quick judgment on the infanticide. On the one hand, a reader has to look back and reinterpret all the events of the first 148 pages differently, as Sethe's murder of her baby changes the meaning of what a reader has understood about Sethe's maternal feelings. Yet at the same time, there is a counter-movement as the content of the past scene of reading fills the present scene of reading. The horror a reader must feel when she learns of Sethe's infanticide has to be experienced in the light of everything she has already learned, through the first half of the book, about Sethe's mothering.

Narrative structure has ethical force. The belated disclosure of the story's central event challenges a reader to rethink all the specifics of Sethe's particular experience of mothering before judging her act. Thus reading becomes a kind of training in contextual ethics. The mind's movement between the first scene of reading and the second scene of reading and back again trains us to defer judgment on a person's actions till we know all the details of his or her life situation.[14] What George Eliot in *The Mill on the Floss* tries to do through direct moral exhortation – telling her reader that "moral judgments must remain false and hollow unless they are checked and enlightened by a perpetual reference to the special circumstances that mark the individual lot" – Morrison accomplishes through the workings of narrative structure alone.[15]

Sethe's Theory of *Nachträglich* Time

Aligning the temporal structure of Laplanche's *Nachträglichkeit* with *Beloved's* narrative form has enabled me to bring out the complex dynamics of reader response, emotional and ethical, to the novel's structure of deferred disclosure. It is, however, the psychoanalytic theories of contemporary trauma theorists mentioned above that best illuminate a different dimension of belatedness in *Beloved*: the temporal displacements that characterize the characters' (especially Sethe's) everyday modes of thinking. Laub and Auerhahn, writing of what we have come to know as PTSD (Post-Traumatic Stress Disorder), explain that traumatic experience so overwhelms the cognitive and affective resources of the subject that it cannot be integrated into memory in the normal way. Hence it returns not as a coherent memory, but as split-off fragments of the traumatic event: "The individual has an image, sensation, or isolated thought, but does not know with what it is connected, what it means, or what to do with it."[16] Already in the first eight pages of the novel, Sethe's consciousness is peppered intermittently with visual images dislocated in time: for example, "the baby blood that soaked her fingers like oil."[17] There is no narration of the event from which this visual image is lifted. An isolated image without context, it can only trouble and confuse the reader, in a readerly imitation of the way that Sethe herself is troubled by a fragment of memory without a context that would give it meaning. Sethe's consciousness is at the mercy of such fragments:

> The plash of water, the sight of her shoes ... and suddenly there was Sweet Home rolling, rolling, rolling out before her eyes, ... it rolled itself out before her in shameless beauty. ... It shamed her – remembering the wonderful soughing trees."[18]

Not "she remembered," but "there it was."[19] The fragment of the plantation where Sethe and her enslaved companions suffered intrudes itself without Sethe's volition, outside her conscious control. The visual fragment interrupts Sethe's present-day life without warning, "rolling, rolling, rolling out before her eyes" of its own accord. As van der Kolk says, "a flashback can occur at any time, whether they are awake or asleep ... There is no way of knowing when it's going to occur again or how long it will last."[20]

Because the traumatizing event originally overwhelmed the subject and escaped the ordinary processes of narrative memory, it is not processed by either the conscious or unconscious structures which would ordinarily weave the new event into networks of association drawn from the subject's prior experience. So the past event emerges not as refined and reshaped by memory, but as a literal replay of events: "The sensory fragments of memory intrude into the present, where they are literally relived."[21]

Sethe herself articulates a similar theory of the time of trauma.
I was talking about time. It's so hard for me to believe in it. Some things just stay. I used to think it was my rememory.... But it's not. Places, places are still there. If a house burns down, it's gone, but the place – the picture of it – stays, and not just in my rememory, but out there, in the world.... the picture of what I did, or knew, or saw is still out there. Right in the place where it happened.... Where I was before I came here, that place is real.... what's more, ... if you go there and stand in the place where it was, it will happen again; it will be there for you, waiting for you.... even though it's all over – over and done with – it's going to always be there waiting for you.[22]

Sethe's view of traumatic temporality resembles van der Kolk's in its emphasis on the literalness of traumatic recall. The traumatic event is not remembered; rather, it is happening again – now, in the present: "If you go there and stand in the place where it was, it will happen again."[23] In the different discourse of trauma theory, van der Kolk describes this experience of the past occupying the present moment: "Dissociation is the essence of trauma. The overwhelming experience is split off and fragmented, so that the emotions, sounds, images, thoughts, and physical sensations related to the trauma take on a life of their own. The sensory fragments of memory intrude into the present, where they are literally relived."[24] Rather than remembering the sensory fragment, a traumatized person experiences it as if it were occurring in the present: rather than calling up a memory, he relives it. This temporal jolt to consciousness may well cause terror in the traumatized subject. Being suddenly placed in an entirely different temporal arena, where one relives a moment of another time, radically alienates the subject from her present reality. When we remember that one of the revisiting split-off sensory fragments that troubles Sethe is "the baby blood that soaked her fingers like oil,"[25] we become aware of just how alienating an involuntary reliving of a traumatic event might be. Such a sensory fragment (broken off from the scene of infanticide) has to alienate a woman who identifies as mother – indeed, as a mother who devotes herself selflessly to her children's wellbeing.

The Skewed Temporality of Trauma

Belatedness is thus the hallmark of trauma, both in Laplanche's notion of *Nachträglichkeit* and in contemporary trauma theory. A confusion of the past with the present also governs Sethe's relationship to her children, and more specifically to Beloved. When Sethe recognizes the baby girl she killed in the nineteen-year-old woman who calls herself Beloved, she constructs a belated fantasy structure for her and her revenant baby to inhabit. "Nobody will ever get my milk no more except my children," says Sethe,[26] quitting her job and separating from her lover Paul D so she can devote herself exclusively to Beloved (and to her living daughter Denver). Ecstatic to have recovered her lost baby, Sethe overfeeds Beloved while "Beloved lapp-[ed] devotion like cream."[27] Breastfeeding is a metaphor, not a literal reality. Yet it expresses an overcloseness, an exclusive devotion to the child that is temporally inappropriate now that the baby, embodied in Beloved, is nineteen and Sethe herself past the age of reproduction.

The hyperconnection implied by the nursing metaphor turns destructive. The mother gives all while the daughter takes all, so that Beloved becomes "bigger, plumper by the day" while Sethe's "flesh" grows "thin as china silk,"[28] in a grotesque exaggeration of the mother feeding her baby with her own substance.[29]

In Sethe's understanding of her relation to Beloved, Sethe's body has returned to the moment before the infanticide. As in Laplanche's notion that trauma typically has deferred effects, Sethe's maternal devotion to Beloved would have been appropriate in the moment before the infanticide. For in that moment the baby was a nurseling. The baby died too early, and the nursing comes too late. Sethe is dislocated in time, living through the belated temporality of *Nachträglichkeit*.

Sethe's Distant Mother

Sethe's memories of her own mother provide a historical context for understanding Sethe's overinvestment in nurturing her children. Such memories are sparse, and they return in fragments. It is clear that even when Sethe was a nursing baby who needed her mother's milk, her mother was caught between the demands of two systems: the plantation system of slave labor and the system of infant nurturance. Her mother's labor in the master's fields filled up her mother's time, so that there was literally no time for her baby.[30] Sethe is never able to say that she missed her mother, but she is able to recover the rage she felt as an infant deprived of mother's milk.

> I'll tend her [Beloved] as no mother ever tended a child, a daughter. Nobody will ever get my milk no more except my own children. I never had to give it to nobody else ... Nan had to nurse whitebabies and me too because Ma'am was in the rice. The little whitebabies got it first and I got what was left. Or none. There was no nursing milk to call my own. I know what it is to be without the

milk that belongs to you; to have to fight and holler for it, and to have so little left . . . Beloved . . . She my daughter. The one I managed to have milk for and to get it to her even after they stole it.[31]

Sethe's reminiscence of having no mother's milk to call her own interweaves with her insistence that she overcame all obstacles to get her milk to Beloved – and always will: "The milk would be there, and I would be there with it."[32] Sethe's connection of baby Sethe's lack of milk with her promise to provide nurturance for Beloved without stint and without end indicate, in the now familiar metaphors of breastfeeding, that Sethe's excessive mothering is her way of compensating for a childhood without a mother:[33] her children will never have to suffer even for a moment from maternal absence.[34]

Sethe's scattered recalls half-hide, half-reveal her mother through a concrete language of material signifiers: a hat and a scar. When Sethe, in a final scene with Paul D, grieves her losses, she mentions that "she couldn't find her [mother's] hat anywhere."[35] "Why a hat?" a reader might wonder – Why not "She couldn't find her mother anywhere?" The answer seems to be that Sethe, in the "couple of times" she saw her mother, could barely perceive her in the distant rice fields. What distinguished her mother was not her face, but "a cloth hat as opposed to the straw ones" the other women wore.[36] A reader has to do some work in order to remember and bring together the dispersed occasional mentions of the hat, and then she has to interpret: Sethe's daily suffering from maternal distance is condensed in a material signifier, the hat. Sethe recalls having only one sustained conversation with her mother:

> She opened up her dress front and lifted her breast and pointed under it. Right on her rib was a circle and a cross burnt right in the skin. She said, "This is your ma'am. This," and she pointed. "I am the only one got this mark now. The rest dead. If something happens to me and you can't tell me by my face, you can know me by this mark." . . . "Yes, Ma'am,' I said. 'But how will you know me? How will you know me? Mark me, too," I said.[37]

The "mark" here is not just a mark, but a brand, and the mother's breast shelters it: the breast intended for the nurturance of her child is dedicated instead to the signifier that marks her as the master's property. Compressed in this linkage of breast and brand is much historical information on slave mothering. In the contest between the slave child's need for nurturance and the master's need for field labor, the master wins.

Why would it be so urgently important that Sethe recognize her mother's scar? The reason must be that Sethe has spent so little time with her mother that she would not recognize her face. In the slavery situation, the press of labor leaves so little time for the child to see her mother's face that she would not recognize it were the mother to be killed along with other rebel slaves. So the desperate mother must improvise a sign for her child to "know her by."

The key word in this exchange is "know." The mother wants Sethe to "know" her body through the brand, and the child Sethe anxiously repeats the query, "But how will you know me? How will you know me?" The mother intends "know" to signify "recognize," but in context, the word "know" reverberates with the sadness of the slave child who does not and cannot know her mother, but only the mark of the master's possession. As Sethe tells Beloved, "I didn't see her but a few times out in the fields . . . By the time I woke up in the morning, she was in line. If the moon was bright they worked by its light . . . She didn't even sleep in the same cabin most nights I remember. Too far from the line-up, I guess."[38]

Recent feminist archival work on slave mothering supports Morrison's account. Slave women

> labored eleven to thirteen hours of each day, excepting Sunday, for the master, and their days' work in the fields was supplemented by spinning, weaving, and sewing tasks in the evenings . . . More often than not, the work requirements that slaveholders and overseers imposed on them . . . made it impossible for mothers to carry out . . . personal maternal work.[39]

As a slave child, Sethe experienced maternal abandonment not just in the traumatic moment of her mother's death, but as a fact of daily life. Readers are left to make the connection for themselves between the ever-distant mother of Sethe's childhood and Sethe's excessive claim that she can provide her children with a constant, unfailing, unchanging maternal presence.

The Skewed Time of Collective Trauma: The Middle Passage

The dislocated time of trauma that haunts Sethe's house at 124 Bluestone Road pertains to more than the individual tragedy of Sethe and the baby she killed. The larger collective dimension that always doubles the personal in *Beloved* is suggested by Baby Suggs's answer to Sethe's idea that the family could move house in order to escape the haunting of her dead child. Baby Suggs responds, "Not a house in the country ain't packed to its rafters with some dead Negro's grief."[40] From this perspective, Sethe's house is nothing special: temporal displacement affects the home of every African American, filling the present with the grief of the past. It is slavery, and in particular the Middle Passage, that haunts the heart of the novel.

The Middle Passage is evoked by the monologue where Beloved speaks not in the voice of Sethe's lost daughter, but in the voice of a child on a slave ship during the Middle Passage.

> I am always crouching the man on my face is dead ... in the beginning the women are away from the men and the men are away from the women storms rock us and mix the men into the women and the women into the men that is when I begin to be on the back of the man for a long time I see only his neck and his wide shoulders above me ... he locks his eyes and dies on my face.[41]

Since Morrison does not identify these scattered perceptions as observations of life on a slave ship or tell how Beloved came to be there or give any coordinates of time and place, readers are baffled: we have no idea where we are. We experience a readerly version of the disorientation of the African captives who were thrown into the slave ships without explanation and suspended outside boundaries of time or space. Contemporary historian of slavery Stephanie Smallwood suggests some of the reasons for the captives' disorientation. Because "Africans relied on the regular cycle of climatic events to locate themselves in time," and because the vast space of the Atlantic was outside their experience and knowledge, they experienced an "unparalleled displacement" on the ships: "Always in motion but seeming to never reach any destination, the ship plowed forward in time without ever getting anywhere, always seeming to be in the same place as the day before. It was as if time were standing still."[42] In both historical and fictional contexts, temporal dislocation marks the presence of trauma.

Beloved subjects the reader, too, to a temporal and spatial disorientation that mimics that of the captives on the slave ships. In the passage quoted above, the fragmented syntax and absence of punctuation robs the reader of known demarcations. And the sentences baffle a reader's expectation of specific and measured time: the child narrator on the slave ship speaks always in the present tense. Events that occurred in the past are given the same temporal status as events in the present: "In the beginning the women are apart from the men"; each subsequent event is assigned the same tense: "storms rock us and mix the men into the women that is when I begin to be on the back of the man." There is no sense of a cause-and-effect sequence, no sense of a progression through time. The unchanging present tense conflates past with present, as in the time of trauma.

The second paragraph of the monologue explicitly describes this atemporal present:

All of it is now it is always now there will never be a time when I am not crouching and watching others who are crouching too I am always crouching The man on my face is dead ... the men without skin bring us their morning water to drink we have none.[43]

The continuous present tense indicates formally that we are in the time of trauma, where the past fills the present moment ("All of it is now it is always now"). Indeed, the child's experience of being on a slave ship long ago interrupts, without preface or explanation, the present-day moment of the narrative, in which Sethe, Denver, and Beloved are speaking. Like the invasive images from her traumatic past that surged into Sethe's mind, without warning and without context, in the early pages of the novel, the text mimics the unwanted interruption of traumatic memory. But in conjunction with the Middle Passage, "the four-hundred-year holocaust that wrenched tens of millions of Africans from their Mother, their biological mothers as well as their Motherland, in a disorganized and unimaginably monstrous fashion," the dislocation of time means something larger than the belated temporality that afflicts the single individual Sethe.[44] Now it is historical memory, collective memory, that fills the present moment of reading – the heretofore "unspeakable" memory of the Middle Passage, framed in the fragmented, discontinuous images of traumatic remembrance.

For whom then, and where, does this belated temporality, this *Nachträglich* reality, intervene? It would have to intervene in the world of the reader, where during the reading process the voice of the child on the slave ship of the past interrupts and disrupts the present-day conversation among Beloved, Denver, and Sethe. And it is evidently the African American reader whom Morrison was addressing in this memory retrieved in fragments from a traumatic past. For Morrison indicates in a 1993 interview with Angels Carabi that she had future African American readers in mind when she created the Middle Passage monologue. After remarking on the striking absence of the Middle Passage from African American folklore and tale, Morrison says:

I understand that omission, because to dwell on [the Middle Passage] would perhaps paralyze you to the point of not being able to ... survive daily experience. It was too painful to remember, yet I had the impression that it was something that needed to be thought about by ... Afro-Americans. With *Beloved*, I am trying to insert this memory that was unbearable and unspeakable into the literature ... It was a silence within the race. So it's a kind of healing experience. There are certain things that are repressed because they are unthinkable and the only way to come free of that is to go back and deal with them.[45]

In Morrison's language of the "repression" of "unspeakable" things we see again Morrison's familiarity with and affinity for psychoanalytic thinking. More specifically, Morrison's faith in the "healing" power of putting trauma into verbal form recalls Freud's faith in the "talking cure." But while Freud sought to uncover the singular individual experience at the core of a patient's neurosis, Morrison seeks instead to articulate the collective trauma at the heart of African American history. As she says in the quoted passage, she put the Middle Passage into a narrative form in order to help African American readers to deal with the unspeakable pain of the past.

Notes

1. Toni Morrison, *Beloved* (New York: Alfred A. Knopf, 1987) and Jean Laplanche, *Life and Death in Psychoanalysis*, trans. Jeffrey Mehlman (Baltimore: Johns Hopkins University Press, 1976).
2. *Nachträglichkeit* is variously translated as afterwardsness, deferred action, après-coup. For a comprehensive history of the term in Freud's writings and in the works of several modern psychoanalytic theorists, see Friedrich-Wilhelm Eickhoff, "On *Nachträglichkeit*: The Modernity of an Old Concept," *The International Journal of Psychoanalysis* 87, no. 6 (2008): 1453–69. See also Deborah Browning, "Laplanche on Après-Coup: Translation, Time and Trauma," *Journal of the American Psychoanalytic Association* 66, no. 4 (2008): 779–94. Among literary critics who use the term as a central concept, see Charles Bernheimer, "Kafka's Ein Landartz: The Poetics of *Nachträglichkeit*," *Journal of the Kafka Society of America* 11, no. 1–2 (1987): 4–8, Greg Forter, "Freud, Faulkner, Caruth: Trauma and the Politics of Literary Form," *Narrative* 15, no. 3 (2007): 259–85, and James Mellard, "Faulkner's 'Miss Emily' and Blake's 'Sick Rose:' Invisible Worm, *Nachträglichkeit*, and Retrospective Gothic," *Faulkner Journal* 2 (1986): 37–45.
3. See Cathy Caruth, "Introduction," *Trauma: Explorations in Memory* (Baltimore: Johns Hopkins University Press, 1995), 3–12, Dori Laub and Nanette Auerhahn, "Knowing and Not Knowing Massive Psychic Trauma: Forms of Traumatic Memory," *International Journal of Psycho-Analysis* 74, no. 2 (1993): 287–302, and Bessel Van Der Kolk, *The Body Keeps the Score: Brain, Mind, and Body in the Healing of Trauma* (New York: Penguin, 2014).
4. Toni Morrison, *Playing in the Dark: Whiteness and the Literary Imagination* (New York: Vintage Books, 1992), v.
5. Erik Erikson, *Childhood and Society*, 2nd edition (New York: W. W. Norton, 1963), 247.
6. Laub and Auerhahn, "Knowing and Not Knowing Massive Psychic Trauma," 287.
7. Toni Morrison, "A Bench by the Road: *Beloved* by Toni Morrison," in *Toni Morrison: Conversations*, ed. Carolyn Denard (Jackson: University of Mississippi Press, 1989), 49.
8. Elissa Schappell, "Toni Morrison: The Art of Fiction," in *Toni Morrison: Conversations*, ed. Carolyn Denard (Jackson: University of Mississippi Press, 1989), 62–90.

9. *Beloved*, 210–17.

10. See Philip Page, *Dangerous Freedom: Fusion and Fragmentation in Toni Morrison's Novels* (Jackson: University Press of Mississippi, 1995), James Phelan, *Reading the American Novel 1920–2010* (Oxford: Wiley-Blackwell, 2013), and Maggie Sale, "Call and Response as Critical Method: African-American Oral Traditions and *Beloved*," *African American Review* 26, no. 1 (1992): 41–50. Mae Henderson shows the complexities of Morrison's presentation of the infanticide, "Toni Morrison's *Beloved*: Re-membering the Body as Historical Text," in *Comparative American Identities: Race, Sex, and Nationality in the Modern Text*, ed. Hortense Spillers (London: Routledge, 1991), 72–80. Andrea O'Reilly gives a positive reading of the infanticide: Andrea O'Reilly, *Toni Morrison and Motherhood: A Politics of the Heart* (Albany: State University of New York Press, 2004).

11. See Sigmund Freud, "Project for a Scientific Psychology" (1950), *SE* 1: 411–16 and Jean Laplanche, *Life and Death in Psychoanalysis*, trans. Jeffrey Mehlman (Baltimore: Johns Hopkins University Press, 1976), 38–43.

12. The many dimensions of slavery that inhabit Beloved have given rise to a host of different and fascinating interpretations of this complex figure. See Brooks Bouson, *Quiet As It's Kept: Shame, Trauma, and Race in the Novels of Toni Morrison* (Albany: State University of New York Press, 2000), Martha Cutter, "The Story Must Go On and On: The Fantastic, Narration, and Intertextuality in Toni Morrison's *Beloved* and *Jazz*," *African American Review* 34, no. 1 (2000): 61–75, Cynthia Dobbs, "Toni Morrison's *Beloved*: Bodies Returned, Modernism Revisited," *African American Review* 32, no. 4 (1998): 563–78, Jennifer FitzGerald, "Selfhood and Community: Psychoanalysis and Discourse in *Beloved*," *Modern Fiction Studies* 39, no. 3/4 (1993): 669–87, Rebecca Ferguson, "History, Memory and Language in Toni Morrison's *Beloved*," in *Feminist Criticism: Theory and Practice*, ed. Susan Sellers (Toronto: University of Toronto Press, 1991): 109–27, Sheldon George, *Trauma and Race: A Lacanian Study of African American Identity* (Waco: Baylor University Press, 2016), Pelagia Goulimari, *Toni Morrison* (London: Routledge, 2011), Deborah Horvitz, "Nameless Ghosts: Possession and Dispossession in *Beloved*," *Studies in American Fiction* 17 (1989): 157–67, La Vinia Delois Jennings, *Toni Morrison and the Idea of Africa* (Cambridge: Cambridge University Press, 2008), Linda Krumholz, "The Ghosts of Slavery: Historical Recovery in Toni Morrison's *Beloved*," *African American Review* 26, no. 3 (1992): 395–408, Linda Koolish, "'To Be Loved and Cry Shame:' A Psychological Reading of Toni Morrison's *Beloved*," *MELUS* 26, no. 4 (2011): 169–95, Christopher Peterson, "*Beloved*'s Claim," *Modern Fiction Studies*, 52, no. 3 (2006): 548–69, Kevin Quashi, *Black Women, Identity, and Cultural Theory: (Un)Becoming the Subject* (New Brunswick: Rutgers University Press, 2004), Justine Tally, "The Morrison Trilogy," in *The Cambridge Companion to Toni Morrison*, ed. Justine Tally (Cambridge: Cambridge University Press, 2007): 75–91, Teresa Washington, "The Mother-Daughter Àjé Relationship in Toni Morrison's *Beloved*," *African American Review* 39, no. 1/2 (2006): 171–88, and Jean Wyatt, "Giving Body to the Word: The Maternal Symbolic in Toni Morrison's *Beloved*," *PMLA* 108, no. 3 (1993): 474–88.

13. *Beloved*, 10.

14. For different perspectives on *Beloved*'s narrative structure, see Philip Page, *Dangerous Freedom: Fusion and Fragmentation in Toni Morrison's Novels* (Jackson: University Press of Mississippi, 1995), Eusebio Rodriguez, "The Telling of *Beloved*," *The Journal of Narrative Technique* 21, no. 2 (1991): 153–69, Rafael Perez-Torres, "Knitting and Knotting the Narrative Thread – *Beloved* as Postmodern Novel," *Modern Fiction Studies* 39, no. 3/4 (1993): 689–707, and Molly Abel Travis, "Beyond Empathy: Narrative Distancing and Ethics in Toni Morrison's *Beloved* and J. M. Coetzee's Disgrace," *Journal of Narrative Theory* 40, no. 2 (2010): 231–50.

15. George Eliot. *The Mill on the Floss* (New York: New American Library, 1965), 521.

16. Laub and Auerhahn, 292.

17. *Beloved*, 10.

18. *Beloved*, 7.

19. See Naomi Morgenstern's similar understanding of this passage: Morgenstern, "Mother's Milk and Sister's Blood: Trauma and the Neoslave Narrative," 104.

20. van der Kolk, 67.

21. Ibid., 67.

22. *Beloved*, 36.

23. Ibid., 36.

24. van der Kolk, 66.

25. *Beloved*, 5.

26. Ibid., 200.

27. Ibid., 243.

28. Ibid., 239.

29. See Loraine Liscio's critical analysis of Morrison's use of mother's milk: Loraine Liscio, "Beloved's Narrative: Writing Mother's Milk," *Tulsa Studies in Women's Literature* 11, no. 1 (1992): 34–35. Stephanie Demetrakopoulos focuses on the destructive effects of Sethe's mothering, especially to her own growth as an individual: Stephanie Demetrakopoulos, "Maternal Bonds as Devourers of Women's Individuation in Toni Morrison's *Beloved*," *African American Review* 26, no. 1 (1992): 52.

30. See Jean Wyatt, *Love and Narrative Form in the Later Novels of Toni Morrison* (Athens: University of Georgia Press, 1993), 49–54 for a detailed historical account of the breastfeeding practices imposed on slave mothers, both on small holdings and on large plantations in the Antebellum South. In their remarkably precise and comprehensive discussions of the conditions in which slave mothers breastfed their infants, recent historians of slavery have shown that because of the excessive demands for mothers' labor in the fields, mother's milk was indeed a scarce resource on Southern plantations.

31. *Beloved*, 200.

32. Ibid., 16.

33. Among Sethe's interwoven obsessions with the lack of her own mother's milk and her determination to provide milk forever, unstintingly, to her own children, are flashes of traumatic memory connected to an event that returns forcefully to focus Sethe's attention even more desperately on her milk, the symbol of her maternity: "[My milk] was took from me – they held me down and took it"; "I

managed to have milk for [my baby] even after they stole it; after they handled me like I was the cow" (200). These scattered references refer to a moment when Schoolteacher, the owner of Sweet Home, commands his nephews to take Sethe's milk: "those boys came in there and took my milk ... held me down and took it" (19). One held her down while the other sucked her breast. In addition to the shock of the physical violation, the mammary rape is devastating because it both dehumanizes Sethe – she is milked like a cow – and, more important to a woman who identifies as a mother, steals the milk that is the mark of her motherhood. This is the milk that her body produces for her baby, signifying the inviolable, biologically necessary connection between mother and child. The violation symbolically robs Sethe of the motherhood that enables her to resist the dehumanizations of slavery. The form of these memories, surging up to interrupt Sethe's reverie on mother's milk in discontinuous fragments of the event, indicates their traumatic force. (See Henderson, "Toni Morrison's Beloved: Re-membering the Body as Historical Text" for an astute analysis of this mammary rape.)

34. Jill Matus makes a similar connection between Sethe's longing for a mother who would be present and protective and the excesses of her own mothering, adding a further inference about the intergenerational transmission of a certain kind of mothering under slavery: "Through Sethe's emerging memories of her mother, Morrison suggests a genealogy of mothering under slavery that would logically produce the excesses and extreme forms of Sethe's maternal subjectivity." See Jill Matus, *Toni Morrison* (Manchester: Manchester University Press, 1998), 111. Barbara Schapiro and Evelyn Schreiber also generalize the damaging intergenerational effects of Sethe's deprivation to all those damaged by the system of slave mothering. See Barbara Schapiro, "The Bonds of Love and the Boundaries of Self in Toni Morrison's *Beloved*," *Contemporary Literature* 32 (1991): 194–210 and Evelyn Schreiber, *Race, Trauma, and Home in the Novels of Toni Morrison* (Baton Rouge: Louisiana State University Press, 2010).

35. *Beloved*, 272.

36. Ibid., 272, 30.

37. Ibid., 61.

38. Ibid., 60–61.

39. Stephanie Shaw, "Mothering Under Slavery in the Antebellum South," in *Mothering: Ideology, Experience, and Agency*, eds. Evelyn Nakano Glenn, Grace Chang, and Linda Rennie Forcey (New York: Routledge, 1994), 245–46.

40. *Beloved*, 5.

41. Ibid., 210–12.

42. Stephanie Smallwood, *Saltwater Slavery: A Middle Passage from Africa to American Diaspora* (Cambridge: Harvard University Press, 2007), 131, 132, 135.

43. *Beloved*, 210.

44. Barbara Christian, "Fixing Methodologies: *Beloved*," in *Female Subjects in Black and White: Race, Psychoanalysis, Feminism*, eds. Elizabeth Abel, Barbara Christian, Helene Moglen (Berkeley: University of California Press, 1997), 364.

45. Angels Carabi, "Toni Morrison's *Beloved*: 'And the Past Achieved Flesh,'" *Revista de Estudios Norteamericanos* 2 (1993): 105.

PART II

In Society

6

ZEHRA MEHDI

Remembering Violence and Possibilities of Mourning

Psychoanalysis, Partition Literature, and the Writings of Sa'adat Hasan Manto

The train was stopped. The ones from the other religion were dragged out one by one, then shot or killed by swords. After they were done, the attackers turned to the remaining passengers in the train and distributed, milk, fruit, and halwa among them.[1]

Mehman Nawazi (Hospitality), *Siyah Hashiye* (Black Margins), Manto (1948)

Literary theorist, Cathy Caruth explains trauma as a wound whose story can never be fully known; "this truth, in its delayed appearance and its belated address cannot be linked only to what is known, but also to what remains unknown in our very actions and our language." This is the reason Sigmund Freud turned to literature to describe traumatic experience since "literature, like psychoanalysis, is interested in the complex relation between knowing and not knowing."[2] Shoshana Felman, literary theorist, and psychoanalyst and Holocaust survivor, Dori Laub, similarly claim in their study of the Holocaust that literature, like psychoanalysis offers a testimony of historical trauma, which "will be understood as a mode of truth's realization beyond what is available as a statement."[3] If psychoanalytic therapy listens to the unsaid and the unspoken in speech, then literature narrates that which cannot be merely written or recorded.[4]

This chapter aims to highlight another psychoanalytic role of literature in the study of historical trauma – remembering what is forgotten in the writing of history. Discussing the Partition of the Indian subcontinent in 1947, this chapter examines how in the historical denial of Partition violence, literature, namely the writings of Sa'adat Hasan Manto perform the psychoanalytic role of remembering the genocidal violence whose memories have been repressed in the writing of Indian history.[5] Instead of providing accounts of

109

sectarian conflict, Manto's stories capture the gruesome nature of violence itself, challenging the predominant narrative of Partition as a consequence of communal strife between Hindus, Muslims, and Sikhs. His stories reveal the banality of violence that pervaded across communities erasing the distinctions between victim and perpetrator, highlighting the impossibility of accepting that communities ravaged themselves. In remembering Partition violence, Manto's writing opens up possibilities of mourning Partition not only as a loss, which Hindus, Muslims, and Sikhs suffered as communities, but as a collective loss incurred by all of them as they were split into Indians and Pakistanis in Partition; it is the loss of a collective identity of belonging to one community of South Asians.

Drawing similarity between literature and psychoanalysis in the exploration of historical trauma, Felman and Laub write that "psychoanalysis and literature have come both to contaminate and to enrich each other."[6] Even as they lend each other the vocabulary of trauma, it is in their contamination that they are most useful. In the exploration of historical trauma, literature and psychoanalysis become fluid, often seeping into each other's disciplinary boundaries. While psychoanalytic case discussions often develop as literary narratives portraying the complexity of human emotion, there is a reluctance in identifying literary narratives having the potential to facilitate psychic processes of healing. Discussing how the writings of Sa'adat Hasan Manto remember the repressed violence of Partition, and offer possibilities of mourning, this chapter demonstrates the psychoanalytic potential of literature in healing the wounds of trauma. It is no surprise that for several Partition survivors, who found themselves unable to remember their experience of Partition, Manto's stories were cathartic.[7] Like an analyst, Manto not only remembered their personal loss but also uncovered a larger matrix of social suffering that evaded historical consciousness.

The Other Side of Independence

August 15 is celebrated as India's Independence Day marking the end of two centuries of British colonial rule in 1947. From the Prime Minister's national address commemorating the sacrifices of the freedom fighters in India's struggle for Independence to movies honoring the martyrdom of political leaders and revolutionaries, August 15 is a victorious reminder of India's freedom from the humiliation and exploitation of colonialism. It is a day of triumph. It is also the day that the subcontinent was partitioned into India and Pakistan, following unprecedented genocidal violence across Hindu-Muslim-Sikh communities in which millions perished. More than twelve million people were displaced as Partition led to the largest mass migration in history, creating an overwhelming refugee crisis, and eventually inaugurating the "category of the citizen"[8] that essayed the dilemmas of belonging to newly formed nation states. August 15 is also the day of mourning families and friends who were lost in "one of the greatest convulsions in human history."[9] It is a reminder that communities, friends, neighbors, who had cohabitated for generations, subjected each other to "an intense sadistic brutality."[10] Thus, August fifteen is not only a reminder of India's victory in freedom but also of its loss in the violence of Partition.

There has been, however, a historical refusal to narrate violence, superseded by an attempt to preserve the glory of Independence by ritual celebration "ritual celebration of the sons who won the freedom – while systematically consigning the Partition to oblivion."[11] Focusing on "the high politics"[12]—the reasons that led to the Partition, historians render the violence of Partition as an anomaly to the otherwise successful freedom struggle by often describing it as madness that "temporarily" gripped the nation.[13] Identifying the violence as "irrational" and "exceptional," historians not only failed to engage with the human cost of Partition but also ended up denying the violent origins of the nation.[14] The impetus to preserve the "nonviolent" image of Gandhian India not only dominated the writing of nationalist history, but also affected the historical memory of Partition itself. The Partition museum founded in 2018 "dedicated to preserving the memory of the Partition – its victims, survivors and legacy"[15] is curated to honor the contributions of migrants to their new nation.[16] Instead of becoming a collective space to mourn the losses whose throbbing reminders persist in present history,[17] it is a celebration of how people got over their grief and suffering.[18] Even as "violence must sit at the core of any history of Partition,"[19] the discussion of the way that violence altered the lives of the subcontinent remains disturbingly absent from the Partition museum.[20]

Any attempt to remember Partition means "recalling the dark side of Independence, a moment of loss…which was immeasurable," for what was lost – "could not be articulated, sometimes not even named."[21] This unnamed loss was the loss of the collective identity in the division of the subcontinent. Independence became free India's "chosen glory"[22] where the large group identity of an Indian was nationalized by idealizing the success of the freedom struggle in which the violence *in* Partition – in the negation of existing identities by the creation of new identities – was cast away from the collective pride of being Indians leaving South Asians unable to mourn the loss of their shared identity – their "Indianness" – in Partition.[23] Division of the subcontinent premised on religious difference gave a new meaning to being Muslim, Hindu, and Sikh; these communities which identified themselves as Indians in their struggle against

Western colonialism were now split between being Indian and Pakistani.[24] Partition effectively erased a possibility of collective coexistence amidst communities as they recognized each other now belonging to "the enemy nation."[25] Apart from the violence *of* Partition, partitioning of the subcontinent is a traumatic event in itself that must be remembered to be recovered.

In his essay, "Death of an Empire" political psychologist, Ashis Nandy writes how the violence of Partition is repressed in the consciousness of South Asia. Nandy writes "South Asia still seems unprepared to face the genocide that accompanied the birth of Independent states in the region."[26] He explains how in the celebration of its freedom, Partition violence is not only rendered invisible but "disowned and carefully banished"[27] from historical writing and public memory. Even as the past is anaesthetized in its historicizing, explains Nandy, there is "no guarantee that it will not return like Sigmund Freud's unconscious. Unless the new generations of South Asians are willing to work through the painful memories of partition violence,"[28] they will not be able to mourn Partition.

Psychoanalysis and Repressed Violence of Partition

The essence of repression, explains Freud lies in "turning something away, and keeping it, at a distance from the conscious";[29] *"return of the repressed"* is the "failure of the defence."[30] When repression fails, the painful event, which was pushed into the Unconscious,[31] "returns" to consciousness in the form of secondary and unrecognizable derivates. Freud links symptom formation with the return of the repressed clarifying how "it is not the repression itself, which produces symptoms, but that these latter [unrecognizable derivates – symptoms] are the indication of the *return of the repressed.*"[32] Symptoms are also an indication that repression is never complete and the failure of repression is "an attempt at recovery"[33] of that which has been repressed; the neurotic symptom, repetition compulsion is an example of the return of the repressed.

In "Remembering, Repeating and Working Through," Freud explains that a patient unable to remember the painful event, instead engages in repetition compulsions that bear some unrecognized association with the repressed material. The repressed event is "reproduce[d] it not as a memory but as an action";[34] the patient repeats it without knowing that he is repeating it and thereby remembers it through repetition. Freud explains how analysis enables the patient to remember by "work through it, to overcome it, by continuing, in defiance of it,"[35] thereby allowing the painful repressed material manifested in the neurotic symptom of repetition to re-enter the consciousness without being "acted out." Since repression is never complete, according to Freud, nothing is ever forgotten but the patient does not say "I've always known it; only I've never thought of it,"[36] that is, it has never been conscious. In other words, working through is a psychoanalytic process aimed at enabling the patient to remember that which is not quite forgotten. Applying these psychological theories to the political trauma of the Partition would require communities to remember those memories of the Partition that they have always known but are unable to bring to their consciousness. To the extent that the memories continue to be repressed, they would need to be worked through in some fashion to be understood consciously – and even integrated into the identity of the parties who have suffered the trauma.

Communal conflict in Independent India only repeats the violence as an on-going action but does not reproduce the memory underlying Partition violence, which continues to be repressed. In acting out what happened during Partition but not recalling it, communal strife largely between Hindus and Muslims, but also Hindus and Sikhs, narrates the "trauma of Partition" as inter-communal conflict with violence as the "obvious" manifestation of religious differences. In his essay, "In Defense of the Fragment," historian Gyanendra Pandey explains how historical discourse on communal violence has been able to capture the moment of violence only with great difficulty because "violence itself is taken as 'known,'" needing no further investigation. Religious difference becomes the assumed context of communal clashes warranting no inquiry into the "contours of violence"[37] which is why besides being an aberration in the historiography of India, violence has also been absent *in* it.

The repressed violence of Partition returns in the surge of communal riots post 1947, where the violence bears an uncanny similarity to the violence of partition, namely the acts of sexual violence. Feminist scholar, Urvashi Bhutalia's work *The Other Side of Silence*, recovers the voices of women in Partition and narrates the overlaps between the 1984 Sikh massacre and the 1947 Partition.[38] The Sikh pogrom in Delhi "resurrected the ghost of Partition"[39] as women began sharing their experiences of horrific sexual abuse, rape and abduction; for several women "1984 felt just like 1947." Abduction and rape were used as "a tool to articulate religious/national enmity"[40] across communities discussed largely in the Partition writings of Amrita Pritam-Pinjar, *The Skeleton*,[41] Raj Gill, *The Rape*,[42] and Bapsi Sidhwa, *Ice-Candy-Man*;[43] sexual assault as an aggressive act of communal revenge persisted in later instances of communal violence such as the 1989 Bhagalpur riots in Bihar;[44] the 1992–1993 Bombay riots;[45] the 2002 anti-Muslim pogrom in Gujarat.[46] The pervasive sexual violence that targets women to dishonor communities is often considered a consequence of "the failure to address the outcome of violence during 1947";[47] for many scholars "Partition resurfaces as a repressed historical memory"[48] as its legacy "provides a backdrop against which to place unresolved conflicts and continued expressions of hatred and commission of atrocities."[49] Working through the resistance of communal violence will allow us to remember perhaps the unspeakable story of Partition violence, which cannot be a record of what some people did to others; it is the "repressed record of what South Asians did to themselves."[50]

Remembering Partition violence requires South Asians to recall what happened within communities. It means confronting how the boundaries between victim and perpetrator blurred, and most victims of Partition[51] violence fell in what Holocaust survivor, Primo Levi called "the gray zone." In *The Drowned and the Saved*, Levi writes about how "the network of human relationships in the Lagers was not simple: it could not be reduced to the two blocks of victims and persecutors"[52] as there existed in the Lager some Jews who collaborated with the Germans against other Jews. The gray zone refers to an area of moral ambiguity where the distinctions between good and bad collapse, and victims merge with their perpetrators through their collaboration with the persecutor. The memory of how "many victims of partition became perpetrators,"[53] is repressed in the collective consciousness of the nation that persists in describing the violence of Partition as communal – between different religious communities — and, thus, never having to face the atrocities communities subjected upon themselves. Working through would require different communities to not only remember intracommunity violence but would upend the articulation of Partition violence as communal leading to a rethinking of the central role that religious difference occupies in not just history of Partition but also in contemporary communal strife.

Descriptions of violence as sectarian allow communities to "disown their memories"[54] of violence and project these memories onto the "other community," reinforcing the binary between victim and perpetrator. Unable to remember the violence in its inception, the nation has been consequently unable to mourn Partition, whose "ghosts" "continue to haunt concepts of democracy in the nation-state."[55]

In "Mourning and Melancholia," Freud explains mourning as a "reaction to the loss of a loved person, or to the loss of some abstraction which has taken the place of one, such as one's country, liberty, an ideal and so on."[56] The "work of mourning" involves de-attaching (de-cathecting) from the loved object and grieving its loss. However, Freud's paper does not discuss the circumstances in which the loss happens; it begins with the existence of loss, not the origins of it. Melanie Klein's depressive position offers insights into origins of losses that are inflicted upon the self. In her theory of the inner life, Klein explains how inside and outside remain porous for the infant such that bodily sensations are felt as attacks from outside. For the infant, the breast of the mother is experienced as nurturing when available, and persecutory when absent. The internal object (breast) is split into good and bad under persecutory anxiety, which Klein calls the paranoid-schizoid position; splitting allows the object to survive. This split must be resolved, though, in order for the infant to develop psychologically. This integration of good and bad occurs in what Klein refers to as the depressive position, where the infant realizes that the nurturing and the persecutory object are the same; it leads the child to restore the object in their inner world.

To extrapolate upon this model for our purposes, the violence caused by Partition in the spatial division of subcontinent ruptured all sense of national belonging where South Asians lost shared cultures and common languages. This might be understood in light of the infantile splitting because with the creation of new identities, Indians were left with what cinema scholar Bhaskar Sarkar calls "truncated identities," with "a compounded sense of loss encompassing, among other things, an internalized sense of lack and inferiority, the loss of a familiar assumptive world, the loss of self-determination and of control over one's destiny."[57] Shared cultures and common languages that were once generative and connective are now painful and divisive, promoting projection of bad feelings, which extend into violence. In order to repair these "truncated identities," thus working with and through the trauma and reclaiming that generative relationship, that was psychically divided, the people must move culturally toward the depressive position, mourning the Partition. South Asians, by such moves, acknowledge violence within communities and reintegrate the lost sense of common language and culture. The reason this may indeed work is expressed in Klein's identification of the culpability necessary in this developmental move toward the depressive position in "Mourning and Its Relation to Manic Depressive States." Here she draws upon Freud's work to explain how once the patients reach depressive positions, they can mourn the loss of the loved object, and "experience emotions – sorrow, guilt, and grief, as well as love and trust."[58] Mourning for Klein is not only for the loss of the loved object but also for our culpability of having caused it pain and suffering. Without accepting culpability there can be no working through. However in the on-going trauma of Partition, the Citizenship Amendment Act (2019) is the latest manifestation of this inability to mourn, accept guilt and to work through, in which the State does not acknowledge persecution within communities,[59] and grants citizenship to minorities from post-Partition Islamic nations to right the "wrongs of Partition." Thus "the work of mourning" Partition is yet to be done. It is through remembering, what they did to themselves that different communities will recognize their underlying similarities, and perhaps come together to mourn their collective loss of a communal identity as Indians in British India, instead of registering losses as Hindus and Muslims.

In the absence of historical narratives being able to "own" the violence of the "birth trauma of India and Pakistan [the nation],"[60] and official records unable to "reflect their pain and agony their fear and afflictions, and their sense of dismay disillusionment,"[61] it is literature that performs the psycho-analytic task of remembering that which no one is able to remember – the abject violence of Partition. Capturing the fragmentary, spasmodic, and unremittingly violent expressions of Partition in Urdu short stories, Sa'adat Hasan Manto's writings[62] not only remember the moral descent of society into depravity and become the "documents of barbarism,"[63] that resist civilizational forgetting, but also capture the "colossal human tragedy of the partition and its continuing aftermath"[64] thus allowing for possibilities of mourning.

Writings of Sa'adat Hasan Manto and Remembering Violence

Salman Rushdie calls Sa'adat Hasan Manto the "undisputed master of the modern Indian short story," who wrote "low-life fiction"[65] and earned the ire of his critics for writing about prostitutes, beggars, criminals, and the insane, who lived at the margins of society; Manto's literary expanse includes a novel, five series of radio plays, three collections of essays, two collections of personal sketches, besides twenty-two collections of short stories.[66] Manto was a celebrated writer of Bombay cinema in the 1930s and 1940s until he reluctantly migrated to Lahore in 1948.[67] "The cata-clysmic and self-devouring violence of Partition would jolt Manto – and the male characters he created – out of their comfort zones"[68] of writing cinematic narratives; he came out with his first collection of Partition stories, called "Siyah Hashiye" ("Black Margins"), two months after his migration. The collection has thirty-two aphoristic sketches depicting vio-lence through individual acts, or even "fragments of individual actions"[69] that are powerful evocations of the "sheer horror and human brutality that marked nation-formation in 1947."[70]

Unlike the redemptive literature[71] of early Partition years, usually evinced in novels, the genre of short stories had the "exorcising power"[72] to uncover the extent of the breakdown of norms in horrifying, often graphic detail; Manto's writing best exemplifies this genre.[73] He is the only person who breaks through the massive wall of silence and captures something of the culture of violence – the complete breakdown of communities, and neigh-borliness — the psychopathic and sadomasochistic components of violence, and the costs of violence paid not only by victims but also by their perpetrators.[74]

Most Partition literature, namely autobiographical memoirs, etched distinct boundaries between victims and perpetrators and depicted perpetrators as "communally charged elements" from the "other community," and never members from the same group; Manto contests this in his short story, "Khol Do" ("Open it") where the victim and the perpetrator belonged to the same community.

The story begins with Sirajuddin, a Muslim man looking for his daughter, Sakina, who has been missing for days. After frantically searching for her in the refugee camps, he seeks the help of young Muslim volunteers working in the camps, who promise to find her. Though the volunteers find Sakina the same day wandering on the highway looking for her father, they do not bring her to the camp. Instead they abduct her and rape her for days. During all this time, when Sakina remains their captive, they assure Sirajuddin that they are committed to their search of his daughter and will bring her back at the earliest. Weeks go by, but there is no sign of Sakina. Distraught by her prolonged absence, Sirajuddin finds his daughter in the hospital; she is suspected to be dead. Upon examination it is discovered that she has been subjected to rape repeatedly. When the doctor asks the nurse to "open it" – that is, the window in the dark hospital room, Sakina numbly opens her trousers, as if obeying demands of the rapists.

Unlike any other story of Partition, the sexual violence in "Khol Do" does not transpire between communities where women are made targets of avenging communal dishonor; rather rape and the rapist belong to the same community – both are Muslims. "Khol Do" challenges the description of Partition violence as essentially a religious conflict – there was no religious difference between the volunteers and Sakina.[75] In contesting the account of Partition as "communal" violence occurring only "between" communities, Manto's writings narrate the nature of violence without identifying religion to mark the distinctions between victim and perpetrator. In "Siyah Hashiye," which horrifically exhibits an equality of violence through sexual assault against women, with the exception of one sketch, all the characters are nameless and have no "religious markers." Their identity reveals the pervasive nature of "collective violence" where all communities participated equally. The only binary that sustains through the unfolding of violence is the one between men and women. In this sense, the true victims of violence were women who become objects of torture across communities, nations, and faiths. Anthropologist, Veena Das' writings on women abducted during Partition[76] elucidates how women were what Giorgio Agamben described as "true witnesses"[77] of Partition, whose testimonies continue to evade language. Analyzing the paradox in the ending of "Khol Do," where the father rejoices his daughter being alive, unable to recognize her repeated subjection to rape, Das and Nandy comment how the story captures the trauma of Partition that lay in the loss of language of sexual violence; the father cannot speak because "the language itself has become brutalized."[78]

In absence of names or any identity markers, Manto's sketches uncover the essence of violence, which lies in its banality. Political theorist, Hannah Arendt describes how ghastly crimes, like the Holocaust, are not necessarily committed by psychopaths or sadists, but by ordinary people who were following State orders; it is in their ordinariness that actions, which are otherwise considered evil, are rendered banal.[79] While Partition was not State sponsored like the Holocaust, its violence was unmistakably banal. Ordinary people committed horrendous acts, even within their own communities. Stories in "Siyah Hashiye" capture this banality in fragments of violence through the figure of the perpetrator whose appetite for abject violence coexists with his ability to express emotions other than rage; rioters and murderers in these stories are not sadists, or perverts who are consumed by frenzy and cannot be remotely imagined as human. Rather they are people who offer glimpses of their humanness amidst their gruesome acts as they express apology, disappointment, leniency, exhaustion, and care through bleak ironies, and dark humor, a typical feature of Manto's writing. In "Siyah Hashiye," cryptic sketches transpire as brief monologues, and conversations between anonymous people, often written in a single line.

For example, "Aaram ki Zarorat" ("The Need to Rest") brings alive the exhaustion of violence when a man declines to kill further saying he is "tired and needs to rest."[80] "Ulhana" ("Reproach") captures the sense of disappointment of the rioter as he complains of not having "torched houses properly."[81] "Safai Pasand" ("The Need for Cleanliness") points out the aesthetics of cleanliness amidst a killing spree where the rioters argue about not killing a man in a train carriage for it would "mess up the compartment."[82] Mishtake ("Mistake") depicts the sense of apology of the man, who exclaims "Oh! I am sorry" on realizing that he has sliced a man from his own community,[83] and "Narmi" ("Leniency") shows the leniency of rioters who listen to the plea of a man, and "not rape his daughter in front of him," but place her with other abducted women.[84]

In such stories, Partition violence is not extraordinary: perpetrators of the violence are ordinary people across all religious communities. They kill with impunity. Considered "abnormal" by Manto's contemporary Urdu writers,[85] they were for Manto what Arendt would call "terrifyingly normal."[86] In "Thanda Gosht" ("Cold Meat"), Manto will humanize the perpetrator further by positing him as a victim of what people during the

Partition did to themselves.[87] In this story, Ishwar Singh is stabbed to death by his lover, Kalwant Kaur, who suspects infidelity as he fails to make love to her haunted by the memory of raping a dead girl. "As the dagger, he had used to killed six people pierces his flesh, memory of the cold body of the dead girl floods his mind and breathing his last he too becomes cold meat."[88] "Thanda Gosht" dovetails interpersonal violence of jealousy within the Partition violence of rape, murder, and necrophilia where the cold dead body becomes the site of collective violence, which not only belongs to the victim of rape but also her rapist; cold meat becomes a testament of the culture of violence pervasive during 1947 where everyone became a killer, and even killers became victims. Manto was charged for obscenity in "Thanda Gosht," and was accused even by members of the Progressive Writers Association for his "sick characters,"[89] the majority of whom were "abnormal"[90] and morally deranged; his texts were condemned as perversions [91] "influenced by decadent intellectuals such as Sigmund Freud."[92] Critical of the insistence on recouping a moral order by his contemporary Partition writers, Manto saw it as their unwillingness to accept that something fundamentally had changed about the society in Partition.

By his own analysis, then, Manto's stories were optimistic, unlike what his critics said, because they showed the "true face of the society,"[93] something that everyone had come to inhabit together. Rather than pass judgments about human failings, Manto "pushes us to rethink those historical trajectories whose unfolding and perspectives are already known and urges us to appreciate lived experiences and practices howsoever messy and unpredictable they may be."[94] Instead of reading Ishwar Singh as a narcophiliac, in him lies the potential for regenerative transformation, as the character is able to realize what he has done and is killed by the same dagger that he used to kill others. Thus, Singh dies with the weight of knowing the truth of his actions. Exploring this regenerative potential requires communities to remember their own violence confronting which is by no means an easy task. In "Ghaate Ka Sauda" ("Losing Proposition"), "the young men are horrified when they realize that they have slept with a woman of their own community";[95] unable to face it, they resort to begging and pleading with the man, whom they purchased her from, to take her back.[96] It is this fear of knowing what "we" have done as a community that gets repressed such that all instances of violence are perceived to be perpetuated by the "outsider" – Hindu, Muslim, Sikh – and thereby are located outside one's own, and in the "other" community thereby absolving communities to explore the trajectories of violence within. This paranoid-schizoid splitting and projection of all "bad" (violence, sexuality) onto the other group, while retaining all good (morality, innocence) for one's own group persists to sustain "othering" to preserve ingroup narcissism.

Indian American psychoanalyst, Salman Akthar explains this othering in the name of religious difference in post-Partition India as postcolonial "villain hunger" where "the universal tendency to externalize aggression"[97] after the departure of the common enemy – the British – led Hindus to identify Muslims in India as villains, who were responsible not only for Partition, but also all instigations of violence in India thereafter. Blaming the "other" kept the community in a shared paranoid-schizoid position, preventing each from identifying their own aggression and recognizing intra-community violence. The pain of the split was projected outward without recognizing that the persecutory object is also the lost object: they must mourn that divide in order to find commonality once again. Thus, reaching the depressive position, a more integrated cultural feeling for these groups, would necessitate working through the memories of Partition, as Nandy pointed out earlier, and perhaps change the repetitive othering of communities in the name of 'communal riots' in contemporary South Asia. This will herald the hoped-for contribution of psychoanalytic clinical theory informed by literature to the amelioration of social trauma and its psychological impact on an entire nation.

Working Through and the Task of Mourning

Remembering our own violence during Partition will allow for possibilities of mourning. It will allow communities to recognize the losses they have unleashed upon their own members, and how they have ridden themselves to the edge of annihilation. Mourning the losses that they have inflicted within their own boundaries will help communities to not lie bound to the narcissism of minor differences,[98] but rather strive to unite. Collectively, they may undertake the task of mourning the loss of their communal identity in Partition, which was not only replaced by religious identities of being Hindu, Muslim, Sikh, but subsumed under national identities of becoming Indian and Pakistani. Here again we may turn to Manto's "Toba Tek Singh" for a story of loss of identity through the figure of the madman.[99]

Approximately, three years after Partition, the newly formed governments of India and Pakistan decide to exchange "lunatics" ; Mulsim "lunatics" in Indian asylums, and Hindu and Sikh "lunatics" in asylums at Pakistan were returned to Pakistan and India respectively. As different "lunatics" analyze the Partition discussing where boundaries of the new nations would lie, some fear that they will be sent to the "wrong side of the border." Bishan Singh, a Sikh man, known as Toba Tek Singh by other "lunatics," after his ancestral village, remains preoccupied about knowing which side of the border his village would lie. He is sent to India and is told at the newly formed border that Toba Tek Singh was now a part of Pakistan. Singh rushes back toward the "other side" but is stopped at the border itself. Refusing to move from the border, Toba Tek Singh collapses after hours of standing on a piece of land, between India and Pakistan, which had no name.

Describing the exchange of "lunatics" between the newfound nation states, and their transfer to the appropriate side of the border, "Toba Tek Singh" uses the vocabulary of insanity to illustrate the incomprehensibility of Partition. The confusion among "lunatics," were they in Hindustan or Pakistan? "If they were in Pakistan today, where was Hindustan," and most urgently, how "could they [sic] be on what was Hindustan yesterday and be in Pakistan today, without moving at all,"[100] shows not only the lack of clarity about the spatial divisions but also points to the bleak conceptual divisions of Partition. What was Hindustan and Pakistan, after all? How was someone Hindustani yesterday and Pakistani today? Raising these questions of identities, the story "mercilessly taking apart the larger territorial logic of the Partition"[101] reveals how creation of nations in the name of religion failed to contain the religious diversity manifested in shared social and collective practices of the subcontinent.[102] In its attempt to forge identities premised only on religion, Partition in fact inaugurated monolithic religious identities of Hindus and Muslims in the name of Indians and Pakistanis. Bishan Singh's refusal to enter the Indian territory is his refusal to accept Partition, which was unable to recognize the communal identity of a village as a shared social space to which people of all faiths belonged:[103] religious identities in the village were fluid and incorporated local and regional rituals. Through his death at the border, in no man's land, the story captures the irretrievable loss of Partition – the loss of belonging to places, which can have no name, which can no longer exist except in a madman's refusal.

"Toba Tek Singh" is considered the "master text of Partition"[104] because it not only "fastidiously detailed in its examination of the shifting borders of madness and insanity in a world that has come unhinged"[105] in Partition, but more so because it is an allegory of Partition that narrates how division of the subcontinent fractured identities where people lost their villages, *mohallas*, and other collective spaces of communal belonging. The death of Toba Tek Singh is analyzed as the "closure of possibilities," a "negation of the inevitability of partition" in sharp contradiction with the invocation of collective insanity to explain accounts of violence.[106] However, in narrating the poignant tale of loss this story bears witness, in Cathy Caruth's terms by becoming the "belated address" to what is known but also what remains unknown in the trauma of Partition. For collective loss manifests as individual loss, this story shows that such a merger opens up possibilities of mourning of the collective within the individual. Mourning collective losses will not only redefine binaries but also allow communities to reconfigure themselves.

To work through the repressed violence of Partition, which returns in the form of communal riots in contemporary India, we need to mourn the loss of collective identities, which communities once shared, and lost together. An inability to mourn this loss leads communities to continuously expunge themselves of all culpability of violence and persist in locating it in the other community, keeping alive the embittered culture of violence locked in divided identities, and geographies. As Freud reminds us, "we may say that the patient does not *remember* anything of what he has forgotten and repressed, but *acts* it out. He reproduces it not as a memory but as an action; he *repeats* it, without, of course, knowing that he is repeating it."[107] Manto narrates the story of society that no one wants to remember yet continues to repeat: the story in which we are the victims, dragged out of the train and killed; the story in which we are the killers, who pull our swords, and seal our own lips. No healing is possible, Manto seemingly cautions, unless we are willing to mourn the violence in our collective losses and examine how as victims, we are also capable of being killers.

Notes

1. See Sa'dat Hasan Manto, "Mehman Nawazi," in *Siyah Hashiye* (Lahore: Maktab-i-Jadeed), 28. I would like to thank Rudra Mohan Guha Biswas for his valuable feedback, and Vera J. Camden for her unconditional support in what seemed like an impossible writing.
2. Cathy Caruth, *Unclaimed Experience: Trauma, Narrative and History* (Baltimore: Johns Hopkins University Press, 1996), 4.
3. Dori Laub and Shoshana Felman, *Testimony: Crisis of Witnessing in Literature, Psychoanalysis, and History* (New York: Routledge, 1991), 15–16.
4. Virginia Woolf reminds us in *A Room of One's Own* that she will create a fiction to tell truths that cannot be captured by mere recitation of facts, as she states, "fiction here is likely to contain more truth than fact ... lies will flow from my lips, but there may perhaps be some truth mixed up with them" (London: Hogarth Press, 1929), 4. These truths are what allow for transformation of lives in society.
5. The memories of Partition violence follow a slightly different trajectory in the history writing of Pakistan. See the work of Ashok K. Behuria and Mohammad Shehzad, "Partition of History in Textbooks in Pakistan: Implications of Selective Memory and Forgetting," *Strategic Analyses* 37, no. 3 (2013): 353–65; and Ananya Jahanara Kabir, *Partition's Post-amnesias: 1947, 1971, and Modern South Asia* (New Delhi: Women's Unlimited, 2013).
6. Laub and Felman, *Testimony*, 15–16.

7. Tarun K. Saint, "The Long Shadow of Manto's Partition Narratives: 'Fictive' Testimony to Historical Trauma," *Social Scientist* 40, no. 11/12 (2012): 53–62.
8. Vazira Fazila-Yacoobali Zamindar, *The Long Partition and the Making of Modern South Asia: Refugees, Boundaries, Histories* (New York: Columbia University Press, 2010).
9. P. R. Brass, *The Production of Hindu-Muslim Violence in Contemporary India* (Seattle: University of Washington Press, 2003).
10. Ian Talbot and Gurharpal Singh, *The Partition of India* (Cambridge: Cambridge University Press, 2009), 67.
11. Ravikant Saint, "Partition: Strategies of Oblivion, Ways of Remembering," in *Translating Partition*, eds. Ravikant and Tarun K. Saint (New Delhi: Katha, 2008), 160.
12. Asim Roy, "The High politics of India's Partition: The Revisionist Perspective," in *India's Partition: Process, Strategy, and Mobilization*, ed. Mushirul Hasan (New Delhi: Oxford University Press, 1993), 102–32.
13. Ian Talbot, *Divided Cities: Partition and its Aftermath in Lahore and Amritsar, 1947–1957* (Karachi: Oxford University Press, 2006), 53.
14. Gyanendra Pandey, *Remembering Partition: Violence, Nationalism and History in India* (New York: Cambridge University Press, 2001).
15. Arjun Bhatia, "Partition Museum Project: Creating a Refuge for the Memories of Partition," *South Asia @ LSE*, March 10, 2017, https://blogs.lse.ac.uk/southasia/2017/03/10/partition-museum-project-creating-a-refuge-for-the-memories-of-partition/
16. Lady Kishwar Desai, "The Partition Museum is our Tribute to the Resilience and Courage of Those Who Migrated," *South Asia @ LSE*, December 19, 2017, https://blogs.lse.ac.uk/southasia/2017/12/19/this-is-the-worlds-first-and-only-partition-museum-and-our-tribute-to-the-resilience-and-courage-those-who-migrated-lady-kishwar-desai/
17. Salman Akhtar, A Partition museum, *Times of India*, January 02, 2008, https://timesofindia.indiatimes.com/edit-page/A-partition-museum/articleshow/2667150.cms. For the impossibilities in imagining a national museum see Anindya Raychaudhuri, "Demanding the Impossible: Exploring the Possibilities of a National Partition Museum in India," *Social Semiotics: The Cultural Politics of Memory* 22, no. 2 (2012): 173–86.
18. This celebration of resilience is the central theme of the latest book on Partition circulated at the Partition museum at Amritsar. The book is Mallika Ahluwalia, *Divided by Partition: United by Resilience: 21 Inspirational Stories from 1947* (New Delhi: Rupa, 2018).
19. Yasmin Khan, *The Great Partition: The Making of India and Pakistan* (New Haven: Yale University Press, 2007), 129.
20. For a different view on the Partition museum see Kamayani Kumar, "Present in Past: Partition of India," 2 *Café Dissensus*, 1 (2018). Retrieved from https://cafedissensus.com/2018/12/28/guest-editorial-past-in-present-partition-of-india/
21. Urvashi Bhutalia, "Introduction," in *Partition: The Long Shadow*, ed. Urvashi Bhutalia (London: Penguin, 2014), viii.

22. Vamik D. Volkan, "On Chosen Trauma," *Mind and Human Interaction* 4 (1991): 3–19.

23. Volkan, "Gods Do Not Negotiate: A Psycho-Historical Look at Terrorism," in *Before and After Violence: Developmental, Clinical and Sociocultural Aspects*, ed. Salman Akhtar (Lanham: Lexington Books), 41–56.

24. While Pakistan became an Islamic nation with significant Muslim migration from north India, as a secular nation with a Hindu majority, India witnessed large- scale Hindu and Sikh migration from what was now called Pakistan.

25. Duncan McLeod, *India and Pakistan: Friends, Rivals, or Enemies* (Burlington, VT: Ashgate, 2008).

26. Ashis Nandy, "Death of an Empire," *Sarai Reader* 2 (2002): 20, Retrieved from http://southasia.ucla.edu/history-politics/independent-india/death-empire-ashis-nandy/

27. Ibid., 20.

28. Ibid., 21–22.

29. Sigmund Freud, "Repression" (1915), *SE* 14: 147.

30. Freud, "Further Remarks on the Neuro-Psychoses of Defence" (1896), *SE* 3: 169.

31. In his essay on "Repression," Freud deploys the notion of pressure to demonstrate the three levels of repression – primary repression, repression proper, and return of the repressed and the way they intrapsychically move between the unconscious and conscious. In describing them through the notion of "pressure" Freud in this paper, makes repression a mechanism. See Freud, "Repression," *SE* 14: 141–58.

32. Freud, "Repression" (1915), *SE* 14: 154.

33. Freud, "Psychoanalytic Notes on an Autobiographical Account of a Case of Paranoia" (1911), *SE* 12: 71.

34. Freud, "Remembering, Repeating and Working Through" (1914), *SE* 12: 150.

35. Ibid., 155.

36. Ibid., 148.

37. Gyanendra Pandey, "In Defense of the Fragment: Writing About Hindu-Muslim Riots in India Today," *Representations* 37 (1992): 27.

38. Urvashi Butalia, *The Other Side of Silence: Voices from Partition of India* (Durham: Duke University Press), 1998.

39. Pallavi Chakravarthy, "The Story of Partition from the Official and the Alternate Archives," in *Partition and Practice of Memory*, eds. Churnjeet Mahn and Anne Murphy (Switzerland: Palgrave Macmillan), 91–113.

40. Arunima Dey, "The Female Body as the Site of Male Violence During the Partition of India in Bapsi Sidhwa's 'Ice-Candy-Man'," *Complutense Journal of English Studies* 26 (2018): 27.

41. Amrita Pritam, *Pinjar: The Skeleton and Other Stories* (New Delhi: Tara Press, 1950).

42. Raj Gill, *The Rape* (New Delhi: Sterling Publishers, 1974).

43. Bapsi Sidhwa, *Ice-Candy-Man* (Minneapolis: Milkweed Editions, 1988).

44. Pandey, "In Defense of the Fragment."

45. Radhika Subramaniam, "Culture of Suspicion: Riots and Rumor in Bombay 1992–1993," *Transforming Anthropology* 8, no. 2 (2008): 97–110.

46. Tanika Sarkar, "Semiotics of Terror: Muslim Children and Women in Hindu Rashtra," *Economic and Political Weekly* 37, no. 28 (2002): 2872–76.

47. Tarun K. Saint, *Witnessing Partition: History, Memory, Fiction* (New York: Routledge, 2010), 173.

48. Jisha Menon, *The Performance of Nationalism: India, Pakistan and the Memory of Partition* (New York: Cambridge University Press, 2013), 1.

49. Christiane Hartnack, "Roots and Routes: The Partition of British India in Indian Social Memories," *Journal of Historical Sociology* 25, no. 2 (2012): 244–60.

50. Nandy, "Death of an Empire," 22.

51. The category of victim here does not include women who experienced horrendous sexual violence during Partition, which I will take up further below.

52. Primo Levi, *The Drowned and the Saved* (New York: Simon and Schuster, 1986), 26.

53. Saint, *Witnessing Partition*, 44.

54. Nandy, *An Ambiguous Journey to the City*, 105.

55. Radhika Mohanram, "Specters of Democracy/Genders of Specters: Cultural Memory and India's Partition," in *Revisiting India's Partition: New Essays on Memory, Culture and Politics*, eds. Amritjit Singh, Nalini Iyer, and Rahul K. Gairola (Lanham: Lexington Books, 2016), 5.

56. Freud, "Mourning and Melancholia" (1917), *SE* 14: 243.

57. Bhaskar Sarkar, *Mourning the Nation: Indian Cinema in the Wake of Partition* (Durham: Duke University Press, 2009), 6.

58. Melanie Klein, "Mourning and Its Relation to Manic-Depressive States," *The International Journal of Psychoanalysis* 21 (1940): 153.

59. The Act grants Indian citizenship to all religions excepting Muslims residing in Islamic nations within South Asia on grounds of religious persecution. It however does not recognize Ahamadiya and Shia persecution in Pakistan, the Rohingya genocide in Myanmar, Tamil persecution in Sri Lanka, or executions of atheists in Bangladesh.

60. Nandy, *An Ambiguous Journey to the City*, 116.

61. Mushirul Hasan, *India Partitioned: The Other Face of Freedom*, vol. 2 (New Delhi: Roli Books, 1995), 9.

62. All excerpts from Manto's short stories have been translated by the author from the original Urdu publication.

63. Walter Benjamin, *Illuminations* (New York: Harcourt, Brace Jovanovich, 1968). In "Theses on the Philosophy of History," Walter Benjamin writes how "there is no document of civilization which is not at the same time a document of barbarism," *Illuminations*, 256.

64. Sugata Bose and Ayesha Jalal, "1947: Memories and Meaning," in *Modern South Asia: History, Culture and Political Economy*, 2nd ed. (New York: Routledge, 2004), 198.

65. Salman Rushdie, "Damme, This Is the Oriental Scene for You," *The New Yorker* (June 23, 1997): 52.

66. Manto is one of the most translated Partition writers. For a collection of writings in English see Sa'adat Hasan Manto, *Mottled Dawn: Fifty Sketches and Stories of Partition*, trans. Khalid Hasan (New York: Penguin, 1997), and Manto, *Bitter Fruit: The Very Best of Sa'adat Hasan Manto*, trans. Khalid Hasan (New York: Penguin, 2008). Those interested can watch the movie on his life and writings called "Manto" available on Netflix.

67. See "Shyam: Krishna's Flute" in Manto, *Stars from Another Sky: The Bombay Film World of the 1940's* (New York: Penguin, 1998), 53–77. His migration to Lahore brought a steady decline in his fame and finance though most of his best stories were written here.

68. Priyamvada Gopal, *Literary Radicalism in India: Gender, Nation and Transition to Independence* (New York: Routledge, 2005), 101.

69. Aamir R. Mufti, *Enlightenment in the Colony: The Jewish Question and the Crisis of Postcolonial Culture* (Princeton: Princeton University Press, 2007), 202.

70. Suvir Kaul, ed., *The Partitions of Memory: The Afterlife of the Division of India* (Bloomington: Indiana University Press, 2002), 247.

71. Dominick LaCapra, *Writing History, Writing Trauma* (Baltimore: Johns Hopkins University Press, 2001), 78.

72. George Lukács, *The Theory of the Novel: A Historical-Philosophical Essay on the Forms of Great Epic Literature*, trans. Anna Bostock (Cambridge, MA: MIT Press, 1989), 50–51.

73. All short stories have been summarized by the author from the original Urdu publication.

74. Nandy, "Death of an Empire," 16.

75. Manto does not only collapse the victim and perpetrator intercommunity boundary to highlight intracommunity violence through themes of sexual violence but also takes up the larger context of violence itself in *Mishtake* (Mistake) and *Islaah* (Mistake Removed) about men killed by men from their own community.

76. Veena Das and Ashis Nandy, "Violence, Victimhood, and the Language of Silence." In *The Word and the World: Fantasy, Symbol, and the Record*, ed. Veena Das (New Delhi: Sage Publications, 1986), Veena Das, "The Figure of the Abducted Woman: Citizen as Sexed," in *Life and Words: Violence and Descent into the Ordinary* (Berkeley: University of California Press, 2007).

77. Giorgio Agamben, *Remnants of Auschwitz: The Witness and the Archive*, trans. Daniel Heller-Rozen (New York: Zone Books, 1999).

78. Saint makes this observation about Das and Nandy's analysis of "Khol Do" in *Witnessing Partition*, 193. The original text is Veena Das and Ashis Nandy, "Violence, Victimhood, and the Language of Silence." In *The Word and the World: Fantasy, Symbol, and the Record*, ed. Veena Das (New Delhi: Sage Publications, 1986).

79. Hannah Arendt, *Eichmann in Jerusalem: A Report on the Banality of Evil* (New York: Viking Press, 1968).

80. Manto, "Aaram ki Zaroorat," in *Siyah Hashiye* (Lahore: Maktab-i-Jadeed, 1948), 61.

81. Manto, "Ulhana," in *Siyah Hashiye*, 35.

82. Manto, Safai Pasand," in *Siyah Hashiye*, 62.

83. Manto, "Mishtake," in *Siyah Hashiye*, 21.

84. Manto, "Narmi," in *Siyah Hashiye*, 15.

85. Kamran Asdar Ali, "Progressives and 'Perverts': Partition Stories and Pakistan's Future," *Social Text* 29, no. 3 (2011): 8.

86. Arendt, *Eichmann in Jerusalem*, 252.

87. Manto, *Thanda Gosht* (Lahore: Sang-e-meel Publishers, 1950), 95–96.

88. Manto, *Thanda Gosht*, 96.

89. Humari Tehreek, Anjuman Taraqi Pasand Musanafeen Lahore Ke Hafta War Ijlas" ("Our Movement, the Weekly Meeting of the Progressive Writers Association Lahore"), *Naqush*, 5 (February 1949): 179.
90. Ibid.
91. Ali, "Progressives and 'Perverts'," 9–10.
92. Ahmad Nadeem Qasmi, "Kuch to Kahiye" ("Say Something"), *Nuqush* 9 (1949): 6.
93. Manto, "Afsana nigar aur Jinsi Masail," in *Mantonama* (Lahore: Sang-e-Meel Publications, 2007), 685.
94. Ali, "Progressive and 'Perverts'," 13.
95. See Manto, "Ghaate ka Sauda," in *Siyah Hashiye*, 24.
96. Ibid., 24.
97. Salman Akhtar, "Hindu-Muslim Relations: India," in *The Crescent and the Couch: Crosscurrents Between Islam and Psychoanalysis*, ed. Salman Akhtar (Lanham: Jason Aronson, 2008), 249.
98. Freud, *Moses and Monotheism* (1939), SE 23: 1–138.
99. Manto, "Toba Tek Singh" (Lahore: Sang-e-meel publishers, 1954), 14–16.
100. Manto, "Toba Tek Singh," 15.
101. Mufti, *Enlightenment in the Colony*, 201.
102. Shail Mayaram, *Resisting Regimes: Myth, Memory and the Shaping of Muslim Identity* (New York: Oxford University Press, 1997).
103. Sukeshi Kamra, "Ruptured Histories: Literature on Partition (India, 1947)," *Kunapipi* 25, no. 2 (2003): 111.
104. Mufti, *Enlightenment in the Colony*, 201.
105. Ibid.
106. Saint, *Witnessing Partition*, 255–56.
107. Freud, "Remembering, Repeating, and Working Through," 150.

7

BEATRIZ L. BOTERO

Latin American Violence Novels
Pain and the Gaze of Narrative

This chapter[1] builds on Gustavo Pellón's classification in "The Spanish American Novel: Recent Developments, 1975 to 1990," which distinguishes four new trends: the historical novel, the detective novel, the documentary novel, and the marginal novel.[2] While Pellón's categories are descriptive, they are not discrete, functioning more as markers to identify important trends within the continuum of documenting history narratively through shared tropes of detecting, investigating, and testifying to marginalized, otherwise hidden experiences within the community of Latin American "violence" novelists. As such, these categories provide a way to organize and identify experiences that yield to psychoanalytic interpretations of violence. Narration, observation, and interpretive distance render this body of fiction accessible to the psychoanalytic critic.

The novelists considered here all rely on a first-person narrator, whose subject's gaze is directed at their own pain and the pain of others. They invite psychoanalytic interpretation on a continuum of voyeurism/exhibitionism and sadism/masochism. The subject observes, seeks, investigates with their gaze directed at the self and at the self and other; exhibition and inspection are reciprocal. Thus, these roles, and the categories they inhabit, can be reversed. In these novels pleasure can be exchanged with pain and the one who looks may be looked at and the one who inflicts the pain may become the victim. There is power and might in this intractable dynamic made visible in Latin American violence novels.

Let me further explain these psychoanalytic concepts before using them as tools to analyze the Latin American novels whose power and might I want to explore in this chapter. Sigmund Freud, in "Instincts and Their Vicissitudes" (1915), touches on these concepts when explaining a defense mechanism referred to as "Reversal into the Opposite" as follows: "Reversal of an instinct into its opposite resolves on closer examination into two different processes: a change from activity to passivity, and a reversal of its content."[3] This mechanism applies when a forbidden and unacceptable conscious desire is changed into an acceptable one in order to be tolerated and then expressed. For example, voyeurism refers to sexual excitement obtained from observing objects that are deemed erotic, usually the naked human body, some sort of sexual activity, or other actions or images that might be attached to masturbatory fantasies. Exhibitionism, also considered as paraphilia (from the Greek *para*, on the margins, and *filia*, love), involves sexual arousal achieved by exposing one's nakedness in public, or again some sexually charged display. The exhibitionist wants to be seen and, in so doing, a voyeur is beckoned to be attentive and witness the exhibitionist's act. If we follow Freud's logic that what occurs is a reversal of instincts, the voyeur inverts their desire to be exposed by watching the exhibitionist. These are two sides of the same coin. And it may also be said that sadism and masochism, for their part, are also conjoined conceptually as well as experientially: you cannot have one without the other. There is power and might in this intractable dynamic in Latin American literature. The same goes for pleasure and pain: one depends upon the other. Let me explain further.

Freud interrogates the instinctual search for pleasure and avoidance of pain in *Beyond the Pleasure Principle* when he posits that humans universally go "beyond" the search for pleasure, seeking at the deepest level through pain a return to an earlier state of things to "inorganic" matter or death itself as a cessation of consciousness.[4] Thus, Freud identifies the "death drive" – or Thanatos – clinically through his observation that patients have a "compulsion to repeat" and return to traumatic, painful events. On the one hand, there is a need to discharge Eros that comes from the individual seeking pleasure, on the other hand, the compulsion to repeat, which Freud identifies as a method of taking control of a traumatic event that aims to regulate pleasure, while containing painful memory: "Each fresh repetition seems to strengthen the mastery they are in search of." There is an inherent gratification of the instinctual drives in repetition, whether in mastery of trauma or as a means of pleasurable engagement, as he continues: "Nor can children have their *pleasurable* experiences repeated often enough, and they are inexorable in their insistence that the repetition shall be an identical one."[5] The mastery of pain here implies a mastery of pleasure as well.

In "The Economic Problem of Masochism," Freud writes that sadism's turning back "against the self, regularly occurs where a *cultural suppression of the instincts* holds back a large part of the subject's destructive instinctual components from being exercised in life."[6] The question that underlies all cultural activity is how the individual will discharge the energies of Eros and Thanatos, "two elemental pugnacious forces in the mind . . . locked in eternal battle."[7] For the purposes of this chapter, one possible answer will be reading novels in which death and pain are part of the repetitive plot. In, for instance, a detective's aggressive investigations, the death drive is performed in front of the subject, the viewing subject as well, of course, as the reader herself. For both, such looking relieves the tension between the drives, bringing pleasurable resolution to the painful tensions of an unfolding drama. The commercial success of this type of literature is immense, and quite obviously depends upon repetition of familiar formulas that, like the child's demands for repetitive pleasures, observe expected conventions. In Colombia and Mexico, this subgenre of the detective mystery is widely – and wildly – popular; in fact, there are hundreds of novels of this sort. The schematic voyeurism-exhibitionism/sadism-masochism in the novels I explore in this chapter places focus on concepts that imply an observing subject fixing its gaze on the world; it acknowledges that we are in constant repetition, learning how to deal with the levels of violence and pain, which, in essence, is translated into how to deal with the Eros and Thanatos, depicted (almost invoked) by Freud as Greek gods, locked in a perpetual agony of strife.

Whereas Freud considers these instincts in a clinical sense, let us not forget that the concepts of sadism and masochism come from literature, specifically the French writer Marquis de Sade (1740–1814) and the Austrian writer Leopold von Sacher-Masoch (1836–1895). Born from literature, *sadomasochism* was coined as a descriptive term to describe the union of pleasure and pain, humiliation and elevation, within human interactions. However, neither masochism nor sadism is exclusively sexual, in the conventional sense. Pain can be found in the relationship that the subject has with the Other, with the world, and with herself. And for such a subject the narrative of psychic or physical pain can become obsessive. Of the three types of masochism that Freud recognizes in "The Economic Problem in Masochism" (1924),[8] moral masochism is the one that interests us here, since it is dissociated from sexual activity per se and the subject does not realize how his or her own actions lead to suffering as part of the satisfaction of the libido. To understand the pleasure behind masochism, an apparent contradiction that Freud notes from the beginning, we must know that underlying suffering there is a subject with his or her own history, a subject who probably does not want to lose the love of the Other for any reason, even when this implies danger for the self. René Laforgue explains this in terms of superego anxiety, or the "eroticization of anxiety."[9] There is an internal desire for punishment, a guilt generated by the forbidden (Oedipus complex),[10] which, due to the use of the defense mechanism of "reversal into the opposite," later defined by Anna Freud as "reaction formation,"[11] results into sadism against the self.

In a letter to Wilhelm Fliess, Freud conveys the way that traumatic material "in the form of memory-traces being subjected from time to time to a *re-arrangement* in accordance with fresh circumstances to a *re-transcription*"[12] is narrated by the subject. In the same way that the child enters a world in which verbal and nonverbal language already exist, forcing the child to rework and decode communication signs and symbols to understand and internalize them, so too in narration the author re-elaborates history in an attempt to offer a perspective that facilitates comprehension of historical facts, not only for the author but also for the audience, and indeed, for society. Literature becomes useful here in our understanding because it locates pain and re-narrates what was once unspeakable, newly found in a continuum of two times: the moment in which it occurred and the moment in which is narrated. The novels I am considering in this chapter, so popular and so powerful in Latin American countries, are perforce premised on traumatic pain, both individual and social. Hence the four mechanisms I am considering (voyeurism-exhibitionism, sadism-masochism) define the narrative rhythms of this literature and influence the identity of the narrated and narrating subject.

Pain and the Narrative Gaze

Now, let us turn to the points of contact between the above theoretical concepts and Latin American literature from 1975 to 1990 and beyond. Historical and police-detective novels function generally in the voyeur mode as the character is looking for a criminal whose violence is variously displayed for the reader who looks back at violence without having to experience it themselves. Documentary novels rely on both the exhibition-ism and voyeurism because of the way in which the body of the marginal is represented within the history of a nation. There is an exhibitionistic quality to reclaiming these bodies by which the reader becomes a voyeur of historical violence both implicating the reader and making them con-scious of this history. The fourth group mentioned by Pellón[13] and that I dub Marginal Novels (Women, LGTBQ+, migration, narco novels, novels that discuss minorities) particularly gratify the exhibitionist sense, insofar as they display the lives of otherwise hidden characters, while they permit the reader an opportunity to explore and exhibit within their own fantasies those libidinal desires otherwise pocketed in such marginal characters. Nevertheless, it behooves us to mention that all novels I am considering can overlap in the ways that they reflect these psychoanalytic categories. Therefore, novels classified as historical, detective, documentary, or marginal can navigate, for instance, between categories, voyeur or exhibitionist, depending on the narratorial point of view.

Historical Novels and the Power of the Gaze

Historical novels serve the voyeuristic mode because they look at the official history of the nation within which the plot occurs. The narrator may go in search of something, a fact that caused pain, an event that changes the nation's history;[14] or there is a police officer looking for a fugitive seeking clues to resolve the fundamental problem of a death. The theme, the characters, and the plot of the novel revolve around national pain. This follows a tradition in Latin American literature of retelling historical events from an individual perspective that does not always align with "the official history." *Rosario Tijeras*[15] (1999) by Colombian Jorge Franco, in this sense, brings historical moments to the readers that provide a background in which the action takes place when characters remember the war against drugs in the city: "It is true that the city had 'heated up.' The unrest was suffocating us. We were up to our necks in dead people by now. Every day, bombs weighing hundreds of pounds would wake us, leaving an equal number of people burned by the same fires and of buildings reduced to their skeletons."[16] Such traumatic social memories loom large among Latin American writers for whom, inevitably there is a revisionist tendency. History that was official is now re-narrated in order to obtain different perspectives: Contemporary authors review the methods of narration, incorporating cutting-edge techniques in some cases and mixing genres and their basic structures in others. Either way, they incorporate historical data with news and radio-television commentaries in the text, thereby dissolving the fine line between reality and fiction.

Numerous authors have contributed to this historical category, most notably Nobel Prize winner (1982) Gabriel García Márquez with *El General en su laberinto* (1989) which shows the pain of the General Bolívar in both his body and in the history re-counted from that perspective.[17] Sharing such blending of the physical with the historical but also adding the magical unfolds in the Cuban novel *El reino de este mundo* (1949), by Alejo Carpentier.[18] His work partakes of the interesting literary movements in Latin America during the twentieth century – magical realism – not only because the novel tells the story of the antislavery and anticolonial insurrection during the Haitian Revolution of the late eighteenth century, which is intertwined with the character of Mackandal and his powers of ubiquity and zoomorphism, but also because Carpentier's magical realism gives space to the region's mythologies.[19] Magical realism refers to an artistic expression that has a special way of weaving historical threads by incorporating the folkloric, mythical, and religious substrate of Latin American culture. The authors incorporate the reality of violent cities using magical elements to explain reality in this type of narration that, like the historical novels mentioned above, blurs the fine line between reality and fiction to generate doubt in the reader as to whether or not something is actually happening.[20] Such repetition, but with a difference this time, aims to master the traumatic colonial history of Latin America. The voyeurism of these novels places the reader in abeyance from the actual trauma while still bearing witness.

According to Ryukichi Terao, "[f]ictionalization becomes an auxiliary method to modify the historical fact so that its historical meaning (for the author) appears in a more illustrative way."[21] García Márquez's *Cien años de soledad* (1967) provides the perfect example of the binary and blurry relationship between reality and fiction in the case of the 1928 Banana Massacre (*La matanza de las bananeras*). García Márquez admitted to having increased the number of victims to give a more dramatic effect to the text, yet, today, the number of 3,000 dead is what Colombians believe to be true.[22] The pain of the nation is present in the novel, and the reader is observing the history from the perspective of the main character. The uses of magic, revelatory but also mystifying, enhance the psychic pain revealed in the violence and trauma of the narrative renderings of characters' psyche and social complexity.

Police and Detective Novels

Police and detective literature in Latin America also utilize and catalyze voyeurism. The main character seeks out something, a clue or a criminal, in order to look directly at them as the voyeur would. The desire here is to see and find pleasure in the revelation. These novels whose explicit violence marks the entire narration are often full of historical incidents within their plot, and there is always a character who looks for something to explain how stability has been interrupted. It is this character who inhabits the place of the voyeur.[23] Historical facts in these novels generally are narrated from the point of view of the detective, as the subject, offering another possible explanation of a murder or historical event. The narration includes details of the moment when the pain is inflicted, the moment when the inevitable bullet or blade is piercing the body.

If with magical realism the objective truth of history is blurred in an effort to weave illustrative ties to mythical substrates of meaning, in the police or detective narrative, this double discourse between the official-mass media story and the unofficial-independent and individual version is key for understanding the blurring of what is real and what is fiction. In the police or detective novel, there is repetition without exhaustion of the spectacle of death; representation can be different in each case, but the message is the same: the law is broken, there is a crime, there is a dead person, there is a body exhibiting trauma and pain (more or less visible), someone is looking for answers and there may or may not be resolution of the enigma. The blurring of fact and fiction may offer reprieve in Márquez's writing, but it can be used against others. Other novels that can be considered part of this trend, blurring knowledge, reality, and resolution, include those which remove the reader even further from certainty by providing a protagonist who is neither a police officer nor a detective but is an inquirer – an everyman – who is nonetheless looking for something.[24] In the novels from Colombia, such as Mario Mendoza's *Cobro de sangre* (2004) and Nahum Montt's *El eskimal y la mariposa* (2004) where national identity has a double discourse in that some public leaders have denied important facts, including an internal war or governmental participation in political murders ("Sí hay guerra, señor presidente"),[25] the main character is looking for a new perspective of the facts. As in the case of *Delirio* (2004) by Laura Restrepo (Colombia), the protagonist, Aguilar, searches for the keys to help him discover what is driving his wife's madness as the capital, Bogotá, is being bombed by drug cartels.

Testimonial Novel and Personal Engagement

In testimonial novels or documentary literature, using Pellón's terms, the relationship established with the body is twofold. The protagonist, who generally occupies the periphery of society revisits the past remembering what was silenced: documenting violence that was done to the body and the pain that is now exhibited. Such literature can be characterized as exhibitionist, yet it is reparative because after revealing the pain, the story re-narrates the event through historical discourse. To invoke Freud's insights: in an effort to master the traumatic history, to make it visible for a new generation and *through literature*, the events are put into language that the reader can take into themselves.

In 1957, the Argentine novelist, Rodolfo Walsh published *Operación Masacre*, a nonfiction novel/narrative journalism that combines the techniques of journalistic investigation, literary narrative, and testimony.[26] Such combinations, and especially the testimonial character also characterizes the work of Roberto Bolaño (Chile) whose work relies upon investigative reporting of an epidemic of female homicides and fictional elaboration. Published in 2004, the year after his death, his novel *2666* depicts four academics who set out in search of an elusive German writer, while incorporating a voyeuristic chapter cataloging an interminable list of women murdered on the border of Mexico. "It was thanks to this priest, the second and last time they met at the church, that Sergio González learned that crimes other than the Penitent's were being committed in Santa Teresa, crimes against women, still mostly unsolved."[27] This section on "the crimes" refers to the femicides in Ciudad Juárez, which we know still occur with impunity.[28]

Histories of cities and of nations are thus told through testimony to catastrophes (wars, tragedies, and trauma) and their consequences. The tension between giving or receiving pain must in the relationship between the I (or self) and the Other pervade such testimonials.[29] Michel Foucault, himself a documentarian of corporate and state violence, shows the collective surveillance of unspoken rules of how to show the body in public, implying the power behind the gaze: the one who looks is the one who holds the power: "visibility is a trap."[30] We revolve around the idea of pain that helps heal mourning from ruptures or losses.

If the one who looks, as Foucault implies, is indeed the one who has the power, then the reader's engagement in these novels must be investigated. The reader's engagement with the narrative of pain connects with their own pain. The reader's engagement with characters of the novel are part of the dialectic of sadomasochism. The reader observes the pain of a character in the novel and feels and reacts to that pain. National catastrophe resonates with personal memory. This is one way in which the reader enters an identification and connects with the facts narrated in the literary text. It is affected by the pain of the protagonist or with the history of the country. The reader seeks the pain of the victim who exhibits his or her suffering and in the act of reading there is pleasure, especially when reaching the resolution of the conflict: whoever has inflicted pain receives the deserved pain. Bruno Bettleheim's study of fairy tales puts into narrative our most primitive desires as he writes,

> It is not that the evildoer is punished at the story's end which makes oneself in fairy stories an experience in moral education, although this is part of it. In fairy tales, as in life, punishment or fear of it is only a limited deterrent to crime. The conviction that crime does not pay is a much more effective deterrent, and that is why in fairy tales the bad person always loses out.[31]

The difference here is that testimonial novels appear to focus more on punishment and less on moral education.

Marginal Novel: A Reading of *Rosario Tijeras*

The final category, consisting of works characterized by Pellón as marginal, displays the most exhibitionistic position of pain in that they wait for the Other's eye to observe. This group includes the voices of women, homosexuals, and other minorities who appear more consistently in novels after the 1990s (including in works referred to as indigenous novels, migrant novels, and narco novels).[32] The major difference between the historical-detective novel, which relies more on a voyeuristic perspective, and the marginal novel, which relies on exhibitionism is that the former category engages with the verifiable – history that has been recorded. The past is reconstructed via the news, photos, comments, and more recently, the Internet. In contrast, the latter category speaks from a marginal position, that of a body that has historically been obliterated, ignored, or sought to be made invisible by society or the government. As a result, the body that does not appear in history books, or only does so on the periphery, is represented in a strong-visual way, where violence is explicitly represented in an exhibitionistic way. From the position of the marginal, this type of narrative has something new to say with respect to the same basic problems of inequality in society; even if the author has no intention of social protest (*denuncia*), they speak to a society eager to understand the complexity of its own moment. While exhibitionistic, the representation of the violated body serves to reclaim that which was lost. It is in the repetition that the pain can be mastered. Within this category, we find novels, which discuss victims of dictatorship in the Southern Cone of South America, which includes Argentina, Uruguay, Paraguay, and Chile. This moment in history was witness to governmental creation of a new type of body that is neither dead nor alive, just disappeared.[33] This no-body is represented in marches with photos, the visual expression of the real body.[34]

In an effort to move these problem texts that disappear like the bodies they represent, to, as it were, center stage, I will focus the rest of this chapter on a reading of *Rosario Tijeras*, a marginal novel related to women and narco-narratives. There is an urgent need for a psychoanalytic reading of this and other such novels as they depict and also interpret the individual and social determinants of the suffering contained in the world of this novel.

Marginal Women and Narco-Narratives

José Franco's *Rosario Tijeras* exemplifies both the particularity and the general applicability of psychoanalysis as it applies to the violence novels of Latin American writers. Containing elements of all of Pellon's categories, *Rosario*'s narrative gaze partakes of the pain and pleasure continuum, while self-consciously reflecting upon the documentary claims of the text itself which depicts the doomed fate of the marginal women who populate the criminal underworld. As an exhibitionist novel, *Rosario* displays in the body of the text and in the body of the main character, an affinity with violence.

136

Rosario Tijeras' very name captures the tensions of trauma: the Christian name Rosario invokes the rosary, the religious beads used to pray to the Virgin Mary while the surname symbolizes the scissors that Rosario herself ultimately wields, turning violent against the man who raped her at the age of thirteen. The violence at the heart of this novel, rooted in trauma and now navigated through the containing gaze of narration and display will yield further insights into the larger, complex cultural context of Latin American literature. Rosario, whose trauma predicated her violence is herself ultimately killed, yet her death is less a punishment for crimes and more an inexorable finale. The narrator leaves the reader with an image of painful beauty rather than a moral precept: "I wasn't capable of raising the sheet, someone else lifted it. And if they hadn't told me, I would have thought she was sleeping. She slept like that, with the peaceful look she didn't have when she was awake. 'Even death becomes you.'"[35]

Jorge Franco's novel was an immediate success: *Rosario Tijeras* "sold out its first edition in one week and by some accounts has since become the second-best selling Colombian novel of all time, after *Cien años de soledad*."[36] Today *Rosario Tijeras* is considered part of a large corpus of novels responding to the world of the drug dealer. From a societal perspective, the prefix *narco* denotes horror and crime. This kind of literature conveys the criminal life to the rest of the public; it lays out how the world of drugs works: the routes, the movements, the *sicarios's* assassinations of public figures, the torture, the luxury. Money is come by quickly within a society marked by the near-impossibility of social ascent. The representation of the pain in pleasure reading is itself complicated and shows how even the act of rewriting history can re-inscribe the violence as something desirable as the narcos become wealthy. The prefix also normalizes the horror that it denotes. Yuri Herrera,[37] in a conference in Santiago de Chile, discussed this normalization in the narco *corrido*, which refers to the music of the criminal world and drug dealers, and the narco *ruta*, which indicates the transformation of the routes, arteries that connect cities yet leave a trail of dead bodies, torture, and disappeared (bodiless – *desaparecidos*). In *Rosario Tijeras*, the police are searching for her all over the city: "[The officers] With the coolness they'd learned, started their interrogation as though I were the criminal and not the others. Why did I kill her, what did I shoot her with, who was the dead woman . . . ."[38] The police question Antonio, but the attempted murder remains unresolved. Still, the act of placing blame on this man as a culprit without any evidence turns him into an exhibit, revealing sadistic fantasies.

In the narco world, the dead body carries a message. For example, some bridges in Latin American cities have been used to send messages with the bodies of the murdered displaying signs of torture (El Universal

Newspaper).[39] Each major narco has had a signature style of killing and this signature functions as a narration that portrays reality from the perspective of the criminal. Rosario, too, has her style. She kisses before she kills. Narco narratives share characteristics with the Spanish picaresque novel. These include the rogue main character, the first-person narrator, the hungry protagonist. Money is the only important thing in protagonists' lives, and moralism or determinism rules without redemption, such that the rogue goes to prison or dies. Rosario is not the exception. The narco novel (as discussed by Rutter-Jensen) or the *sicaresque* novel[40] narrates the drama behind narco violence.[41] Rosario is a *sicaria*, a woman who kills for money as she seduces.

Rosario's kiss serves an important function here psychologically because for Freud, the mouth is the first stage where libidinal energy takes form. This means that the origin of the pleasure focuses on that area of the body – in terms of child development this is the infant's first connection to the world, and it is the part of the body over which they have the most control. Thus, Rosario uses the kiss as a signifier for her "work." On some occasions, Rosario does not speak because her vulgarity and rudeness lead to social rejection; thus, she mimics the language of the social class to which she desperately aspires, failing every time. Here she masochistically silences herself because of the social class dynamics. She takes on the role of sadist though when she wants to kiss her future victims. Her mouth and entire body are displayed shamelessly exhibited. The mouth lures the taker to death: "I think they deserve a kiss before dying";[42] "while she was being kissed, she confused the pain of death with that of love."[43] The mouth curses and yet it also prays. It is perhaps of such confusion that Rosario has no actual voice in the novel: that is, the reader hears her voice only in dialogues, never internally.[44] The weight of the text is on Antonio, the narrator, yet it is her body that is on display appears battered, violated, in pain. One sign of bodily pain arises when Rosario records a thin cut in her arm for each murder she commits. Although not visible because she covers them with a black ribbon, the scars ensure Rosario repeatedly sees the victims "tattooed" on her body, as well as the abuse of drugs that brings her almost to death until her friend saved her.

Franco does not simply use Rosario's mouth in a sexualized sadomaso-chistic dynamic. Rather, as noted before, sadomasochism can emerge in the form of psychic pain. She eats too much out of guilt. After engaging in criminal activity, she locks herself in her room and eats, full of guilt, until she becomes fat. That is, each time Rosario kills someone, she puts on weight.[45] She hides herself away to eat, engulfed by fear, only to then stop eating in a kind of abjection:

She wouldn't go outside for weeks at a time. She ordered in candy, desserts; she devoured everything she came across. Sometimes, people would see her step outside only to return home shortly with her hands full of food. She wouldn't speak to anyone, but everyone, seeing her pack on the pounds, deduced that she was in trouble. Around three or four months after the crime, she stopped eating and began to lose weight. She kept the sweaters with which she covered up her pounds and went back to her tight blue jeans, her exposed midriffs, her bare shoulders. She went back to being as beautiful as one always remembered.[46]

The mouth helps represent Rosario's pain since introjection is not only about nutrition-food but also about introjecting the world around, as Freud describes in the oral phase.

Even so, Rosario drastically – violently – puts on and loses weight. She hides and everyone "sees" the pounds; then she sheds them. Sadism and masochism, in regard to eating serves as a mistreatment of the body, to the point that desire from the Other is no longer in tension between subject and Other (insofar as eating produces a fat body that does not meet socially accepted standards for desire). Em Farrel, in *Lost for Words: The Psychoanalysis of Anorexia and Bulimia,* discusses the distortion of body image as well as the idea of mortality.[47] The mother and later society track the quantity of food ingested by the baby and then the adult. This practice is more acute with women. In social events, the subject observes the Other managing food quantities, the shape of the body of the Other, and the shape of their own body in the mirror.

As a woman, having a "perfect" body is crucial in order to be part of the social infraorder of the drug business.[48] The contrast between rich and poor is extreme; fear is expressed through violence and excess as part of the narcos lifestyle. The narrator describes the life of hit men (*sicarios*)/narcos who prove how "macho" they are in an environment in which small mistakes in hierarchical obedience are met with death. The Eros and Death drives are manifested in these young people who know that they will soon face a violent end.[49] This is why they live a life full of adrenaline.

Finally, castration becomes the last signal to the body in this novel. As mentioned above, Rosario Tijeras' very name suggests her castrating powers over men. Her boyfriend, the narrator, Antonio, suffers when she compares him and all his parts to another: "Emilio's is bigger than yours." He falls silent and begins to cry. In the midst of his crying that he proclaims: "A pair of scissors is what your pussy is, Rosario Tijeras."[50] Her castrating comparison obviously invalidates, indeed, obliterates the one person who loves her. She uses her mouth to castrate and Antonio; his response, of course, invokes the *vagina dentata*, thus returning us to Freud's theory of castration anxiety. Freud writes, "The most significant portion of it [Narcissism], however, can be singled out in the shape of the 'castration complex' (in boys, anxiety about the penis – in girls, envy for the penis) and treated in connection with the effect of early deterrence from sexual activity)."[51] If Rosario has been silenced by others, she herself silences them in return, demonstrating how the sadomasochistic dynamic can shift and furthermore reveals its rootedness in mastering traumatic history. Rosario oscillates between sadist and masochist so easily, demonstrating that the sadist uses these acts as a defense. Here it seems we can say that her sadistic use of the kiss is a response to the masochistic position she is placed in because of her social standing, which has at its core an infant-like helplessness.

We can say in conclusion, that Latin American violence novels use violence through re-inscription in a hopeful act of witnessing that may become reparative for the reader. From the standpoint of psychoanalysis, both masochism and sadism are part of the human repertoire, but repetition serves as a re-inscription of the traumatic event and serves as a way to master a traumatic history. Revealing a more inclusive reality wherein pain represented in art can be the meeting point between humans, in the end what we learn from reading the four intersecting categories of Latin American novels is that pain connects humans, even as humans seek to mediate pain through what Freud has called the pleasure principle. Reading novels can help display and dismantle the paths – and pathologies – that determine our existence, allowing the invisible to become visible so that we may discover for ourselves new paths to follow to new places.

Notes

1. I am indebted to the volume editor, Vera Camden and her editorial assistant, Valentino Zullo, for their insightful contributions throughout the development of this work.
2. The marginal novel "[gives] voice to the experience of women, homosexuals, and Jews." Gustavo Pellón, "The Spanish American Novel: Recent Developments, 1975–1990," in *The Cambridge History of Latin America Literature*, eds. Roberto González Echevarría and Enrique Pupo-Walker (Cambridge: Cambridge University Press, 1996), 282.
3. Freud, "Instinct and Their Vicissitudes" (1915), *SE* 14: 127.
4. Freud, *Beyond the Pleasure Principle* (1920), *SE* 18: 38.
5. Ibid., 35.
6. Freud, "The Economic Problem of Masochism" (1924), *SE* 19: 170.
7. Peter Gay, *Freud: A Life for Our Time* (New York: W. W. Norton & Company, 1998), 401.
8. The three types are: sexual excitation, expression of the feminine nature, and as a norm of behavior, moral masochism, Freud, "The Economic Problem of Masochism," 155–70.

9. René Laforgue, "On the Erotization of Anxiety," *International Journal of Psycho-Analysis* 11 (1930): 312–26.

10. Sacha Nacht, "Introduction to Le Masochisme," in *Essential Papers on Masochism*, ed. Margaret Ann Fitzpatrick Hanly (New York: New York University Press, 1995), 18–34. "Psychoanalytic studies have shown that masochism is derived from the aggressive forces by a turning round of these against the subject. This mechanism brings into play the guilt complex and its result: the need to be punished, that is, to suffer" (32).

11. See Anna Freud, *The Ego and the Mechanisms of Defense*, revised ed. (New York: International Universities Press, Inc, 1966), 43–44, 47.

12. Freud, Letter 52 to Wilhelm Fliess (December 6, 1896), *SE* 1: 233.

13. Pellón, "The Spanish American Novel," 279–302.

14. The voyeur is the narrator as well as the original historian and is the reader. All are present in the chain of voyeurism.

15. Jorge Franco, *Rosario Tijeras* (New York: Seven Stories Press, 2004).

16. Franco, *Rosario Tijeras,* 67.

17. The novel traces General Simón Bolívar's last trip up the Magdalena River from Bogotá to the coastal city of Santa Marta in 1830; at the time of the journey, Bolívar was already ill and looking to leave the country he had governed. Gabriel García Márquez, *The General in His Labyrinth*, trans. George Colbert (New York: Vintage International, 1990).
Another example can be *La fiesta del chivo* (2000) by Peruvian Mario Vargas Llosa, winner of the 2010 Nobel Prize, which explores the assassination of the dictator Rafael Trujillo in the Dominican Republic from the point of view of the daughter of a powerful follower of the regime.

18. Alejo Carpentier, "Prologue to The Kingdom of This World," In *Magical Realism: Theory, History, Community*, ed. Lois Parkinson Zamora and Wendy B. Faris (Durham, NC: Duke University Press, 1995), 75–88. Gabriel García Márquez is considered one of the more important figures of this literary movement.

19. A good example of this religious syncretism in *Aura* (1962), by Carlos Fuentes (México), is in the novel, the sacred and the profane coincide in the body of Aura, who is a beautiful young woman and four days later a toothless old lady.

20. See Wendy B. Faris, "Scheherezade's Children: Magical Realism and Postmodern Fiction," *Magical Realism: Theory, History, Community*, ed. Lois Parkinson Zamora and Wendy B. Faris (Durham, NC: Duke University Press, 1995), 163–90.

21. Ryukichi Terao, *La novelistica de la violencia en América Latina* (Mérida, Colombia: Universidad de los Andes, 2005), 100.

22. There is no consensus on the number of victims. According to some, the figure is twenty-nine; for others, such as General Cortés Vargas, author of the massacre, the number is forty-seven. For the United States Embassy, it is more than 1,000. For more information on this, see Eduardo Posado Carbó, "La novella como historia: cien años de soledad y las bananeras," *Boletín Cultural y Bibliográfico* 35, no. 48 (1998), 3–19. Other examples of this voyeuristic relation with history can be found in Rubem Fonseca (Brazil) in his novel *Agosto* (1990) or *Adiós muchachos* (1999), by Sergio Ramírez (Nicaragua).

23. Two examples of this category come from Colombia. Mario Mendoza's *Cobro de sangre* (2004) and Nahum Montt's *El eskimal y la mariposa* (2004) introduce the assassination of Colombian presidential candidates, namely Jaime Pardo Leal in 1987, Luis Carlos Galán in 1989, and Bernardo Jaramillo Ossa and Carlos Pizarro Leongómez both in 1990, as well as the fall of the infamous Pablo Escobar.

24. In the so-called Latin American Boom, some novels developed their plot around this point. The most well-known example is Julio Cortázar's (Argentina) *Rayuela* (1963), which opens with "Would I find La Maga?" The novel ultimately seeks the identity of the character, first in Buenos Aires and then in Paris, where the limit between "here" and "there" is vague – a technique learned from the artistic currents (the isms) of the mid-twentieth century. Jorge Luis Borges and Adolfo Bioy Casares, writing together as H. Bustos Domecq, published some detective stories where the crime is observed, and like a jigsaw puzzle, the pieces unite in front of the reader to solve the case.

25. Chloe Rutter-Jensen, "Sí, hay guerra, Señor Presidente," *Revista Semana*, June 2, 2005, www.semana.com/portada/articulo/si-guerra-senor-presidente/70763-3

26. Rodolfo Walsh, *Operation Massacre*. trans. Daniella Gitlin (New York: Seven Stories, 2013).

27. Robert Bolaño, *2666*, trans. Natasha Wimmer (New York: Farrar, Straus and Giroux, 2008), 378.

28. Daniel Hernández Guzmán, "Más allá de los feminicidios: violencia y cuerpo femenino en 'La parte de los crímenes' de Roberto Bolaño," *Cuadernos de Literatura* 20, no. 4 (2016): 633–47.

29. Jacques Lacan, *Ecrits: A Selection*, trans. Alan Sheridan (W. W. Norton & Co., 1977); G. C. Spivak, *Can the Subaltern Speak* (New York: Macmillan, 1988). In using "Other" here, we refer to Jacques Lacan's conceptualization of the importance of the profound relationship between the I and the Other as well as Gayatri Spivak's "Other"; Spivak coined the term "othering," which is used primarily within the discourse of colonialism. See Gayatri Chakravorty Spivak, "The Rani of Sirmur: An Essay in Reading the Archives," *History and Theory* 24, no. 3 (1985): 247–72.

30. From the sociological perspective see more in Michel Foucault, "Society Must be Defended" in *Lectures at the Collège de France, 1975–1976*, trans. David Macey (New York: Picador, 1997) and in Foucault, *Discipline and Punish: The Birth of the Prison* (New York: Random House, 1977). Foucault introduced the idea of biopolitics as the collective surveillance of unspoken rules of how to show the body in public, implying the power behind the gaze: the one who looks is the one who holds the power in the prison and the panoptic, where he said that "visibility is a trap." The intervention of this variable cannot be ignored in this analysis.

31. Bruno Bettelheim, *The Uses of Enchantment: The Meaning and Importance of Fairy Tales* (New York: Vintage Books, 1989), 9.

32. The novels recreate pain and help the reader deal with the pain of colonization, of violence in the way that the LGBTQ+ novels give a person a place to both find themselves and to come to terms with their own repression, abuse, internalized homophobia.

33. General Videla said in a press conference during the military government which he commanded: "They are neither dead nor alive – they disappeared." Archivos Políticos, "Ni muerto ni vivo … está desaparecido" ARCHÍVOS POLÍTICOS, April 1, 2015, YouTube video, 0:29, www.youtube.com/watch?v=ASMPYgoYueU

34. One such case is that of Chilean writers including José Donoso in *Casa de campo* (1978). Donoso's novel has been seen by many critics (Carlos Cerda, Myrna Solotervsky, Augusto C. Sarrochi, Flora González Madri, Enrique Luengo, and Mayra E. Bonet, among others) as a metaphor for the Pinochet dictatorship. Isabel Allende (Chile) in her book *La casa de los espíritus* (1982) where the female characters not only open the concepts of inside/private – outside/public but are the ones who keep the house together despite the surrounding violence, torture, and murder.

35. Franco, *Rosario Tijeras*, 167.

36. Franco's novel was adapted for film and television with great success. A. Valbuena, "Rosario Tijeras." Film notes. ¡Viva! 12th Spanish and Latin American Film Festival, Manchester, March 31, 2006.

37. Catedra Abierta Roberto Bolaño, "Yuri Herrera – 'Semántica del luminol: La resignación de los espacios [...]'," April 20, 2017, YouTube video, 44:38, https://youtu.be/GPl_DxcHZuU.

38. Franco, *Rosario Tijeras*, 23.

39. "Era funcionario el Hombre colgado de puente en Tijuana," *El Universal*, October 9, 2009, vanguardia.com.mx/erafuncionarioelhombrecolgadodepuenteentijuana-415797.html

40. Such as *Lazarillo de Tormes* – anonymous – (1554) or *Guzmán de Alfarache* (1599) by Mateo Alemán, two major works that place outlaw life at their center of the narration.

41. Rutter-Jensen, "Reproductive Monologue: Fernando Vallejo Against the World," *Journal of Iberian and Latin American Studies of Australasia* 12 (2006): 33–53; H. A. Faciolince "Entrevista con Héctor Abad Faciolince," interview by J. A. Orrego Universidad EAFIT, Medellín, Colombia July 4, 2006, www.escritoresyperiodistas.com/NUMERO27/jaime.htm; and E. von der Walde, "La novella de sicarios y la violencia en Colombia," *Revista Iberoamericana* 1, no. 3 (2001): 27–40.

42. Franco, *Rosario Tijeras*, 35.

43. Franco, *Rosario Tijeras*, 5.

44. For more on this, readers should consult Beatriz L. Botero, ed., *Women in Contemporary Latin American Novels. Psychoanalysis and Gendered Violence* (London: Palgrave, 2018). One way to analyze the reason why women give up their voice can be explained from the concept of *sujet supposé savoir* as used in J. Lacan, *Les quatre concepts fondamentaux de la psychanalyse*, ed. Jacques-Aain Miller (Paris: Le Seuil, 1973).

45. In her essay on Franco's novel, Aldona Bialowas argues that "Franco Ramos's heroine, an ideological amalgamation of femme fatale, 'action babe,' and Colombian girl-next-door, has hit the right note among the present-day public because she aptly mirrors the relation between global cultural mythology and local circumstances," "Towards the Latin American Action Heroine: The Case of Jorge Franco: *Rosario Tijeras*," *Studies in Latin American Popular Culture* 24 (2005): 17–35.

46. Franco, *Rosario Tijeras*, 14.
47. Em Farrel, *Lost for Words: The Psychoanalysis of Anorexia and Bulimia* (Port Townsend, WA: Process Press, 1995).
48. In Mexico, narco novels have their own space in national literature. Yuri Herrera's *Los trabajos del reino* (2004) and Elmer Mendoza's *Balas de plata* (2008) depict violence so its horror can be perceived as part of daily life. The list is vast. Same happens in Colombia, where *La virgen de los sicarios* (1994) by Fernando Vallejo and *Rosario Tijeras* (1999) by Jorge Franco are two of the best-known Colombian versions of this subgenre.
49. A literal translation of the title of a few Colombian works tellingly expresses how short life is: *We Were not Born for Seed* (1990) by Alonso Salazar, *El "pelaito" ("kid") that did not last* (1991) by Víctor Gaviria (who also directed the movie *Rodrigo D, No Future* [1990], which addresses the same topic).
50. Franco, *Rosario Tijeras*, 170.
51. Freud, "On Narcissism: An Introduction" (1914), *SE* 14: 92. For a contemporary discussion of penis envy and castration anxiety, see Mari Ruti, *Penis Envy and Other Bad Feelings: The Emotional Costs of Everyday Life* (New York: Columbia University Press, 2018).

8

ADELE TUTTER

A Man and His Things
Bruce Chatwin's Utz

There are three conditions which often look alike
Yet differ completely, flourish in the same hedgerow:
Attachment to self and to things and to persons, detachment
From self and from things and from persons; and, growing between
them, indifference
Which resembles the others as death resembles life
    – T. S. ELIOT, "Little Gidding"[1]

The ugliest men loved the most beautiful things.
    – BRUCE CHATWIN, *Utz*[2]

The legacy of overly eager, psychoanalytic theory-bound approaches to literature is summed by psychoanalyst Maurits Katan, who cautioned,

> [t]o conceive of a novel as a dreamlike fantasy pertaining to the personal past of the author is to risk one's reputation. When one has the audacity to continue with an analysis of the story, it is practically synonymous with sacrificing one's head.[3]

Surely this warning also reflects the inclination, shared by many creative persons and critics alike, to disavow the inevitable autobiographical content of works of art, be it clear or cryptic – a perspective that sacrifices not only psychoanalysis' power as explanatory metapsychology and hermeneutic method, but also the singular value of the work of art as a means to understand human nature. For to the extent to which the artist is an acute and perceptive observer of himself and others, the study of the artist in relation to his art can elucidate not only unique aspects of their individual psyche, but also those that are more generalizable. If art imitates life, it also illuminates it.

The foundation of the science of the mind is the individual case history, which, when collected and studied, reveals patterns and trends that allow the

* This work was made possible by a generous grant from the Research Foundation of the International Psychoanalytic Association.

Figure 8.1 Johann Joachim Kändler, hard paste porcelain. The Metropolitan Museum of Art, the Lesley and Emma Sheafer Collection, Bequest of Emma A. Sheafer, 1973. 1974.356.355. Image: https://commons.wikimedia.org/wiki/File:Harlequin_with_jug_MET_DP-12395-012 .jpg. Public domain, copyright https://creativecommons.org/publicdomain/zero/1.0/ *Harlequin*, Meissen, 1738

mapping of psychology, normal and abnormal. I will argue that the category of the case study can be expanded to include literary "cases" – with qualifications, because fictional characters are artificial constructs that should not be confused with the "real" people they are so often taken to be. Yet the literary character may be understood a container of projected parts of the author's self either too private or too problematic to disclose more openly, and more safely expressed behind the obscuring screen of fiction. Within this proposition, literary fiction affords a privileged window into the mind – in particular, the unconscious fantasies and beliefs that underlie and often inexplicably drive human motivations, behavior, and relationships. As example, a psychoanalytically informed reading of Bruce Chatwin's final novel, *Utz* (1989), contextualized within his life and work, will permit the interrogation of the tangled relationship between man and the things he owns and collects: a curiously under-theorized aspect of human nature.

Traditionally preoccupied with the self and the interpersonal world, psychoanalysts have paid scant attention to man's interactions with the material environment, as if his inner and outer realms were subjectively boundaried and separable.[4] It has fallen to philosophers,[5] anthropologists,[6] and modern geographers,[7] among others, to approach the physical universe and the things in it having meaning and import beyond their traditional function, for example, as symbols.[8] "Thing theory," as outlined by critical theorist Bill Brown, holds that we begin to see objects as the *things* they are when they lose their usual function: a dirty window, a broken tool.[9] Implicated here is a quality of attention that delves beyond considerations of surface to address substance, history, and construction: an attitude that overlaps compellingly with the psychoanalytic. In contrast to other disciplines, however, psychoanalytic inquiry allows privileged access to the elusive world of fantasy – critical to any contemplation of man and his things.

As a thing, the figurative work of art is particularly interesting as it "functions" to represent something else – to *not* be that which it represents. *Utz* engages these dialectics in a series of reverberating paradoxes. Its eponymous protagonist collects rare Meissen porcelain, mainly figurines of stock theatrical characters from the Commedia dell'Arte; identifiable by their stereotypical gestures and other iconographic markers, they are, and are not, people.[10] Shutting himself off from the external world, Utz retreats into a private, tightly circumscribed fantasy life formed around and populated by his porcelain figurines. As a citizen of Communist Czechoslovakia, he would forfeit his collection were he to defect to the West; thus, while he controls the things he buys and sells, they in turn control him. The novel's setting in a totalitarian state can be read as a metaphor that magnifies Utz's auto-imprisonment, but I argue that it is more powerfully understood as a seamless extension of its inhabitant, a comment on the fluidity of the personal and the political. Fluid, too, is the boundary between things and people: the limitations on personal freedom imposed by Utz's figurines emblematize those imposed by the human relationships they represent – a tension that becomes clearer once *Utz* is read as a constellated self-portrait of aspects of its author.

Starting in his twenties as a porter at Sotheby's, Bruce Chatwin was within a few years appointed director of two major departments (Antiquities and Impressionist Art); there, he cultivated a love for artifacts that speak of remote histories and cultures. He also gained the practiced detachment of the connoisseur; preternaturally able to distinguish the real from its representation, his keen eye detected forgeries and reconstructions that slipped by others. Moving from auctioneer to buyer, Chatwin maintained an intense relationship to the antiquities that he famously collected, yet would regularly take off and travel the globe for months at a time, leaving behind not only his precious collection, but also his wife – a persistent oscillation that points to a profound conflict at the heart of his attachments. But rather than qualify Chatwin's charged relationship to things as extreme or pathological, I will consider it the leading edge of more ordinary phenomenon, and view its parodic exaggeration in *Utz* as a lens that magnifies our view onto the otherwise ubiquitous – which, perhaps because of this very quotidian quality, has resisted sustained psychoanalytic interest.

***

Since his death, Chatwin's work has been both sanctified in a documentary by Werner Herzog[11] and subjected to the inevitable, albeit deserved post-colonial critique.[12] Attempts to understand his oeuvre in relationship to the man in any psychological depth are lacking; the dutifully thorough biography of Chatwin by his friend, Nicholas Shakespeare[13] and other personal remembrances offer few insights into the scintillating, enigmatic man who left people breathless as he "passed them by like a comet."[14] Tellingly, an author is the exception to the rule in Chatwin studies: W. G. Sebald, who characterizes Chatwin's strangely disparate, prematurely attenuated collection of five novels as belonging to "no known genre."[15]

> [T]hey move along a line where the points of demarcation are those strange manifestations and objects of which one cannot say that they are real, or whether they are among the phantasms generated in our minds ... collections of facts, dream books, regional novels, examples of lush exoticism, puritanical penance, sweeping baroque vision, self-denial, and personal confession ... where reality is constantly entering the realm of the metaphysical and miraculous, and the way through the world is taken from the first with an eye fixed on the writer's own end.[16]

This excerpt of Sebald's all-too-brief appreciation identifies three critical elements in Chatwin's prose: the tension between "lush exoticism" and "baroque" excess on the one hand, and "puritanical penance" and "self-denial" on the other; the preoccupation with mortality that constitutes a primary lens; and the elements of fantasy, organized around "manifestations and objects," that transform his works from the "travel books" that they are often classified as into something completely different. The autobiographical aspect of his fiction responsible for much of this categorical confusion is just one example of the play between reality and fantasy that Sebald observes.

Utz epitomizes all of these tensions. In contrast to Chatwin's previous narrative excursions into exotic adventure, his fifth and last novel, written while the author was terminally ill with AIDS, is a highly compact work of precise, nearly perfect prose.[17] With the clipped economy of the auction catalogue, *Utz* reflects the author as a collector whose self is formed around his attachments to precious things, which, like the Romantic poet's Grecian urn, connect him to life and death. Whereas Chatwin's first autobiographical novel, *In Patagonia* (1977), made his fabled restlessness iconic, *Utz*, by contrast, confesses of a different side of the man, held captive by home and the things in it in a deeply divided pull.

***

Chatwin leaves a clue to *Utz* in plain sight in its simple dedication, "For Diana Phipps." Born into the supranational aristocracy of Czechoslovakia, Diana Phipps (b. 1936) and her parents, Count and Countess Leopold Sternberg fled Častolovice, their ancestral Bohemian castle, not once, but twice: first, after the Nazi invasion of 1939, and again, after the Communist coup of 1948. Diana Sternberg married an American financier, Michael Phipps, and settled in London, where she became an interior designer known for her flair and wit. But, and strangely for someone worthy of a dedication, Phipps is absent from Chatwin's biography and archive, and appears only once in his published correspondence – and then in a letter to someone else.

In January 1988, Chatwin wrote in a letter to Susannah Clapp, who edited *Utz*, that he wished to show the newly finished manuscript:

> to my friend Diana Phipps, who is a Czech – and had first hand [sic] memories of Prague until 1949 when she and her family left – to Vichy! (except that they went to Paris instead). One the few facts I have about my model for *Utz* is that he did go annually to Vichy – until 1968.[18]

Left unmentioned are the other salient "facts" about Phipps that he used to model *Utz*, including the forfeiture of its protagonist's inherited castle to the Communists. Utz's castle is not named, but is located in Kostolec, a Bohemian town that exists in reality, and which boasts not one, but two castles. The fact that one of them is Phipps' home, Častolovice, indicates both contiguity and contrast between Phipps and *Utz*; neither are incidental. Phipps is the author of the best-selling *Affordable Splendor: An Ingenious Guide to Decorating Elegantly, Inexpensively and Doing Most of It Yourself*,[19] a manual for creating domestic splendor with less than splendid resources. It was a skill learned the hard way: an aristocrat in exile, Phipps refashioned, in her home and those of others, an approximation of her personal paradise lost, the glamor and fancy of the castle she once called home. In placing Utz's castle in proximity to Phipps, Chatwin announces that his narrative is a variation on hers: *Utz* embodies the longing for a lost past, and the attempt to recreate it by reconstituting the present with the things of the past, and which survive, symbolize, and animate it.

The contrast embedded in the contiguity lies in how the two handled that longing. Unlike Utz, the exiled Phipps professed no desire for the valuable things of her childhood, preferring imitations created with fabric and a glue gun: "[t]hings to last a lifetime have always depressed me. They're so final, so binding. Better to spend less in the first place and furnish with fantasy than spend a lifetime stuck with the same boring investment."[20] And although she ultimately returned to Častolovice, Phipps rationalizes this as something of an accident.[21]

> I have no sentimental feelings about the place at all . . . I realized from the work that I've done for all my life, that one could make it look a bit better. But I don't have any feelings of nostalgia or feelings about the families and so on. I just saw it as a job.[22]

In a parallel elision Chatwin in his letter to his editor neglects the link between Utz's and Phipps' castles. We can thus read his cryptic dedication as an expression of a longing to repair loss; the inability to satisfy that longing; and the subsequent need to repudiate it. For whether decorating a flat or manufacturing a fiction, any recreation of the past, even when restored with authentic things, is ultimately only a simulacrum, a diorama furnished with fantasy.

✳✳✳

Aptly enough, Chatwin begins his last book – *Utz* – with the funeral of its protagonist – a morbid theme immediately offset by "the first signs of spring."[23] In true Chatwinian fashion, he evokes these changes with striking visual imagery, a "minor avalanche" of melting snow sliding from a tiled roof. Humor, too, lightens the mood – the janitor who fills in for the missing organist plays a dirge composed of "two sonorous chords he had learned the day before."[24] Further departing from melancholy, the first reference to Czech Communism is heavily aestheticized: Utz, a man of refined taste, had specified his coffin to be draped with white carnations, and "had not foreseen the wreath of Bolshevik vulgarity that had been placed on top," a gaudy composition of red.[25] Chatwin with marvelous economy thus introduces his theme – mortality – as well as the three defensive strategies he enlists against it: ironic comedy, the quest for enduring life and the aesthetic pleasure of rarefied taste. These are in turn condensed and embodied in the tragicomic figure of the collector, the inanimate objects he collects, and the permanence they promise.

As fragile as porcelain, these fortification against mortality and mourning are shattered by the entrance to the funeral of Marta, "Utz's faithful servant" who "arrived at the church "shaking with grief" and "almost fell onto the slushy cobbles." There is nothing funny, beautiful, or ironic about this woman with her "leatherette" purse and disfigured feet, her shoes slit open "to relieve the pressure on her bunions."[26] Adding to her degradation, when the service is over, the funeral attendants rudely "shove the moaning Marta by the shoulder blades, towards the waiting limousine."[27] Her grief – the result of her love – cannot be mocked or aestheticized. And it is precisely in her prevailing capacity to love and grieve that the character of Marta will emerge as a central redemptive figure in Utz's narrative as the mystery of his passions unfolds.

After the opening funeral vignette, the unidentified narrator of *Utz* launches into an intimate first person narrative, explaining that he first met the mysterious Utz in Prague, where he traveled to conduct "historical research" for a journalism assignment, an article that he intended "to be part of a larger work on the psychology – or psychopathology – of the compulsive collector."[28] A seductive proposition to the knowing reader, this statement implicates a self-analytic motivation for the author, with some uncertainty as to whether (or how much) "psychopathology" might be uncovered. The narrator seems to already have a theory about this: "Emperor Rudolf II's passion for collecting exotica" was, "in his later years, his only cure for depression." The narrator singles out items from Rudolf II's *Kunstkammer* (later termed the Ambras Collection) that, as those familiar with Chatwin's collection will recognize, bear correspondences with his prized possessions.[29] Regardless of the author's conscious intention, it is clear at least that the collectors the narrator means to study – Rudolf, certainly, but also Utz – hold a mirror to the author.[30]

***

As Chatwin describes in *In Patagonia*, his actual journey to this remote, wind-flattened land at the bottom of the earth was inspired by an artifact collected in a cave there by Charles Milward, his grandmother's cousin, who gave it to her to keep for posterity in her *Kunstkammer*: a tattered piece of petrified skin. It was not, as the young Chatwin was first led to believe, from a brontosaurus, but from a mylodon, an extinct giant sloth. Milward was one of several merchants in the Chatwin family with a penchant for ships and skullduggery, an attractive legacy for a child such as Chatwin reared on a diet of adventure books. In his telling, as a boy he was transfixed by the fragment of "brontosaurus" skin in his grandmother's china cabinet, but when after her death he sought to claim it, he learned that what was to him a valuable totem of his legendary uncle's exoticism and derring-do had long been discarded. Chatwin specifies that he traveled to Patagonia, Milward's old haunt, not only to retrace his steps, but also to recover the skin, now lost, that his uncle had found there. Yet we cannot forget that the treasure was not the exalted dinosaur fossil, as he had once believed – a family fable punctured, painfully and publicly, by a schoolmaster. And while in his text Chatwin states that his pilgrimage to the mylodon cave was successful, the reader is not so convinced. *In Patagonia* circles around this now-famous quest for a material piece of family lore. Its contested origin set conspicuously aside, the reclaimed trophy of daring adventure, the reader is given to understand, will catalyze a lifetime of collecting – an artifact that reinstitutes the myth.[31]

Just as Chatwin was transfixed by the mylodon skin in his grandmother's china cabinet, the young Kaspar Utz is "bewitched" by something more aesthetic in his grandmother's china cabinet: a Meissen figurine of a Harlequin.

> His taut frame was sheathed in a costume of multi-coloured chevrons. In one hand he waved an oxidized silver tankard; in the other a floppy yellow hat. Over his face there was a leering orange mask. "I want him," said Kaspar.[32]

In her quest for higher social status, Utz's grandmother, born into a prosperous merchant family, converted from Judaism to Catholicism – offending her neighbors, who, as proper citizens of the Habsburg Empire, "were affronted that a woman of her race should affect the outward forms of aristocracy."[33] Her wealth, and the things it bought – including, if we are to believe Utz, a peerage – allowed her to rejoice "in the thought that her fortune would go in increasing after her death."[34] But while the "outward forms" of the visual culture of aristocracy – a castle and its trappings, such as the Meissen porcelain – were real enough, the nobility they meant to signify was not.

Chatwin, born into a solidly middle-class family, also acted the part of the aristocrat, a role that came to him naturally. If forever pained by the residue of a Birmingham accent, he was blessed with devastating good looks, effervescent intelligence, and an unsurpassable gift for gab which, along with his brokerage of precious things at Sotheby's, gave him privileged entrée to high society; he escorted Jacqueline Onassis to the opera and had affairs with James Ivory and Jasper Conran, among other illuminati. In purchasing precious things, he like Utz's grandmother consolidated his claim to the collecting class. Indeed, for Chatwin as for Utz's grandmother, the "outward forms" of aristocracy allowed him to construct a protective persona, what Bick in 1968 termed a "second skin."[35] This skin was a porcelain one, not one debased by the humiliation suffered when his schoolmates ridiculed his father's van that smelled of pig and laughed at his erstwhile brontosaurus skin. Chatwin demonstrates that the things that comprise the "outward forms" of a lost past may also be recruited to materially resurrect lost illusions of that past – or to construct a wholly alternative one.

***

Utz's grandmother initially refused to gift the Harlequin to her grandson. But,

> [f]our years later, to console him for the death of his father, the Harlequin arrived from Dresden in a specially made leather box, in time for a dismal Christmas celebration. Kaspar pivoted the figurine in the flickering candlelight and ran his pudgy fingers, lovingly, over the glaze and brilliant enamels. He had found his vocation: he would devote his life to collecting – "rescuing" as he came to call it – the porcelains of the Meissen factory.[36]

It is thus death and loss that precipitates Utz's compulsion to collect – or "rescue" – the porcelain that only the wealthy could afford to hoard. His attempt to reconstitute long-dispersed noble collections reignites his grandmother's claim to an aristocracy eradicated by "revolution and the tramp of armies."[37]

If Utz's refined porcelain figurines are the antithesis of Milward's nodular, hairy fossil, *In Patagonia*'s satisfying narrative of return screens far fewer satisfying memories of childhood. Born in 1940, Chatwin's early years were wartime years that depleted his family's modest resources. Until he was five, Chatwin only saw his father, who enlisted in the British Navy in 1941, during his infrequent brief leaves. Wanting for father and husband, money and security, he and his mother, perpetually on the move, lived with a succession of relatives; "home" was never apt to feel secure.[38]

Chatwin undoes such insecurity in "Your Father's Eyes Are Blue Again,"[39] a short remembrance that binds the father who left him during the war to the literal reversal of loss. While its title refers to one miraculous restoration – the color of his father's eyes after cataract surgery, its text concerns another, his father's unexpected reunion with *The Aireymouse*, a sailing rig that belonged to *his* father (Chatwin's grandfather), a would-be inheritance that had to be sold upon his death.[40] Now recovered, and in need of extensive restoration, Chatwin prays that his father will once again "sail on *Aireymouse*."[41] The love of things, and their meanings, are inherited, Chatwin seems to say; just as his father's (undone) loss of *Aireymouse* screens and contains the loss of his own father, the recovery of the fossilized skin – simultaneously representing and materializing Chatwin's connection to a man he never knew, the buccaneering Charles Milward – screens the boyhood loss of another Charles, Bruce's father, Charles Chatwin.

For his father, Chatwin writes, the loss of the boat "was the loss of a lover."[42] Confirming that he also experienced the wartime absence of his idealized father, "a man who has never known the meaning of dishonesty,"[43] as "the loss of a lover," he details in "My Father's Eyes" his bedtime ritual of kissing his father's photograph whenever he was away – a tender act followed by a somewhat less tender "first memory" of him:

> on my third birthday, the 13th of May 1943. He took us bicycling near Flamborough Head, the grey Yorkshire headland that Rimbaud may have seen from a brig and put into his prose-poem *Promontoire*.
> He rigged up an improvised saddle for me on his crossbar, with stirrups of purple electric wire. I pointed to a squashed brown thing on the road.
> "What's that, daddy?"
> "I don't know."
> He did not want me to see something dead.
> "Well, it looks to me like a piece of hedgehog."[44]

Sparkling images of sailing ships and blue eyes brought back to life could not undo his father's inability to shield his small son from the "squashed brown thing" that even to a child was not even a complete hedgehog, but a piece of one, a fragment of an animal no longer an animal but a dead "brown thing." The scrap of mylodon skin, on the other hand, is immortalized, a venerated legacy. To the extent to which things are able to both signify and mitigate loss, they negotiate the dual poles of life and death.

***

Writing in 1973, Chatwin observes, "[t]hings appear to be vital to us; to be without them is to be lost and deranged."[45] The dialectic of the animated inanimate pervades the pages of Utz. The narrator reluctantly admires the "boisterous" modeling of the Meissen master Kaendler, siding with Utz against the critic Winkelmann – "who, in his 'Notes on the Plebian Taste in Porcelain,' would supplant [Kaendler's] plebian vitality with the dead hand of classical perfection."[46] Chatwin would have been quite familiar with the trove of Meissen held in the Ashmolean Museum in Oxford, a favorite stomping-ground. Of particular note is one large glass vitrine crammed with Meissen figurines – several of them, Harlequins – which may have inspired the scene in which similar figurines in the museums of Dresden "seemed to beckon Utz into their secret, Lilliputian world – and also to cry for their release."[47]

They also cry to be brought alive. Writing in his own scholarly publication, "The Private Collector," Utz avers that museumized things:

> suffer the de-natured existence of an animal in the zoo. In any museum the object dies – of suffocation and the public gaze – whereas private ownership confers on the owner the right and the need to touch ... the passionate collector, his eye in harmony with his hand, restores to the object the life-giving touch of its maker.[48]

Like the artist, so does the "passionate collector" animate the inanimate, infusing dead material with sensuous, "life-giving touch." Utz does not seem confused by this as he lectures the narrator on the fine line between Meissen and man:

> "So you see," said Utz, "not only was Adam the first human person. He was also the first ceramic sculpture."
>
> "Are you suggesting your porcelains are alive?"
>
> "I am and I am not," he said. "They are alive and they are dead."[49]
>
> Later, the narrator persists:
>
> "So you do think the porcelains are alive?"
>
> "I do and I do not," [Utz] sniggered. "Porcelains die in the fire, and then they come alive again" ... if, to the eighteenth-century imagination, porcelain was not just another exotic, but a magical and talismanic substance – the substance of longevity, of potency, of invulnerability – then it was easier to understand why the King [Augustus the Strong] would stuff a palace with forty thousand pieces ... Porcelain, Utz concluded, was the antidote to decay.[50]

Moreover, Utz notes, "the search for gold and the search for porcelain had been facets of an identical quest: to find the substance of immortality."[51] For things to provide an illusory protection from death, porcelain is the ideal substrate.

✳✳✳

As Utz knows, things can be used to shield one from the reality of life, as well as that of death. He plays with his Commedia dell'Arte figures with no little slippage between the real and its unreal representation, manipulating the porcelain "Madame Pompadour in a lilac dress scattered with roses" that sings "the aria from Lully's 'Acis and Galatea' which she had sung in real life."[52] Galatea, of course, is also the name given by Pygmalion to the woman that he sculpted so realistically, she came alive; likewise, Utz finds two porcelain clowns "as funny in porcelain as they were supposed to have been in real life."[53] Marta's reappearance brings him back to that "real life," but "the moment her back was turned he reentered his world of little figures. His face lit up."[54] Utz, too, comes alive.

In the street, away from his private enclave, Utz's pessimism surfaces. His bitterness surprises the narrator:

"I hate this city," [Utz] said.
"Hate it? How can you hate it? You said it was a beautiful city."
"I hate it. I hate it."
"Things will get better," I said. "Things can only get better."
"You are wrong. Things will never get better."[55]

But some "things" are good enough, at least for now: as the narrator watches him twirl and play with his porcelain figurines, he realizes that Utz,

too, was dancing; that for him, this word of little figures was the real world. And that, compared to then, the Gestapo, the Secret Police and other hooligans were creatures of tinsel. And the events of this somber century – the bombardments, blitzkriegs, putsches, purges – were, so far as he was concerned, so many 'noises off'.[56]

When Communist apparatchiks force an inventory of his collection, Utz is forced to confront the real possibility of losing his "miniature family."[57] He considers emigrating and procures a prescription to a spa in Vichy. On the night he is to leave, he gazes at the laid table:

as he surveyed the sparkling Swan Service plates, the salt cellar, the cutlery with the chinoiserie handles – he came close to believing in his fantasy that this was the 'porcelain palace' and that he himself was Augustus reincarnate.[58]

The seductive (re)construction of court life with the artifacts of "The Porcelain Century" afford a genuine luxury: refuge from the ultimate irony, the exquisite prison that was Communist Prague. There is no Gestapo or Secret Police in the Commedia dell'Arte, only the reincarnation of the Augustus the Strong: a Baron – not a nouveau riche posing as one. Nor was "Baron von Utz" a subjugated subject of a totalitarian state, but a tyrannical director of his Meissen court, an insular cocoon of erotic excitement, power, and pleasure, staffed by a troupe of porcelain players and a court jester, the Harlequin that inaugurated his Porzellankrankheit ("porcelain sickness"), that peculiar malady of nobility. Indeed, Utz is a cold opportunist when seeking to expand his empire, and

welcomed the cataclysm that flung fresh works of art onto the market. "Wars, pogroms, and revolutions," he used to say, "offer excellent opportunities for the collector." ... Kristallnacht was another. In the same week he hastened to Berlin to buy porcelain, in US dollars, from Jewish connoisseurs who wished to immigrate. At the end of the War he would offer a similar service to aristocrats fleeing from the Soviet Army.[59]

Here, one remembers Diana Phipps: when fleeing Nazism and Communism, the survival of her family depended upon the "service" of those who, like Utz, acquired their priceless heirlooms at the ridiculous discounts occasioned by catastrophe. She is the unseen moral compass of *Utz*, and an important, ironic counterpart to her fictional legate. Both Phipps and Utz have lost a castle, each a victim of fate and theft. Unlike Countess Diana Phipps Sternberg, however, Utz's inherited nobility was purchased. Unlike Phipps, he continues to need to purchase and reinstate its "outward forms," emblematizing the thief, the opportunist, the trickster who relieves people like Phipps of theirs. This strategy involves moral compromise, a Faustian bargain – one which Phipps, in her refusal to collaborate and in her acceptance of reality, does not engage. But Utz cannot tolerate reality, and for this he will sacrifice personal and political integrity. For Utz, as for his grandmother, things mediate between reality and fantasy, and between inner and outer worlds; they materially furnish and thereby stabilize a fantasy life in which things do "get better" – in the present, surely, and also past and future.

✳✳✳

In some views, any collector of ethnographic antiquities is a thief. Chatwin's tenure at Sotheby's initiated him into the transactional, corruptible world of buying and selling antiquities, which finds representation in the name "Utz," which in German carries "any number of negative connotations," including "cardshark" and "dealer in dud horses."[60] Tellingly, Chatwin takes pains to mitigate Utz's ruthlessness, which might have cut too close to the bone. Hence, while "the rumours were true" that Utz "had helped in the activities of Goering's art squad," this was justified, as "by doing so he had been able to protect, even to hide, a number of his Jewish friends ... What, after all, was the value of a Titian or a Tiepolo if one human life could be saved?"[61]

Chatwin himself, on the other hand, had no greater good to serve, and grew sickened by feeding the appetites of others. After returning from leave from Sotheby's and before he left for good, he wrote James Ivory:

> Two days in the auction room brought back a flood of gruesome memories ... The nervous anxiety of the bidder's face as she or he waits to see if she can afford to take some desirable thing home to play with. Like old men in nightclubs deciding whether that can really afford to pay that much for a whore. But things are so much better. You can sell them, touch 'em up at any time of the day, and they don't answer back.[62]

The ability of things to elicit erotic pleasure, alongside the fact that they can be bought, allows them – especially human figurines – to function as "whore." Utz exhibits a chilly callousness when he inquires, with greedy relish, how much the narrator imagines his things are worth on the rarefied Meissen market.

Utz's eroticized connoisseurship began early: "'What,' Utz's mother asked the family physician, is this mania of Kaspar's for porcelain?' 'A perversion, he answered. 'Same as any other'."[63] The "perversion" would endure.[64] Without irony, the narrator links his misplaced passion for miniature objects to the failure of his youthful sexual campaign: his attempts to emulate Augustus the Strong's sexual conquests left him sadly mocked by girls who "collapsed with giggles at the miniscule scale of his equipment."[65] Giving him compensation for small "equipment," the needed illusion of virility, his miniscule figurines are even smaller; the narrator relates how, as Utz showed him his vast collection, he "came up behind me, breathing heavily. 'Beautiful, no?'"[66] Utz is also aroused by the narrator's story of a man who "collects" human dwarves, which, along with figurines, are miniatures, a category that offers a microcosmic, alternative reality with the reassuring containment of dominating control.[67]

Like prostitutes and things, slaves are also bought and sold. Indeed, in a potential allusion to slave-trading, the narrator speculates that Utz sold confiscated Meissen on behalf of the Communist state through his safe deposit box in Switzerland.[68] Luckily for Utz, porcelain is immune to the vicissitudes of morality, and its subjugation and sale elicits no guilt. But his faithful maid Marta is a different matter. Her role as something of a slave – essentially, an indentured servant – resonates with Prague's quintessential legend of the golem that Rabbi Loew made from mud and brought to life because, according to Utz, he "wanted a servant without paying wages."[69] The narrator discusses the golem, a servile being neither animate nor inanimate, just before he describes meeting Marta, "a solid woman dressed awkwardly in a maid's uniform" who addresses Utz as "Herr Baron."[70] On cue, she serves canapés in a room of mirrored glass that holds his prized Meissen, "a 'dream palace' multiplied to infinity, through which human forms flitted like insubstantial shadows." In comparison, Marta's movements are "so lifeless and mechanical you would have thought that Utz had created a female golem."[71] While both Meissen and Marta exist in perpetual servitude to Utz, he sees the Meissen as more human.

The narrator gives us to understand that Utz sacrifices his freedom in order to keep his collection: the collector of things under his control is ultimately controlled by his desire – or need – for them: when a friend suggests that "they both flee to the west, Utz pointed to the ranks of Meissen figurines, six deep on the shelves, and said, 'I cannot leave them.'"[72] There is thus no little tension when we learn that when he reaches Vichy, he becomes "desperately homesick," yet "hadn't given a thought for the porcelains. He could only think of Marta, alone, in the apartment,"[73] full of

> remorse for having left her: the poor darling who adored him; who would lay down her life for him; her passionate heart that beat for him, and him only, concealed under as mask of reserve, of duty and obedience.[74]

Marta understood Utz's need for the "outward forms," and "insisted on the details: the sauce in the sauceboat; the starching of the shirt-cuffs; the Sèvres coffee cups on Sunday – for a coffee composed of roasted barley and chicory!"[75] Thus, although the narrator reports that his was his "severe case of Porzellankrankheit" that "prevented him from leaving for good,"[76] it seems it was Marta, who intuits his need for the Meissen – and not the Meissen per se – that pulled him to abandon the capitalist playground of the West. And it is her that keeps him in Prague: Utz ponders the fact that Marta, who knew only Czech, would be "a fish out of water" if they defected together.[77] He cannot take her, but he cannot leave without her.

Thereafter, Utz compromises. In what doubles as an accurate description of Chatwin's own pattern of travel, he undertakes yearly trips to Vichy "to breathe the fresh air of freedom," only to "bolt for home like a man pursued by demons."[78] But there, he eventually suffers

> acute claustrophobia, from having spent the winter months in close proximity to the adoring Marta: to say nothing of the boredom, verging on fury, that came from living those months with lifeless porcelain.[79]

Here lies exposed the fault line in the otherwise stable fantasy: the alienation and boredom incurred by exchanging human relationships for an artificial world populated by *lifeless porcelain*.

Utz was no saint in returning to Marta, however; there were simply no longer any contenders for his love. Reminiscent of earlier attempts, at the spa in Vichy – which cannot but evoke a compromised morality – the refined, beautiful woman with whom he imagines falling in love rejects him. Try as he might, the aging Utz could no longer reconstitute. in real life "the moods and facets of the 'Porcelain Century': the wit, the charm, the gallantry, the love of the exotic, the heartlessness and light-hearted gaiety."[80] Famously possessive of these very qualities, Chatwin did approximate something of the "Porcelain Century" with the coterie of wealthy friends that he collected. He enjoyed extended stays at their villas in the South of France and the Greek islands, and they put up with his imperious entitlement (he never helped and paid for nothing). As much as he expected to be served by them, apparently he served them, too, letting them borrow on his cachet: a beautiful, mercurial, androgynous, endlessly entertaining thing, much like his porcelain equivalent – "The Harlequin . . . the arch-improviser, the zany, trickster, master of the volte-face . . . [who would] grin through his orange mask, tiptoe into bedrooms, dance in the teeth of catastrophe."[81] The Harlequin, beloved for his surface and performance, is little more than a servant, a slave – a thing. Judging from how fast he went from being enamored of the newest fashionable destination to being contemptuous with it, the fabled "restlessness" that Chatwin sought to justify as a superior way of life seems instead a response to inescapable boredom, akin to Utz's – the emptiness of a life wanting for intimacy, constancy, and depth.

***

Chatwin suggests why Utz is unable to engage more intimately with the peasant woman who offers him what his "lifeless" porcelain cannot: no Dresden figurine, her human imperfections, indeed her humanity itself, disappoints. Missing her on an annual trip to Vichy, Utz nevertheless

> knew that, once he got back, the porcelains would re-exert the power of snobbery. The ladies of the Dresden court would turn their vitreous smiles on Marta, dismissing her to the kitchenette – where she would sit, patiently, in her shabby maid's uniform and black stockings with holes at the knee.[82]

Chatwin would never disclose his sexual orientation with his family, fearing it would be met with similar disappointment, even mortification, and denied that he had AIDS, "the gay plague," to the end. His own marital dissatisfaction may have been less a result of narcissistic "snobbery" than his barely closeted homosexuality. And, while his wife Elizabeth may have preferred gardening and rearing sheep to glittering repartee, Chatwin appears to have had great respect and love for her.

In Chatwin's fictional reflections, Marta, like Elizabeth, was earthly, maternal. As a girl, Utz rescued her from a mob that mocked her for having a pet gander. He took her in as a servant; ever grateful, she spent her life repaying him with unstinting pleasure. Eventually, he married her, if only to keep the two-room apartment that housed his collection; likewise, their final romance blossomed only when he could no longer lure other women to his bedchamber. They bond even further after he suffers a stroke, sharing the special intimacy of dependency; likewise, Elizabeth cared for Chatwin in his final months, his skeletal body ravaged by AIDS. Unlike Utz and underclass Marta, it could be said that it was Elizabeth who initially "rescued" Chatwin, her family wealth affording him status, upward mobility, and the stability of a country home. Yet she understood him as Marta understood Utz, tolerating his prolonged absences, the reckless purchases that left them financially unstable, and his numerous homosexual affairs. When Marta, "her heart in shreds,"[83] spends the night in the railway station while Utz entertains an overnight guest, Chatwin suggests some awareness that for him, as for Utz, "these arrangements suited no one except himself."[84] Marta remains Utz's servant even after she becomes his wife. Her loyalty for the man who rescued her unquestionable, and her love for him unconditional, the martyrdom this entails is inscribed in her very name. Marta is the moral counterpoint to Utz: like Phipps, her integrity is uncompromised; like Elizabeth, she "stayed the course," an "eternal Columbine" to Utz's Harlequin.[85]

***

Turning back to the beginning of Utz, at the end of its first six pages the narrator reports that the article on collecting that occasioned his trip to Prague "came to nothing. I remember the episode as a very enjoyable holiday, at the others' expense."[86] Chatwin leaves some clues to an even harsher self-indictment. Near the end of *Utz* the narrator meets a young garbage collector who he imagines may have collected some of the Meissen he believes Utz destroyed in his final days "An energetic young man with laughing eyes," he personifies Utz's orange-masked Harlequin: "The light lit [the garbage collector's face] into an orange mask." His garbage truck is an anthropomorphized extension of its master: "An orange arm shot forth from the truck; clamped its claws around the lip of the bin" and "jettisoned the contents into the vehicle's belly . . . from inside the truck cane the noise of gnashing, crushing, churning, compressing and the shriek of metal teeth." The subsequent dialogue suggests that the narrator, a writer standing in for the author, identifies with this chimeric avatar of destruction. The garbage collector asks the narrator:

> What am I doing here?
> "I'm a writer," I said.
> "So am I," he said.[87]

This *mise en abîme* reveals *Utz* as a finely refracted portrait of the author.[88] He is the narrator, a writer who writes to understand what he observes, and makes some of it up; and he is Utz, a dubious "Baron" obsessed with the things that furnish his fantasy world. At the same time, he is the living embodiment of the Harlequin, a dazzling persona to be desired and collected; unmasked, however, he is a garbage collector that consumes and destroys everything he desires. These facets coalesce as the narrator envisions the collector's last days: "in reviewing his life during those final months [Utz] regretted having always played the trickster":[89] the collector is a Harlequin himself, and all of his things and all of his tricks are garbage, or worse.

Near the end of *Utz*, the narrator surprises the reader with a "revised version of the story," adding a happy ending to the tale of Utz and Marta who against all odds "passed their days in passionate adoration of each other, resenting anything that might come between them." Although it is retold with certainty, it remains unclear exactly what has been changed in this "revised version" of their final chapter. In particular the narrator tries but fails to find evidence for the rumor that Utz shattered his collection, a deliberate ambiguity that marks it as a *fantasy*. The fantasy of an idealized love for a flawed but real woman allows the fantasy of disposing his fraudulent figures, defusing them of their toxic power. After Marta "embraced [Utz] as a true wife," the porcelain proxies for intimate connections lose their glazed sheen, becoming disposable "bits of old crockery that simply had to go."[90]

"The work of art as fetish emerges when the activating sorrow has been repudiated," writes Julia Kristeva:[91] when representations of the human figure function as replacement, rather than remembrance, they preclude, rather than facilitate the work of mourning. Diana Phipps mitigated the loss of her castle by recreating its aura not with replacements, but with *representations* – evident imitations with which she "furnished with fantasy." It is a very different thing to use things in place of *people*. Whereas Phipps's parents survived the Nazi and Communist scourges, Utz lost his father – and with him, it seems, an entire past, a loss he attempted to erase with the carefree, laughing figurine. Porcelain people would thereafter reconstitute his object-related world. Rather than grieving loss, Utz parlayed it into gain: "the deaths, in quick succession, of his mother and grandmother, allowed him to bid against a Rothschild."[92] Chatwin, too, lost his father, once to war, and again when he was sent to boarding school. There, he made his first significant acquisition, an antique French chair – a "form of mourning" that echoes the form of the person it is meant to hold.[93]

In the narrator's fantasy, Utz attempts to reverse his literally dehumanizing substitution of people with things by destroying his collection. Rescuing his virtue by rectifying his treatment of Marta, he elevates her status from servant to the worshipped focus of his life. Chatwin did something similar when, at end of his life, he in a giving frenzy dispersed his private collection among his closest friends; simultaneously, he embarked on a manic buying spree, intent on building a new collection for Elizabeth: like the Harlequin, an antidote for her imminent loss. Bestowing on her the mantle of collector may also reflect a fantasy of immortal reincarnation in his wife's visage. In the last lines of the novel, Marta recognizes Utz in a rainbow. Gazing at his atomized specter, she tells the narrator, "*Ja! Ich bin die* Baronin von Utz."[94]

The elderly "Baroness von Utz" has a new white gander; like Diana Phipps, her nobility needs no accouterment. The name "Kaspar Utz" invokes Kaspar Hauser, the boy who in myth was raised in a cellar without language. Utz tells us in actions that which only the author puts into words. And it is only in words, in the fantasy embedded in fiction, that Chatwin enacts what he could not in life – the literal breaking of his bonds to the things that distracted him from, if not displaced from more demanding and more vulnerable intimacies. The writer of fiction breathes life into fantasy, animating it with a palpable, believable reality. Thus, does Chatwin immortalize in literature a dying wish to renounce his transgressions, transforming them into an act of sacrificial reparation.[95]

Notes

1. T. S. Eliot, *Collected Poems 1909–1962* (New York: Harcourt Brace Jovanovich, 1981), 205.
2. Bruce Chatwin, *Utz* (London: Viking, 1989), 9.
3. Maurits Katan, "The Origin of 'The Turn of the Screw,'" *Psychoanalytic Study of the Child* 21 (1966): 584–85.
4. The Anglophone psychoanalytic literature boasts but two articles addressing the topic of collecting apart from hoarding, Scott C. Schwartz, "Narcissism in Collecting Art and Antiques," *The Journal of the American Academy of Psychoanalysis* 29, no. 4 (2001): 633–47 and Peter Subkowski, "On the Psychodynamics of Collecting," *The International Journal of Psycho-Analysis* 87, no. 2 (2006): 383–401. Two book-length psychological studies of the topic are limited by a lack of psychoanalytic sophistication: Werner Muensterberger, *Collecting: An Unruly Passion. Psychological Perspectives* (Princeton: Princeton University Press, 1994) and William McGuire, *Bollingen: An Adventure in Collecting the Past* (Princeton: Princeton University Press, 1982). Indeed the interest that psychoanalysts have shown in collections and collectors tend, predictably enough, to focus on Freud and his antiquities and considerations of attachments to material things have been approached as symptoms of pathology. For example, Janine Burke, *The Sphinx on the Table: Sigmund Freud's Art Collection and the Development of Psychoanalysis* (New York: Walker and Company, 2006).
5. See Gaston Bachelard, *The Poetics of Space*, trans. Maria Jolas (Boston: Beacon Press, 1958); Walter Benjamin, *The Origin of German Tragic Drama*. Translated by John Osborn (London: New Left Books, 1977); Maurice Merleau-Ponty, *The Merleau-Ponty Aesthetics Reader: Philosophy and Painting*, edited by Galen A. Johnson and Michael B. Smith (Evanston, IL: Northwestern University Press, 1993).
6. See Arjun Appadurai, ed., *The Social Life of Things: Commodities in Social Perspective* (Cambridge: Cambridge University Press, 1986).

7. Patrick Devine-Wright and Lynne C. Manzo, eds. *Place Attachment: Advances in Theory, Methods and Application* (London: Routledge, 2014).

8. See this author's essay on the photographer Josef Sudek for an initial attempt to integrate psychoanalytic theory with contemporary thinking about things, Adele Tutter, "Angel with a Missing Wing: Loss, Restitution, and the Embodied Self in the Photography of Josef Sudek," *American Imago* 70, no. 2 (2013): 127–90.

9. Bill Brown, "Thing Theory," *Critical Inquiry* 28, no. 1 (Autumn 2001): 1–22.

10. For all its intrinsic interest, in the single psychoanalytic study that addresses *Utz* (or, for that matter, its author at all), Katz (2007) understands the things its protagonist collects as little more than fetish items; further, she concentrates not on the novel itself but on its filmed interpretation, and steers clear of the autobiographical ramifications of Chatwin's text.

11. Werner Herzog, director, *Nomad: In the Footsteps of Bruce Chatwin* (London: Sideways Film, 2019).

12. See Debbie Lisle, *The Global Politics of Contemporary Travel Writing* (Cambridge: Cambridge University Press, 2006) and Joe Moran, "Primitivism and Authenticity in Bruce Chatwin's Travel Writing," *Prose Studies: History, Theory, Criticism* 22, no. 3: 91–104.

13. Nicholas Shakespeare, *Bruce Chatwin: A Biography* (London: Nan Talese, 2000).

14. W. G. Sebald, "The Mystery of the Red Brown Skin: An Approach to Bruce Chatwin," in *Campo Santo*, Anthea Bell, trans. (New York: Modern Library, 2005), 173. Similarly, Clapp's moving remembrance of her editorial relationship with Chatwin contains few surprises, and while colorful, the single volume of his letters (guardedly edited by Shakespeare and Chatwin's widow, Elizabeth) reveals little about his inner life. Similarly, Susannah Clapp's moving remembrance of her editorial relationship with Chatwin contains few surprises, and while colorful, the single volume of his letters (guardedly edited by Shakespeare and Chatwin's widow, Elizabeth) reveals little about his inner life, *With Chatwin: Portrait of a Writer* (New York: Knopf, 1997); Bruce Chatwin, *Under the Sun: The Letters of Bruce Chatwin*, edited by Elizabeth Chatwin and Nicholas Shakespeare (New York: Viking Penguin, 2011). Moreover, Chatwin's archive in the Bodleian Library at Oxford, unsealed in 2014, is utterly devoid of other clues as to what drove his attitude to things or his compulsive collecting.

15. Sebald, "Mystery of the Red Brown Skin," 173. Allan Hepburn (2010) comes closest to a psychological understanding of Chatwin's literary treatment of things in *Utz* and elsewhere.

16. Sebald, "Mystery of the Red Brown Skin," 174.

17. Hepburn, *Enchanted Objects*.

18. Chatwin, *Under the Sun*, 497–99. Chatwin uses the pronoun "he" to refer to Phipps, perhaps in his mind rendering her gender ambiguous for the purposes of his fiction.

19. Diana Phipps, *Affordable Splendor: An Ingenious Guide to Decorating Elegantly, Inexpensively and Doing Most of It Yourself* (New York: Random House, 1981).

20. Jane Anderson, "Decorator Diana Phipps Finds Shortcuts to Luxury," *Christian Science Monitor*, February 23, 1982. www.csmonitor.com/1982/0223/022307 .html, accessed May 24, 2020.

21 Phipps states "I never decided to come back [to Častolovice]. As a result of a book that I wrote about interior decoration, and how to do it inexpensively, I had the honor that Olga Havel, the first wife of the president asked me to come and help them in the Prague Castle in 1990" (Mikule 2004, n.p.). Aged forty-eight, Chatwin died just after *Utz* was published, just before the Velvet Revolution liberated Czechoslovakia in November 1989; he did not live to see Phipps return to Častolovice for the third time to restore to their former perfection the repatriated castle and grounds returned to her in shambles. Martin Mikule, "Častolovice – a castle that is living," Blog, Radio Prague International (blog), Aug. 25, 2004, www.radio.cz/en/section/spotlight/castolo vice-a-castle-that-is-living.

22. Mikule, "Častolovice," n.p.

23. *Utz*, 7.

24. Ibid., 8.

25. Testimony to his memory for details, Chatwin with razor-sharp perceptiveness skewers the singularly morbid and droll absurdity of the denizens of Communist Prague, visited over two decades before writing the novel. Superficially entertaining and light but deadly serious, the book mirrors its author.

26. *Utz*, 9.

27. Ibid., 10.

28. Ibid., 12.

29. Thus, "Montezuma's headdress of quetzal plumes" (*Utz*, 13) recalls one of Chatwin's "hangings of blue and yellow parrot feathers, possibly made for the back wall of thePeruvian Sun Temple and supposed to date from the fifth century AD," *Anatomy of Restlessness: Selected Writings, 1969–1989*, edited by Jan Born and Michael Graves (New York: Viking Penguin, 1996). Chatwin in a 1967 letter to his wife Elizabeth writes admiringly of Montezuma's headdress, *Letters*, 97; he bought his own "feathers" with their wedding money. More prosaically, Rudolf II's "gold-mounted coco-de-mer" (*Utz*, 13) is a nod to the author's personal (but not gold-mounted) specimen, the source of some private humor, Chatwin, *Letters*, 187.

30. Chatwin invites a guilty self-comparison to Rudolf II, who neglected his state affairs, dabbled with astronomers and alchemists, and imagined himself "a hermit in the mountains" (14): Chatwin himself impulsively left Sotheby's to pursue a degree in archaeology he never finished; spent years researching and writing a book on nomadic life that was never published; and, smitten by the cloistered monks in the remote cliff monasteries in Greece, just before his death suddenly converted to Greek Orthodoxy, stipulating in his will that his ashes be scattered on Mount Athos.

31. Indeed, the skin provides the title of Sebald's essay and is the awe-inspiring centerpiece Werner Herzog's hagiographic film on Chatwin, *Nomad: In the Footsteps of Bruce Chatwin*.

32. *Utz*, 18.

33. Ibid., 17–18.

34. Ibid., 18.

35. Esther Bick, "The Experience of the Skin in Early Object-Relations," *The International Journal of Psychoanalysis* 49, no. 2–3 (1968): 484–86.

36. Ibid., 19.

37. Ibid., 51.

38. From this perspective, the solid, implacable lure of home in *On the Black Hills* appears a wishful construct.

39. Chatwin, "Your Father's Eyes Are Blue Again," in *What Am I Doing Here* (New York: Viking Penguin, 1989).

40. As Chatwin hoped, after extensive restoration *The Aireymouse* did sail again. For more on this historic ship, see www.nationalhistoricships.org.uk/register/745/airy-mouse

41. *Utz*, 11.

42. Ibid., 10.

43. Ibid., 9.

44. Chatwin, *What Am I Doing Here*, 9–10. The reference to Rimbaud's *Promontoire* is surely multiply determined. It is worth noting that Rimbaud was, like Bruce Chatwin, a libertine and a homosexual, a man of art and commerce, and an avid explorer of Africa and the Near East. He was also suspected of slave-trading, the significance of which will soon be clear.

45. Chatwin, *Anatomy of Restlessness: Selected Writings, 181*.

46. *Utz*, 50.

47. Ibid., 20.

48. Ibid., 20.

49. Ibid., 42.

50. Ibid., 111–12.

51. Ibid., 109.

52. Ibid., 53.

53. Ibid., 54.

54. Ibid., 55.

55. Ibid., 115.

56. Ibid., 114.

57. Ibid., 58.

58. Ibid., 61.

59. Ibid., 21.

60. Ibid., 16.

61. Ibid., 24.

62. Shakespeare, *Bruce Chatwin,* 179.

63. *Utz*, 20.

64. The perversity is, of course, a classical Freudian one: the fetishistic substitution of the "thing" for something else that is missing – traditionally the penis, but other things, real or perceived, that one lacks or has lost.

65. *Utz*, 20.

66. Ibid., 51.

67. In Bachelard's words, "I feel more at home in miniature worlds, which for me, are dominated worlds ... To have experienced miniature sincerely detaches me from the surrounding world, and helps me to resist dissolution of the surrounding atmosphere, " Bachelard, *The Poetics of Space, 161*.

68. Chatwin's second novel, *The Viceroy of Ouidah* (1980), reinforces the nascent equivalence between Utz's figurines and human slaves. A Brazilian man travels to Dahomey (now Benin) to deal in slaves – a collector of dehumanized men. Amassing a fortune, he is named Viceroy of the capital city of Ouidah, another title gained by less than noble means.
69. *Utz*, 44.
70. Ibid., 47–48.
71. Ibid., 49.
72. Ibid., 25.
73. Ibid., 82.
74. Ibid., 83.
75. Ibid., 84
76. Ibid., 90.
77. Ibid., 83.
78. Ibid., 89.
79. Ibid., 88.
80. Ibid., 50–51.
81. Ibid., 114, ellipsis and emphasis in original.
82. Ibid., 87.
83. Ibid., 137.
84. Ibid., 89.
85. Ibid., 152.
86. Ibid., 12.
87. Ibid., 147.
88. See Freud, "Dostoevsky and Parricide" (1928), *SE* 21: 173–94. for an acute analysis of the author's tendency to split and distribute parts of himself between different characters.
89. *Utz*, 125.
90. Ibid., 152.
91. Julia Kristeva, *Black Sun*, trans. L. Roudiez (New York: Columbia University Press, 1989), 9.
92. *Utz*, 21.
93. Jeffrey K. Ochsner, "Meditations on the Empty Chair: The Form of Mourning and Reverie," *American Imago* 73, no. 2 (2016): 131–63.
94. *Utz*, 82.
95. Hannah Segal provides a useful reading of the seminal work of Melanie Klein on art as reparation, "A Psychoanalytic Approach to Aesthetics," *International Journal of Psychoanalysis* 33 (1940): 196–207. See Melanie Klein, "Mourning and Its Relation to Manic-Depressive States," *International Journal of Psychoanalysis* 21 (1952): 125–53.

9

JOSIE BILLINGTON

The Uses of Literature and Psychoanalysis in Contemporary Reading Groups

This chapter is concerned with the value of psychoanalytic thinking and procedures in understanding the experience of reading literature in groups. The intention is to suggest not that shared literary reading performs the function of psychoanalysis, but that it creates conditions not unlike what Freud calls the psychoanalytic situation or "deal": "total honesty in return for complete discretion," in order to give to the analysand "the knowledge [he or she] lacks."[1]

Context

Over the last decade, the Centre for Research into Reading, Literature and Society, a collaboration of literary and linguistic specialists with health experts in Medicine and Psychology at the University of Liverpool where I have been based, has researched the mental health benefits of a specific model of Shared Reading which has been pioneered and delivered by UK charity, The Reader.[2] Shared Reading groups are distinct from conventional book clubs.[3] The material is not read in advance nor confined to contemporary works. Nor is the material chosen for its targeted relevance as in self-help bibliotherapy[4] or in reading interventions which seek to treat particular cases, conditions or moods.[5] Rather, poems, short stories and novels from the literary heritage down the ages are read aloud, together, live, and the reading is regularly interrupted for group members to share thoughts and responses. Currently there are 600 Reader groups across the UK and in Europe, in health and social care contexts, and community and secure settings, including drug and rehabilitation centers, prisons, hospitals, drop-in centers in local medical practices, dementia care homes, facilities for looked-after children, schools, and libraries. CRILS' multi-disciplinary published studies have shown the value of Shared Reading in relation to mental health in community and health-care settings[6] – specifically depression,[7] dementia,[8] and chronic pain[9] – as well as in prison and secure environments.[10] Such research has been crucial not only for convincing often skeptical mental health service providers of the power of a "soft" intervention for chronic, long-term conditions but for laying the foundation for a theory of literary reading and mental health.[11] This endeavor has increasingly led away from medical and psychological paradigms which emphasize outcomes to psychodynamic models concerned with complex inner processes.[12]

In what follows, I identify four key areas to demonstrate where and how the processes of shared literary reading and psychoanalysis richly intersect. In so doing, I draw on an invaluable (and, as far as I know, unique) body of data collected by CRILS in the course of multiple research studies. These are (with the informed consent of all participants) filmed, sound-recorded, and transcribed Shared Reading sessions, together with (recorded and transcribed) individual interviews with group members in which they were able to witness their own participation and re-inhabit the feel of significant but small passing moments.[13]

Reading, Free Association, and Not Knowing in Advance

"Psychoanalysis as a form of therapy," writes Adam Phillips, "works by attending to the patient's side effects, what falls out of his pockets once he starts speaking. ... Undergoing psychoanalytic treatment is, rather like reading a powerful work of literature, a leap into the relative dark. No one can ever know beforehand the effect it will have."[14] The inadvertent, unexpected, and often unwanted "side effects" of shared literary reading are witnessed plentifully and powerfully in participant testimony.

> I went in there, not knowing; I didn't know I was going to come across that. I was totally taken aback and it felt so important. I felt it mattered and should be pursued.
>
> I felt quite – quite emotional there – and wasn't expecting to. The reading just touched something in me. I had no idea where that was going to go.
>
> The poem kind of short-cut into a feeling when I was least expecting it. It just happened quite – suddenly.[15]

When a literary text "matters," it catches the reader pre-cognitively, beneath the level of preconception or considered response ("I went in there not knowing"; "I had no idea where that was going"). The effect is invariably experienced as an involuntary emotional and neo-physical connection. "It got to me"; "a powerful poem sort of hits you in the face"; "the reading can get to feelings really quickly"; "the poem really zeroed in on my feelings, laid them bare"; "just touched something in me." These sudden, live, unexpected short-cuts to often dormant inward matter are the result, in the first place, of the poetry being read aloud performatively, as a near and intimate emotional–vocal presence: "things become more 3D and more alive"; "certain words, sort of jump out at you"; "it seems to resonate"; "it got into me"; "it strikes home."[16] The voiced text, at such moments, acts as a quick trigger to the kind of subterranean experience which psychoanalysis goes in search of.

In the psychoanalytic situation, said Freud, the analysand "has to put at our disposal all the material that its self-perception offers it":

> He has to tell us everything that his self-observation yields to him, everything that comes into his mind, even if it is unpleasant for him to say it ... If he succeeds in switching off his self-critical mechanism ... he will give us a wealth of material – thoughts, associations, memories – that are already under the influence of the unconscious, indeed are often directly derived from it.[17]

In Shared Reading, literature acts as a stimulus to this unconscious material not so much by switching off the self-critical mechanism as by short-circuiting it and switching *on* what lies outside or beneath it. Let me offer here some brief representative examples, some of which I will draw on throughout the chapter. The examples are taken from different reading groups across a range of studies, but, in each case, the reader has been diagnosed with a mental health difficulty (depression) sometimes associated with a physical condition. None of the readers referred to in what follows has any formal education or experience in reading literature.

Lois, a young woman in her early twenties is attending a community reading group. She is suffering some significant neurological impairment from a traumatic accident where she came into contact with an electric fence while living in South Africa. It is during a reading of Robert Frost's "The Road Not Taken" that she speaks for the first time about the difference her accident made to her life. "If I hadn't gone, I would still probably be wanting to go here, wanting to go there. At the same time, would I have the same mentality as now? Perhaps something worse could have happened. Or I could have been worse if it had been easier." Then, suddenly:

> But if anyone was thinking of going and doing exploring, I'd say, don't do it, don't do this, don't do that. I'd be awful if if ... I'd be awful if I ever had ... if I ever had ... if I ever had ... if I ever had ... if I ever had ... children. Because I'd be like, you're not doing *that*.[18]

The stutter occurs on the "if," the poem's own key word ("I doubted if I should ever come back"[19] is the closing line of the penultimate stanza). Lois's neurological disability meant that she occasionally had problems with fluent speech. But here Lois's intermittent speech problems come under the most intense emotional strain, as she stutters five or more times "if I ever had" before poignantly managing to complete the sentence with – "children." As a result of her accident the possibility within that "if" is unlikely to be fulfilled. It is the kind of admission which is as difficult and "unpleasant" to say as it might be unbearable to think. In one so young, it is a thought that might need to be suppressed simply for Lois to carry on. But I use the example here because it offers a model of the sudden inarticulacy, in place of default or automatic norms of thought and speech, which characterizes and signals those instances where significant psychic matter is "touched," in much the same way as happens in psychoanalysis.

> What is distinctive about the practice of psychoanalysis is that the patient is encouraged to tell the story of his sufferings in a way that makes it impossible to tell a story. . . . The free-associating speaking patient must not be in search of the right word; indeed, getting it right, finding the words for what he has to say, is the problem not the solution.[20]

In my next example, Toby, whose depression accompanies his severe chronic physical pain, is reading Elizabeth Bowen's short story "The Visitor," in which a young boy, whose mother is dying, is waiting for the news that she is dead. He hears a large clock "tick out."

> Sixty of these ticks went to make a minute, neither more nor less than sixty, and the hands of the clock would be pointing to an hour and a minute when they came to tell Roger what he was expecting to hear. Round and round they were moving, waiting for that hour to come.[21]

Toby, who normally sits back in his chair, upon hearing this moment in the story, leans forward and extends his arm across the table, in imitation of the clock hand, as he speaks: "I used to look at the clock when I was a child and try to will the second hand to stop." "Why, was that because of something you didn't want to happen?," the group leader asks. "Yes," says Toby, looking down, covering his face, leaning back. The momentary silence which follows is almost palpably full of something amorphously un-nameable or too emotionally powerful to be fitted into words. Witnessing a video-recording of this moment later at interview, Toby related his response to the child's helplessness in relation to his own experience of a prolonged period of abuse when he was young. The story did not simply stir "painful memories," he said. "The pain is still there, locked away inside." The interviewer ventured that this pain – like his chronic pain itself – is a hidden, secret thing. "Yes," he said. "Those two things – no one can ever see them."[22]

While not the same as free association – formally, it can be very different – what I am calling inarticulacy is nonetheless operating in the same area, freeing the psyche from default norms or constraining patterns of thought and releasing from "locked-away" debilitating restraint, unfinished business or unpurged residues of lived experience. As psychoanalyst Christopher Bollas explains: "Through free association Freud knew he had found a new form for being spoken to by the self ... The therapeutic genius of this method is that it quite naturally breaks down the paralyzing authority of any symptom or pathological structure."[23] In Shared Reading, the "break-down" can sometimes be quite literal at the level of language, where the authority of straightforward speech is replaced by a kind of dumb pointing ("That bit there" said one reader in relation to a half-line – "myself almost despising" – from Shakespeare's Sonnet 29)[24] or simply by the words of the poem as they are read aloud. Of his experience of reading haltingly and with quiet care Robert Herrick's "To Anthea, Who May Command Him Anything," one reader, Donald, said afterwards at interview: "I was shaking inside. Certain words touch nerves with me [pointing to the poem on the page and reading] – 'Heart as soft, heart as kind'.[25] Really good things, which I've not had. Softness, kindness, I like those traits."[26]

Across all of these instances, what is abundantly evident is the vital centrality of the literature in producing a situation analogous to a psychoanalytic one. First, the reading aloud of the poem or story creates a resonant "atmosphere"[27] or, as Freud put it of the "surrender" to free association, "a special attitude of the attention" ("quite different from reflection, and which excludes reflection").[28] The literary text provides "a grounded centre ... 'as though there was a power in the middle .... pulling us in'"[29] for immersive concentration and sustained attentive "listening." Second, the literature in such instances helps to give material body to realities otherwise hard to hold or contemplate. A poem or story at once contributes to the "holding" environment of the reading group and itself "holds"[30] the trouble or emotion it "hits" in the reader.

Interpretation and Story: Writer-Reader-Therapist

One might say that the virtue of Shared Reading's primary reliance on the literary stimulus to disclose unconscious material is that the process is freed (to borrow Bollas' words), from the "authority" of *the therapist*. As both Bollas and Phillips emphasize, the latter can be radically at odds with the practice upon which it relies. Freud's free-associative method, writes Bollas, was subversive not only of the Western mindset (which "privileges mental adventures ... mediated by custodians of consciousness") but of the very certainties of psychoanalysis. "Analysts have the somewhat thankless task of supporting a process that undermines the intellectual sanctity of analytically acquired truths."[31] "A psychoanalysis bent on understanding people is going to be very limited," says Phillips, because Freud's "golden rule of free association points us in two directions at once" – the possibility of profound "intelligibility" on the one hand and equally profound "bafflement" on the other.[32]

Arguably, Shared Reading aids the psychoanalytic project while avoiding some of the contradictions inherent within its process. For what typically happens in Shared Reading, is that a poem or prose passage "lands" on someone. Why? No one knows, and no one tries to understand in the conventional way. The process is entirely unpredictable, and save for the loose informal rules which operate within the group,[33] non-governable. No one has the "answer."

But what possible help can literary reading be to the inward life it awakens without an external intelligence to guide it? And is it not dangerous to open up psychic wounds in the absence of a therapist who can skillfully manage such irruptions? This is where the centrality of the literature is once again crucial. As one psychiatrist running a reading group in a high-secure hospital put it, "the book becomes the expert."[34]

Let me return, by way of illustration, to what happened in the group session in which Toby, reading Bowen's "The Visitor," became particularly attuned to the child's anxiety about the impending news of his mother's death. "The loss is going to be a great big thing in his little life; I think I'd want to run and hide, want to escape."[35] It is important to remember that, while the significance of Toby's reaction was palpably and incontrovertibly present in the room, intensifying its atmosphere, nobody in the group knew (or knows) why this passage resonated personally and powerfully for him, not even the group leader. Indeed, the question which elicited this reaction ("Why, was that because of something you didn't want to happen?") arose spontaneously out of the moment's mutual attentiveness, and was not intended therapeutically to target painful memory. It was in a similarly informal way, nonetheless, grounded in the formal structures of the text, that Toby's "secret" pain seemed to be ameliorated itself at the end of the session without need of the group leader's explicit intervention.

At the close of the story, when the boy-protagonist expects his father to tell him the terrible news, his father holds out to him instead, a picture-postcard from his aunt, depicting the bay of Naples: "Blue sea, infinitely smooth and distant ... Behind the land, behind everything, the clear fine line of a mountain went up into the sky ... This was the blue empty space, Heaven, that one came out into at last, beyond everything."[36] Toby said:

I'm thinking about his father as well. The little boy doesn't know how his father's thinking. But I think the father can see what's happening with the little boy. It's like his way of being able to give the child comfort. You really feel for the father, don't you?[37]

Both in the course of the story, and here in the same single moment – "I'm thinking about his father *as well*" – Toby (himself a father) is now distributed between his own child and adult selves. Occupying, imaginatively, the father he is at the same time giving comfort, vicariously, to the child. The therapeutic alliance, says Bollas, warrants entry into a "highly complex psychic theatre" in which the analysand is "deconstructed by projections, diverging self-experiences, shifting moods, eventful thoughts and allegorical personages" and "oscillates between two mental positions," that of the "simple self" "inside" the experience" and "the organising intelligence that gives it meaning."[38] I am suggesting that, in this instance of reading, unsafe personal matter is at once released, as well as richly held or contained, by an analogous alliance between story and reader. Fascinatingly, through the novel's own generously shifting movement between different centers of being, Toby occupies two "insider" positions (father, son) which are mutually supportive "outsiders" to one another. It is worth noting, also, that the story absolutely fulfills the requirement for "neutrality" or suspended judgment on the part of the therapist which the therapeutic alliance exacts.[39] The literary text cannot know and does not care whether one needs its help or not.

My primary intention here is not to suggest that literary reading might do the job of psychoanalysis better than psychoanalysis can. On the contrary, I am seeking, via these comparisons with the psychoanalytic situation, to offer a more congenial paradigm than those currently available, for what literary reading, and specifically shared literary reading, can achieve, therapeutically speaking. Psychological models, focusing on the usefulness of reading to encourage theory of mind, stress the capacity of fiction-reading to promote "empathy" with other points of view, "putting oneself in another's shoes."[40] The thinking exerted in literary reading groups at such moments, however, is deeply (ontologically and emotionally) engaged rather than merely intellectually or morally mobile. Crucially, this thinking – dispersed as it is among separated centers of being who are nonetheless held together in the same world as in the same story – is virtually in collaboration with the novelist. The analogy rightly proposed by J. M. Coetzee between analyst and author ("Both are occupied with the exploration, description and analysis of human experience, with finding linguistic and narrative structures within which to contain [it]"),[41] here holds good when transposed to *reader* and *author*.

It is in recognition of such collaboration between the literary work and its reader that Paul Ricouer defines narrative as "not a static structure, but an operation, an integrative process." Every story dynamically mediates between "two kinds of time," "time passing and time enduring." To compose a story is to draw "integration, culmination, configuration" from "a succession of incidents":

> The process of configuration does not complete itself in the text [but] is completed only in the reader ... in the living receiver of the told story. ... Through their imaginations, readers belong to both the horizon of experience of the work and that of their own real action. ... The sense and reference of the story well up from the intersection of the world of the text and the world of the reader, [making] possible the reconfiguration of life through the narrative.[42]

Ricoeur's notion of the reading process as poised (transformatively) in and out of continuous narrative, in a "welling up" in-between the life and the literary story, helps to explain why moments of significance in Shared Reading – Lois's in relation to poetry as much as Toby's in relation to fiction – can feel like fragments of experience suddenly turned, momentarily, into lyric wholeness. Indeed, such instances offer specific empirical examples in support of Ricouer's psychoanalytic theory of literary reading. Here is one final moment relating to Toby, one given retrospective power and significance by Toby's later disclosures at interview. The group is reading the conclusion to John Steinbeck's *Of Mice and Men,* where Lennie, the child-like man, has inadvertently killed the wife of his employer, Curley, and has fled in panic:

> The sun streaks were high on the wall by now, and the light was growing soft in the barn. Curley's wife lay on her back, and she was half covered with hay.
> It was very quiet in the barn, and the quiet of the afternoon was on the ranch. ... A pigeon flew in through the open hay door and circled and flew out again. ...
> As happens sometimes, a moment settled and hovered and remained for much more than a moment. And sound stopped and movement stopped for much, much more than a moment.[43]

Toby's response to this scene was insightful for his own self-analysis; he remarked: "Even though Lennie's gone, we're left looking at that feeling, that atmosphere in the barn. That's the feeling Lennie has got inside himself. The pigeon flying in and the advance of day – isn't that showing you nature just going about its daily business. Life continuing as it normally does as if this bad thing hasn't happened. You could see the world going on as normal but what had happened to you might feel unbelievable, you know, hard to accept."

"It is a big problem for me," Toby said further in an interview, "that I can't keep hold of everything. The reading helps things, certain things, to stay in my mind. Normally I wouldn't be able to do that: I would be lost." What reading demonstrably does for Toby here is "hold together" two complexly related-but-distinct experiences: on the one hand, the feeling that trauma leaves behind "inside"; on the other hand, the further trauma produced by having to carry on, with that inside, as though one were just the same. Again, at no point is this confessionally exposing or explicit. Toby is not "put on the spot." But nor is the moment psychically risk-free. Toby is the "living receiver" of his own and the story's pain, each bearing witness to the other. This is powerfully "implicit" therapy,[44] doing its own work hiddenly in the moment of reading, and only known to have been therapeutic through recognition afterwards. "The reading is helping me. I am actually having a go – to make sense of things. It gives me time to come through the fog."[45]

Thinking

The reading examples I have given are instances of what Wilfred Bion called the "really real," and which he designated "O"[46] in recognition that no ordinary definition or discourse would serve for what exists antecedent to or beneath language and cannot be "contained" by it. O cannot be truly known except by experience or discovery. The really real is immersively lived, experienced in absorption, phenomenologically steeped in itself. In Shared Reading, "O" is often marked by a "full silence," in which speakers abandon a thought or leave it uncompleted and at which gestures often take over. At these "stops" or "hangings," something emergent seems not so much blocked as to continue to exist suggestively and unspoken in the resonant atmosphere of the group without a ready-made category or framework.[47]

It is precisely at such moments, says Bion, that thinking, or rather proto-thoughts begin. These inchoate, half-commenced thoughts (like Lois's stuttering "if" or Toby's "yes") originate in the pre-verbal, undigested experience which Bollas called the "unthought unknown," and which Bion called "beta" elements. These unmetabolized experiences need to be operated on, converted, digested, given a substance by thinking ("alpha function"), and thus be made available for use and translation into action as "alpha elements."[48] It is an axiom of Bion's theory that the inability "to "think" with one's thoughts" is a catastrophic "deprivation of truth" where truth is "essential for psychic health." "Failure to eat, drink or breathe properly has disastrous consequences for life itself. Failure to use the emotional experience produces a comparable disaster in the development of the personality." But Bion also knew that thinking one's thoughts – thinking O – could be almost impossibly hard to achieve. Indeed, for Bion, the discovery of psychoanalysis, was itself a symptom of the fact that thinking and the tasks of self-knowledge had been forced upon a mental "apparatus" which is ill-suited and undeveloped for the purpose.

> An apparatus existed and had to undergo, still has to undergo, adaptation to the new tasks involved in meeting the demands of reality by developing a capacity for thought. The apparatus that has to undergo this adaptation is that which dealt originally with sense impressions relating to the alimentary canal.[49]

In digesting experience, humans have to rely on primitive psychic processes belonging to a phase of development which the complexity of reality has long outgrown. Real thinking "is embryonic even in the adult and has yet to be developed fully by the race."[50]

Thus a key matter for Bion was that the thinking *tools* at our disposal (for the analyst as well as the analysand) – our mental or verbal "containers" for the experience of reality – are liable, in the very effort at containment, to falsify or misrepresent through over-definition or inadequate frameworks: "The verbal expression can be so formalized, so rigid, so filled with already existing ideas" that "the container can squeeze everything 'out of' the contained."[51] Or the "pressure" exerted by the contained, may have such force and vitality relative to the verbal formulation, so that the container disintegrates or is destroyed.[52] The "vocabulary forged" in psychoanalytic practice "serves, though inadequately" in negotiating between these two possibilities of over-rigidified and exploded meaning, because the process and persons are fully present. "In mathematics, calculations can be made without the presence of the objects ... but in psychoanalytic practice it is essential for the psychoanalyst to be able to demonstrate as he formulates. This is not possible as soon as the conditions for psychoanalysis do not exist." Significantly, Bion singled out "poetic and religious expression" as alone achieving "durability and extensibility," containers in which uniquely "the carrying power of the statement has been extended in time and space."[53]

A representative example of that carrying power is witnessed, here, when Carol, a young woman recovering from drug addiction, first encounters John Clare's "I am":

> I am – yet what I am none cares or knows;
> My friends forsake me like a memory lost:
> I am the self-consumer of my woes – ...
> And yet I am, and live – like vapours tossed

Into the nothingness of scorn and noise,
Into the living sea of waking dreams,
Where there is neither sense of life or joys,
But the vast shipwreck of my life's esteems; ...

I long for scenes where man hath never trod
A place where woman never smiled or wept
There to abide with my Creator, God,
And sleep as I in childhood sweetly slept,
Untroubling and untroubled where I lie ...[54]

Carol said immediately, "It has really – hit me; right there [points to heart],
the whole poem." As the group began to discuss the distress in the first two
stanzas, the need for the release of something like a suicidal death in the final
stanza, Carol suddenly left the room, returning some minutes later, saying,
amidst restrained tears:

> The way this is to me, I exist at the moment ... I am. But I am not– [Another
> group member adds, supportively: 'Living']. I am literally vapours, the noth-
> ingness of what-have-you, and I feel like a shipwreck, and things I used to
> esteem in my life are no longer there, and I have been forsaken by a lot of
> people, so I am a bit of a memory lost, no one really cares or wants to know.
> And it's interesting what was said about suicide because, I don't want to
> commit suicide, no, but I want to be at peace ... and go back to that innocent
> childhood or you know that kind of untroubled place.[55]

Carol is not so much "quoting" from the text, as inhabiting the emotional
reality of the poem, which itself is coming to life again in her. When Carol
repeats the words of the poem, it is as though they are not only entering her
own heart ("right there") but coming from it at the same time – finding her
own deep text. It is an important example of how poetry has potential at
once to "hit" or find inner trouble *and* help unfold it into articulate
expression.

The problem of finding the right word, says Bion, "is analogous to that of
the sculptor finding his form in the block of his material, of the musician
finding the formula of musical notation within the sounds he hears, of the
man of action finding the actions that represent his thoughts."[56] It is hard,
struggling work; it is, Bion suggests, one of the most profoundly creative
acts of being alive. It is why we people who are not artists might need
literature as a language to think in. The dumb marks on the page come to
life when we read with all the emotional reality – the really real, the
unspoken O that originally summoned them – yet with the verbalized
capacity to take in and hold that pain for longer than humans ordinarily can.

Holding

I close by proposing two possible consequences of literary Shared Reading's capacity (as I suggested earlier) to offer a "holding environment," in Winnicott's sense, for difficult experience.

Participants of Shared Reading groups often explicitly value how literature permits them not to think of themselves as "cases." "Oh I'm not going mad, someone else has had this experience. Somebody else is feeling that way."[57] For these readers, literature widens and enriches the human norm, accepting and allowing for troubles, traumas, and inadequacies as part of a continuum of existence, related not to a pathological "case" but to the whole spectrum of normative human being. In a reading group for older adults, a recently widowed woman, Ona, in late middle-age, responds to Dorianne Laux's poem "For the Sake of Strangers," in which the grieving speaker recounts her feelings of emptiness and her urge to fall "away from the world"[58] even as she is required to push on. Ona says:

> She sounds to me like a person who's had a terrible loss ... and that feeling ... disengaged to the world I ... I ... I remember that feeling ... and I walked about like she's walking about now. I was aware of things but not aware of things. I wasn't part of it. It's a horrible, horrible feeling ... The words in the poem "No matter what the grief, its weight,/ we are obliged to carry it" ... I'm afraid I know that. I can't say I don't know that because I do.[59]

As though indeed afraid, Ona has previously found it difficult to speak of the death of her husband. The poem helps her here not by prescribing any "cure," nor by simply alleviating the pain. Rather it at once transmits and witnesses grief, shares the "weight" of emotion, making a momentary community of suffering amid an experience which is otherwise utterly isolating. It is as though the poem "finds" Ona emotionally in the same way as, within the situation the poem depicts, the individual kindnesses of people in the crowd – a young boy, a woman, a child, all strangers – "reach toward" the grieving one, keeping her "from the edge."[60] And versions of these strangers are literally present for Ona in the uniquely intimate space for shared emotional meditation created within a literary reading group.[61] One critical finding is that the "group" does "not really exist save as a static or notional unit until, through the text, connections are made between one individual and another."[62] As one person, now another, becomes the "realizer" of a poem or story, or as the text catalyzes the release of (often unrealized or unliberated) personal matter into shared external expression, the conventional boundaries between personal and public, private and social become porous. "*Inner* lives come *out*, and come out *together*."[63] This dynamic, wherein the literary work and the reading group bring the subject in relation to themselves within the small-group community, offers a perspective and reparative opportunity that is missing from the psychoanalytic consulting room.

For ordinary people in difficult or volatile situations, it is as if a poem or story performs an equivalent of what D.W. Winnicott called crucial "acts of human reliability."

> The way the mother fits in when rocking the child, the sound and tone of her voice, all communicate long before speech is understood. We received a silent communication over a period of time that we were loved in the sense that we could rely on the environmental provision and so get on with our growth and development. ... The continuation of reliable holding [is present in] the ever-widening circle of family and school and social life.[64]

"We are believing people," says Winnicott, on the strength of "reliable holding"[65] which Winnicott describes here as originating with the mother's loving physical and vocal presence. Literature's widened paradigm and language, especially as it is delivered in the read-aloud mode of Shared Reading – intimately voiced, living, present – offers its own version of "human reliability" and life-supporting belief. A group-leader recalls how one reader, Eve, on listening to Edward Thomas's poem "Adelstrop," "after a long silence began to speak but only in the words of the poem as if musing at the possible meaning."[66]

> Yes. I remember Adlestrop –
> The name, because one afternoon
> Of heat the express-train drew up there
> Unwontedly. It was late June.
>
> The steam hissed. Someone cleared his throat.
> No one left and no one came
> On the bare platform. What I saw
> Was Adlestrop – only the name.[67]

"No one left and no one came," Eve repeated. "That's how it is for me. I don't know if there is anyone there. I put words out but I don't know if there is anyone really there to pick them up. There's no evidence. One can't be sure. One hopes. 'No one left and no one came.'[68] No it seems I am quite alone, but I trust there is someone there to receive it."[69] In these instances, the literature seems to offer "a vocalized place" for "something not fully known or named – or not even had ['It seems ... I trust'] – to be momentarily held and realised."[70] After another silence, as if in witness of that trust, Eve read the poem's final stanza:

And for that minute a blackbird sang
Close by, and round him, mistier,
Farther and farther, all the birds
Of Oxfordshire and Gloucestershire.[71]

"I hear birds outside sometimes early in the morning," said another group member: "That's a good sound." "Mistier," said another, "has to do with one bird starting and the others all join in." "The group then talked with enthusiasm of the birds all coming into song together," the group leader recalls, "as they themselves in their own way did at that point."[72] "Nothing I am capable of is just me . . . somebody enabled me to get to the place I am."[73] "An emotional experience cannot be conceived of in isolation from a relationship."[74] In ways akin to the mother's "reliable holding" of the child, Shared Reading offers at such times an adult equivalent of the "facilitating environment" which renews "the line of life."[75]

Martha Nussbaum has proposed that a literary text can act as a "transitional object": "When we have emotions of fear and pity towards the hero of a tragedy and his reversal, we explore aspects of our own vulnerability in a safe and pleasing setting."[76] Ricoeur's assertion that literature "proposes to the imagination for meditation sample cases which constitute thought-experiments,"[77] is also posited, as we have seen, on the text's occupying what Winnicott called the "third part of a human being's life." This "third" area consists not of an "inside and outside" only, but of "an intermediate area of experiencing, to which inner and outer life both contribute."[78] In Shared Reading, as the foregoing examples have demonstrated, the third area is three-dimensionally present. What strikes observers time and again, is how the reading group constitutes a "protected space,"[79] an "invisible shield."[80] It has led psychotherapists and psychiatrists to emphasize how Shared Reading imitates and (re)-creates (sometimes for the first time) the intimacy of a close human voice speaking or reading to one's needs – "the way the mother fits in when rocking the child, the sound and tone of her voice." "When every word and every line is a close, vocal-emotional presence, the primary emotion involved will almost inevitably be closer to earlier life before adult stress patterns took hold or hardened into ill health" [David Fearnley, Ashworth Hospital, UK]. "We can't regrow brains, but [in Shared Reading] we *can* provide an experience which patients can internalize – that is social and in some way equated to early childhood experience of attachment and safe relationship" [Nick Benefield, Lead, National Personality Disorder Team, UK].[81] The suggestion is that Shared Reading might offer an adult version of pre-verbal relationship, reaching back to a period or condition prior to trauma, before damage set in, getting underneath habitual categories and frames, those of identity as well as of mental health condition.

Notes

1. Sigmund Freud, *An Outline of Psychoanalysis* (London: Penguin, 2003), 201–02.
2. See: www.thereader.org.uk; Jane Davis, "Introduction" in *A Little Aloud: An Anthology of Prose and Poetry for Reading Aloud to People You Care For*, ed. Angela Macmillan (London: Random House, 2010), 7–19; Jane Davis, "The Reading Revolution" in *Stop What You're Doing and Read This!* (London: Vintage Books, 2011), 115–36.
3. Jenny Hartley, *The Reading Groups Book* (Oxford: Oxford University Press, 2002).
4. Debbie Hicks, "An Audit of Bibliotherapy/Books on Prescription Activity in England," *Arts Council England and the Museums Libraries and Archives Council* (2006).
5. Susan Elderkin and Ella Berthoud, *The Novel Cure: An A–Z of Literary Remedies* (Edinburgh: Canongate, 2013); Jonathan Bate, Paula Byrne, Sophie Ratcliffe, and Andrew Schuman, eds., *Stressed, Unstressed: Classic Poems to Ease the Mind* (London: Harper Collins, 2016).
6. Ellie Gray, Gundi Kiemle, Philip Davis, and Josie Billington, "Making Sense of Mental Health Difficulties Through Live Reading: An Interpretative Phenomenological Analysis of the Experience of Being in a Reader Group," *Arts & Health* 8, no. 3 (2016): 248–61.
7. Christopher Dowrick, et al., "Get into Reading as an Intervention for Common Mental Health Problems," *Medical Humanities* 38, no. 1 (2012): 15–20.
8. Josie Billington, et al., "A Literature-based Intervention for Older People Living with Dementia," *Perspectives in Public Health* 133, no. 3 (2013), 165–73; Eleanor Longden, et al., "An Evaluation of Shared Reading Groups for Adults Living with Dementia: Preliminary Findings," *Journal of Public Health* 15, no. 2 (2016): 75–82.
9. Josie Billington, Grace Farrington, et al., "A Comparative Study of Cognitive Behavioural Therapy and Shared Reading for Chronic Pain," *Medical Humanities* 43, no. 3 (2017): 155–65.
10. Josie Billington, "Prison Reading Groups in Practice and Theory," *Critical Survey* 23, no. 3 (2012), 67–85; Josie Billington, Eleanor Longden, and Jude Robinson, "A Literature-based Intervention for Women Prisoners: Preliminary Findings," *International Journal of Prisoner Health* 12, no. 4 (2016): 230–43; Jude Robinson and Josie Billington, "Prison Reading Groups," in Billington, *Reading and Mental Health*, 155–90.
11. Josie Billington, Philip Davis, and Grace Farrington, "Reading as Participatory Art: An Alternative Mental Health Therapy," *Journal of Arts/Community* 5, no. 1 (2014): 25–40; Eleanor Longden, et al., "Shared Reading: Assessing the Intrinsic Value of a Literature-based Intervention," *Medical Humanities* 41, no. 2 (2015), 113–20.

12. Josie Billington, *Is Literature Healthy?* (Oxford: Oxford University Press, 2016); "Inner Voices: Literary Realism and Psychoanalysis," in *The Faces of Depression in Literature*, ed. Josefa Ros Velasco (New York: Peter Lang, 2020), 165-80.

13. Josie Billington, et al., "Developing Innovative Qualitative Approaches in Research on Reading and Health," in *Reading and Mental Health*, ed. Josie Billington (London: Palgrave, 2019), 191–240.

14. Adam Phillips, *Side Effects* (London: Hamish Hamilton, 2006), xi–xii.

15. See Philip Davis and Josie Billington, "'A Bolt Is Shot Back Somewhere in the Breast' (Matthew Arnold, 'The Buried Life'): A Methodology for Literary Reading," in *The Edinburgh History of Reading*, ed. Jonathan Rose and Mary Hammond (Edinburgh: Edinburgh University Press, 2020), 4 vols, Vol 2 *Modern Readers*, 283–305 and Billington, et al., "Developing Innovative Qualitative Approaches in Research on Reading and Health."

16. Billington, et al., "Developing Innovative Qualitative Approaches in Research on Reading and Health."

17. Freud, *An Outline of Psychoanalysis*, 202.

18. Quoted in Billington, *Is Literature Healthy?*, 93.

19. Edward Conney Lathem, ed., *The Poetry of Robert Frost* (New York: Henry Holt, 1988), 105.

20. Phillips, *Side Effects*, 56–57.

21. Elizabeth Bowen, *Collected Stories* (London: Vintage, 1999), 129–30.

22. See Josie Billington, Grace Farrington, et al., "A Comparative Study of Cognitive Behavioural Therapy and Shared Reading for Chronic Pain" (University of Liverpool: Centre for Research into Reading Literature and Society, 2016), 75.

23. Christopher Bollas, *The Mystery of Things* (London: Routledge, 1999), 2, 21.

24. John Kerrigan, ed., *William Shakespeare: The Sonnets and A Lover's Complaint* (Harmondsworth, Middlesex: Penguin Books, 1999), 91.

25. Christopher Ricks, ed., *The Oxford Book of English Verse* (Oxford: Oxford University Press, 1999), 144.

26. Phillip Davis and Josie Billington, "The Very Grief a Cure of the Disease," *Changing English Special Issue: Uses of Poetry* 23, no. 4 (2016): 396–408, 406.

27. For extended discussion of "atmosphere" and "listening," see Billington, *Is Literature Healthy?*, 54–56, 91–94.

28. Freud, "The Premises and Technique of Interpretation," in *Introductory Lectures on Psychoanalysis*, ed. James Strachey (London: Penguin Books Ltd., 1976), 136.

29. Longden et al., "Shared Reading," 115.

30. Freud, "The Premises and Technique of Interpretation," in *Introductory Lectures on Psychoanalysis*, ed. James Strachey (London: Penguin Books Ltd., 1976), 136.

31. Bollas, *The Mystery of Things*, 1–2.

32. Adam Phillips, *In Writing: Essays on Literature* (London: Random House, 2016), 145, 263.

33. Gray, et al., "Making Sense of Mental Health Difficulties," 252–53.

34. Billington, et al., "Reading as Participatory Art," 28–29.

35. Billington, Farrington, et al., "A Comparative Study of Cognitive Behavioural Therapy and Shared Reading for Chronic Pain," 2016, p. 55.

36. Bowen, *Collected Stories*, 140.

37. Billington, Farrington, et al., "A Comparative Study of Cognitive Behavioural Therapy and Shared Reading for Chronic Pain," 2016, p. 55.
38. Bollas, *The Mystery of Things*, 6–7.
39. Ibid., 13.
40. See for example: Lisa Zunshine, *Why We Read Fiction: Theory of Mind and the Novel* (Columbus: Ohio State University Press, 2006), 159–64.
41. J. M. Coetzee and Arabella Kurtz, *The Good Story* (London: Vintage, 2016), vii–viii.
42. Paul Ricouer, *On Psychoanalysis* (Cambridge: Polity, 2012), 188–89, 193.
43. John Steinbeck, *Of Mice and Men* (London: Penguin, 1994), 91.
44. Longden, et al., "Shared Reading," 116.
45. See Billington, Farrington, et al., A Comparative Study of Cognitive Behavioural Therapy and Shared Reading for Chronic Pain, 2016, for the source of these extracts.
46. W. R. Bion, *Attention and Interpretation* (London: Maresfield, 1970), 26.
47. Davis and Billington, "A Bolt Is Shot Back Somewhere in the Breast," 283–305.
48. Bion, *Second Thoughts* (London: Maresfield, 1967), 117.
49. Bion, *Learning from Experience* (London: Maresfield, 1962), 57.
50. Bion, *Learning from Experience*, 42, 56–57, 84.
51. Bion, *Attention and Interpretation*, 107.
52. Bion, *Second Thoughts*, 141.
53. Bion, *Attention and Interpretation*, 1–2.
54. Eric Robinson, ed., *John Clare: Major Works* (Oxford: Oxford University Press, 2008), 361.
55. Quoted in Davis and Billington, "A Bolt Is Shot Back Somewhere," 287.
56. Bion, *Learning from Experience*, 116.
57. Davis and Billington, "A Bolt Is Shot Back Somewhere in the Breast," 295.
58. Dorianne Laux, *What We Carry* (Brockport, NY: Boa Editions, 1994), 23.
59. Philip Davis, Fiona Magee, Kremena Koleva, and Thor Mangus Tangeras, "What Literature Can Do," *University of Liverpool: Centre for Research into Reading, Literature and* Society (2016): 25.
60. Laux, *What We Carry*, 23.
61. Dowrick, et al., "Get into Reading as an Intervention for Common Mental Health Problems," 18–19; Longden, et al., "Shared Reading," 117; Billington, Farrington, et al., "A Comparative Study of Cognitive Behavioural Therapy and Shared Reading for Chronic Pain," 2017, 163; Billington, et al., "Developing Innovative Qualitative Approaches in Research on Reading and Health," in *Reading and Mental Health*, 201–02.
62. Billington, et al., "Cultural Value: Assessing the Intrinsic Value of The Reader's Shared Reading Scheme," *University of Liverpool: Centre for Research into Reading, Literature and Society* (2015): 35.
63. Longden et al., "Shared Reading," 119.
64. D. W. Winnicott, *Home Is Where We Start From* (New York: W. W. Norton and Company), 147–49.
65. Winnicott, *Home Is Where We Start From*, 147.
66. Davis, et al., "What Literature Can Do," 38.
67. Matthew Hollis, ed., *Selected Poems of Edward Thomas* (London: Faber, 1964), 36.

68. Hollis, *Selected Poems of Edward Thomas*, 36.
69. Davis, et al., "What Literature Can Do," 39; Josie Billington and Mette Steenberg, Literary Reading and Mental Wellbeing', in Arthur Jacobs and Donald Kuiken, *The Handbook of Empirical Studies of Literature* (Berlin: De Gruyter, 2021), 408.
70. Billington, et al., "Developing Innovative Qualitative Approaches in Research on Reading and Health," in *Reading and Mental Health*, 198–99.
71. Hollis, *Selected Poems of Edward Thomas*, 36.
72. Davis, et al., "What Literature Can Do," 39.
73. Winnicott, *Home Is Where We Start From*, 148.
74. Bion, *Learning From Experience*, 42.
75. Winnicott, *Home Is Where We Start From*, 144.
76. Martha C. Nussbaum, *Upheavals of Thought* (Cambridge: Cambridge University Press, 2001), 271–72.
77. Ricouer, *On Psychoanalysis*, 190.
78. D. W. Winnicott, *Playing and Reality* (London: Tavistock Publications, 1971), 3.
79. Gray, et al., "Making Sense of Mental Health Difficulties," 252–54.
80. Robinson and Billington, "Prison Reading Groups," in *Reading and Mental Health*, 161.
81. David Fearnley and Grace Farrington, "Reading and Psychiatric Practices," and Nick Benefield, "On Not Falling Apart," in *Reading and Mental Health*, ed. Billington, 323–29, 419–31.

PART III

In Sight

10

EMMY WALDMAN

Frames of Mind
Comics and Psychoanalysis in the Visual Field

The visual form of comics has much to teach psychoanalysis about the psychic power of images. As French psychoanalyst Didier Anzieu proclaimed in 1989, squinting over the horizon of the twentieth century, "psychoanalysis has a greater need of people who think in images than of learned scholars, scholiasts, and abstract or formalistic thinkers."[1] We find this proclamation prefacing Anzieu's classic book, *The Skin-Ego*, whose namesake concept – or thought-image – brings the body back to the center of psychoanalytic inquiry by suturing it to the Freudian ego, as a literal "skin for thought." While Anzieu does not mention comics in *The Skin-Ego*, he also wrote the introduction to a literary critical book on one of the most popular European comics of the twentieth century, Belgian cartoonist Hergé's *Adventures of Tintin*.[2] The distinguished psychoanalyst's interest in this particular visual form of mass culture foretells the conjoined fates of psychoanalysis and comics the present chapter seeks to trace. Cartoonists meet Anzieu's "need" in myriad and creative ways, developing the comics form as a medium of thinking in images – images that conjure regions of unconscious feeling inaccessible to language, and open hermetic internal worlds to creator and reader, patient and caretaker alike.

Comics and graphic narratives today are more popular than ever. Accounts of personal and historical traumas that would be difficult to imagine in words alone have been captured throughout the twentieth century in comics form, first and perhaps most notably in Art Spiegelman's still-shocking Holocaust comic book, *Maus*, a combined autobiography and biography that presents the survivor testimony of Spiegelman's father, Vladek, with Jews as mice and Nazis as cats. As a form that captures stories of lived experience for so many, comics is ideally suited to psychoanalytic literary study. This chapter traces the history of repeated encounters and interactions between the discourse of mental healthcare and comics. Now in our own day this form which was so denigrated is gracing the covers of elite journals; educators on both sides of academic campuses bring comics into classroom settings as informational and accessible resources. At the same time, the comics field welcomes a growing number of autobiographical comics and graphic narratives that take up some of the most sobering subjects of mental health and personal as well as social trauma, channeling what cartoonist Justin Green calls the inbuilt "double vision" of the medium – its stereoscopy of pictured action and verbal overlay in thought bubbles, speech balloons, and narrative text boxes – to represent complex, fractured, chaotic, ambiguous, or otherwise hard-to-describe psychic realities.[3] This chapter thus further describes how the turn to visual media as a force for capturing contemporary culture may be understood from a psychoanalytic perspective.

All has not always been well between the psychoanalytic establishment and comics. After World War II, comics responded to the shocking horrors emerging out of Europe with new genres, many geared toward GIs and veterans. Lurid war, crime, and horror stories registered the unmastered anxieties repressed by conformist 1950s high culture. In 1954, psychiatrist Fredric Wertham unleashed his best-seller, *Seduction of the Innocent: The Influence of Comics Books on Today's Youth*, which claimed that comics were turning the nation's youth into illiterate delinquents. On April 21, 1954, a Senate Judiciary subcommittee tasked with investigating the causes of juvenile delinquency summoned Wertham as its star witness. Wertham's testimony was catastrophic for comics. In an effort to forestall government censorship, comics publishers adopted a strict, and sometimes preposterous "self-regulatory" code, including such stipulations as: "in every instance shall good triumph over evil."[4] This Comics Code ended comics' "Golden Age" of unfettered expression and ushered in the "Silver Age" of the superhero.

One title that warrants special mention during this transition into a morally instructive mission for popular comics is *Psychoanalysis*, which restaged the traumas of world history as private psychodrama (1955). Scripted by Daniel Keyes and drawn by Jack Kamen – the same talented artist responsible for EC's bestselling horror, crime, and suspense titles – *Psychoanalysis* advertises stories of "People Searching for Peace of Mind through … PSYCHOANALYSIS," inspired by the personal analyses of Gaines and Feldstein.[5] Each issue documents another week of sessions, following three patients who come through the analyst's revolving door. As the editors themselves acknowledge at the outset of the series, in their editor's note, "Id Bits," the portrait of psychoanalysis made by *Psychoanalysis* takes a number of liberties. Patients move agitatedly about the room; the couch is a prop. The anonymous psychoanalyst *"actively* guides" his patients to their breakthrough insights. Meanwhile, psychosomatic symptoms melt away at the touch of an explanation, so that the treatment arc is telescoped into just four sessions. The handsome psychoanalyst, who bears a striking resemblance to Clark Kent, rewrites the analyst as superhero, or the superhero as analyst: resolving symptoms faster than a speeding bullet, leaping patients' defenses in a single bound. Yet despite its crude stereotypes of psychoanalytic theory and practice – the parents are always to blame – *Psychoanalysis* flirted suggestively with how the comic-book format could be used to portray, graphically and dramatically, the methods of psychoanalysis.

But what is repressed will return; and the cultural unconscious that had gained expression in shocking horror comics took new shape on the coattails of the Code. The repressed unconscious anxieties that horror comics of the 1940s had symptomatically expressed found new expression in the comix underground that emerged in the 1960s and early 1970s. In this period comics stood divided between the mainstream, commercial comics and the self-published or "underground" comics, which were known as "comix" – the "x" indicating their adult, "x-rated" content. An outcropping of the underground left-wing press more generally, the underground comix movement reinvented comics as an "adult" medium. In 1968, Robert Crumb launched the underground movement by peddling his self-published comic book *ZAP* #1 (labeled "Fair Warning: For Adult Intellectuals Only") on Haight Street with his wife; the pair even sold copies to pedestrians out of a baby carriage. Rejecting mainstream commercial standards and strictures, underground comix also rejected "house drawing styles," embracing instead an "auteurist" model of production that went hand-in-hand with the construction of idiosyncratic unconscious worlds. Known for his bulbous, grotesque female forms and a meticulous, tightly controlled line quality, Crumb visualized every sort of sexually perverse, racist, bigoted, materialist fantasy and exorcised his own fears, gripes, and sexual neuroses in stories that seemed to tap directly into the discontents of a generation.[6]

Crumb and his followers in the comix underground set the table for the rise of the "graphic novel," a development relevant to psychoanalysis because the very form was born of a desire to document private, interior states – especially those produced by mental disease.[7] The founding comics narrative that can be considered a "graphic novel," Justin Green's *Binky Brown Meets the Holy Virgin Mary*, communicates the author's own experience of debilitating obsessive-compulsive disorder; in this sense, it anticipates cartoonist Alison Bechdel's visualization of her own childhood OCD in her bestselling *Fun Home* (2006), now a Tony Award-winning Broadway musical.[8] In 1972, Green – whose discovery of a little cartoon by Robert Crumb in a tattered European underground paper had inspired him to abandon a career in painting and join the vital underground comix movement – published the forty-four-page, stand-alone *Binky* on cheap newsprint, through Last Gasp

Eco-Funnies. As Green later recalled, he was driven by "an internal necessity to define the psychic components of a specific condition" for which he had no official diagnosis at the time.[9] (The title ironically stages a hero-meets-villain plot, although the fight is not with the Madonna herself, but rather with Binky's own internal demons.) "With *Binky Brown*," cartoonist Chris Ware observed of McSweeney's deluxe 2009 edition of the book, "comics went practically overnight from being an art form that saw from the outside in to being one that sees from the inside out."[10]

In terms especially pertinent to a discussion of comics form, Green describes his OCD as "a spatial and temporal relationship with Roman Catholic icons, architecture, and doctrine that has been resounding in my life for almost forty years."[11] Comics is a form that produces meaning and causality through the careful arrangement of objects and figures in space, as Hillary Chute has argued in her keen analysis of Green. In this way, comics can map the anxious causal narratives that determine Green's mental landscape, and which coalesce around the position of his own body in a space brimming with phantasmatic threats. Additionally, *Binky* shows how the work of comics itself gains energy from the compulsive spatial preoccupations its pages do not so much purge as refocus and redirect. Against the common notion that making art is "cathartic," an easy purging of difficult emotions – perhaps the psychological counterpart to Catholic confession, as an unburdening of sin – Green suggests that the craft of cartooning offers rather a mode of assimilation, containment, and integration: it requires "the precision of a jeweler along with the fortitude of a cobbler," he writes; it involves placing little pieces together into a multipartite material construction that rebuilds cognitive and emotional meaning.[12]

Binky chronicles Green's childhood struggle with obsessive-compulsive disorder and Catholic guilt in a surreal, allegorical style that allows him to externalize and animate the bizarre, compulsive commands he fights to suppress. In one scene, Binky botches his special way of going down his front stairs: we see his "routine" diagrammed on the steps; in the next panel, the staircase, now with eyes, a mouth, and clutching hands, grabs Binky from behind and yells, "Come back here!" And Binky, who attends a strict Catholic school, obsesses most intensely over the consequences of his "impure" thoughts directed at the Virgin Mary. In the comic, these sexual thoughts radiate as literal "pecker rays" or "penis rays" from his genitals, crisscrossing through space to pierce their sacred objects; the cat's cradle of lines can be seen as a parody of the orderly orthogonals in a linear perspective scheme. The device also puts an ironic twist on the conventional depiction of the Annunciation in Christian art, whereby a single golden ray – usually a delicate line of gold paint – falls across the Virgin, impregnating her. Later, as Binky's obsession morphs and intensifies, the rays begin to project from every appendage. His fingers and toes transform into surreal penises; eventually, even inanimate objects reassemble before his eyes as engorged genitals. The proliferating penis rays visualize preoccupying *thoughts* as *graphic marks*, while underscoring the connection between vision and the body by rendering visual rays as penis rays.[13]

On the introductory splash page, "A Confession to My Readers," Green himself appears with his feet and hands bound, dangling upside down over a scythe positioned right at his crotch, like a needle about to scratch a record.[14] Ave Maria warbles from an old phonograph. Gripping his pen between his teeth, he inscribes a page with the comics boxes we are about to read. The text of his confession is contained in a speech bubble that has been nailed to the wall; the bubble, which bulges with veins, like an engorged penis, states the book's twofold intention: to "purge" the author of his compulsive neurosis; and to use the "easy-to-understand comic book format" to liberate other "tormented souls" from their own neuroses, so as to tie together "all we neurotics" into "a vast chain of common suffering." The image expresses and makes melodramatically literal the double bind of confession – while binding him once more to the Catholic faith he claims to have renounced, Green's comics confession further seems to participate in the compulsive neurosis he would purge (thus the speech bubble becomes a penis). Through the metaphor of the "vast chain of suffering," however, Green suggests how the comics format, through its very power to visualize metaphors, can reach and unite a community of those suffering from "invisible" mental disorders. Green's statement serves as an early "graphic medicine" manifesto.[15]

Comics' visual grammar itself tracks with the visual, fragmentary, and repetitive experience of trauma. It is no accident that such a broad swath of autobiographical graphic novels recount and attempt to account with traumatic experiences and historical traumas. In a crisp definition that has become canonical, Cathy Caruth defines trauma as "precisely to be possessed by an *image* or event" (italics mine).[16] Geoffrey Hartman writes that trauma "seems to have bypassed perception and consciousness, and falls directly into the psyche," where "its exceptional presence" relates to its having been "registered rather than experienced."[17] In comics, too, images seem to sear themselves directly onto the mental retina. Responding to Wertham's attack on comics, Spiegelman notes how the infamous "injury-to-the-eye" motif penetrates to the core of what comics does. "I concede that this isn't Mother Goose," he writes of Plastic Man creator Jack Cole's panel showing a hypodermic needle piercing the protagonist's eye: "but I find the panel (part of a dream sequence, incidentally) emblematic of the comic book's visceral power to pass the reader's analytical defenses and pierce the brain."[18] In a public conversation, Spiegelman further described how the visual domain in comics "has to do with the body – with the things that can't be articulated in other ways."[19]

As a form where the illusion of time is created, or broken, through the juxtaposition of images in space, comics articulates what influential French second generation Freudian André Green calls "eclaté" ("shattered") time – the exploded time of psychic life.[20] Comics frames remain materially and conceptually accessible on the page, in contrast to film, which snatches its frames away at a fixed rate of millimeters per second; for this reason, comics can make profoundly legible the Freudian "hypothesis of the time-lessness of the unconscious, which is nothing more than the timelessness or its traces and cathexes, endowed with mobility."[21] In comics, then, as in the psychoanalytic session itself – steered by the analysand's dream-like, freely associative speech – the tripartition of past/present/future may be represented as a purely present manifestation at any given moment. In comics, as in psychoanalysis, the past is not hidden behind the present; it infiltrates it, giving it modes of organization and its own special character.

The cartoonist who perhaps has revealed this most convincingly is Spiegelman. His memoiristic work consistently explores intergenerational trauma – the impact of his parents' trauma on his own life – and exemplifies how the work of comics relates to psychoanalytic categories of memory and repetition. In the *annus mirabilis* of 1972, Spiegelman produced the first pieces toward his Pulitzer Prize-winning Holocaust comics narrative, *Maus*.[22] *Maus* brought comix out of the underground and into the main-stream as a respectable form. Spiegelman claims that without the personal, confessional mode *Binky* innovated, "there could have been no *Maus*."[23] And at the heart of *Maus*, about his parents' trauma, is Spiegelman's own. Spiegelman's mother, Anja Spiegelman, took her own life in 1968, months after Art himself had been hospitalized for a psychotic breakdown. Spiegelman chronicles his mother's suicide and its immediate aftermath in his 1972 underground comic, "Prisoner on the Hell Planet: A Case History," drawn on scratchboard in a German Expressionist style that seems etched with anger. "Prisoner," originally published in a small underground publi-cation, is reprinted in its entirety at the heart of *Maus I*, where it breaks with the rest of the narrative temporally and stylistically.

The mother's loss is the unfinished business of *Maus*. At the outset of his 2008 experimental comics *kunstlerroman* "Portrait of the Artist as a Young %@%*!" – inspired by his underground-era work, a collection of which Pantheon re-editioned in 2008 – Spiegelman returns to the subject of his mother. "Portrait" opens by conjuring an intriguing sequence of childhood memories that situate maternal loss at the origin of his becoming the cartoonist he became. On the first page of "Portrait," little Art and his mother are playing a popular drawing game: Art makes a scribble – the same spiral that forms the third character in the last "word" of the book title – and hands it to Anja to turn into a representational picture. She compulsively draws another iteration of the "same old face" she always draws: the profile of a thin-lipped woman with closed eyes. She draws an unconscious avatar, who does not (cannot?) return her son's look. Then Anja makes a scribble for Art (random, jaggy – very unlike the smooth and composed spiral of her son). He draws an adorable cartoon duck in a sailor's cap. But Anja is too worried to play further: her husband isn't home yet.[24] The mother-child idyll breaks down: "Breakdowns" is the title of Spiegelman's 1978 underground collection, the cover of which is reproduced alongside the scribble game sequence on the first page. The absorptive moment is ruptured by the mother's creative inhibitions, by the symbolic intrusion of the father, by Anja's own war-haunted past. Here the emotional subtexts shaping the mother-child encounter gain graphic form through their shared production of lines on paper.

The vignette is introduced by two more panel images featuring the spiral scribble: an image of Spiegelman as a vaudeville clown slipping on a banana peel (the spiral figures the motion line of his tumble), and a surreal portrait panel of Spiegelman with the spiral scribble for a face. Each "Portrait" strip begins a portrait cameo of one "face" of the artist, rendered in a different graphic style, which together produce a constantly shifting, kaleidoscopic psychological portrait of the artist in the self-interpretative act – attempting (according to the noir-style voiceover of his midget detective character, Ace Hole) "to locate the traumas that shaped and misshaped him."[25] Here, we see how the scribble Spiegelman's child self makes for the mother to complete gives him his identity as a cartoonist – the cartoonist who is constantly slipping over his own history – even as it destroys his recognizable features. While the looped spiral line is the icon for drunkenness and confusion in the lexicon of comics, as W. J. T. Mitchell tells us, the spiral line or vortex itself has been "the signature of the artist since Apelles and Hogarth, the sign of transformation and empathetic doodling."[26]

This encounter between the young artist and his mother also stages a (suggestively missed) encounter between psychoanalytic theory and comics. British psychoanalyst Donald Winnicott adapted the same popular drawing game into a psychotherapeutic technique for use in initial consultations with his child patients. This game would later be regarded as Winnicott's "most famous technical invention," although the analyst referred to it much more simply – as a game he "liked to play with no rules," or "the squiggle game."[27] "Portrait" becomes a kind of squiggle game the adult artist plays with and by himself, yet which casts the reader in the maternal – and by extension, psychotherapeutic – position. The "active" reader recruited by the participatory comics form turns rough marks into story, dream-residue into meaningful presence. The space of the drawing pad, and the realm of the visual more broadly, is proposed as a powerful, even compulsory site of memory and history-construction – memory and history-construction as moreover collaborative, interlocutionary activities – where the past is preserved but also transformed. The artist's drawing pad offers up a leaden signifier of the past, the unexpurgated spiral – a remnant of former marks and spaces, a lingering gesture (like a motion line etched in the air) – for transformation: "Ha! Turn *THIS* one into something!" says the young "%@&*!" to his mother, and to his adult self.[28]

As the repeating spiral mark itself announces, repetition is central to comics. Repetition carves comics' formal contours and creative procedures. (Spiegelman further highlights this by repeating panels and even whole sequences across the pages of "Portrait," adding different captions or, in the self-reflexive finale, mixing up the colored overlays used to print the panels to turn the images into defamiliarized abstractions.) At the most basic level, to move the story forward, another panel must be drawn and filled. Such a painstaking process of drawing and redrawing can seem almost mad – a form of repetition-compulsion, similar to the urge to repeat in OCD. And yet, comics also repeat to remember and transform; they side with Freudian remembrance, with "working through," over amnesial "acting out."[29] Quoting Jacqueline Rose, Hillary Chute writes that "the encounter between psychoanalysis and artistic practice draws its strength from 'repetition as insistence, that is, as the constant pressure of something hidden but not forgotten – something that can only come into focus now by blurring the fields of representation where our normal forms of self-recognition take place'"[30] Chute argues that comics – especially by women – make this mode of repetition evident, as the "work of (self)-interpretation is literally visualized; the authors show us interpretation as a process of visualization (93)."

The very *panelization* of the comics page implies interpretation, a *nachtraglich* (belated) resignification of past events. Specifically, as the careful selection and curation of moments in frames titrates what can or should be seen, comics requires immense condensations and compressions that cannot happen without some degree of assimilation, of processing. By situating images within a meaningful order, through words and pictures, the comics panel or box (a word evocative of a literal container) itself becomes a therapeutic container for the symbolic repetition of trauma, rather than a vector or agent of traumatization. What Wilfred Bion (1970) calls "containment," similar to what Donald Winnicott calls "holding," refers to the containing environment (originally just the mother) into which elements of the self can be projected and then transformed, given back in a way that solidifies the contours of self and precipitates self-actualization and self-understanding.[31] Containment/holding further provides an apt metaphor for the psychological work performed by the framed, spatial envelope of the comics form, offering perhaps a second psychic skin: a prosthetic extension of Anzieu's skin-ego – a psychic envelope that interfaces with the world. Even so, it is important to recognize that comics is not simply a form of therapy, as cartoonist Lynda Barry is fond of reminding the students who come to her creative workshops. "Therapy is like *this*, and this is very old," she says about the process of drawing.[32]

Another cartoonist who reveals the aptness of comics for psychoanalytic work is Alison Bechdel, the acclaimed author of *Fun Home: A Family Tragicomic* (2006) and *Are You My Mother? A Comic Drama* (2012), the latter of which reflects on Bechdel's relationship with her mother, using Winnicottian theory as an organizational matrix. Both Bechdel and Spiegelman situate filial play, or its traumatic interruption, at the origins of their professional careers. Spiegelman once compared obsessively rewriting the same phrases over and over again – trying to get his father's testimony to fit into the tiny boxes of the comics page – to the hypergraphia of a mental ward inmate (as Spiegelman himself was in 1968). Joking about her own labor-intensive book projects, Bechdel claims that one must be "clinically insane" to be a graphic novelist.[33] In interviews and lectures, the queer cartoonist – who won a MacArthur Foundation "Genius" grant in 2014 for redefining the form of contemporary memoir and expanding the expressive possibilities of the graphic form – characterizes her autobiographical cartooning as a less virulent expression of the OCD that overtook her childhood diary at age eleven, when, petrified of bearing false witness to the people and things she wrote about, she began obliterating her own autobiographical texts, and most vigorously the pronoun "I," with ritualistic symbolic markings. "I do like to describe my drawing process as a barely harnessed obsessive-compulsive disorder," she said in one interview.[34]

When it comes to creating her graphic memoirs, Bechdel follows a very elaborate procedure, one thoroughly textured by repetition. This process includes not only redrawing, by hand, all the archival images exhibited within her pages, but also using her digital camera to set up photographs of herself posing (sometimes in costume!) as all the characters in her narrative, including her past self, and her parents. Though Bechdel blames this technique on "an utter failure of imagination," her fastidiousness is more than a cartoonist's basic fieldwork, gathering reference materials for the accurate rendering of figures in space.[35] She enters the subjectivity, the psyche of her characters by "inhabiting" their gesture and feeling the weight of each pose in her own body. "As I am doing these poses which are really just quick drawing aids, there is a kind of interesting emotional thing that happens as I have to impersonate these characters," she muses. "I would like to think it gives me an emotional intimacy that filters into my drawing. I don't know if that happens, but it is just like I *have* to do it."[36] Putting a name to the "weird acting ability" her writing requires, Bechdel calls herself a "Method cartoonist."[37]

Indeed, Bechdel's "method cartooning" pushes the medium of comics toward theater; it steers narrative toward mimetic imitation. We can see this consilience of comics and theater in the ad hoc genres of the "tragicomic" and the "comic drama," which Bechdel uses to subtitle *Fun Home* and *Are You My Mother?* respectively. The processual basis of Bechdel's comics as a kind of auteurist psychodrama may also shed some light on the success of *Fun Home*'s stage adaptation, which sold-out on Broadway and won multiple Tony Awards. Bechdel's process makes palpable the link between the body and the psyche, indeed the body in the grip of its compulsive repetitions, which Spiegelman had also adumbrated with reference to *Maus*: "it's necessary for me to reenact every single gesture, as well as every single location present in these flashbacks," Spiegelman said.[38] In this sense, Bechdel's emphasis on the gestural body revives the archaic, physiological or somatic idea of "mimesis" evoked by Walter Benjamin. This is the meaning of mimesis defined – put in *play* – by Walter Benjamin in his 1933 essay on the mimetic faculty, which argues that man's ability to perceive likeness is nothing more than the rudiment of a powerful compulsion to imitate and become other.[39] Benjamin's foremost example is that of a child's powerful compulsion to perform similitude to objects: to play at becoming a train, for example. By her own avowal, Bechdel's mimetic comics are skeins of competing instincts. Her role reversals can seem aggressive: efforts to co-opt and seize back agency and control. In this strange, auteurist psychodrama, Bechdel functions as patient-protagonist, doctor-director, and the audience, dramatizing events from her past so as to integrate and control the unmastered feelings contained within them. "I am literally in my basement recreating my childhood," Bechdel said, somewhat sheepish. "But I feel like this is my way to the outside world. And that when I'm writing about my family, my family is like a little country. It is like a little state and I'm trying to ... overthrow it. So it is a kind of political act even as it is very intimate."[40]

The imbrication of the visual image with the very body of the perceiver in Bechdel is key to the jointly political and psychoanalytic labor her work performs. Bechdel renders all the materials she reproduces from her family

198

archives – photographs, newspaper clippings, childhood drawings, a gorgeous, illustrated page from Dr. Seuss – with painstaking realism, contrasting with the simplified contours she deploys elsewhere in her books. This "mimetic" style of rendering is itself crucially related to touch. Beyond the fact that Bechdel often figures her own hands holding the documents she copies, fine linear hatching is schooled by touch; it models the topography of a sensory surface, the ridges, wrinkles, and folds. "I often feel, when I'm drawing," Bechdel said, in terms resonant with Anzieu's "skin-ego,"

> that the line I'm making on the paper is a way of touching the people and things I'm drawing ... The paper is like skin. And when you're drawing comics, you have to physically touch every square inch of every page you're working on. That feels really different from writing. It's possible for a novelist to write a whole book and never really touch the paper.[41]

Whether "behind the scenes," in the basement studio of her Vermont home, "recreating her childhood," as she puts it, or rather through the optical tactility of drawing, in her staging of the space of the printed page, Bechdel's mimetic performances are ways of contacting – of being in touch with – the things she copies.

Early in *Are You My Mother?*, Bechdel reproduces a fascinating sequence of snapshots of herself as a three-month-old infant being held by her mother (Figure 10.1). This photographic sequence, a series of five or six snapshots all seemingly taken in a single sitting – but then scattered across various boxes and albums – seems to capture the genesis of Alison's mimetic practices: her mother is cooing at her, and she is precisely mirroring the shape of her mother's mouth. Later in her book, in the chapter entitled "Mirror," which deals with the psychoanalytic figure of the mirror from Lacan to Winnicott, Bechdel delves into a theory that helps us grasp what is happening in this filial mirroring play. Winnicott's late paper on the "mirror-role" of the mother in early child development evolves his earlier, instinct-based model of holding (the infant at breast) into one rooted in the visual field: Winnicott writes that the mother's ability to reflect back what she sees in her child's face – her ability to give the child the sense that she or he is seen (and therefore exists) – is essential for the development of the child's self. From this perspective, Bechdel's mirroring play with her mother illustrates the relational context within which the self is formed.

But it also illustrates something else being formed: a graphic narrative. In her voiceover, Bechdel observes that there is no way of knowing the photographs' order without the sheet negatives, which she does not have. So she constructs her own order. This is itself deeply psychoanalytic work:

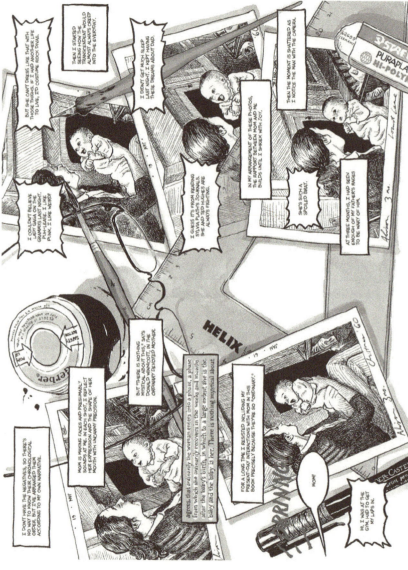

Figure 10.1 Double Spread from *Are You My Mother? A Comic Drama* by Alison Bechdel. Copyright © 2012 by Alison Bechdel. Reprinted by permission of Houghton Mifflin Harcourt Publishing Company. All rights reserved.

"by transforming the past into a history," writes Christopher Bollas, "the psychoanalyst creates a series of densely symbolic stories ... generating constant and continuous associations."⁴² Here, Bechdel gathers the scattered, disconnected fragments of the sequence together and arranges them – top-down, left-right, according to the conventions of western reading – across one arresting, full-bleed, double-page spread. Instead of a page of comics panels, we see the photographs, grouped in pristine disarray, covering a meticulously drawn, trompe l'oeil ("fool the eye") tableau of Bechdel's working space, nested with the assembled tools and props of the cartoonist's trade: a helix triangle, ink – in a Gerber baby food jar! – a brush and fountain pen, a pair of glasses, and a rubber eraser. Rather than fetishize these photos by placing them together in some gilt-covered photo album, Bechdel shows us the creative, haptic memory-work she performs with and around them as the work of comics. In fact, Bechdel turns these photos into a species of comic, or proto-comic – the very seed of the text we are reading: on this unconventional page, the photographs serve as panels, with the white borders around the images as gutters.

The arrangement further functions as a psychoanalytic allegory, casting Alison and her mother in the universal roles of mother and infant. It is a parable of the child's premature transition from pre-oedipal unity to triangular oedipal conflict. Through her comics, as in the après-coup of an analysis – the deferred action of attributing meaning, often traumatic meaning, to the past – Bechdel reconstructs and gives meaning to this archaic moment of rupture. As she tells it, the baby's delight builds and builds, until suddenly she becomes aware of the presence of her father, offstage, with the camera, and the moment is ruined. Bechdel concludes the sequence with a shot of baby Alison staring warily out over her mother's shoulder at cameraman and reader alike, mouth pursed up into a worried little "o." Here, the unpredictable figure of the father disrupts ("shatters," like a mirror?) the visual encounter which is formative of the self.

As in the opening episode of Spiegelman's "Portrait," the father's entrance puts an end to the filial play and interferes with the basic experience of parental holding. "The picture of me looking at the camera feels like a picture of the end of my childhood," Bechdel laments.⁴³ All the self-censorship and doubt (her analyst calls it "undoing") that plagues Bechdel as an adult cartoonist seems to enter the picture in the little rubber eraser at the bottom right of the page. But at the same time and on another level, the trauma of this interference assumes the quality of a "primary scene" in Bechdel's professional development. Like the memoir of which it is the germ, the narrative of the photos is a "comic drama," in the sense that it has, as *Maus* has, a qualified happy ending, a "happy, happy ever after."

Similar to Spiegelman's *Maus*, *AYMM* is a story of survival, which performs the life instinct as the quest not so much for the mother, but for the self. It is no accident that the ink pot is a Gerber baby food jar. Bechdel feeds herself as well as her pen with her ink. Recreating what Winnicott would call the "environment-mother,"[44] the physical and psychic care, originally condensed on the mother, that envelops the infant, Bechdel wrests care and cure from the comics' material form. Making comics becomes a form of visual incorporation, a drinking-in with the eyes, related to the gustatory feed. "If I'd had different parents," Bechdel mused,

> I would probably not have needed to write these books about my parents. But I'm glad I had the parents I did, I'm grateful for all the ways that they both oppressed and nurtured me as an artist, and I'm glad I've been able to climb out from underneath their thumbs.[45]

Commenting on the comic strip that made her name as a cartoonist, *Dykes to Watch Out For*, about the daily lives of a group of lesbian friends, Bechdel claimed that her motivation to make work comes from her sense of lacking "an accurate reflection" in the "cultural mirror."[46] She did not see popular images of lesbians like her; so, in *Dykes*, she created her own. In *AYMM*, Bechdel reflects on the psychology of the act of reflection itself, exploring how not seeing a reflection of herself in her childhood home led her to become the particular autobiographical cartoonist she became. Originally, Bechdel had thought to write about the relationship of the self to the other in the abstract, using her love life; then, helped along by her discovery of object-relations theory, and Winnicott especially, she saw how her relationship with her mother was the paradigm for her relationship with her analysts, as well as for her romantic attachments. In the text that overlaps this double page, Bechdel reflects on her decision to include her daily phone conversations with her mother within the book. Like the psychoanalyst, who finds tendentious meaning in the psychopathologies of everyday life, she observes the "transcendent" within the everyday. This is to see, finally, how the personal can transcend itself to become universal: how Bechdel's story can hold a mirror to her readers.

The past two decades have seen a dramatic uptick in comics that address topics of mental illness. These titles – by and for those suffering from mental disabilities, as well as those who treat them – continue to expand the horizons of literature and of psychoanalysis in productive ways. *New Yorker* cartoonist Jason Katzenstein's graphic memoir, *Everything is An Emergency* confronts Katzenstein's OCD.[47] This honest, often hilarious book once more reveals the fraught and multidimensional connection between comics and forms of compulsive behavior: Katzenstein's book grew out of his Exposure Response Prevention (ERP) therapy. Its pages were drawn in the interval between an anxiety-producing exposure – such as touching his shoe and then his face – and the performance of a compulsive ritual – washing up. This charged space between exposure and response can be thought of as a metaphorical gutter, a space of constitutive absence that interrupts the narrative of emergency "written" by Katzenstein's disorder. Katzenstein's comics-making, which began as a stop-gap measure to hold off a compulsion, opens a space where his disorder's inexorable causal narrative of emergency can be deconstructed, unwoven, figured otherwise – and where the compulsion to make meaning can be rerouted. Crucially, Katzenstein describes his book as an outgrowth of the group therapy that held him accountable throughout his treatment. In fact, he narrates his story *to* but also *for* – on behalf of – a community of fellow sufferers, making their invisible suffering visible and legible. At the height of an international pandemic, as the health of the world depends on our empathetic imagination, the so-called "art of the empathetic doodle,"[48] as Chris Ware put it, may be more important now than ever.

Notes

1. Didier Anzieu, *The Skin-Ego*, trans. Naomi Segal [Originally published as *Le Moi-peau*, Paris, 1995] (London: Karnac, 2016), 6. On the "skin-ego" in comics, see Vera J. Camden, "'Cartoonish Lumps': The Surface Appeal of Alison Bechdel's 'Are You My Mother?,'" *The Journal of Graphic Novels and Comics* 9, no. 1 (January 2018): 93–111.
2. Didier Anzieu, "Essai sur la création graphique et la mis en scène de ses enjeux dans l'œuvre d'Hergé" in *Tintin Chez le Psychanalyste* (Paris: Aubier, 1985).
3. Justin Green, "Afterword," in *Binky Brown Meets the Holy Virgin Mary* (San Francisco: McSweeney's, 2009), 51–63.
4. For a comprehensive discussion of the history of the code and its disastrous consequences for comics, see Amy Kiste Nyberg, *Seal of Approval: The History of the Comics Code* (Jackson: University of Mississippi Press, 1998), 166.
5. For a discussion of the history of the *Psychoanalysis* comics, see Valentino L. Zullo, "Keeping Horror in Mind: Psychoanalysis and the 'New Direction' of EC Comics," *The Journal of Popular Culture* 54, no. 4 (2021): 868–90. As EC editor Al Feldstein told interviewer Steve Ringgenberg, "*Psychoanalysis*, which Bill [Gaines] and I had come up with as part of our 'New Direction' after we were censored out of the horror because we had both been going. I was in analysis and he was in analysis. It was the '50s thing to do when you had a little money and you had problems." Steve Ringgenberg "An Interview with Al Feldstein," *The Comics Journal* 177 (May 1995): 90.
6. See Chute, *Why Comics*, 95–108.
7. "Graphic novel" was born of publishing and marketing copy; but the term has become the most widely recognized name for any expressive, long-form graphic narrative that exists between book-covers.

8. The first book to proclaim itself a "graphic novel" was Will Eisner's *A Contract with God*, which bore the words "a graphic novel" on the cover. Published by Baronet Press in 1978, *A Contract with God* tells of poor Jewish immigrants in a series of four interlocking vignettes.

9. Justin Green, "Binky Brown Meets the Holy Virgin," *Justin Green's Binky Brown Sampler* (San Francisco: Last Gasp, 1995), 8.

10. Cited in Chute, *Why Comics*, 211.

11. Green quoted in Chute, *Why Comics*, 253.

12. Green quoted in Chute, ibid., 254.

13. Justin Green, *Binky Brown Meets the Holy Virgin Mary* (San Francisco: McSweeney's 2009).

14. Green, *Binky Brown Meets the Holy Virgin Mary*, 1.

15. The recent international "graphic medicine" movement, founded by an interdisciplinary community of academics, healthcare providers, authors, artists, and fans of comics and medicine, explores the interaction between the medium of comics and the discourse of healthcare, broadly conceived. In 2015's *Graphic Medicine Manifesto*, the inaugural volume in the Graphic Medicine series published through Penn State University Press, six doctors, nurses, and professors map the growing field of graphic medicine in scholarly essays and visual narratives. Comics that fall under the "graphic medicine" umbrella include narratives by patients that depict the complex, subjective experience of illness, as well as comics by and for doctors and nurses about patient care and medical education.

16. Cathy Caruth, *Trauma: Explorations in Memory* (Cambridge, MA: Harvard University Press, 1995), 4–5.

17. Geoffrey H. Hartman, "On Traumatic Knowledge and Literary Studies," *New Literary History* 26 no. 3 (Summer 1995): 537.

18. Art Spiegelman, "Forms Stretched to Their Limits," *The New Yorker* (April 19, 1999).

19. W. J. T. Mitchell and Art Spiegelman, "Public Conversation: What the %$&# Happened to Comics?" in Hillary Chute and Patrick Jagoda, eds., *Comics and Media* (a special issue of *Critical Inquiry*) (Chicago: University of Chicago Press, Spring 2014), 20–35.

20. André Green, *Time in Psychoanalysis: Some Contradictory Aspects*, trans. by Andrew Weller [Orig. pub. as Le Temps eclaté [Cairn International, 2000] (London: Free Association Books, 2002).

21. Green, 11.

22. Art Spiegelman, *Maus I: A Survivor's Tale: My Father Bleeds* History (New York: Pantheon, 1986); Spiegelman, *Maus II A Survivor's Tale: And Here My Troubles Began* (New York: Pantheon, 1992).

23. Art Spiegelman, "Introduction," *in Binky Brown Meets the Holy Virgin Mary*, by Justin Green (San Francisco: McSweeney's, 2009), n.p.

24. Art Spiegelman, *Breakdowns: Portrait of the Artist as a Young %@&*!* (New York: Pantheon, 2008), n.p.

25. Spiegelman, *Breakdowns*, n.p.

26. W. J. T. Mitchell, "Comics as Media: An Afterword," *Comics & Media*, 270.

27. Adam Phillips, *Winnicott* (Cambridge, MA: Harvard University Press, 1988); D. W. Winnicott, "The Squiggle Game" (1968), in Winnicott, *Psychoanalytic*

Explorations, eds. Clare Winnicott, Ray Shepherd, and Madeleine Davis (London: Karnac Books, 1989), 301–02 (Phillips, 15; Winnicott, 301–02).

28. Spiegelman, *Breakdowns,* n.p.

29. See Sigmund Freud, "Remembering, Repeating, and Working Through" (1914), *SE* 12: 145–56.

30. Hillary Chute, *Graphic Women: Life Narrative and Contemporary Comics* (Columbia University Press, 2010), 20–21 (228).

31. See D. W. Winnicott, *Playing and Reality* (London: Tavistock, 1971): W. R. Bion, *Learning from Experience* (London: Karnac Books, 1984).

32. Dan Kois, "Lynda Barry Will Make You Believe in Yourself," *The New York Times Magazine,* October 27, 2011.

33. Margot Harrison, "Life Drawing," *Seven Days,* June 1, 2006.

34. "Video of Alison Bechdel," HoughtonMifflinBooks.com. www.houghtonmifflin books.com/booksellers/press_release/bechdel/#video

35. Harrison, "Life Drawing."

36. "Public Conversation, May 19, 2012: Alison Bechdel and Hillary Chute," *Comics & Media,* 203–19, 218.

37. Harrison, "Life Drawing"; Bechdel again describes her "method cartooning" in Lydia Polgreen. "Alison Bechdel Misses Feeling Special," *New York Times Magazine,* May 13, 2015.

38. *Art Spiegelman: Conversations,* ed. Joseph Witek (Jackson, Mississippi: University Press of Mississippi, 2007), xiv.

39. Walter Benjamin, "On the Mimetic Faculty," in *Selected Writings, 1926–1934,* trans. by Rodney Livingstone and others, eds. Michael W. Jennings, Howard Eiland, and Gary Smith (Cambridge, MA: Belknap Press, 1999).

40. Alison Bechdel and Hillary Chute, "Public Conversation," *Comics & Media,* 218.

41. Hillary Chute, *Outside the Box: Interviews with Contemporary Cartoonists* (University of Chicago Press, 2014), 179.

42. Christopher Bollas, "The Functions of History," in *The Christopher Bollas Reader* (London: Routledge, 2011), 134.

43. Bechdel, *Are You My Mother?,* 45. For further discussions of these images and the concept of the psychoanalytic allegory, see Vera J. Camden, "Alison Bechdel's Mystic Muse: A Psychoanalytic Allegory," in *The Muse: Psychoanalytic Explorations of Creative Inspiration* (New York: Routledge, 2016), 229–74.

44. D. W. Winnicott, "The Development of the Capacity for Concern" in *The Maturational Processes and the Facilitating Environment: Studies in the Theory of Emotional Development* (London: Hogarth Press and the Institute of Psycho-Analysis), 75–78.

45. Alison Bechdel, *Outside the Box* 185.

46. See Alison Bechdel, *The Indelible Alison Bechdel: Confessions, Comix, and Miscellaneous Dykes to Watch Out For* (Firebrand Books, 1998), 209.

47. Jason Adam Katzenstein, *Everything Is An Emergency* (New York: Harper, 2020).

48. Chris Ware, *Comics: Philosophy and Practice Poster* (Chicago: University of Chicago Conference, 2012).

11

ELLEN HANDLER SPITZ

Psychoanalysis and Children's Literature
Spotlighting the Dialogue

I

With the goal of stimulating further imaginative exchange, this chapter lightly examines several contributions to the well-established interdisciplinary dialogue between psychoanalysis and children's literature.[1] For our purposes, children's literature is stipulated here to include references to literature written about as well as for children. A possible first category of dialogue that springs to mind is interpretation and criticism. Handled knowledgeably, skillfully, and delicately, psychoanalysis has been used with profit by critics when interpreting children's books. A wealth of knowledge[2] based on decades of theory, infant research, and clinical experience has illuminated children's books and been brought to bear on them in a variety of ways. Pioneer Bruno Bettelheim (1976) will serve as prime exemplar. Second, when psychoanalysis is directly experienced as treatment, it can play the muse to authors and artists of children's books.

Maurice Sendak's oeuvre stands as a notable testament here. In a third type of exchange, we might reverse direction so that psychoanalysis becomes the recipient rather than the source of influence. Let's picture psychoanalysis in the student's seat, astride Mark Hopkins's legendary log, while the opposite place is occupied by a children's book or books, functioning as teacher.[3] In this version of the interdisciplinary dialogue, clinical work and psychoanalytic understanding stand to benefit from children's literature rather than the other way around. Beatrix Potter and Elena Ferrante will serve to illustrate this type of encounter.

All of the above negotiations risk going awry because of overarching claims, misconceptions, or reductionism, the latter being the steel trap and cardinal sin of applied psychoanalysis. These are normal risks, however, whenever we juxtapose fields that are related but different in their aims, contents, histories, and language. Nonetheless, as Freud[4] averred in 1908, the insights of creative writers (and artists) offer rich bounty to psychoanalysts, just as psychoanalysts bring unique lenses to authors whose literary pursuits concern our inner lives, be it those of adults or children.

The very notion of a child's inner life, however, brings us up short when we consider that our forebears did not understand childhood as we do. It took centuries in the west to realize that children actually have psyches with wishes, fears, and judgments and are born neither tabula rasa[5] nor miniature adults.[6] From ancient Egypt and Mesopotamia, from the Graeco-Roman and the Judeo-Christian worlds, through the Middle Ages, and up to the dawn of early modern Europe, little material evidence of children's actual lives survives. We have a dearth of documentation concerning children's activities or products. The ancients and the medievals kept nothing made by children and almost nothing made for children; such items were deemed inconsequential. Children's stories, children's drawings, and children's play, all of which have become contemporary subjects of interest and scholarly research as well as of exhibitions and collections, suffered centuries of neglect.[7] Today's assumptions that children evolve developmentally along circuitous internal and external paths of interwoven cognitive, emotional, and social experience with strong emotions and acute perceptions replace centuries of disinterest. My caveat here is that the age-old cultural dismissal of childhood continues to underlie what is now taken, nominally, for granted. This being so, psychoanalysis, with its aim of probing the psyche at all stages of human life, has an indispensable part to play.

Just to illustrate and complicate this picture, I would like to cite two contrasting thirteenth-century fabliaux from what we now call northwest France. Fabliaux are short comic medieval tales written in Old French. Almost never do they mention children.

L'Enfant noif,[8] however, tells of a woman seduced by priest when her merchant husband is away on a long journey. Eventually, she gives birth to a child and, when her unsuspecting husband returns, he questions her. The baby, she explains, came from a melting snowflake. The husband says nothing but, scheming to get rid of the bastard, he bides his time. When the boy (who is given no voice whatsoever in the story) reaches age fifteen, the husband takes him away, presumably to teach him his trade, but sells him into slavery in Sicily and returns home to inform his wife that, in a heat wave, the boy melted away. Thus, the story typifies the use of a child as a prop, as chattel, as the butt of humor, with no subjectivity or agency, not to mention any inner life.

Let's fast forward now to the twentieth century and consider the psychoanalytically modulated work of Alice Miller. Miller, in several persuasive and highly influential books,[9] describes a poignant syndrome in which children are treated by their parents as mere narcissistic projections, devoid of their own volition. In Miller's descriptions, we may discern an elaborated afterlife of this age-old mode of (dis)regarding childhood and seeing the child as an object.

A second fabliau indicates a far rarer strand in the cultural tapestry. *De celui qui bota la pierre*[10] tells of another lubricious priest, who visits a pretty woman when her husband is away, in this case, tilling the fields. She welcomes the prelate seductively and kicks a large stone in the yard, whereupon the priest declares that if she does that again he will f**k her. She does so, and he does so. By the hearth, a toddler watches as the priest jumps on his mother and they tussle. After the priest is gone, the husband returns and stoops in the yard to move the stone. The child cries out: Papa, do not do that, for the priest will return and do to you what he did to Mama before. Thus, here, we see, contrastingly, a rare and genuine engagement with a child's mind. This fabliau, we might say, actually foreshadows Freud's claim that adult sexual intercourse is interpreted by small children as frightening and unwanted aggression.

While early modern and Enlightenment authors engaged to an extent with childhood, Rousseau's *Émile* of 1762 being perhaps the outstanding example,[11] it was the early nineteenth century, with Wordsworth's lyrical poems[12] on subjective experience in boyhood and continuing through nineteenth-century Romanticism,[13] on into the twentieth century, that recognized the child's mind as a serious subject worthy of study. Thus, the actual study of childhood began to emerge from prior relative obscurity. Seminal work by such figures as psychologist Jerome Bruner,[14] building on earlier pioneering studies by Jean Piaget,[15] claimed that even the youngest children construct their own mental worlds.

Psychoanalysis appeared on the horizon between Romanticism and the advent of cognitive developmental psychology, and it started with an understanding of children based entirely on projections backward in time on the part of adults.[16] This understanding, which initially focused exclusively on psychosexual development, came from memories and fantasies reported by Freud's adult patients during treatment. Shortly, child psychoanalytic work with case studies was undertaken, albeit not by Freud. Freud's colleagues and followers, including Hermine Hug-Hellmuth, Anna Freud, Melanie Klein, D. W. Winnicott, Margaret S. Mahler, René Spitz, and Erik Erikson,[17] among others, contributed over the first three quarters of the twentieth century an enduring legacy of rich theoretical material. It would be no exaggeration to say that their contributions, taken en masse, opened the eyes not only of the discipline of psychology per se but of the public at large. Now the luminous, intricate, sometimes terrifying landscapes and dreamscapes that comprise children's inner worlds began to be scrutinized – a terrain that had already been visited in literary form over a century before, in poems and novels.

It was psychologist Bruno Bettelheim who, as mentioned above, took psychoanalysis in hand like spade and used it to unearth buried truffles of meaning in the centuries-old European fairy tales of his youth.[18]

II

Bruno Bettelheim's[19] award-winning book *The Uses of Enchantment* (1976) claims that fairy tales (he is particularly concerned with the multiply edited volumes compiled by the Grimm Brothers of Kassel, Germany)[20] present life's existential dilemmas in simplified form. Assuming, erroneously, that these tales were intended principally for the education and edification of children, Bettelheim writes about them as if they were hidden guides to child psychology. He reads them as symbolic displacements of core issues in child development. Overreaching in his zeal and never hesitant, Bettelheim occasionally trumpets interpretations that strain credulity. His ideas, consequently, have been satirized as flagrant examples of psychoanalytic dogmatism. I find those judgments harsh. An example of one of his more far-fetched notions is his assertion that the mutilation of Cinderella's sisters' feet (a savagery promulgated by their monomaniacal mother in order to make them fit the iconic slipper) should be interpreted as a form of female castration. Other insights of Bettelheim's, on the other hand, hit the bull's-eye. His interpretation, for example, of Little Red Riding Hood as a young girl on the cusp of reluctant and ambivalent sexual awakening, new to the excitements and anxieties of heterosexual desire, seems just right. Bettelheim believes that exposure to fairy tales can actually enable children to work through their anxieties and, therefore, promote emotional growth. He bases his interpretations on Freudian theory exclusively but tempered by his own clinical experience; he served from 1944 to 1973 as Director of the Orthogenic School at the University of Chicago.

Prominent literary scholar Marina Warner[21] accords Bettelheim considerable respect, whereas, Jack Zipes,[22] another leading expert in the field, is more wary. My view is that Bettelheim merits high praise for his groundbreaking volume, which set in motion one important strand of the interdisciplinary dialogue under consideration here. His attunement to intrapsychic conflict and above all his staunch refusal to deny close attention to the darker aspects of the tales he analyzes tales stands as a bulwark against contemporary childhood educators, who would sanitize children's cultural lives and "protect" them from malice by showering them with trivia and banality. Malice haunts the fairy tales, as it does life, and Bettelheim, to his credit, holds that for children to encounter it safely displaced in stories may serve them well in the future. Arguing for this, he brings to mind the work of psychoanalytically informed child psychologist Selma Fraiberg, whose landmark book of 1959, *The Magic Years*, makes similar claims. Let's take an example. In the Grimm Brothers' 1812 volume of tales, an unwise friendship between a cat and a mouse ends by the cat deceiving the mouse and eating her. This plot occurs, as well, in the fables both of Aesop and La Fontaine and, with species altered, in a Russian version, where a scorpion stings a frog who foolishly carries him across a river, thereby causing them both to drown, since, as the scorpion confesses before expiring, it is in the nature of a scorpion to sting. Neither Bettelheim nor Fraiberg would deny children access to these tales because they portray valuable truths. Candor grounds Bettelheim's analyses, and his psychoanalytic refusal of pablum is as valuable for adults today as it is for children.

Bettelheim insists, furthermore, with sensitivity to both psychic and aesthetic experience, that it would be wrong to "explain" to children the symbolism implicit in fairy tales or indeed, in any of their storybooks. Like Bruner, mentioned above, who taught that children construct their own worlds, Bettelheim knows that children must generate their own interpretations and that these will evolve as they do.[23] He insists, moreover, that to "explain" a story is to rob it of the mystery essential to its appeal. A seasoned psychoanalyst, similarly, knows not to jump the gun by interpreting rather than allowing insights to emerge over time from a patient's own evolving comprehension.

What Bettelheim does not see clearly, I think, is how his own manner, often quite ham-handed and doctrinaire, tells against the value of his offerings. Like premature interpretations, which he would be the first to deplore, his dicta can seem off-putting to his readers and result therefore in resistance. This observation may serve as a gentle caveat to other psychoanalytic critics who would speak to a general audience. Reticence, the use of qualifying modifiers, and a dash of humility may help disarm defenses and allow kernels of truth to be absorbed.

Bettelheim, without a doubt, would have disapproved of and probably scorned contemporary attempts to soften and refashion fairy tales according to today's "politically correct" rubrics. One example of this practice is *The True Story of Rumpelstiltskin*,[24] in which child readers are mollycoddled. To keep them from fearing or loathing the eponymous baby-stealing trickster dwarf, this psychologically naïve picture book cooks up a sentimental backstory meant to make children sympathize with and pity its title character. The results, predictably, are disastrous. The plot is undermined and all thrill is siphoned off. What was once the mesmerizing edge-of-your-seat tale of Rumpelstiltskin crumples like a popped balloon. Psychoanalysis helps explain why: the exquisitely playful pleasures of safe mastery over virtual dangers have been obliterated.

III

Maurice Sendak, like a number of other paragons in the pantheon of children's literature (Hans Christian Andersen, Lewis Carroll, Robert Louis Stevenson, J. M. Barrie, Beatrix Potter, P. L. Travers, C. S. Lewis, and Margaret Wise Brown), was childless. For inspiration, Sendak drew on a bygone childhood of his own, which festered within his mind, raw and accessible.[25] That childhood, which began in 1928, was spent in marginal health, in a Brooklyn Jewish/Sicilian neighborhood, with ravaged working-class immigrant parents whose efforts were spent rescuing overseas Polish Jewish relatives from the impending doom of World War II. Sendak translated this childhood gradually into books, which, particularly in the decades from 1960 to 1981, galvanized the field of late-twentieth century American children's literature. He laid bare authentic features of childhood that had previously been ignored, denied, or papered over. His art opened floodgates that, by now, have been almost thoroughly broken through. What Sendak let in were the dark fantasies and quintessential loneliness of childhood.

Just previous to and during Sendak's creation of his most psychologically penetrating and successful as well as controversial books, he was undergoing psychoanalytic treatment.[26] That this pivotal experience failed to impact his work would be hard to believe. For obvious reasons of confidentiality, the impact cannot be proven, but we can unwaveringly infer it. Sendak knew and was able to represent the profound sense in which every child, from time to time, perceives himself to be alone – an outsider – and feels the need to retreat into some private space, some nook, or secret hiding place, which are precisely what Sendak's books themselves provide for certain children. His books can function as such even when being read aloud by an adult. His gifts as artist and writer, informed – as I am claiming – by psychoanalysis, led him to discover pictorial as well as narrative means of portrayal. Furthermore, we must add, for historical context, Sendak's recognition and revelation of childhood subjectivity coincided with the very decades when American psychoanalysis was enjoying its heyday.[27]

Let's engage briefly with Sendak's trilogy: *Where the Wild Things Are* (1963),[28] *In the Night Kitchen* (1970), and *Outside Over There* (1981). Their protagonists, Max, Mickey, and Ida are child characters who exist within solitary psychic worlds, and at the end of their stories they remain isolated and apart. All three, at least momentarily, feel misunderstood, unrecognized, and insufficiently loved. Before Sendak's revolution, such dystonic feelings had rarely been explored – certainly not overtly – in the pages of a picture book. Yet, these feelings are experienced by even the most cherished child; for who has not suffered, now and then, the emotional unavailability of one or both parents?

In *Where the Wild Things Are*, Max's mother (who, like Kafka's insect,[29] is never depicted and is thus a fertile field for projection) grows angry at him for his naughtiness and sends him to bed without supper. In *In the Night Kitchen*, Mickey's parents are presumably together in their own room and unresponsive when he hears the "racket" that angers him: "QUIET DOWN THERE!" he shouts. In *Outside Over There*, Ida's father is away at sea, and her depressed mother ignores both her and a baby sister. In each story, as the plot unfolds, Sendak limits his child protagonist's sensibility such that he or she remains solely within a world of private fantasy.

As we follow the trajectories and dénouements of each of these stories, we note the theme of escape: Max sails away; Mickey flies away; Ida turns away and vanishes out a window. When each fantasy ends, we are reassured – perhaps not very believably – that things are fine now. Max's dinner is there, even though he and his mother have not reestablished any direct communication. Mickey is carefree and dry in his bed even though he is still clueless about the noise that upset him and kept him awake in the dark.

Ida's papa loves her still, even though it is not certain he is still alive, and his letter has charged her to take care of her mom and baby sister indefinitely. To accompany each of these "benign" endings, Sendak provides imagery that silently undercuts it: Max has food, true, but no suggestion of his mother's arms or smile. Mickey appears smug, hugging his bottle solipsistically to himself. Ida, in profile, wiggles her big bare feet, fondles strands of her own hair; she wears a distracted expression as though words about her bravery fail to move her.

Estrangement lies at the heart of Sendak's legacy. By leaving his protagonists alone (Johnny and Pierre from *The Nutshell Library*[30] belong here too), Sendak assures his child readers that they are not alone. Children who enter the realms of his picture books find understanding, and, in that important sense, they are not wholly disconnected or lost. When it works, each book creates, borrowing Winnicott's term, a viable holding environment.[31]

Sendak was edited by Ursula Nordstrom, the formidable doyenne of American children's literature during her reign as Editor in Chief of juvenile literature at Harper and Brothers (now Harper Collins). Nordstrom discovered Sendak, promoted his work, and fought fiercely with him, as she did with all her authors, over details. In *Where the Wild Things Are*,[32] Max returns to his room to find his dinner "was still hot," but Nordstrom rejected that line.[33] She argued it would be more plausible to say, "it was still warm."

Sendak dug in. "'Warm' doesn't burn your tongue," he countered. "There is something dangerous in 'hot.'" Sendak, of course, won. His gut conviction of the rightness of "hot" smacks of psychoanalytic attunement. A mother's love can remain constant, but it cannot be pure – unmixed with the possibility of displeasure and anger. There is an intimation here also that, while Max's "hot" anger has abated; it can easily recrudesce. "Hot" vibrates with ambivalence. Sizzling and discordant, it ends Sendak's best book with panache.

IV

If psychoanalysis can, in turn, learn from children's literature, many teachers spring to mind. Our first is Beatrix Potter, whose astonishing fame burst suddenly upon her with *The Tale of Peter Rabbit* (1902). Potter, born in 1866, was the shy, lonely daughter of well-to-do London parents. London publisher Frederick Warne, following the wild success of Helen Bannerman's *Little Black Sambo*, published by a rival house in 1899, itched to surpass it. He hesitated but finally accepted the unknown Potter's first effort, her *The Tale of Peter Rabbit*. It proved a runaway hit. Potter had modeled her title character on a pet rabbit called Peter Piper, who was familiar to Noel Moore, the son of her former governess and first recipient of the story in letter form. Curious, greedy, disobedient, clever, and irresistibly lovable, Peter Rabbit dwells under a fir tree dangerously close to Mr. McGregor's garden, in which his hapless father had perished.

Partly to undo that trauma, Peter, in a sky-blue jacket with brass buttons, pursues an ill-starred raid on Mr. McGregor's vegetable garden. Surviving just barely, he pops up again in Potter's later tales, for after the success of Peter, she continued writing, occasionally producing two books a year. In cousin Benjamin's story, Peter manifests considerably less bravado for, as children quickly discover, timidity often follows terror.

Potter's thirty-odd books, most of them scaled to a 4"× 6" format for small hands to hold, are sparing of word. They feature a limned pantheon of named, speaking, dressed-up mice, pigs, ducks, frogs, fox, badger, and rabbits all delicately rendered in pastel water colors and ink. Translated into more than thirty languages, they are said to be among the best-selling children's books of all time.

What can Potter teach psychoanalysis? What is it about her work that confers its staying power? Not mere charm and artistry. Nor can we chalk it up to canny commercialism as years went by. A staunch realism pervades it: an unsentimental, clear-eyed approach to life that gives her pages an emotional kick far beyond the pretty fancies of her compatriots Randolph

Caldecott and Kate Greenaway. Wise, unflinching truth is what grabs children, and Potter dishes it out. She toys, moreover, with the uncanny.[34]

Real and surreal, her painstakingly observed lake shores, gardens, and country interiors are sites of rebellion. Children get it. Potter punts hard-hitting lessons ensorcelled from the constraints of her own family life, her intimacy with nature's indifference, and the bruising hypocrisies of Victorian society. We should, however, notice how the tenderness and delicacy of her pastel-colored illustrations of acutely observed animals and scenes serve to mitigate harshness and to render her characters both appealing and emotionally accessible.

Let's peer into Potter's pages so as to discover her revelations of children's inner worlds. Old Brown is a long-suffering owl who wants to sleep. Finally, pushed beyond endurance by incessant ambient noise, he bites off the fuzzy tail of annoying, chattering Squirrel Nutkin. No quarter there. No pulling back for fear of children's tender sensibilities. Naughty Peter Rabbit gets chased by Mr. McGregor with a rake, and Potter's page shows us the tines. The Flopsy bunnies are kidnapped and nearly skinned to line a coat, rescued barely in the nick of time. The "bad mice," Tom Thumb and Hunca Munca (Potter's actual pets, initially rescued from a trap and carried about in a box, the latter eventually falling to her death from a chandelier) destroy a doll house out of bitter disappointment when they learn that the appealing-looking doll food it contains is not real. (Betrayal leads to destructive vengeance.) And, like most children, Potter's animal characters are burdened by their clothes. Aunt Pettitoes practically strangles Pigling Bland with a scarf as she sends him outdoors. Poor Tom Kitten is cruelly squeezed into an outgrown jacket by his mother Tabitha Twichit, an avatar, quite possibly, for the author's tyrannical and possessive mother.[35] Thus, Potter's strongest stories face childhood vulnerability, fear, and humiliation head on.

Could it be coincidence that Potter's lifespan – almost year for year – overlaps that of Sigmund Freud, who, after all, began building his theories of psychoanalysis by studying gifted Viennese women who suffered constraints similar to those imposed on Potter in London? Like many Victorian girls and women of her class, Potter chafed under harsh reins pulled taut by family and society. Not encouraged to grow up, tutored at home, lacking independent means, she lived with her parents until she was in her forties. She dined with them daily and moved seasonally with them from city to country.

In relation to them, she remained a child. Her younger brother Bertram once said their mother would have had them pushed in a perambulator indefinitely. Potter drew strength from a beloved, rebellious grandmother (a Unitarian Dissenter), from her own innate curiosity about the natural world, and from her insatiable need to sketch and record it.

Capitalizing on remarkable gifts, she adapted. Always the dutiful daughter, she kept a coded journal and eventually transposed her unvoiced mutiny onto the pages of her children's books.

In addition to never forgetting what it is like to smart from powerlessness, Potter, as noted above, like many other children's authors, remained childless. Indeed, childlessness may have liberated her (and others) from felt obligations to spare the supposedly fragile sensibilities of youthful readers. Respecting their honesty, she gives them hers. Potter's nurturing needs were fulfilled by multiple pets, including several hedgehogs variously called Pricklepin and Mrs. Tiggy-Winkle. Although many of her books began as picture letters addressed to children far away, one senses she is always talking to a vital part of her own former self – a practice typical of the finest children's authors, especially those who never cross the divide into parenthood. Potter's lonely London childhood was relieved by summers in Scotland and in the beautiful Lake District, where she wandered in boots, gathering specimens of insects and small mammals as well as mushrooms, which particularly intrigued her; there, she sketched constantly from nature. Her literary and artistic achievements are inseparable from an indomitable spirit, a horror of self-pity, a fierce honesty, and a sardonic wit, which allowed pent up frustrations to break free.

From Beatrix Potter's life and work psychoanalysis can learn, beyond the previously implied lessons, to re-focus its gaze on to what matters most today, namely, our human relations with planet earth, for, as more and more children remain indoors and in vehicles, ignoring the natural word, their eyes and fingers glued to robotic gadgets, screens, and other electronic devices, the fauna and flora Potter loved go unheeded.

Potter offers children the tender, the trenchant, and the cruel; she makes us wonder at our precarious place in the world. The British Isles have produced many fine women authors for children – Edith Nesbit, Enid Blyton, P. L. Travers, J. K. Rowling, but Beatrix Potter whispers wisely to the very youngest. Her unique perspective merits prominence in this dialogue.

V

Hugely popular contemporary Italian novelist Elena Ferrante wrote a children's book, *The Beach at Night*, translated into English in 2016 by Ann Goldstein.[36] It curried scant favor in the American press. It would not be an exaggeration to say it was vilified.[37] I would like to claim a place for it in this dialogue. A doll named Celina, left behind on a beach at the end of the day by five-year-old Mati, tells what abandonment feels like. The story is told in her voice, that of an anthropomorphic toy. Abandonment – a child's deepest fear – plays out within blurry, intimate, triadic bonds between a little girl Mati, her doll Celina, and her mother. With short, direct sentences, Ferrante unfurls a catalogue of woe. Being neglected comes first, as Celina watches Mati leave her to go play with Minù, the new kitten her visiting father has just brought. Humiliation comes next. Rejected and cast off on the sand, Celina suffers maltreatment by Mati's grumpy brother, who dumps burning sand on her. Physical discomfort follows, and then terror, as the family leaves the beach without her. Daytime over: the sky changes color. A "Mean Beach Attendant" with a huge rake frightens her and flings her onto a pile of trash. Fear morphs into sadness and then anger. Worried about being hurt or broken, Celina remembers Mati's former love for her. Envy comes barreling in, as she pictures the kitten who has supplanted her. Spitefully, she imagines spoiling him. Vindictively, she pictures him having bouts of diarrhea and herself vomiting on him so Mati will be compelled to forsake him – a wonderfully apt image since little girls, expected by their mothers to be clean, may believe themselves unlovable when they are not.

Loneliness and boredom ensue, then confusion. The Mean Beach Attendant ignites a fire to burn residual beach trash, including the discarded doll. Celina, at first, uncomprehendingly welcomes its warmth because the sunless beach has grown cold. Gradually, she recognizes that the fire which pleases her can destroy her. When it scalds her dress, she chides (as to a naughty pet): "Bad fire."

Ferrante partakes here in the time-honored tradition of dolls coming to life in children's books. Without tracing the theme all the way back to Ovid's Pygmalion, we could cite Collodi's *Pinocchio* of 1883 or Margery Williams's 1922 *The Velveteen Rabbit*.[38] Other long-lived examples include Rachel Field's 1929 Newbery Award-winning *Hitty*, in which a doll carved from magical wood recounts her hundred-year journey, and the ever-beloved *Raggedy Ann* stories of c. 1900, in which a stuffed rag doll with a candy heart from grandma's attic survives nocturnal escapades based on author Johnny Gruelle's observations of his daughter Marcella. And, of course, Pixar's *Toy Story* of 1995, by John Lasseter. Ferrante mines this vein in several of her other works, including *The Lost Daughter* and *My Beautiful Friend*. Her pages, however, portray the toy characters in nightmarish settings fraught with anxiety.

Rarely do books for children plumb the intensity of feeling to which youngsters are prey. Maurice Sendak's oeuvre, as per above, represents an exception. Ditto Ferrante's. Like Jezibaba or Medea,[39] Ferrante dips into the cauldron without gloves, seizes fears, yanks them out, and thrusts them under the glaring strobe lights of her prose. In so doing, she performs a service not unlike that of Sendak, whose *Where the Wild Things Are* unfastens a door and shoves us in, or, better yet, pushes us in and closes the door fast behind us. Ferrante's Mean Beach Attendant, replete with lizard-like moustaches and nasty ditties updates the ogre or bogeyman of European folk tales. Ferrante's grasp of truth informs her slender book. No emotion in *The Beach at Night* is foreign to young children because, as she knows but as many continue to deny, even the youngest have active inner lives despite a paucity of words with which to report on it. Fear, envy, confusion, longing, disappointment, anger, and sadness are all poignantly felt. That said, where better to practice coping than in the pages of a story book? Children who encounter danger there, especially with adults present, can do so safely. If intense emotional exploration is seen as a boon in art and literature for grown-ups, should it not be made available to children?

The Beach at Night offers what, for some children, may provide an occasion for feeling afraid but also practicing mastery, while for others, undeniably, its scenes may prove too hard to bear. Parent, teacher, librarian, or therapist (each with a specific child at hand) can make that call together, and this in itself constitutes valuable learning. As I have written elsewhere,[40] some of the best reading aloud consists of "conversational reading," during which pauses are taken, questions asked, and feelings explored.

Abandonment tops the list of terrors. An undergraduate astonished me in class once by nailing the most abject horror of Hans Christian Andersen's "The Little Match Girl." Not darkness, she whispered, not freezing cold, not starvation. It's the fact that the little girl can't go home. Cast out, she dies on an empty city street alone.

Ferrante plots Celina's abandonment with exquisite care. Good turns into evil and then reverses. Mati's love for her doll Celina morphs into rejection. The hot beach becomes cold at night. The comforting fire harms what it warms. A sea wave saves Celina from the fire but engulfs and nearly drowns her. The aptly colored black and white kitten starts as a rival for Mati's affection but ends up being the creature who saves her, brings her home, and becomes, at the book's end, her friend. Mati's father, kindly giver of the kitten, serves as foil for the other adult male character, the Mean Beach Attendant, who nearly annihilates her.

These turnabouts match a young child's mental life, where perceptions reverse in a flash. The hand that caresses stiffens into a spank. The angry grimace softens into a twinkle. Lacking analytical ability and information, children find the world both magical and terrifying.[41]

Darkness matters. Night is when mysterious events take place. And Ferrante uses the beach elsewhere in her work, especially in *The Lost Daughter*, where her protagonist "rescues" a doll forgotten on a beach and then holds on to it, unable to bring herself to return it to the child who longs for it. As in *The Beach at Night*, *The Lost Daughter* blurs boundaries between girl and doll, and mother and daughter, boundaries breached again by Ferrante in the opening pages of *My Brilliant Friend*, where two girls play with their dolls, conversing with them and imitating each other like miniature characters in a Pirandello play until the one with the ugly doll throws the other's beautiful toy into a dark cellar. A paradigmatic moment in *The Lost Daughter* occurs when the narrator, a mother of two faraway grownup daughters, anxiously watches a young mother on the beach with her little girl and a doll. Eavesdropping, she listens as the names of mother, daughter, and doll all seem to mingle and merge: Nina, Ninù, Niné, Nani, Nena, Nennella, Elena, Leni. Switching back and forth from childish to grownup voices as they play, the observed mother and daughter make the mute doll "speak" as if it were both mother and child. Envious of their easy fluidity and yearning for lost moments in her own life, the narrator finds the scene unbearable. Unhinged, she rises to intervene, willing it to stop.

In *The Beach at Night*, the sky has turned dark; no stars or moon appear, and the abandoned doll Celina recalls her little mistress Mati telling her in her mother's voice, "If you catch cold, you'll get a fever." Suddenly, the doll understands: Mati is repeating her mother's words "because Mati and I are also," as Ferrante writes, "mother and daughter." Celina's next thought is surely what Aristotle would have called a peripeteia. Celina comprehends that, because of these identifications, Mati cannot possibly have forgotten her. She has not been abandoned! A child encountering the story will get this. On the penultimate page, Mati, having Celina back, hugs her with a face wet with tears.

Ferrante's small miracle never lets up. Right there on the beach, in the sand, each of us – as the sun goes down – is led through the dread of abandonment. But, closing the book with a child, she and we may suddenly experience a sharp sense of gratitude for those who abide with us and gratitude to Elena Ferrante for daring to startle us with this immersion into the fragility of love.

VI

Among all that has gone missing, apologetically, in my foregoing brief essay are surely merriment and the joy, silliness, and nonsense of childhood, represented *con brio* in myriad children's books. With these in hand, psychoanalysts, who deal with pathos, might expand their purview to include the heartening resiliency of youth, its ever-renewing hope, and its *joie de vivre* – which are perhaps the quintessential gifts youth brings to age and children's literature to psychoanalysis.[42] And, in conclusion, we might opine that psychoanalysis, as a discipline, has been far less concerned with joy than with gloom. Perhaps a better balance is due. Despite Tolstoy's off-quoted assertion that all happy families are alike, the complexity of human life cannot be understood only from the perspectives of trauma and dysfunction. Children's literature, like the last entity to emerge from Pandora's casket, may point, therefore, in an auspicious direction.

Notes

1. For further reading, see PEP (Psychoanalytic Electronic Publishing) database. See Seth Lerer, *Children's Literature: From Aesop to Harry Potter* (Chicago: University of Chicago Press, 2008), and Kenneth Kidd, *Freud in Oz: At the Intersections of Psychoanalysis and Children's Literature* (Minneapolis: University of Minnesota Press, 2011).

2. *The Psychoanalytic Study of the Child*, an important annual journal, founded in 1945 by Anna Freud, Heinz Hartman, and Ernst Kris, contains articles on childhood and psychoanalysis, occasionally on children's literature.

3. James Garfield, American President (1881) and a graduate of Williams College, said famously of his teacher that the ideal college would be Mark Hopkins sitting on one end of a log and a student on the other.

4. Sigmund Freud, "Creative Writers and Daydreaming" (1908), SE 9: 141–54.

5. See John Locke, *An Essay Concerning Human Understanding* (London: 1689); the notion itself can be traced back to the ancient Greek Stoic philosophers.

6. See Philippe Ariès, *Centuries of Childhood* (New York: Vintage Books, 1962), who explores this theme admirably through the lenses of the visual arts.

7. By now, there is a vast bibliography on children's art and on the juvenilia of famous writers and artists. Among the most famous and best documented are the juvenilia of the Brontë children. With regard to exhibitions, see: Marina Warner, *Only Make Believe: Ways of Playing*, 2005 catalogue, Compton Verney, England; see also, my "MoMA and Child: The Century of the Child; Growing by Design 1900–2000," Museum of Modern Art, New York City, https://artcritical.com/2012/09/24/century-of-the-child/

8. See Nathaniel Dubin, trans., *The Fabliaux: A New Verse Translation* (New York: Liveright Publishing: 2013).

9. Alice Miller, *The Drama of the Gifted Child: The Search for the True Self* (London: Faber and Faber, 1979).

10. See note 8.

11. For example, see John Bunyan's *A Book for Boys and Girls: Or, Country Rhimes for Children* in *The Miscellaneous Works of John Bunyan, Vol. 6: The Poems*, edited by Graham Midgeley (Oxford: Oxford University Press, 1980). Bunyan's book is meant first of all to teach, of course, but does exemplify the intense interest in the inner lives of children generally held by the early modern dissenters. Special thanks to my astute editor, Vera Camden.

12. See William Wordsworth, "Now We Are Seven" (1798); "The Prelude" (1799); "Ode: Intimation of Immortality from Recollections of Early Childhood" (1802).

13. Among the many nineteenth-century novels featuring child characters, see Charles Dickens and George Eliot. Children's literature flourished in the Victorian era; see John Ruskin, Charles Kingsley, Lewis Carroll, George MacDonald, and Edward Lear. Moralizing gave way gradually to fantasy, nonsense, and merriment.

14. Jerome Bruner, Jacqueline J. Goodnow, and George Austin, *A Study of Thinking* (New York: Wiley, 1956), 330; Jerome Bruner, *The Process of Education* (Harvard University Press: 1960); Jerome Bruner, Rose R. Oliver, and Patricia M. Greenfield, *Studies in Cognitive Growth* (New York: Wiley: 1966); Jerome Bruner, *Processes of Cognitive Growth: Infancy* (Worcester, MA: Clark University Press, 1968).

15. Jean Piaget, *The Language and Thought of the Child* (New York: Harcourt Brace, 1926) (*Le Langage et la pensée chez l'enfant*, 1923), and Jean Piaget, *The Child's Conception of the World* (London: Routledge and Kegan Paul, 1928) (*La Représentation du Monde Chez L'enfant*, 1926).

16. By way of exception, note the case of "Little Hans." Freud, "Analysis of a Phobia in a Five-year-old Boy" (1909), *SE* 10: 1–150.

17. The following are selected sources for the authors mentioned. For Hug-Helmuth, see *The Published Works of Dr. Hermine Hug-Hellmuth* [Letter], *Journal of the American Academy of Child Psychiatry* 25, no. 4 (1986): 580. For Anna Freud, see *The Ego and Mechanisms of Defense*, 1937; *War and Children* (with Dorothy Burlingham), 1943, and *Normality and Pathology in Childhood*, 1968; for Melanie Klein, see *The Collected Works of Melanie Klein*, 4 vols., 1975, Hogarth Press (especially, vol. 4: *Narrative of a Child Analysis*); for D. W. Winnicott, see *Collected Papers: Through Paediatrics to Psychoanalysis* (London: Tavistock, 1958) and *Playing and Reality* (London: Tavistock, 1971); for Margaret S. Mahler, see *The Selected Papers of Margaret S. Mahler*, Vols. 1 and 2, 1979 (*The Psychological Birth of the Human Infant and Separation-Individuation*); for René Spitz, see *No and Yes* (New York: International Universities Press, 1957) and *The First Year of Life*, 1965 (New York: International Universities Press); for Erik H. Erikson, see *Childhood and Society*, 1950, and *Identity: Youth and Crisis*, 1968.

18. Bruno Bettelheim, *The Uses of Enchantment: The Meaning and Importance of Fairy Tales* (New York: Vintage, 1976).

19. This discussion of Bettelheim draws on a section of my article, " Revisiting Fairy Tales" in *Contemporary Psychoanalysis*, 52, no. 3 (2016): 478–88.

20. See my "The Irresistible Psychology of Fairy Tales," *The New Republic*, December 28, 2015. https://newrepublic.com/article/126582/irresistible-psychology -fairytales

21. See Marina Warner, *From the Beast to the Blonde: Fairy Tales and Their Tellers.* (New York: Farrar, Straus and Giroux, 1995); Marina Warner, *Wonder Tales* (New York: Farrar, Straus and Giroux, 1996); Marina Warner, *No Go the Bogeyman: Scaring, Lulling and Making Mock* (New York: Farrar, Straus and Giroux, 1999).

22. See Jack Zipes, ed. *The Victorian Fairy Tales: The Revolt of the Fairies and Elves* (New York: Routledge, 1984); Jack Zipes, ed. *Don't Bet on the Prince:*

Contemporary Feminist Fairy Tales in North America and England (New York: Routledge, 1986); Jack Zipes, ed. *The Complete Fairy Tales of the Brothers Grimm* (New York: Bantam Books, 2003).

23. In the first chapter of my *Inside Picture Books* (New Haven: Yale University Press, 1999), I offer several examples of children's idiosyncratic, often psychologically revelatory, and astute interpretation of text and pictures.

24. Liesl Shurtliff, *Rump: The (Fairly) True Tale of Rumpelstiltskin* (New York: Yearling Book, 2013).

25. This discussion of Sendak draws on my remarks on the occasion of his death, "Remembering Maurice Sendak ...," The *New Republic*, May 9, 2012. https://newrepublic.com/article/103200/sendak-wild-things-death-bumble-poetchildren

26. See Obituary of Maurice Sendak, "'Fresh Air' Remembers Author Maurice Sendak," NPR, May 8, 2012. www.npr.org/transcripts/152248901

27. Psychoanalytic ideas which find expression in Sendak's work might well include "oral aggression" (Freud), "identification with the aggressor" (Anna Freud), "the good enough mother" (D. W. Winnicott), "denial of loss, triumphing, and spoiling" (Melanie Klein), "magical thinking" (Selma Fraiberg), "separation/individuation" (Margaret S. Mahler), "basic trust" (Erik Erikson). My claim here is not that Sendak read or knew these concepts himself but rather that these concepts would have formed the background of a psychoanalytic therapy undertaken over many years and as such become available for use by the artist unconsciously in his creative work. See my *Inside Picture Books* (New Haven: Yale University Press, 1999), 123–34, for examples.

28. See my analyses of *Where the Wild Things Are* and *In the Night Kitchen* in my *Inside Picture Books*.

29. Franz Kafka, *Metamorphosis*, 1913; published originally in German, widely available in English translation. At the start of this story, the human protagonist, Gregor Samsa, has turned into an insect, and Kafka expressly directed his publisher not to have the insect depicted visually by any illustration. The precise size, shape, color, and species are left to each reader's imagination.

30. Maurice Sendak, *The Nutshell Library* (New York: Harper and Row, 1962).

31. D. W. Winnicott (see above note 16) developed the notion that the physical holding and cuddling of a baby by the parent produces salutary psychological effects reproducible by the calm trusting presence of the child's caregiver and, later in life, by a good therapist. I argue here that the children's books themselves can, under some circumstances, provide an analogous "holding environment."

32. For this excellent interpretative suggestion regarding the "heat" of a mother's love, I wish to express my indebtedness to Vera Camden, personal communication.

33. This exchange between Sendak and Nordstrom is reported by Katherine Rundell, "Story Time: Five Children's Books Everyone Should Read," The *Guardian*, July 26, 2019.

34. Freud has written a 1919 essay on "The Uncanny," which explores the psychological origins and ramifications of the experience of suddenly finding something that is unfamiliar seem weirdly familiar and, conversely, something well-known feels oddly strange.

35. See Linda Lear, *Beatrix Potter, a Life in Nature* (New York: St. Martin's Press, 2007).

36. This discussion draws on my "A New Discussion of Elena Ferrante's The Beach at Night," *School Library Journal*, February 15, 2018. http://blogs.slj.com/afu se8production/2018/02/15/guest-post-a-newconsideration-of-elena-ferrantes-the-beach-at-night/

37. See Nora Krug, "The Latest Elena Ferrante Controversy: Her Children's Book, The Beach at Night," *Washington Post*, October 13, 2016. See also, Maria Russo, "Elena Ferrante's Picture Book Embraces the Dark Side," *The New York Times*, October 12, 2016.

38. Margery Williams, *The Velveteen Rabbit (Or How Toys Become Real)*, illustrated by William Nicholson (New York: Doubleday & Company, 1922).

39. Jezibaba (or Baba Yaga) is of Slavic folkloric origin – a menacing, enigmatic, deformed old woman, a witch, imagined often, as dwelling in a cabin on chicken legs. Medea is the sorceress of ancient Greek mythology who helps Jason to obtain the Golden Fleece by murdering and dismembering her brother, and who eventually kills her own two young sons when betrayed later on by Jason (see the plays by Euripides and Seneca by that name and also Ovid's *Metamorphoses*, Book 7).

40. See my *Inside Picture Books*, 7–22.

41. For an unequalled description of these turnabouts, see Selma Fraiberg, *The Magic Years* (New York: Scribner, 1959), a psychoanalytically informed classic on child development from zero to age five.

42. See my "Gleaning Wisdom from 11 Sources," Fuse 8, *School Library Journal*, March, 28, 2019, http://blogs.slj.com/afuse8production/2019/03/28/guest-post-imagination-and-picture-books-gleaning-wisdom-from-11-sources-by-ellen-handler-spitz/

12

VICKY LEBEAU

Reflections on Psychoanalysis and Class
Andrea Arnold and Donald Winnicott

Preamble

Psychoanalysis, class: on the face of it, not a promising conjuncture. Psychoanalysis may be one of the central interpretative frameworks of modern Western cultures, but there is a widely held view that it is has little, if anything, to say about lives that fail to "fit" within its frames: class, as Lynne Layton, Nancy Caro Hollander, and Susan Gutwill have put it, is one of its last taboos.[1] Above all, psychoanalysis – including its modified forms, psychoanalytic psychotherapy and psychodynamic psychotherapy – is expensive; its costs, in terms of both time and money, put it beyond the reach of the majority of people. As Joanna Ryan argues in her groundbreaking *Class and Psychoanalysis: Landscapes of Inequality*, published in 2017, "lack of money is a powerful aspect of class exclusion from psychoanalysis. ... To a large extent, it structures the whole field."[2]

It's a stark claim, extending the question of access to psychoanalysis from that of who can afford to see an analyst to who can afford to become one. Money, or the lack of it, excludes most of us from the field. The training is long, expensive, and difficult to do outside of major urban centers. That demographic alone imposes enormous constraints on who can consider training: like the issue of money, this is a material fact with the consequence that relatively few psychoanalysts can draw on their own experience of working-class life and identity in their practice. Class remains a lacuna; there is, as one practitioner puts it in interview with Ryan, an "almost total denial of class factors."[3]

That working-class men, women and children rarely make it on to the analyst's couch is one of the factors at work in that denial, and the consequent gap in psychoanalytic thinking about class and class inequality. It is not that analysts have never engaged with deprivation and poverty; nor that, as a profession, psychoanalysis actively eschews inclusion (though, at times, it may do).[4] But the profile of its practitioners – both analysts and analysands – can skew its understanding away from the lived experience of class, its

I would like to thank Vera Camden for her incisive comments on this chapter.

expressions of difference and inequality, as a vital aspect of our psychic lives. What has been described as the "psychic life of class" remains unthought and unelaborated: a loss not only to the many excluded from psychoanalytic therapies, but to psychoanalysis itself.[5] As Adam Phillips reflected in interview in 2015, psychoanalysis "has suffered greatly from being such a rarefied and elitist practice, and by being so middle class."[6]

Working against that impasse, Ryan notes how, in attempting to think about psychoanalysis and class, she had to "go outside of psychoanalysis," exploring a range of sociological and psychosocial perspectives on class and class differences.[7] In other words, she had to engage in a form of psychoanalysis "off the couch" – a venture that runs from the very beginning of Freud's discovery of the unconscious mind. From the late 1890s, Freud was wondering about what he describes, in *The Interpretation of Dreams*, as the "practical applicability" of psychoanalysis beyond its clinical setting, a wondering that, at various points in his writings, prompts him toward an interdisciplinary, and collaborative, theory of mind and practice (in our context, his investment in the analyst's openness to the study of cultural forms is of particular interest).[8] Such "extra-mural psychoanalysis" (to borrow psychoanalyst Jean Laplanche's term) is bound to discover its own questions, objects, and practices; it is inter-textual and dialogic, committed to inhabiting the spaces among institutions and disciplines.[9]

It's a commitment that supports the type of initiative sketched out in this chapter: a "conversation" between Andrea Arnold – a contemporary British film-maker, renowned for what she describes as her "passion for the real and the method for filming it" – and Donald Winnicott, a psychoanalyst and pediatrician whose attention to the earliest ties between mothers and babies fostered one of the predominant traditions in contemporary psychoanalysis: the Independent Tradition.[10] It is central to my argument that to open up the (potential) space between psychoanalysis and class requires the provocation of creative and critical works engaged by the living facts of material and symbolic disadvantage. In this context, Arnold's acclaimed short film *Wasp*, released in 2003, is a vital object to think with.[11] *Wasp* is that rare thing: a film about an impoverished single mother, Zoe, made by a woman with lived experience of working-class lives and environments. "I grew up in a working-class family," Arnold has commented in interview, "so you could say I write from what I know."[12] Such forms of knowing are invaluable. "What we rarely found," as Nathan Connolly puts it in his Introduction to *Know Your Place: Essays on the Working Class by the Working Class*, published in 2017, "was the working class allowed to speak for themselves."[13] The difficulty of definition is only part of the problem: it is not easy to stabilize ways in which to describe, and categorize, "class";

people identify in various ways with different, often conflicting, forms of class discourse; the relations among profession, income, housing, and formal education are significant, but not always reliably predictive; like poverty, then, "class" is relative, or relational. It is a lived experience of self and others, self and world – experience that Arnold puts at the heart of her film-making in *Wasp*, bringing to the screen a working-class mother's conflict between caring for her four children and her wish for a "break," a "night out" (what might otherwise be called a "full life").

This chapter reads between Winnicott's idea of the "good-enough" mother and Arnold's imaging of the relation between a working-class mother and her children. It is not that *Wasp* (or any other cultural object) can stand in for a "class"; nor that psychoanalysis can be used to put *Wasp*, or Andrea Arnold, on the couch. But, as an audio-visual object, located in a particular socio-political space and time, *Wasp* carries a class dimension with it – a dimension embedded in its uses of narrative and image, its ways of relating to cinema and its audiences, and in its reception (including Arnold's own reflections on her film-making). On this view, *Wasp* is a singular, but by no means a single, object; it is overdetermined, conflicted and multi-voiced, and poised to support an emerging conjuncture between psychoanalysis and studies in class and culture.

"My Mum Looks Like Victoria Beckham, You Foul Cow!"

That we need women to speak more about mothers has become something of a commonplace over the past few decades: from Adrienne Rich's *Of Woman Born*[14] to Jacqueline Rose's recent *Mothers: An Essay on Love and Cruelty*,[15] the figure of the mother preoccupies feminist as well as psychoanalytic thinking. But what kind of mothers do we listen to? On the whole, not mothers like Zoe, living on the breadline with four young children on a housing estate in Dartford. By contrast, classic in its generative economy, *Wasp* "drops in" on a few hours in the lives of this young family (one of Arnold's privileged methods for satisfying that "passion for the real").[16] "I want to make it feel like we've dropped in on some people's lives," she explains in interview. "With a lot of films, people are sitting on the outside, looking in, but I want the audience to get a bit more intimately involved with what's going on, so that they maybe can experience it a little bit more intensely."[17]

It's a rich, and complex, statement, drawing attention to the invitation offered by Arnold's cinema to enter into the states of being and feeling it explores. On the one hand, it is easy to understand why *Wasp* has been described as an "English working-class, slice-of-life film": less than 30 minutes long, it is at once mundane and extreme, visibly and audibly, frayed at the edges (like the Estuary accents – Kent, Essex, East London – that cue us into the world of the working-class housing estates of southeast England). In this sense, *Wasp* belongs to a tradition in post-war British film-making that brings the social and psychic experience of working-class men, women, and children to the screen: Ken Loach's *Kes* (1969), *Cathy Come Home* (1966), *Ladybird, Ladybird* (1994), *I, Daniel Blake* (2016); Barney Platts-Mills' *Bronco Bullfrog* (1970); Alan Clarke's *Rita, Sue and Bob Too* (1987); Shane Meadows' *A Room for Romeo Brass* (1999), *Once Upon a Time in the Midlands* (2002), *This Is England* (2006); Lynne Ramsay's *Ratcatcher* (1999): the list could go on. Among other things, this is a cinema engaged by the human right to a life that includes more than the bare fact of being alive, its social realist poetics – however naturalistic, these films are always artful – intervening on the side of working-class hopes and dreams (which is not to say that this tradition traffics in happy endings).[18]

On the other hand, Arnold's childhood – as the daughter of a single mother, growing up on an estate in Dartford in Kent in the 1960s and 1970s – has been seen as significant both in relation to this film and to her later *Fish Tank* (the credits to *Wasp* thank the people of Dartford, where it was filmed; *Fish Tank* is set on the then Mardyke Estate in Rainham, Essex).[19] As Sophie Elmhirst comments, Arnold predicted that she would be "on the same estate [as her mother], with a lot of kids probably" – an expectation that casts her cinema as, among other things, embedded in the complex processes of class transition: "I felt my lack of education and accent always held me back in the eyes of the gatekeepers."[20] "The thing about the film industry," as she reflects following the release of *Fish Tank* in 2009, "is that it's incredibly middle class, isn't it?":

> All the people who look at it and study it and talk about – *write* about it – are middle-class, so they always see films about the working class as being grim, because the people in the film don't have what they have. I very much get the feeling that I'm seeing a different place. People at Cannes kept asking me about grim estates and I thought, ugh, I don't *mean* that. I tried not to mean that.[21]

Part of the value of Arnold's cinema is the difference of perspective on which she insists here. Pointing to a stark contrast between how she sees her films – "I very much get the feeling that I'm seeing a different place" – and a critical reception sometimes appalled by the lives she brings into view, Arnold brings the question of class back into focus. As she does so, what she confronts is that the conditions for seeing her films as she does may not be in place, a difficulty that goes beyond an artist's familiar unease with what audiences (readers, viewers, listeners) may, or may not, do with their work. There is a more structural difference, or obstacle, at stake here. Provisionally,

Arnold *sees* differently because she belongs to (at least) two different worlds: on the one hand, the world of her childhood; on the other hand, what she experiences as the "middle-class" world of making and talking and writing about films. It's a form of belonging – divided, dissonant, dissident – that can at once wrack a life, and force new forms of imagining into the fray. "Only if you actually manage to move from one side of the border to the other," writes Didier Eribon, reflecting on his experience of class transition in *Returning to Reims*, published in 2009, "can you get out from the implacable logic of all those things that go without saying."[22]

Like, for example, the implacable logic that casts Zoe as a bad mother. "This woman should not be a mother, and these children should not have these lives": writing in 2007, film critic Roger Ebert's summary response to *Wasp* exposed the task facing Arnold as a film-maker attuned to both the vulnerability, and the viciousness, of a young mother who desires something, or someone, beyond her children. In fact, in his tendentious account of the film, Ebert can stand in for those who see a "different place" to the one Arnold may have thought she was filming:

> She (Zoe) fears having the children taken away from her, and with good reason: During a long day and night, she chats up a former boyfriend, claims she is only baby-sitting the children, takes them home and finds only white sugar from a bag to feed them. Then she brings them along to the pub where she's meeting the boyfriend, parking them outside and rushing out to give them potato chips and a Coke, "to share around." Hour follows hour as she plays pool and is sweet-talked by her date, while the kids wait outside, sad and hungry. The film is notable above all for not underlining its points, but simply making them: This woman should not be a mother, and these children should not have these lives.[23]

If there is one thing that *Wasp* does not do it is to make its point simply (or singly). It is not that Ebert's version of *Wasp* is "wrong"; in fact, he reproduces a common judgment against Zoe that runs through the film. In its opening sequence, Zoe drags her four young children – Kelly, Leanne, and Siobhan, aged roughly 10 to 3, and baby Kai – across the estate to confront another young woman (known only as Bullet Head); barefoot, wearing only her nightdress, Zoe's rage is at once physical, emotional, verbal – "Don't you fuck with my kids"; "No one hits my kids and gets away with it!" – and fueled by an everyday story of conflict between two small girls and their mothers (Leanne has been accused of stealing another girl's crisps). Depending on our own beginnings, we may recognize the scene: in particular, the performative dimension to Zoe's real violence, and the position she seeks to secure as a mother fighting to protect her children (one of the few things she may be able to lay claim to). Equally, Bullet Head's contempt erupts via clichés that immediately establish Zoe's reputation on the estate: "You let your kids run wild; you ain't fit to 'ave 'em! I should call social services on ya!" It's a threat that brings Zoe's attack to a halt, as her eldest daughter, Kelly, moves in to defend her mother. Her mouth wide open, her expression a slack sneer, she fills the screen to confront Bullet Head: "My mum looks like Victoria Beckham, you foul cow!"

At the limits of respectability, then, Zoe is a "bad" mother. It is true – painfully true – that she fears losing her children and that her children are hungry. She is known to neglect them ("Left your kids home alone again have ya?": this is Bullet Head, catching sight of Zoe in the pub); living on the breadline, she cannot feed them: in the family's damp, and grubby, kitchen, there is no food in the cupboards and little money in Zoe's purse. "I want chips!" is a refrain that runs through the film, the children's foraging for food outside the pub precipitating its eponymous crisis: attracted by the sauce smeared around Kai's face, a wasp crawls into his mouth (Kelly has fed her brother and sisters with chips and spare ribs dropped by a group of men as they leave the pub). It's a moment of visceral panic, *Wasp*'s punitive "answer" to Zoe's ruthless, if reluctant, decision to leave her children to play outside the pub. In this sense, *Wasp* does not flinch from the potentially fatal consequences of Zoe's mothering. On the contrary, the wasp's (potential) attack on her baby is intercut with images of Zoe, making out with a young man, Dave, in his car. On hearing her children's screams ("Mum! Mum!"), she rushes to them, in time to see the wasp crawling into Kai's mouth. After an agonizing few seconds, with the camera focused on the baby's face, the wasp re-appears, and flies away. Zoe explodes, shaking Kelly, and screaming in her face: "What's that shit round his mouth?" "I told you to look after him, didn't I?"

Wasp does not flinch from the tragedy of being Kelly at this moment (or from the impossibility of becoming a mother when you are yourself a child). The aesthetic of Arnold's realism demands staying alongside her subjects, keeping us there with them, until we are in the grip of the turmoil generated by a maternal idiom at once passionate and dangerous, devoted and neglectful, playful and depressed. Such an idiom can be difficult to bear – "grim" does not begin to cover it – but that *Wasp* bears with it is a mark of the film's achievement. Throughout we are confronted by the fact that, while Zoe may be a degraded mother – humiliated in, and by, the world – she is still the world to her children. Whether dancing with them outside the pub, racing down the street with pushchair and dolls' pram – "Last one to the bottom of the hill is a plonker!" – or remonstrating with them to "give me a break!" – "It's my first night out in fucking ages!" – she is creating a world for her children to live in that is full of her – her needs, her demands, and her fantasies. Including the fantasy of looking like, of being like, Victoria Beckham: a woman, and a mother, who "has it all" (money, fame, husband). A tiny picture of David Beckham, stuck on the kitchen wall, cues us into that fantasy, and its collision with the reality of Zoe's life on the estate with four young kids and no one around to help her. At one point, as she stands pensively in the kitchen, frustrated by attempts to find someone to babysit her children, the camera alights on that picture of Beckham, zooming in until he is centered on the screen, occupying our field of vision. It's a preoccupation then projected back onto Zoe via a close-up shot that lingers, albeit momentarily, on her face; this is a rare moment of stillness in a film that so often appears to be unable to settle, a pause during which a young woman, a young mother, appears to contemplate the object of her desire – and, by extension, the image of a life she does not have. Noticing a wasp buzzing against the window, Zoe reaches over to open it and sets the creature free.

That the wasp returns in the form of an attack on her baby can be used to symbolize not only the fact of maternal aggression, but the ruthless limits on Zoe's freedom imposed by the everyday realities of her life as a single mother. That *Wasp* wants to know about those realities is evident in its attention to the details of Zoe's day, and to the circumstances that led up to her "parking" her children outside the pub. "What are you doing with all them fucking kids?": that question, as brutal as it is casual, comes at Zoe as she walks home with her children following the confrontation with Bullet Head (Bullet Head's stupefied amazement – "Victoria Beckham my arse!" – is still ringing in our ears). A young man, Dave, hails Zoe from a passing car, drawing up at the side of the road. "I knew it was you!" he tells her as Zoe, leaving her children on a grass verge, approaches him. Dave glances through the windscreen, his expression becoming quizzical, challenging, even contemptuous: "What are you doing with all them fucking kids?" There's a brief pause, no more than a second or two, between this question and Zoe's response, but it goes to the heart of Arnold's film-making. As Zoe hesitates, licking her lips, drawing in her breath, the camera cuts momentarily from her face to her bare toes, flexing to grip the edge of the curb. It's a tiny gesture, but it anchors us in Zoe's somatic and psychic reality: this is a moment of trying to hold on to the promise of a pleasure that has come her way: a "night out," a "break," a drink with a man who desires her. She doesn't want to lose it; she is always close to losing it. "They're me mate's," she replies, defiantly, breathlessly, as Dave smiles sensuously at her. "I'm looking after 'em for her."

Charged with the conflict between eroticism and maternal care, this exchange generates the moral crisis of the film. Zoe is at once a mother who will put her body on the line for her children ("Don't you fuck with my kids!") and a woman who, in a bid to become the object of male desire, will deny any relation to them at all. That male desire is cast in the form of contempt, or aversion, for the ties between a mother and her children is crucial to *Wasp's* psychosocial exploration of mothering, class, and poverty: whether defending or denying her mothering, Zoe stands to lose in the eyes of a world that does not value, or cannot take the measure of, the demands made on her by the work of maternal care. To begin to take the measure of those demands, I want to take a brief detour via Winnicott's writings on the earliest ties between mothers and babies – notably, his attention to the need to understand the stakes involved in "good-enough" mothering and care.

"How Does the Infant Survive Such Conditions?"

"There is no such thing as a baby!": this is, perhaps, Winnicott's best-known aphorism, echoing an Enlightenment investment in the mother-baby dyad as source of love and relationship, self and creativity.[24] It would be difficult to overestimate the significance of this claim to Winnicott's provocations to psychoanalysis in the 1950s and 1960s, as well as the influence of his work on the post-war development of the British welfare state.[25] Embroiled in the work of imagining the very earliest experiences of infantile life, Winnicott conjures the scene of the baby's absolute dependence on the care of others – typically, in his writings, the care provided by the mother:

> [I]f we look at an infant we see an infant in care. The state of not being separated, of not being integrated, of not being related to body functions, of not being related to objects, this state is very real; we must believe in these states that belong to immaturity. The problem is: How does the infant survive such conditions?[26]

"How does the infant survive such conditions?" This is the question that opens up to the world of care, and dependence, at the core of Winnicott's psychoanalysis. How far the baby survives those very real states of non-integration and non-relation at the beginning of life, depends on how far the environment – in Winnicott's terms, the "environment mother" – can protect her against too much exposure to the terrors of having been born. "Continuity of being," along with the mother but not aware of her, is the basic aim of what Winnicott calls the mother-infant "set-up," or the "environment-individual set-up," at the origins of human life. "At the earliest stages the infant and the maternal care," as he puts it, "belong to each other and cannot be disentangled."[27] In fact, nothing less than a reversal of reality takes place via this "set-up" in which the mother's identification with her baby creates an environment, at once internal and external, in which the baby can experience absolute helplessness as a form of illusory omnipotence: what is needed is reliably "there" via the work of another who is not yet recognized as separate from the baby, another who offers a "live, human holding" at once somatic and psychological (at this stage, the two cannot be distinguished).[28] "In her holding function," as psychoanalyst Angela Joyce clarifies, "the mother not only attends physically to her baby's needs but in her mind imaginatively elaborates her baby's experiences."[29]

It is no wonder that you are likely to "talk about" your mother in analysis (even if only by never mentioning her). Or that psychoanalysis – in particular, the Independent tradition – can sometimes find it hard to talk about anything else (what Jacqueline Rose has called the "utter unmovability of the mother" in that tradition).[30] The mother – our first world, our first object, our first "culture" – is always already there under our skin, inhabiting our sensations, alive (or dead) within us, long before we are able to understand who, or even that, she is: the child's first reality, as Joyce McDougall puts it, is the maternal unconscious.[31] It's a sobering claim, especially given Winnicott's attachment to the idea of the "ordinary devoted mother," her capacity to care well, and naturally, for her baby. "I am asking," as he writes in "Mirror-role of Mother and Family in Child Development" in 1967,

> that this which is naturally done well by mothers who are caring for their babies shall not be taken for granted. I can make my point by going straight over to the case of the baby whose mother reflects her own mood or, worse still, the rigidity of her own defenses. In such a case what does the baby see?[32]

"Mirror-role of Mother and Family in Child Development" is a remarkable, often tantalizing, analysis of maternal holding through the play of looking between mother and baby (in this sense, Winnicott is pointing not only to the maternal structuring of the visual field, but to the visual dimension of our earliest experiences of psycho-somatic care).[33] Above all, perhaps, it is in this chapter that Winnicott draws attention to the fact that the baby who is not "held" – reflected, mirrored, "seen" – is a baby who loses the experience of the mother's mind; withdrawn into herself – through illness, or depression, or exhaustion – this is a mother whose "fixed," or rigid, face exposes her baby to an environment that, because it cannot "see" her, forces her into a premature perception of the mother (her needs, her wishes, her feelings). The consequences of such a disruption can be devastating: for Winnicott, the capacity to experience life, to make it real and find it worth living, can happen "only in *relation to a feeling of confidence* on the part of the baby, that is, a confidence related to the dependability of the mother-figure or environmental elements."[34] In other words, being human, having a human life, depends on a psycho-somatic experience of environmental care: the baby needs to be met by another human mind and body – and, by extension, a world in which the mother has a mind to meet her baby with.

"She's a Fucking Nan and She's Got a Better Social Life Than Me!"

It is a (Romantic) commonplace that the child is father of the man.[35] That the child is mother of the woman, mother of the mother, is less often thought. But this is, I think, part of the challenge of Winnicott's writings on mothers and babies, and of the value of his thinking to those of us working on the cusp between psychoanalysis, class, and culture. Class, as Ryan points out, "is a prime example of the past operating in the present" – a prime object, then, for psychoanalysis – and a form of trans-generational experience that can prove remarkably resistant to the forces of social change.[36] In bringing to the fore the earliest ties between mother and baby, Winnicott offers a way into thinking about that resistance, its origins in a potential coincidence between the state of the social environment and maternal states of mind. Reflecting on the idea of the "ordinary devoted mother" in 1966, for example, Winnicott drew attention to one of the primal scenes of trans-generational inheritance: the woman's transfer of her own experience of infancy into that of becoming a mother to her baby. "After all," he notes, "she was a baby once, and she has in her the memories of being a baby; she also has memories of being cared for, and these memories either help or hinder her in her own experiences as a mother."[37]

How far a mother can care for her baby – how far she can bear her baby's helplessness – depends not only on the social environment but on forms of unconscious experience reaching back toward her own infancy and childhood. What remains, for me, most striking in *Wasp* is its capacity to hold the two domains in play – most notably in its depiction of Zoe's attempts, having agreed to meet Dave at the pub, to find someone to look after her children for the evening. It's a scene that takes place in Zoe's kitchen, her increasingly peremptory attempts to care – to feed, to amuse, to distract her children – displaced by the need for a "night out." Trying to placate Kai with a sugared dummy (he spits it out in despair and disgust), Zoe is on the phone to her friends, looking for help. As we look at her hopeless attempts to find food for her daughters (moldy bread, empty cereal packets, and white sugar are pulled from the cupboards), it is apparent that no help is forthcoming: "No, I've asked her already and she can't; she's a fucking nan and she's got a better social life than me." It's a tantalizing comment, unelaborated (Zoe has little credit left on her phone) but resonant. Who is this nan? The woman to whom, it seems, Zoe has turned for help before turning to her friends? It's possible to read this as a trace of Zoe's relationship with her own mother, her children's "nan," a woman now with access to a world beyond kitchen and kids, a world opening onto the pleasures from which Zoe, staring at a tiny photo of David Beckham, risks being shut out. A woman – a mother, a mother of the mother – who is not there to help.

Perhaps. *Wasp* offers only a trace. But in so doing the film embeds the psychosocial question: Who cares for mothers? In particular, for mothers like Zoe, made brittle by a world that doesn't want to know about what they do and why they do it: "This woman should not be a mother, and these children should not have these lives." "I should call the social services on ya!" "What are you doing with all them fucking kids?" The "shoulds" threaten to become overwhelming, but *Wasp* mobilizes a form of symbolization that pulls against any summary judgment. In this context, finally, it's worth going back to the scene outside the pub when, as the wasp crawls out of Kai's mouth, Zoe first explodes in anger, and then breaks down in tears. The soundtrack is dominated by her heavy breathing, and by her children's crying; Kelly weeps silent tears, initially refusing to go near her mother as Zoe attempts to hug and hold her children close to her. As the camera swerves up, following Zoe's gaze, we become aware of Dave, standing behind them. His gaze is steady, bemused, concerned, the camera holding on his face, brightly lit, before cutting, suddenly, to the image of a red ceiling lamp, its warm glow on a dull white ceiling. It's a takeaway, promising chips and Chinese, a promise made good in a series of shots of each child, munching blissfully on chips in Dave's car. Holding Kai close, Zoe is sitting silently in the passenger seat, staring straight ahead, as if petrified. Until Dave speaks: "Why don't we just get 'em home? We'll have a little chat, yeah?"

This is, I think, a transformative moment – a moment of "holding" in, and by, the film. *Wasp* ends on a note, literally, of erotic optimism, using the resources of image and sound to contain the crisis of the film – but also to give Zoe what she wants. As the car pulls off (Dave has to start it twice: a running joke in the film), the children begin to sing: "Hey Baby," a song played over the scene in the pub, now sounding its endorsement of Zoe's desire to be desired as the credits roll and DJ Ötzi's performance takes over: "Will you be my girl?" Who cares for mothers? Perhaps films like *Wasp* that, in wanting to know, and wanting us to know, of Zoe's life, begin the work of understanding the complex web of relations among Zoe and her children, the "environment mother," and the environment.

Notes

1. Lynne Layton, Nancy Caro Hollander, and Susan Gutwill, *Psychoanalysis, Class and Politics: Encounters in the Clinical Setting* (London: Routledge, 2006), 1.

2. Joanna Ryan, *Class and Psychoanalysis: Landscapes of Inequality* (London: Routledge, 2017), 159.
3. Ryan, *Class and Psychoanalysis*, 111.
4. See Ryan's discussion of this issue in *Class and Psychoanalysis*, 3.
5. Diane Reay, "Beyond Consciousness? The Psychic Landscape of Social Class," *Sociology* 39, no. 5 (2005): 911–28.
6. Sian L. Whitehead, "Adam Phillips in Conversation with Psychoanalyst James Mann," SITE for Contemporary Psychoanalysts December 15, 2015, video, 1:02: 37, www.youtube.com/watch?v=lbJOuxpe1q8&feature=youtu.be &fbclid=IwAR1x_rj2jjRr7CFWLV-cBQHpj2Bhb66mNXr9NoLX7FfCSuU4lji4I76yYzI.
7. Ryan, *Class and Psychoanalysis*, 82.
8. Sigmund Freud, *The Interpretation of Dreams* (1900), SE 4: 241.
9. Jean Laplanche, *New Foundations for Psychoanalysis* (Oxford: Blackwell, 1989), 11.
10. Fabien Lemercier, "Andre Arnold: 'A Passion for the Real'," *Cineuropa*, May 14, 2009, https://cineuropa.org/en/interview/108559/
11. *Wasp* is included as a "Special Feature" on the DVD release of Arnold's *Fish Tank* (2009; Curzon Artificial Eye).
12. "Andrea Arnold Interview," *The Scotsman*, August 28, 2009, www .scotsman.com/news/film-andrea-arnold-interview-2467078
13. Nathan Connolly, *Know Your Place: Essays on the Working Class by the Working Class* (Liverpool: Dead Ink Press, 2017), 5.
14. Adrienne Rich, *Of Woman Born: Motherhood as Experience and Institution* (London: Virago, 1997).
15. Jacqueline Rose, *Mothers: An Essay on Love and Cruelty* (London: Faber & Faber, 2018).
16. Lemercier, "Andre Arnold: 'A Passion for the Real'."
17. Graham Fuller, "Social Realism in a Poetic Lens," *The New York Times*, January 14, 2020, www.nytimes.com/2010/01/17/movies/17fish.html.
18. In fact, *Wasp* is in a complex dialogue with Ken Loach's *Ladybird, Ladybird* – a topic I hope to take up elsewhere.
19. As Jonathan Murray comments: "We might even go so far as to see Mia [*Fish Tank*] as an authorial surrogate in several key regards, rather than as an authorial subject pure and simple." Jonathan Murray, "Red Roads from Realism: Theorising Relationships between Technique and Theme in the Cinema of Andrea Arnold," *Journal of British Cinema and Television*, 13, no. 1 (2016): 211.
20. Sophie Elmhirst, "Andrea Arnold's Immersive Cinema," *The New Yorker*, October 8, 2016, www.newyorker.com/culture/persons-of-interest/andrea-arnolds-immersive-cinema.
21. Lisa Mullen, "Estate of Mind," *Sight and Sound*, October 2009, www .michaelfassbender.org/sightsound.html.
22. Didier Eribon, *Returning to Reims* (London: Allen Lane, 2009), 52.
23. Roger Ebert, "Short Subjects Get Oscar Nod and a Big Screen Release," *RogerEbert.com*, February 24, 2005, www.rogerebert.com/reviews/oscar-short-subject-nominees-2005.
24. D. W. Winnicott, "The Theory of the Parent-Infant Relationship," *International Journal of Psycho-Analysis* 41 (1960): 587.

25. For further discussion, see Vicky Lebeau, "Feeling Poor: Donald Winnicott and Daniel Blake," *New Formations: A Journal of Culture, Theory, Politics* 96–97 (2019): 160–75.

26. D. W. Winnicott, "The Parent-Infant Relationship: Further Remarks," *The Collected Works of D. W. Winnicott: Volume 6, 1960–1963* (Oxford: Oxford University Press, 2016), 360.

27. Winnicott, "The Theory of the Parent-Infant Relationship," 587.

28. D. W. Winnicott, "Group Influences and the Maladjusted Child: The School Aspect," in *The Family and Individual Development* (London: Tavistock, 1955), 147.

29. Angela Joyce, "Introduction to Volume 6," *The Collected Works of D. W. Winnicott: Volume 6, 1960–1963* (Oxford: Oxford University Press, 2017), 5.

30. Jacqueline Rose, "Of Knowledge and Mothers: On the Work of Christopher Bollas," in *On Not Being Able to Sleep: Psychoanalysis and the Modern World* (London: Chatto & Windus, 2003), 150.

31. Joyce McDougall, *Theatres of the Body: A Psychoanalytical Approach to Psychosomatic Illness* (London: Free Association Books, 1989), 39–40.

32. D. W. Winnicott, *Playing and Reality* (London and New York: Routledge, 2005), 112.

33. For further discussion see Vicky Lebeau, "Mirror Images: D. W. Winnicott in the Visual Field," in *Embodied Encounters: New Approaches to Psychoanalysis and Cinema*, ed. A. Piotrowska (London and New York: Routledge, 2015), 171–82.

34. Winnicott, *Playing and Reality*, 100.

35. See William Wordsworth's "My Heart Leaps Up" (1802): "The Child is father of the Man;/ And I could wish my days to be/Bound to each other by natural piety."

36. Ryan, *Class and Psychoanalysis*, 6.

37. D. W. Winnicott, "The Ordinary Devoted Mother," in *Babies and their Mothers* (London: Free Association Books, 1988), 6.

PART IV

In Theory

13

JEREMY TAMBLING

Why Literature? Why Psychoanalysis?

Psychoanalysis and literature have become an inseparable if odd couple, and have brought out things in each other that would not have been apparent without their pairing. Vestiges of interchange are numerous. Freud analyzed Gustav Mahler and the American poet, H. D.[1] James Joyce (1882–1941) consulted Carl Jung (1875–1961); Samuel Beckett was analyzed by Wilfred Bion (1897–1979).[2] Freud uses literature in many foundational essays for psychoanalytic theory, including "The Uncanny,"[3] especially E. T. A. Hoffmann's "The Sandman." He puts Sophocles' *Oedipus* alongside *Hamlet*;[4] discusses *Macbeth* and Ibsen in "Those Wrecked by Success,"[5] and *The Brothers Karamazov* in "Dostoevsky and Parricide."[6] He analyzes Wilhelm Jensen's "short tale" about Pompeii, "Gradiva." And though psychoanalysis makes scientific and rational claims, it has leaned more to literature, as will be seen, outstandingly, with the French psychoanalyst Jacques Lacan (1900–1981).

For Freud, literature was not just the wellspring of psychoanalysis but rather engendered our modern world. Hamlet, as a "hysteric,"[7] launches the first of what he calls "modern dramas."[8] *Hamlet* has dominated psychoanalytic discussion since, reappearing with the Hungarian psychoanalyst Nicholas Abraham (1919–1975) who, with Maria Torok (1926–1998) adopted the idea of "cryptonomy," wherein the subject's language contains the repression of the previous generation. Abraham scripted a sixth Act of *Hamlet*; here, the prince's indecision in acting originates from being haunted by his father's "secret" – his own murder of King Fortinbras.[9] Ernest Jones (1879–1958), British psychoanalyst and Freud's biographer[10] wrote *A Psychoanalytical Study of Hamlet* in 1922, amplifying Freud on Hamlet's "Oedipus complex."[11] Drawing on Ella Sharpe (1875–1947), Lacan discusses *Hamlet* in his Seminar VI.[12] His Seminars II and VII return to the Greek tragedies, *Antigone* and *Oedipus at Colonus*. The psychoanalytic theorists and practitioners whose ideas dominate the field, all learned from literature in constructing their metapsychology. Freud, an educated mid-European intellectual, formed by German and European literature, frequently quoting Goethe, for instance, uses this legacy as a reference-point throughout his career in writing what many would see as modern literature. His "case studies" – "Dora,"[13] "Little Hans,"[14] the "Rat Man,"[15] the "Wolf Man"[16] – are modernist biographies.[17] This sampling is hardly exhaustive, but rather representative of the interconnectedness of psychoanalysis and literature, for which this chapter argues.

Freud and Memory

Modern literature interrogates the meaning of memory, conscious and unconscious: Freud began conceptualizing this when writing to Wilhelm Fliess[18] and more particularly in his case studies, such as the Wolf Man,[19] where he posits the present influence of a past traumatic "primal scene."[20] This, which might be the scene of the child's own conception, never witnessed, offstage (= "obscene") constructs repressed thought / memory / fantasy which returns as a symptom. This theory of repressed material returning in thought and producing parapraxes (unplanned, irrational behavior, perhaps), whose source is the unconscious, shows in Freud's sense of *Nachträglichkeit* (deferred action).[21] *Nachträglichkeit* introduces a differential, non-punctual relation between an "event" and its effects. Memory of a contemporary or later event reactivates memory of an earlier one, changing its significance and meaning. For "memory-traces" are "sub-jected from time to time to a *re-arrangement* in accordance with fresh circumstances – to a *retranscription*. ... Memory is present not once but several times over."[22] Analysis must reinterpret, reintegrate the past, and re-member in fantasy the witnessed – or if not witnessed, fantasized – traumatic primal scene.[23]

Freud exemplifies this with his discussion of "Emma," a young girl who came to him; her symptom being that she could not enter a shop alone. A memory from childhood of two visits to a shop during which she was sexually assaulted, was activated upon a third visit to the shop as an adult. For Freud the point is that the significance of the earlier, repeated, traumatic visits only emerges later as "a memory arousing an affect which it did not arouse as an experience because the change brought about in puberty had made possible a different understanding of what was remembered."[24] The "affect" is ambiguous: she experiences both horror and attraction. Emma suffers from an "oppressive bad conscience," since, though assaulted, she still returned to the shop as a girl, as if seductively. It does not correspond to the literal action (the shopkeeper had grabbed her under her clothes) because she interprets that on the third visit as feeling that the shop-assistant was laughing at her clothes. Thus, says Freud, the unspeakable action is replaced by a "symbol-formation."[25] Memory is laid down as a writing within the psyche; clothes-symbolism, invested with "affect" (i.e., her clothes take on an emotional valence), but they are not really the issue as they actually capture and replace a blocked-off memory. This sequence describes a narrative, a *literary* process. If memory-traces exist in the psyche as writing, such writing comprises the "signifier," which is predominant within the subject; and on differentially layered forms of signification, having plural times and meanings, which are resolved as symbolic-formations, attached to non-locatable, non-chronological memories, which carry an affectual weight, but cannot be attached to an unambiguous signified (i.e., meaning). This insight has impacted on literature, disturbing ideas of recognizable cause-and-effect, locating present trouble (i.e., trauma) within a past perhaps impossible to access; it has been fundamental for conceptualizing delayed trauma and PTSD; trauma being perhaps the decisive word for considering the twentieth and twenty-first centuries' wars, bombings, genocides, enforced migrations, and trafficking.

Modernist texts invest in what the text does not /cannot say, probing absences which show ideology (as the symbolic order) lacking coherence in offering an "imaginary" sense of social / individual reality. They mirror Freud's injunction to listen for contradiction, repetition, and omission.[26]

Thus for Fredric Jameson, the Marxist literary critic, the literary text comprises gaps, discontinuities, contradictions, parallel to repressions in thought, resisting the symbolic order through gaps to be read symptomatically, because they speak of what Louis Althusser called an "absent cause" present, however, in the effects: "the whole existence of the structure [here, of the text] consists of its effects." Following Freud, Althusser added that contradictions came from "overdetermination": plural (absent) causes produce multiple textual effects.[27] Reading literature (outstandingly in American "New Criticism") once meant seeing a text whole, investigating the strategies wherein everything coheres in a triumph of artistic "form." Psychoanalysis suggests reading symptomatically, finding the "absent cause" – perhaps something repressed which the author cannot speak of – which is "inaccessible to us except in textual forms."[28] What I will describe later as the "Real," Lacan's term, for what the "absent cause" speaks of, points to personal, or political, or historical, trauma, imprinting the text, whose symptoms reveal traces of a history which Marxism and feminism describe: of class and gender-oppression; just as the literature of madness shows what a culture represses and silences.[29]

After Freud

The psychoanalyst Melane Klein (1882–1960) also turned to literature, but her focus was on the psychic life of children and how their early attachments define the adult mind. She concentrates on infantile fantasies about the mother; the child "introjecting" her (internalizing her) as the "good breast" and "projecting" onto her negative qualities such as the bad breast, reacting to her as a devouring figure by, in fantasy, tearing her to pieces. This fantasy she calls the "paranoid-schizoid" position; in the contrasted "depressive" position, the child makes reparation, characteristically in art, attempting to reintegrate its shattered, split world. Klein presents this in an essay on Aeschylus' *The Oresteia*.[30] She recognizes in her reading that "the greatness of Aeschylus's tragedies – and this would have a general application as far as other poets are concerned – derives from his intuitive understanding of the inexhaustible depth of the unconscious and the ways in which this under-standing influences the characters and situations he creates."[31] Greed and jealousy associate with introjection; envy – hatred of the mother – with projection; envy being illustrated from *Othello*. In the "splitting off" within these childhood fantasies, the child fears the loss of the loved object, and is destructive toward the mother, not seeing her as a whole person.[32] The unconscious was full of aggression and could be destructive, as Julia Kristeva (b. 1941) brings out in her book-length study of Klein.[33] The fear of annihilation needed to be contained by the child and, eventually, the adult. Attuned to the death-drive, Klein shows the subject needing to avoiding depression, self-division.[34] And there is no instinctual urge, no anxiety situation, no mental process which does not involve objects, external or internal; in other words, object-relations are at the center of emotional life.[35] The child, within the sphere of "phantasy," sees not wholes, but fragments, objects which are not quite objects, neither fully interior nor exterior. Klein uses Freud's example of his grandson's *Fort! da!* game wherein he throws a spool back and forth crying out: Fort! (There) and Da! (Gone) attempting to master separation from his mother.[36]

Hence under Klein's influence, D. W. Winnicott (1896–1971 a pediatrician who became a psychoanalyst) turns to the child's first "not me" object in *Playing and Reality* (1971). "Transitional objects" as he calls them, are partial, and let the child move within "potential spaces."[37] This concentration on the mother's overlapping with the child, and on play – which creates symbolizing – has generated literary criticism focused on the growth of love, on children's creativity and play, and ability to discover the power of symbolism, for Klein, "the foundation of all sublimation and of every talent."[38] Literature speaks for desire for integration, making sense out of loss, mourning the loved, lost object. Wilfred Bion (1897–1979), associated with Winnicott and with the "Middle Group," of the British School of psychoanalysis, cites Keats's praise of "negative capability," the avoidance of "irritable reaching after fact or reason," with its potential of psychic disturbance.[39] He asks how the psyche can be a "container" for thoughts: "thinking is a development forced on the psyche by the pressure of thoughts and not the other way round."[40] It is not consciousness that founds the subject, but thoughts; hence the mother, and symbolic objects, are essential to allow thoughts – which are simultaneously nothing, and uncontainably overwhelming – to cohere.

The plurality of psychoanalytic schools means that we cannot think of psychoanalysis as saying any one thing; and if it claims the authority to tell the "truth" about someone – which might make it coercive – for example, in advocating heteronormativity – and uses literature and its stories in proof of such normalizing, it is also questionable whether literature escapes such a will to truth. The literary critic Leo Bersani critiques a "culture of redemption" within Klein. His example is Proust's novel À la recherche du temps perdu, which tries to hold on to the past through memory, recovering it, making art repair inherently damaged, or valueless experience, devaluing, through the aesthetic art-work, historical experience, and art. Bersani claims from this that Kleinian belief in reparation and sublimation devalues, refuses, the violence within sexuality, and the inseparability of civilization and aggression, Freud's theme in Civilization and Its Discontents[41] which argues that civilization functions to control individual / group aggression does so at an exorbitant price by installing guilt and thwarted resentment. Literary theorist, Leo Bersani criticizes the implicit sense that literature reclaims, redeems the past, and that sublimations are "symbolic reparations of damaged experiences … spectral replications of experience." He argues that while "the projections, introjections, and identifications studied by Klein gravely problematize the formation of a bounded ego," her belief in "the restitutive forms of sublimation are tendencies to give back to the subject – and to the objects of the subject's love and hatred – their securely traced boundaries."[42] In other words, psychoanalysis recognizes that aggressivity in sexuality, and in the attempt to form an ego, smashes the ego which civilization needs for its continuance, and if literature is made to establish identity, that betrays these disconfirming effects in the name of a normalizing ideological tendency. Literature (Proust) and psychoanalysis acquire as agenda the consolidation of an identity which has given up on its own sexual desire, making it seek its extinction in "sublimation." Proust's novel values what resists the pull of civilization and sublimation, despite its stated drive to "redeem the past," as in T. S. Eliot's poetry (Ash-Wednesday and Four

Quartets). Bersani prizes the anti-systemic in Proust, and Freud, that which proves that psychoanalysis, like literature, works by perception of irresolvable contradictions, and shatters its certainties.[43]

But psychoanalysis, if it does not need to simply diagnose literature and uncover a single truth, can also uncover the processes that have impacted on literature. Writing trauma, as much modern literature does, contests nineteenth-century "realism" which accepted cause-and-effect, and makes autobiography, and witnessing traumatic events both necessary and yet impossible.[44] Under such a dominion of realism, early twentieth century literary critics used Freud directly, as with Edmund Wilson, whose essay "Dickens: The Two Scrooges" (1941) explored signs of Dickens as not only having /being his own double but as possessed by the idea of the double, a theme from Freud's "The Uncanny."[45] This Freudian methodology was continued by Steven Marcus' work on Dickens in a 1963 essay "Who Is Fagin?," a signature essay for the idea of the double, highlighting the son's aggression toward the father, and the father's toward the son.[46] There emerged many literary critics influenced by such classical psychoanalysis including Norman Holland, Kenneth Burke, and Lionel Trilling who used Freudian ideas to think about post-war democracy, and who were significant for American criticism. In France, an early Freudian critique of Edgar Allen Poe, using his complex life, comes from Marie Bonaparte (1882–1962).[47] This early psychoanalytic criticism read texts alongside psychoanalyses of their writers' biographies. Textual conflicts and ambiguities emerge from the author's life. And here we should note how detective fiction and psychoanalysis interrelate, both being fascinated by crime, encrypted secrets, and the truth of the past, which searches out but also disrupts confident assumptions about memory and reconstruction of past events and their meaning.

Literature and Lacan

I will focus for much of what follows on Jacques Lacan and his influence on the study of literature and psychoanalysis as it became dominant in psychoanalytic literary criticism in the 1960s and beyond. Lacan's positioning of human subjectivity in the realm of language made him a compelling figure for literary theorists and critics. Lacan, a contemporary of Surrealism reads like a baroque poet, as he locates language, not individual consciousness, as the producer of the text (as in Freud, jokes arise unbidden from the unconscious). Lacan's fascination with the language of literature appears throughout his collection of essays, *Écrits* (1966), one example being, "The Function and Field of Language in Psychoanalysis" (1953). In particular, he discusses Edgar Allen Poe's short story "The Purloined Letter" (1955–1956), in an essay[48] as a paradigm of his position. "The Purloined Letter," essay argues that the symbolic order "insists" by its constant repetition within the subject's life, its "letter" (i.e., the signifier) constructing the subject, holding it in place, giving it an apparently consistent identity. The "letter" disallows the subject's autonomy, for in each unconsciously repeated pattern in the story, the self, or better, the subject, is always contained by language and thus "feminized," rendered passive by the "letter" determining, controlling all truth relating to the subject. And psychoanalysis, correspondingly, can know and tell the truth about people's unconscious. Truth appears in how the "letter" within language demands that everything be taken *literally*, and *materially*: each letter (an epistolary letter, the letters of a word) tells.

Influenced by the structural linguistics of Ferdinand de Saussure and Roman Jakobson, and the structural anthropology of Claude Lévi-Strauss, Lacan critiques the earlier view of psychoanalysis starting not with the biographical subject and instead situates language as constructing the subject. This appears in his essay "The Instance of the Letter in the Unconscious, or Reason Since Freud" (1957) which mapped *metonymy* and *metaphor* (literary, traditional rhetorical terms), onto Freud's *displacement* and *condensation*: which Freud said constructed dream-images.[49] Images in dreams formed a "rebus," riddling pictures, the interpretation thereof being a word, or group of words.[50] In condensation, one image combines, or makes several different images cohere, making any one image "overdetermined," or multiple in meanings. It comes from several non-unified sources, which on analysis reveal their difference.[51] Dreams, like literary texts, contain plural meanings because any image (especially any metaphor) derives from multiple sources.[52] In displacement, one word, or image, replaces another with which it associates. Freud had already noted "the antithetical meaning of primary words"[53] – that words mean what they say, and their opposite, this doubleness is structured into language – while *Jokes and Their Relation to the Unconscious*[54] explored unconscious resonances within language because this is the very basis of how jokes surprise or shock: like literature, jokes always reveal more than intended. Further, in discussing the death-drive, Freud argued that language *Fort* (gone) and *da* (here) with Ernst, his grandson's play – substitutes, as symbolism, for the mother's presence.[55] Language, and symbolism starts up in the child's repetitive attempts to master death, the primary absence, identified with the mother, whose importance he carried over from Klein, as much as he took the importance of symbolism, which is, of course, where literature begins.

Lacanians, however, must contend with French philosopher Jacques Derrida's commentary, finding Lacan's interpretation of "The Purloined Letter" simplifying, omitting details in the text because Lacan wants to prove a point from it: that the psychoanalyst, the "postman of truth," is always right in their analysis of a person. Lacan gives the letter a single meaning and this accords with Derrida accusing Lacan of being "phallogocentric" – imposing patriarchally defined single meaning, making the "letter" of psychoanalysis – unlike the letter within literature – unitary, not internally split, saying one thing only. Perhaps, then, Lacan is guilty of downplaying literature,[56] which is Derrida's point in accusing him of being a Cartesian, but the debate between psychoanalysis as a discipline and literature maps onto another between philosophy and literature, where Derrida is antiphilosophy, and literature questions the investment in truth within philosophy / psychoanalysis. Yet the debate may be irresolvable, since Barbara Johnson argued that Derrida's essay on Lacan cannot prove that Lacan subordinated literature to psychoanalysis, making the latter superior as knowing the "truth," mastering interpretation of the literary text. Lacan might be literary and anti-philosophy himself.[57]

In Lacan, the subject begins with the "Imaginary" state, in "the mirror stage," where the subject sees itself as an ideal form, though Lacan points to this as a misrecognition (*méconnaissance*), which nonetheless centers the individuals as absolute and as narcissistic. But the subject must learn to become subject to the signifier, which has no inherent, or natural, meaning; it has a "signified" only because any signifier exists in a differential relationship with other signifiers. The subject is fragmented by the language it uses; each move in language is a further separation from that moment of imagined wholeness. So, for Lacan, within the signifying chain comprising the "symbolic order" of language and culture, each signifier displaces each other in a metonymic sequence (A-B-C); thus signifier B only bears meaning in being neither A or C, though it contains A and C within its unconscious. Interlocking with A or C, it forms the "symbolic order," which is "the law of the father," since it comes with patriarchal authority.[58] The Marxists Louis Althusser and Pierre Macherey identified this order with the power of ideology, as meaning those socially and patriarchally acquired beliefs which seem natural, and incontestable (and which psychoanalysis, no less than literature, challenges). The symbolic order, dominating the subject, imposes language as rational single meaning and gender position. However, since its terms are not positive, but only differential, identity assumed within the "symbolic," entails misrecognition; language speaks, and the subject misrecognizes itself within its displaced/displacing terms. Language, as "a system of differences without positive terms" is marked by an internal "lack"; a lack in "the Other," namely the place of language and of the unconscious. Entry into the "symbolic order" creates and constructs a gap, making poetic language the expression of desire.

Such a gap appears in Hamlet's melancholia, which has an uspecifiable content within it. The melancholic "knows *whom* he has lost, but not *what* he has lost in him"; in mourning the world "has become poor and empty; in melancholia, it is the ego itself."[59] Melancholia identifies with the lost object, with the Other: and rather than what is lost being let go, "the shadow of the object fell upon the ego,"[60] so that the self identifies with the Other, as no thing (no identifiable thing, which is not the same as "nothing"). This "no thing" compares with the *objet a*, and *das Ding* ("the thing") which is the subject of Lacan's Seminar VII: the unnamable object, which leads Lacan to argue that art is organized around "emptiness."[61] Whereas "emotion" assumes the ego producing definable feelings from its own autonomous being, "affect" comes from the Other, in other words, from language, from the symbolic order, itself not complete, but marked by absence. If the self affects itself (in "auto-affection"), that indicates a divided self, the shadow of the Other being within it, an unnamable self "other" to itself. "Affect" originates outside, in "hetero-affection," for what is affected in me is "the other in me"; "what affects me is always something other than myself."[62] If culture and history induce guilt, anxiety, even madness, "affect" is less the self's authenticity than a symptom of what lies at the border between I and the Other.[63] The border between the "Real" and the "Symbolic" is marked by "affect," feelings, or a mood, differing from a cognizable (i.e., represent-able) emotion. As Freud discussed irrationally felt guilt, Lacan calls anxiety an affect.[64] Anxiety, as affectual, lacks a clear, perhaps any, signified, per-haps no signified at all, but still causes insomnia.

The third term, after the "Imaginary," and the "Symbolic," is "the Real": in 1964, Lacan approached this with saying: "In our relation to things, in so far as this relation is constituted by the way of vision, and ordered in the figures of representation, something slips, passes, is transmitted from stage to stage, and is always to some degree eluded in it – that is what we call the gaze."[65] Whatever we read, or see, misses some "thing" missing in the "symbolic order" – which attempts to cover a lack it creates; this, which is nothing, being a "lack," exceeding symbolization, is – almost interchange-ably – "the Real," or "the gaze," and the "*objet petit a*," terms which imply that we are held (as in narcissism) by something fantasmatically elusive, fascinating us.[66] The "Real," preceding language, as a gap, a lack in being outside chronological orderings, makes literary representation (e.g., in "real-ism") impossible, or inadequate. It has a lure of attraction, fascinating, but threatening madness. Language attempting to describe it (as in the literature of mysticism) is baffled, must know no restraints; in Antonin Artaud, or James Joyce, it produces puns, portmanteau words, words elided, or chosen for their absence, like Georges Perec's *A Void*, which never uses the letter "e."[67] Lacan's Seminar X, "Anxiety," finds the *objet petit a* something "irreducible," an excess in the body of the other, as this is the subject of fantasy.[68] This fantastic sense indicates the inadequacy of the symbolic order; it means that literature can never be fully mimetic; thus supplementing our sense that traumatic events show up a crisis of representation anyway. Thus we find in the representation of the slaughter of banana plantation workers in Marquez' *One Hundred Years of Solitude*, or the slave-ship, and slavery itself in Toni Morrison's *Beloved*, or the poetry of Paul Celan.

Lacan, then, grounds his work in the three registers he identifies, the realm of the Imaginary/ Symbolic/ Real all held together in a "Borromean knot" (by three interlocking rings): if one is cut, all fall apart, inducing psychosis. Attention focuses on what happens where the rings intersect. To this arrangement of three, Lacan added a fourth, which binds them with multiple points of intersection, the *sinthome* (punning on "symptom," of which it is an older spelling, St. Thomas Aquinas, saint homme, or "man"). "Sin," and "tomes" (books) Lacan's Seminar XXIII argues, are both embodied in James Joyce's *Finnegans Wake* (1939), making Joyce, and the novel, "symptoms." *Finnegans Wake* articulates unconscious thought, with its running together of word-associations, and linguistic displacements and condensations. The *sinthome* is a mad writing, like *Finnegans Wake*, which saves from madness; it comprises *jouissance*, which is usually translated as "enjoyment" (sexual, beyond what is nameable in social terms – i.e., *Plaisir*). But it includes pain and pleasure, satisfaction deriving from suffering, even anxiety. Joyce, threatened by his father's simultaneous absence and dominance, created, deliberately, a language to avoid psychosis; the *sinthome* challenges the symbolic, which is committed to the father's authority, or to predefined knowledge.[69]

The *sinthome* attempts to cover a gap, which would also be the space of madness. Julia Kristeva articulates this sense of the lost unnamable thing with fear of the mother's real, or fantasized death, and the black depression / dejection/ melancholia this causes.[70] She speaks about "abjection," resulting from the attempt to become self-sufficient in throwing away what speaks of the Other, especially the mother. The mother's body makes the child feel itself an "object"; desire to establish the self as a "subject" produces the "abject," which comes from violently excluding those formless non-things (blood, urine, excrement, tears) which recall the young child's uncertain border with the mother. Attempting to establish such borders, such a defined pure self, engenders a Fascist masculinity.[71]

Culture tends, however, not to affirm lack, but completeness, as in Hollywood-type heroism. Lacan's "The Signification of the Phallus"[72] is relevant here, for the *objet a* relates to the phallus. This argument lays psychoanalysis open to the charge of anti-feminism, as promoting male sexuality, denying the woman a place and a "signifier" (as the phallus signifies male completeness).[73] The problem increases when Lacan strikes a bar through the "the" in "la femme" (the woman) as if saying there is no definition of "woman" which is not in the negative; but here, Lacan invokes a "*jouissance* beyond the phallus.*" If "the phallus" implies having, or possessing in the self fantasmatic wholeness of meaning, then the child's primary discovery is that the mother lacks that, but that it is unnamable. As the subject of primary repression, its lack constitutes desire as for the unknowable, hence unfulfillable. Relationships between the sexes are premised on neither having the phallus; the woman bound to be what she cannot be, the man giving what he has not got (something like a definition of love for Lacan); both sexes sensing, unconsciously, their castration. Freud considered castration a feared male fantasy, making male relationships with women fetishistic, phantasmagoric[74] but since castration in Freud relates to anatomical reality, it implies – problematically – that women are lacking. In Lacan, neither sex has the phallus, though the rhetoric of "the phallus" apparently privileges the male, even if such privilege only comes through patriarchal ideology. Yet the "supplementary" *jouissance* in Lacan, for which he references the mystic writings of women, medieval and baroque, in attempting to speak of a non-conceptualizable "Real" – "no thing" implies, as with Joyce, that writing must push toward the unrepresentable. "The phallus," however, signifies desire for established, single, patriarchal names and meaning.

Beyond Lacan

While the analysis of female hysteria in such literary criticisms led to a deepening of feminist insights into such historical and cultural contexts within literature, some feminisms reject psychoanalysis as patriarchal, depriving women of their bodily identity; this applies to Luce Irigaray, Catherine Clément, and Hélène Cixous; though their work remains Lacanian in its sense of language.[75] Queer theory, as in the work of Judith Butler, and more recently, Mari Ruti, is Freudian in its recognition of the bisexuality of all humans and polymorphous perversity, but follows Michel Foucault's suspicion of psychoanalysis as normalizing – in which he is followed by Gilles Deleuze and Félix Guattari – and begins by questioning why heterosexuality is considered the norm.[76] Examining the distinction between sex (biological) and gender (social) it asks if "sex" is not also socially determined, since biology with its XX and XY chromosome distinctions, may support a regulatory thinking about gender. Newer transgender discourses see all "sex" distinctions as malleable, not necessarily pre-given.

Yet psychoanalysis does speak to LGTBQ+ issues, as with Freud's "Psychogenesis of a Case of Homosexuality in a woman."[77] Like queer theory, it negates thinking that any sexual choice is "natural" or inherently preferable since, especially in Lacan, it denies that either sex has an advantage in being happier in the body, more fulfilled in its desires; sexuality is inhibited by lack and the phallus only figures an unrealizable fantasy of completeness. There can be no "literal" truth about what a body is, or should be. Psychoanalysis, hardly concerning itself with what a man or woman "is," remains, like queer theory, uninterested in identity, as opposed to masculinity and femininity. Lee Edelman supplements Lacan with the neologism *sinthomosexuality*: homosexuality must so braid language to create a space for gay desire in literature, which, perhaps seen in coded forms in Gothic literature, is denied ideological space, being dubbed a "culture of death" (Bersani sees heteronormative, sublimated culture, as that). Edelman calls sexuality that which is "intolerable to the structured self." Living, and writing sexuality, to do that, comes from wresting a space within language.[78]

Psychoanalysis recognizes the human as incomplete. Sexuality names that which, overcoded by the death-drive, incorporates masochism into attempts to solidify itself, remaining, however, not sealed off but invaded by an unknown and uncanny Real, which is "at the centre only in the sense that it is excluded, being the excluded interior."[79] Lacan defines hysteria as a man or woman asking what it is to be a woman when she is denied space within the symbolic order.[80] Hysteria, a nineteenth-century diagnosis, figures in much literary criticism discussing texts which thematize women in terms of their nervous sickness and even madness as in the cases of Bertha Mason in *Jane Eyre* or Jean Rhys' *Wide Sargasso Sea*, the governess in Henry James's *The Turn of the Screw*, or the narrator in Charlotte Perkins Gilman's *The Yellow Wallpaper*. Transgender issues highlight what Lacan says of hysteria – male and female – that the body may not be a given in its relation to a person's "sex," making even transgendering problematic, since neither sex nor body may offer a "natural" home for identity.[81] Here "Gothic" fascination with the ghost, as in the novels just cited, relates to the sense of the subject being ghosted by the past, by the other, by another identity not possessed. That, which will recall *Nachträglichkeit*, turns on uninterpretability. Freud thought dreams finally resisted interpretation,[82] and literary texts, like sexed beings, are not fully interpretable.[83]

Notes

1. Claire Buck, *H. D. and Freud* (Hemel Hempstead: Harvester 1991). H. D. wrote her own *Tribute to Freud* (1956).

2. Didier Anzieu (1923–1999) even argued that Beckett's work recalls and addresses his encounters with Bion. See Didier Anzieu, "Beckett and Bion," *International Review of Psycho-Analysis* 16 (1989): 163–69.

3. Sigmund Freud, "The Uncanny" (1919), *SE* 17: 264.

4. Freud, *The Interpretation of Dreams* (1900), *SE* 4: 26–266.

5. Freud, "Some Character-Types Met with in Psycho-analytic Work" (1916), *SE* 14: 316–21.

6. Freud, "Dostoevsky and Parricide" (1928), *SE* 21: 175–94.

7. Freud, *The Interpretation of Dreams*, 265.

8. Freud, "Psychopathic Characters on the Stage" (1906), *SE* 7: 308–09.

9. Nicholas Abraham and Maria Torok, *The Wolf Man's Magic Word: A Cryptonomy*, trans. Nicholas Rand, foreword by Jacques Derrida (Minneapolis: University of Minnesota Press 1986) and Nicholas Abraham, "The Phantom of Hamlet or the Sixth Act: Preceded by the Intermission of 'Truth'," *Diacritics* 18 (1988), 2–19. The "crypt" develops the idea of the "unconscious," as built out of what consciousness represses. It "encrypts" (hides, buries, and encodes) another's secrets within; this produces, with the Wolf Man's language (1918, *SE* 17: 3–122), a vast polyphonic poem, a "verbarium," in several languages (Russian, German, French, English). These fragments, punningly echoing from language to language, construct the Wolf Man, and what he conceals (for Abraham, the father's rape of the Wolf Man's sister). See Allan Lloyd Smith, "The Phantoms of Drood and Rebecca: The Uncanny Reencountered through Abraham and Torok's 'Cryptonomy'," *Poetics Today* 13 (1992): 285–308.

10. See Ernest Jones, *The Life and Work of Sigmund Freud* (3 vols.) (New York: Basic Books, 1953, 1955, 1957).

11. On the Oedipus Complex, see Freud, "Letter 71" (October 15, 1897), *SE* 1: 265–66. The psychoanalyst André Green thought Freud was fascinated with the theatre above other literary forms, drama showing conflict, not between opposing equal conscious impulses, "but between a conscious impulse and a repressed one"; engaging with neurotic drives (those which deal with the unconscious, and resistances to it). André Green, *The Tragic Effect: The Oedipus Complex in Tragedy*, trans. Alan Sheridan (Cambridge: Cambridge University Press 1979): discussing Oedipus, Orestes, *The Oresteia*; *Othello*, *Iphigenie*; *Bacchae*; Artaud, Hölderlin.

12. Ella Freeman Sharpe, *Collected Papers on Psychoanalysis* (London: Hogarth Press 1950), 203–65, including work on *King Lear* and *the Tempest*.

13. Freud, "Fragment of an Analysis of a Case of Hysteria" (1905), *SE* 7: 1–122.

14. Freud, "Analysis of a Phobia in a Five-Year-Old Boy" (1909), *SE* 10: 1–150.

15. Freud, "Notes Upon a Case of Obsessional Neurosis" (1909), *SE* 10: 153–318.

16. Freud, "From the History of an Infantile Neurosis" (1918), *SE* 17: 1–122.

17. Though seeing his work as scientific, he called the first version of *Moses and Monotheism, The Man Moses: An Historical Novel* (1939), *SE* 23: 3.

18. Wilhem Fliess was a confidant of Freud with whom he theorized many of his defining ideas through their correspondence. See Peter Rudnytsky, *Freud and Oedipus* (New York: Columbia University Press, 1987), 23–37.

19. Freud, "From the History of an Infantile Neurosis," 45.

20. See Peter Brooks *Reading for the Plot: Design and Intention in Narrative* (Cambridge MA.: Harvard University Press 1984).

21. Freud, "From the History of an Infantile Neurosis," 45–47. For "parapraxis" see *The Psychopathology of Everyday Life, SE* 6: 239–40; parapraxes include slips of the tongue, essential within literature, *SE* 6: 100–1.

22. Freud, "Letter 52" (December 6, 1896), *SE* 1: 233.

23. Freud, "Hysteria," *SE* 1: 50–51; "Constructions in Analysis," *SE* 23: 256–69. See Ned Lukacher, *Primal Scenes: Literature, Philosophy, Psychoanalysis* (Ithaca: Cornell University Press, 1986). See my discussion of *David Copperfield* in *Becoming Posthumous* (Edinburgh: Edinburgh University Press 2002), 59–87.

24. Freud, "Project for a Scientific Psychology" (1950), *SE* 1: 356.

25. Ibid., 353.

26. Freud notes that "almost everywhere noticeable gaps, disturbing repetitions and obvious contradictions have come about – indications which reveal things to us which it was not intended to communicate." Freud, *Moses and Monotheism*, 43.

27. Louis Althusser, *Reading Capital: The Complete Edition*, trans. Ben Brewster and David Fernbach (London: Verso, 2015), 343–44.

28. Fredric Jameson, *The Political Unconscious: Narrative as a Socially Symbolic Act* (London: Methuen, 1981), 35.

29. For madness, see Freud on Schreber (note 67); and Gilles Deleuze and Félix Guattari, *Anti-Oedipus: Capitalism and Schizophrenia* trans. Robert Hurley (London: Athlone Press, 1984), who open with discussion of Georg Büchner's *Lenz*, and with Artaud; see also Shoshana Felman, *Writing and Madness (Literature/Philosophy/Psychoanalysis)* trans. Martha Noel Evans (Ithaca: Cornell University Press, 1985). Felman uses Foucault's *History of Madness*, trans. Jonathan Murphy and Jean Khalfa (London: Routledge, 2006), which Derrida criticizes for neglecting psychoanalysis: *Resistances to Psychoanalysis*, trans. Peggy Kamuf (Stanford: Stanford University Press, 1996), 70–118.

30. For Klein, see Nicolette David, *Love, Hate, and Literature: Kleinian Readings of Dante, Ponge, Rilke, and Saurraute* (New York: Peter Lang 2003), 1–40.

31. Melanie Klein, "Some Reflections on *The Oresteia*," in *Envy and Gratitude, And Other Works 1946–1963*, ed. Hannah Segal (London: Vintage, 1997), 299.

32. Melanie Klein, "Envy and Gratitude," in *Envy and Gratitude, and Other Works 1946–1963*, ed. Hannah Segal (London: Vintage, 1997), 182.

33. Julia Kristeva, *Melanie Klein* (New York: Columbia University Press, 2004).

34. See for example, Melanie Klein, "Infantile Anxiety-Situations Reflected in a Work of Art and in the Creative Impulse," *International Journal of Psycho-Analysis* 10 (1929): 436–43.

35. Melanie Klein, *Envy and Gratitude, and Other Works 1946–1963*, ed. Hannah Segal (London: Vintage 1997), 182, 53, and 275–99 for *The Oresteia*.

36. See Freud, *Beyond the Pleasure Principle* (1920) *SE* 18: 13–17. For Klein's discussion of *Beyond the Pleasure Principle*, see "On Observing the Behaviour of Young Infants," in *Envy and Gratitude, and Other Works 1946–1963*, ed. Hannah Segal (London: Vintage, 1997), 121.

37. See Peter L. Rudnytsky ed., *Transitional Objects and Potential Spaces: Literary Uses of D. W. Winnicott* (New York: Columbia University Press 1993).

38. Klein "The Importance of Symbol Formation in the Development of the Ego" (1930) in Juliet Mitchell ed., *The Selected Melanie Klein* (Harmondsworth:

Penguin 1986), 97. Sublimation in Freud means "diversion" of the sexual drive toward "cultural achievement," *Three Essays on the Theory of Sexuality, SE* 7: 178. Marion Milner (1900–1988) follows Winnicott; her evocative book titles (*On Not Being Able to Paint; The Suppressed Madness of Sane Men*) indicate literary interests: *The Hands of the Living God* quotes the title of a D. H. Lawrence poem; *Eternity's Sunrise* recalls Blake.

39. In Britain there was debate between Anna Freud and Melanie Klein about child analysis and the future of the field with many taking sides. The "Middle Group" consisted of those analysts who "did not want to belong exclusively to either the Melanie Klein or the Anna Freud group," Claudine Geissmann and Pierre Geissmann, *A History of Child Psychoanalysis* (London: Routledge, 1998), 235.

40. W. R. Bion, *Second Thoughts: Selected Papers on Psycho-Analysis* (London: William Heinemann, 1967), 111.

41. Freud, "Civilization and Its Discontents" (1930), *SE* 21: 57–146.

42. Leo Bersani, *The Culture of Redemption* (Cambridge, MA: Harvard University Press 1990), 97–98.

43. Bersani shows that "sublimation" of sexuality also sexualizes; he reads Freud's "On Narcissism" (*SE* 14: 69–102) to show that ego-formation sexualizes, disruptively shattering the ego it creates (this questions the validity of identity-politics based on sexual identity). See Bersani's *The Freudian Body: Psychoanalysis and Art* (New York: Columbia University Press 1986), and *Baudelaire and Freud* (Berkeley: University of California Press, 1977).

44. Cathy Caruth, *Unclaimed Experience: Trauma, Narrative, and History* (Baltimore: John Hopkins University Press, 1996).

45. Freud, "The Uncanny," 217–52.

46. Edmund Wilson, *The Wound and the Bow* (London: Methuen 1961), 1–93, Steven Marcus, *Dickens from Pickwick to Dombey* (New York: W. W. Norton 1986), 358–78.

47. Marie Bonaparte, *The Life and Works of Edgar Allan Poe: A Psychoanalytic Interpretation*, trans. John Rodker (London: Hogarth Press, 1971).

48. Lacan, *Écrits*, 6–48.

49. Freud, *Interpretation of Dreams*, 279–309.

50. Freud, *Interpretation of Dreams*, 277–78. William Empson *Seven Types of Ambiguity* (Harmondsworth: Penguin, 1961) used Freud's "condensation" to consider a last, different ambiguity in language, where what is said is the opposite of what is desired (193).

51. See Freud, *Interpretation of Dreams*, 4: 283, and Freud on hysteria, Freud, *Studies on Hysteria, SE* 2: 212, 287–88.

52. Freud, *Interpretation of Dreams*, 307.

53. Freud, "The Antithetical Meaning of Primal Words," *SE* 11: 153–61.

54. Freud, *Jokes and Their Relation to the Unconscious, SE* 8: 1–258.

55. Freud, *Beyond the Pleasure Principle*, 14–17.

56. Malcolm Bowie, *Freud, Proust and Lacan: Theory as Fiction* (Cambridge: Cambridge University Press 1987), 135–63 discusses Lacan's distance from literature.

57. Jacques Derrida, *The Postcard: From Socrates to Freud and Beyond*, trans. Alan Bass (Chicago: University of Chicago Press, 1987), 413–96; Barbara Johnson,

"The Frame of Reference: Poe, Lacan, Derrida," *The Critical Difference: Essays in the Contemporary Rhetoric of Reading* (Baltimore: Johns Hopkins University Press, 1980), 110–46. For documents in the debate see John P. Muller and William J. Richardson, *The Purloined Poe: Lacan, Derrida, and Psychoanalytic Reading* (Baltimore: Johns Hopkins University Press, 1988). See also Sarah Kofman, *Freud and Fiction*, trans. Sarah Wykes (Cambridge: Polity, 1991), 52.

58. See Dylan Evans ed., *An Introductory Dictionary of Lacanian Psychoanalysis* (London: Routledge, 1996).

59. Freud, "Mourning and Melancholia" (1917), *SE* 14: 245–46.

60. Freud, "Mourning and Melancholia," 249.

61. Lacan, *The Ethics of Psychoanalysis*, trans. Dennis Porter (London: Routledge, 1990), 130.

62. Adrian Johnston and Catherine Malabou, *Self and Emotional Life: Philosophy, Psychoanalysis, and Neuroscience* (New York: Columbia University Press, 2013), 20.

63. For views on affect, especially non-psychoanalytic, see Marta Figlerowicz, "Affect Theory Dossier: An Introduction," *Qui Parle* 20 (2012): 3–18.

64. Freud, "Some Character-Types Met with in Psychoanalytic Work," *SE* 14: 332–33, *Civilization and Its Discontents* (1930), *SE* 21: 123–39; Lacan, *Anxiety*, trans. A. R. Price (Cambridge: Polity, 2014), 15.

65. Jacques Lacan, *The Four Fundamental Concepts of Psychoanalysis* ed. Jacques Alain-Miller, trans. Alan Sheridan (New York: W. W. Norton, 1981), 73. The section is called "Of the Gaze as *Objet Petit a*," 83 identifies the real with the gaze.

66. Charles Shepherdson, *Lacan and the Limits of Language* (New York: Fordham University Press, 2008), 1–49, 81–100 discusses the Real, and Lacan on "affect."

67. See Freud on the psychotic Judge Schreber's made-up language, *SE* 12: 35–36; on Schreber and literature see Eric L. Santner, *My Own Private Germany: Daniel Paul Schreber's Secret History of Modernity* (Princeton: Princeton University Press, 1996).

68. In Lacan and in Freud's "Fetishism" (1927), *SE* 21: 149–57, all looking and engagement with others contains something fantasmatic, especially in perceiving sexual difference; see Massimo Fusillo, *The Fetish: Literature, Cinema, Visual Art*, trans. Thomas Haskell Simpson (New York: Bloomsbury, 2017).

69. Luke Thurston, *James Joyce and the Problem of Psychoanalysis* (Cambridge: Cambridge University Press, 2004); Daniel Bristow, *Joyce and Lacan: Reading, Writing, and Psychoanalysis* (London: Routledge, 2016).

70. See Julia Kristeva, *Melanie Klein*, trans. Ross Guberman (New York: Columbia University Press, 2001), 186–91; for the mother and melancholia, *Black Sun: Depression and Melancholia*, trans. Leon S. Roudiez (New York: Columbia University Press, 1989), and *Powers of Horror: An Essay on Abjection*, trans. Leon S Roudiez (New York: Columbia University Press, 1982).

71. On Klein and Kristeva, using, for example, Mary Shelley, see Mary Jacobus, *First Things: The Maternal Imaginary in Literature, Art, and Psychoanalysis* (London: Routledge, 1995), 51–52, 98–99, 110–13, and generally, Mary Jacobus, *The Poetics of Psychoanalysis: In the Wake of Klein* (Oxford: Oxford University Press, 2005). See also Juliana Schiesari, *The Gendering of*

Melancholia: Feminism, Psychoanalysis, and the Symbolics of Loss in Renaissance Literature (Ithaca: Cornell University Press, 1992), and for Mary Shelley, Mladen Dolar "'I shall be with you on your Wedding-Night': Lacan and the Uncanny," *October* 58 (1991): 5–23. Hal Foster, "Armour Fou," *October* 56 (1991), 64–97, discusses Fascist identity and art.
72. Lacan, *Écrits,* 575–84.
73. Jane Gallop, *Reading Lacan* (Ithaca: Cornell University Press, 1985), 133–56.
74. Freud, "Fetishism," 149–57.
75. Toril Moi, ed. *French Feminist Thought: A Reader* (Hoboken, NJ: Wiley-Blackwell, 1987); Peter L. Rudnytsky and Andrew Gordon, eds. *Psychoanalyses/Feminisms* (Albany: SUNY Press, 2000).
76. See Michel Foucault, *The History of Sexuality: An Introduction* (New York: Vintage, 1990).
77. Freud, "Psychogenesis of a Case of Homosexuality in a Woman," *SE* 18: 146–72.
78. Lee Edelman, *No Future: Queer Theory and the Death Drive* (Durham, NC: Duke University Press 2004) 33–66.
79. Lacan, *Ethics* 71, 101, 139.
80. Lacan, *The Psychoses,* trans. Russell Grigg (London: Routledge, 1993), 172.
81. Patricia Gherovici, *Please Select Your Gender: From the Invention of Hysteria to the Democratizing of Transgenderism* (London: Routledge, 2010), and *Transgender Psychoanalysis: A Lacanian Perspective on Sexual Difference* (London: Routledge, 2017).
82. Freud, *Interpretation of Dreams,* 525.
83. For transdisciplinary writers who work with literature and psychoanalysis (as clinicians) see also: Josh Cohen, *The Private Life: Why We Remain in the Dark* (London: Granta Books, 2013); Adam Phillips, *Promises, Promises: Essays on Psychoanalysis and Literature* (New York: Basic Books, 2009); Christopher Bollas, *Meaning and Melancholia: Life in the Age of Bewilderment* (New York: Routledge, 2018). Similarly, see the post-Lacanian writings of Slavoj Žižek; but that is a topic for another essay.

14

LISA RUDDICK

Beyond the Fragmented Subject

In a recent book, Marianne Noble describes the forms of interpersonal contact that are evoked in the works of four antebellum writers. Theoretically speaking, she believes the concept of "human contact" requires vigorous defense. For "today," she says, "scholars tend to be skeptical about the possibility" of "anything we might call human contact." Since "they doubt the existence of authentic selves," they cannot envision two selves greeting each other. Against this background, Noble draws on psychoanalytic theories ranging from object relations to relational psychoanalysis to argue that distinctive selves do exist, and that "attunement to the other's individuality" is possible.[1]

In another recent work, Katherine Ding remarks, similarly, on a "current scholarly malaise with claims of true self-revelation." Unlike Noble, Ding happens to share in this malaise. Her own argument is that "the sense of interiority we [in the West] associate with character, personhood, or identity" is actually just a "performative effect," the result of each individual's "compositional" efforts. Further, the notion that one might disclose a part of one's inner life to another is fatally bound up with "Romantic sincerity," which in turn depends on "an outdated surface/depth model."[2] These ideas will be more or less familiar to those who follow contemporary criticism. While it is hardly the case that everyone in our field adopts a strict antihumanism or posthumanism, these positions are often taken to represent the most sophisticated thinking available on the nature of subjectivity.[3]

For purposes of real life, it is hard to imagine that many members of our profession actually think we must do without "anything we might call human contact." As I write, conditions of self-isolation prevail among nonessential workers in the United States, as states attempt to flatten the curve on COVID-19. During this challenging time, we academics are doing the same things to forestall loneliness that others self-isolating are doing. We reach out via phones and other media to sustain our interpersonal worlds, and by no means scorn what the meditation teacher Tara Brach, commenting on the same crisis, has called "the joy that comes from real, tenderhearted connection during such vulnerable times."[4]

The fact that contemporary literary criticism has so little to say for "real, tenderhearted connection" is not due to any dearth of available theoretical models for describing such a thing. Psychoanalysts in the English-speaking world have for some decades been engaged in a series of rich, evolving conversations regarding the kinds of self-experience and mutual attunement of which human beings are in fact capable, at both the conscious and the unconscious levels. These discussions, many of them associated with relational theory, build not only on clinical findings but also on contemporary neuroscience and infant research.[5] Why has this body of clinically and scientifically informed psychoanalytic theory not interested literary scholars, particularly those whose own work draws on psychoanalysis in one or another of its aspects?

In what follows, I will use the example of Max Cavitch to represent a small cohort of literary scholars who do draw on relational theory. My aim is not just to suggest that this psychoanalytic school offers fine alternatives for those in our field who have little affinity for antihumanism. More pointedly, I will show how the comparison throws into relief the weaknesses of the antihumanist understanding itself. Though my main touchstone will be relational psychoanalysis, that is hardly the only school to offer a potential answer to the pieties of antihumanism. Object relations theory, its precursor, is another good candidate. Were this a longer chapter, I would describe the work of Peter Rudnytsky, Michael Snediker, TreaAndrea Russworm, Nancy Yousef, Alicia Christoff, and David Eng and Shinhee Han – a partial list of contemporary scholars who bring object relations theory powerfully to bear on the interpretation of literary and other cultural texts. My larger point is that it is time our discipline engaged more fully with the range of psychoanalytic theory. Were we to do so, we would quickly recognize what is lost in antihumanism.

Yet as an obstacle to this more capacious inquiry, our field's dominant discourse features a rhetoric that suggests that one cannot depart from the notion of a completely "decentered" or "fragmented" subjectivity without falling into political conservatism. We will see how this rhetoric operates through logical slippages, which serve to spread shame where it does not belong. This manipulative logic is a key delivery system for the "paranoid" thinking Eve Sedgwick long ago identified in literary studies.[6] It has survived by decades the heyday of high theory, living on in conceptual tics that by now seem to call for no justification or even reflection.[7]

A final question I ask in these pages is why our profession should have clung for so long to a view of subjectivity that has these weaknesses. It is not that we lack for theoretical alternatives. Nor, of course, do we lack for literary matrices that could inspire new thinking.

Within literary studies, the privileging of theoretical models that deny the existence of "authentic selves" extends to the subfield of literature and psychoanalysis. The conversation in literature and psychoanalysis is heavily imprinted by the antihumanist models that descend from poststructuralist psychoanalysis, with Jacques Lacan standing as the founding figure.[8] Scholars sometimes do appeal to alternative psychoanalytic models, but in doing so they generally adhere to a small canon, selected on a principle of not offending sensibilities trained on the theory of the decentered subject.[9] For example, the concept of the *observing ego* or the *observing self*, ultimately derived from Freud's own ideas about the ego, remains to the present day a central element of psychoanalytic theory. These terms describe the part of the self that can witness and understand the experiencing aspects of the self, with consequences for a person's stability and psychological growth.[10] Nowadays this mental function is sometimes captured by other terms, such as "reflective function" and "mentalization"; but despite some theoretical variations, the same aspect of subjective life is in the theorists' sights. But contemporary literary criticism, even when drawing on Freud's own theories, generally steers clear of the concept of the observing ego, because of a settled idea that "the ego" and "the self" in all their aspects are fatally bound up with the individual's adaptation to coercive social norms.[11]

Or again, a literary scholar might draw on object relations theory, invoking the theories of D. W. Winnicott or a contemporary descendant such as Adam Phillips or Christopher Bollas. Yet it is vanishingly rare for such a scholar to touch down into the area of Winnicott's thought that involves the "true" and the "false" selves, despite the high regard the psychoanalytic community has for that aspect of Winnicott's contribution.[12] For the concept of the true self clashes with our own profession's skepticism as to the existence of a self, which goes back to high theory's dismissal of "some essence I might be."[13]

When we turn to relational psychoanalysis, which stands at the cutting edge of psychoanalytic thought in the English-speaking world, the discrepancy between our own profession's thinking and that of the analytical community is stark. Few scholars of literature cite relational theory at all. In 2007, Vera Camden, speaking both as a practicing psychoanalyst and as a literary scholar, noted that "most academics act as if the relational turn that ... defines clinical practice today simply never occurred." Camden remarked that our discipline was thus "out of step with the most fruitful and affectively enriching clinical research and practice of our times."[14] In the years since, the discipline has seen glacial, though promising, movement toward an encounter with relational theory, which, again, I will ultimately represent through the example of Max Cavitch.

Progress has been slow because academics find relational psychoanalysis ideologically dissonant. To read relational theory is to find that amid great variety, this school accounts for subjectivity in ways that conflict with the academy's preferred vision of a fragmented, discontinuous subjectivity. However much the relational theorists might question the existence of a static or singular self – thus, in some cases, accounting themselves post-modernists – they suggest that it is beneficial to be able to grasp and integrate some of the facets of one's self-experience.[15] As the psychoanalyst Susan Fairfield writes, "If we imagine a continuum extending from a monolithic, rigid, and undifferentiated subjectivity to sheer random dispersion, it turns out that every psychoanalytic theorist has a mixed model ... with the center of gravity located closer to one or the other end of the continuum but well short of the extremes." Thus, while some relational theorists conceive of selfhood in "plural" terms, they still affirm the need for forms of self-integration. On this score, Fairfield cites the theorist Jessica Benjamin, a "pluralist" who nonetheless affirms, with the psychologist Margo Rivera whom Benjamin here quotes, "a central consciousness that can handle the contradictions of the different voices and different desires within one person [and that represents] the growing ability to call all these voices 'I,' to dis-identify from any one of them as the whole story."[16] I cannot make this point strongly enough: even the most postmodern of contemporary psychoanalysts do not view subjectivity as entirely decentered, as literary criticism in a postmodern psychoanalytic vein does. Fairfield, whose comments I have just quoted, sees this cleavage herself. She notes that she taught comparative literature before embarking on her analytic training; thus she is poised to compare the perspectives of the two fields. What she observes is that the "thoroughgoing postmodern pluralism" that one would think would follow from academic postmodern theory is not "consistent with psychoanalysis" as "currently theorized and practiced," even by those relational psychoana-lysts who conceive of their views as postmodernist.[17]

As a kindred disparity, contemporary Lacanian analysts often interpret Lacan in a manner that assumes the necessity of an ego, presenting a Lacan who would sound oddly conservative (or "humanist") to an ear trained in literary studies. For example, the Lacanian psychoanalyst Raul Moncayo clearly distinguishes "defensive" from "non-defensive forms of ego-functioning." If I may speak telegraphically for readers who know Lacan, Moncayo associates "non-defensive ego functioning" – which he sees as positive – with what Lacan calls "the subject of the unconscious."[18] Yet literary criticism, whether drawing on Lacan or on a different psychoanalytic theorist, seldom makes space for ego functioning in this positive sense. To someone trained in our discipline, the phrase "non-defensive ego functioning" might sound like something pulled from the pages of the long-despised ego psychologists, the very school that Lacan attacked.

What all this means in practical reality is that our profession's commitment to a particular view of subjectivity confines us to a silo that admits only cracks of light from the contemporary psychoanalytic world. This wary behavior is motivated by a widely felt need to protect ideas whose truth our profession established long ago, in the theory era of the 1980s and 1990s. But did earlier critical generations in fact establish the superiority of the model of decentered subjectivity?

Let us make a brief detour into the critical past, to observe a form of tendentious reasoning that has permeated academic discussions of subjectivity since the 1980s. I here discuss a critical example that appeared around the turn of the millennium. It is thus recent enough to have some continuity with contemporary inquiry, but remote enough to belong to a time when Lacan's ideas were still being extensively laid out on the page, rather than simply assumed as a part of the conceptual bedrock as is now the case. In 2003, then, the literary scholar Cynthia Marshall published a piece in *PMLA* in which she described the importance of Lacan for her own account of early modern forms of subjectivity. She remarked that she rejected "the dynamic therapeutic models drawn from object relations and ego psychology." Her brief against those models was that they "delineate the interaction of a clearly posited self and other." She preferred Lacan because "the subject for Lacan is not defined in the humanistic terms of interiority or depth."[19]

Today, these understandings are still widespread, though the current style is to nod to them rather than to elaborate and justify them. Briefly, the idea is that the integrated sense of self that is valorized by object relations theory and midcentury ego psychology is a phenomenon that from the different, Lacanian perspective is just a bundle of Imaginary identifications.[20] A further common complaint against ego psychology in particular, and one that may lie in the background in the present case, is that this school has a conservative tenor, as it associates psychological health with the individual's adaptation to society.[21] From these various considerations, it is thought to follow that when an analyst indebted to either of these two schools helps an analysand to strengthen his or her sense of self, the result is to inhibit the analysand's productive encounter with his or her actual fragmentation (or lack). A final academic commonplace rehearsed in Marshall's remarks is that in historical terms, the experience of cohesive selfhood, along with the sense of having "interiority" and "depth," belongs only to members of modern Western societies; this selfhood supposedly evolved in tandem with early modern "humanism," and in the centuries since has served a toxic bourgeois individualism.

The rising academic generation no longer devotes pages of exposition to these concepts. Yet a normative understanding persists to the effect that cohesive selfhood is an illusion born of Western modernity, and that an affirmation of self-cohesion in any form is tantamount to political conservatism.[22] As far as I can see, that is the only reason that for purposes of psychoanalytic inquiry, object relations theory has a lower prestige in the academic humanities than theories involving an incoherent or a shattered subjectivity. Yet we are here looking at a disciplinary bias rather than a well-reasoned preference. Our profession has somehow avoided the collective conversation that would have carefully weighed object relations against the psychoanalytic models that valorize a fragmented subjectivity, a discussion that among other things would have compared the actual political and social implications of each.[23]

As an index of this bias, innumerable scholars over the years have drawn on the ideas of the psychoanalytic queer theorists Leo Bersani and Lee Edelman, who propose (varying) forms of self-shattering as a means to oppose "the fixity and coherence of the ego's form."[24] In the meantime, the theorist Michael Snediker, who likewise engages in psychoanalytic queer-theoretical inquiry, has had far less influence. Yet Snediker's *Queer Optimism*, published in 2009, offers a brilliant rejoinder to both Bersani and Edelman, using object relations theory as a fulcrum.[25] Snediker's book, while very well received, should have had a cutting impact not just on the conversation in queer theory but on the default understandings of the profession as a whole. Instead, the conversation proceeded largely as before.

Another marker of the same bias is the fact that to the present day, scholars whose thinking accords with antihumanism are allowed to proceed via the most gnomic of references to apparently settled truths. For example, "interiority" and "depth" will be attributed out of hand to the illusory "sovereign subject," and it will be asserted, without explanation, that "the 'I'" is "other to itself."[26] In contrast, those who rely on object relations must provide a scrupulous, linear account of their theoretical framework. My concern, throughout, is with the profession's default understandings, rather than with any monolithic ideology. The question I ask is not "Which ideas has every person in our profession agreed to?" but, more modestly, "Which are the ideas that go without saying, the ones that can be invoked glancingly, without a coherent elaboration or defense?"

In the two decades or so since the "death of theory" was widely pronounced, the same dutiful thinking governs critical movements that on the surface appear new.[27] It is as if the eminences of high theory had among them settled once and for all certain questions regarding the nature of human subjectivity. For example, an article of 2016 that is situated squarely within the movement known as the new materialisms praises a particular literary work for "successfully destabiliz[ing]" the idea of "integrated" selfhood and asserting in its place a "fragmented," "split or posthuman subjectivity."[28] Though the article cites theorists of the posthuman rather than Lacan, the concept of the "split" subject has been a staple of critical discourse since Lacan's thinking first entered the discipline in the late 1970s.

Yet the reasoning that has long supported this idea of a "fragmented" subjectivity rests on a false binary. If the present chapter spreads awareness of this central fault, it will have done its main work. The conceptual sleight of hand I am about to describe has probably always been unconscious; its function in any case is to suppress alternative opinion.

To see how the binary works, let us spend another moment on Marshall's work, again as a sample of ordinary academic discourse produced at a juncture when colleagues were still devoting pages at a time to vindications of Lacanian theory against alternative psychoanalytic models. Marshall's theoretical framework was entirely normative for the moment in which she wrote. Her work was very highly reviewed; when the book-length study associated with the essay I have quoted above was published, colleagues praised not just its readings of early modern texts but also its theoretical apparatus.[29] Gail Kern Paster's blurb, for example, opens as follows:

> Brilliantly employing the insights of Freudian, Lacanian and post-Lacanian psychoanalysis in a series of close textual readings, Marshall demonstrates the early modern self's desire for self-dissolution in the rough textual pleasures of jouissance.

Recall, then, that Marshall criticizes "ego psychology and object relations." Yet neither in the essay I have quoted earlier nor in the book where she makes the same dismissals does Marshall indicate that she has actually read any work from either of these schools. Particularly in the case of object relations, her critique is captious. Marshall rejects object relations theorists on the grounds, again, that they describe "the interaction of a clearly posited self and other." But what would a psychoanalysis look like that did not validate the existence of self and other, and the potential for interaction between the two?

Most practicing psychoanalysts, including Lacanians, would have serious concerns about a person who had no sense of where the self ended and the other began. As it happens, confusions of self and other are often experienced by individuals with the cluster of symptoms commonly diagnosed as borderline personality disorder; these confusions can cause great suffering for these individuals and those close to them.[30] On the other hand, perhaps the force of Marshall's critique is lodged in the word "posited" – "a clearly posited self and other" – on some notion that object relations theory conceives of selfhood in terms of the individual's experience of a "posited" identity, reified and abstract. Yet that by no means describes what one finds when one reads the object relations theorists themselves – Klein, Winnicott, Bion, Fairbairn, and so on.

On one side, then, stands Lacan, whose thinking is taken to be rigorous. On the other side are placed not only the ego psychologists, some of whom arguably did encourage a reified self, but also the object relations theorists. Like much scholarship before and after, this work creates the impression that if one were to try to nudge the conversation at all in the direction of assigning some value to individuation, interiority, and self-cohesion, one would fall in with the conservative ego psychologists.[31] Marshall makes her theoretical case only by caricaturing as the psychoanalytic other everything that lies outside the Lacanian branch of psychoanalytic theory.

It apparently follows that an utter dissolution of selfhood is the only viable alternative to a fantastically rigidified sense of self-coherence. In keeping with this understanding, and in particular reliance on the theories of Bersani, Marshall makes an implausible argument to the effect that certain early modern dramas, in portraying horrifying acts of violence on the stage – the blinding of Gloucester, for example – "shattered" audience members' selfhood, thus giving audiences relief from a then-emergent "bourgeois" self-cohesion.[32] I grant that aesthetic experiences can unsettle our sense of who we are; that can be a part of their appeal. But this disruption must be subtle and manageable, in order to prevent our simply exiting the aesthetic scene in order to avoid severe distress. If one's viewing of a play were instead to lead to a total loss of ego functioning – a different phenomenon from a mere relaxation of self-boundaries – that would surely be a sign that the theatrical experience had reactivated a trauma or brought forward some other underlying disturbance.

To pursue a fictional example, if Shakespeare's Claudius leaves the scene of "The Mousetrap," it is surely because he sees in it a repetition of the traumatic scene of which he himself was the instigator, and of whose theatrical representation he is now the target. But as the narrative evolves, even this blow does not obliterate Claudius' sense of selfhood. He gathers himself, using his full authority as king to clear the room with a simple "Give me some light: away!"[33] (3.2.257). To the extent, then, that this character reads plausibly to us in this moment, it is hard to see why we should believe that the typical reaction of flesh-and-blood audience members in the early modern period to merely theatrical representations of gore and mayhem was that their very identities were shattered.

Today, the dichotomized thinking I have just described continues to control academic discussions of subjectivity. The word "sovereign" has somewhat displaced "Cartesian" as the preferred descriptor for the congealed selfhood that represents one pole. At the other pole, and supposedly truer to the realities of psychic life, stands a subjectivity that is incoherent, fragmented, and incapable of integration. In an important recent work, Rita Felski makes a point similar to mine: "The notion of an inner nature, of a fateful inner self ..., is viewed [by many contemporary scholars] as a naïve Romantic holdover or a nakedly ideological belief in the autonomy and supremacy of the individual." Felski further critiques an academic preference for the idea that "what we think is inside is really outside: our sense of an inner reality is manufactured by external forces, and any sense we may have of our individuality or uniqueness is misplaced."[34]

There is no reason to assume that human self-experience cannot be conceived of except in terms of absolute stability or absolute dispersion. The critical theorist Mari Ruti makes this point in a number of superb recent works, though unlike me she takes a Lacanian route through the problem. Ruti sees Lacan, rightly interpreted, as offering a corrective to the academic thinking that in his name declares "subjective coherence ...bad," and "incoherence ... good." "Many critics," Ruti notes, "promote a stark either/or choice between a fully autonomous subject and the complete pulverization of the subject."[35] She places Edelman, Gilles Deleuze, and Lynne Huffer among the thinkers who have promoted this binary thinking. But on her own reading, Lacan himself, far from "advocating the complete destruction of the subject," thinks in terms of a "middle ground." Thus "[her] Lacan" is not the Lacan, for example, of Edelman, nor of most other literary scholars indebted to Lacan.[36]

In this connection, Ruti and the philosopher Amy Allen have recently compared Lacan's views on psychological life with the those of Melanie Klein, one of the founders of object relations theory. Like Lacan, Klein "offers a conception of subjectivity that occupies a productive middle ground between the rational, autonomous, and transcendental subject of Western metaphysics and the embrace of a radical desubjectivation."[37] In fact, a different version of the present chapter might have challenged the antihumanist pieties by charting a conceptual course from Klein herself, though Sedgwick's Kleinian critique of "paranoid" criticism, and on to Allen and then the remarkable work of the contemporary psychoanalyst Donald Carveth.[38] Though Carveth's subject is not the academic humanities, I believe his theories offer a rich potential resource for those who wish to find a path past the conceptual blockages in our own field.

Alongside Lacanian theory thus construed, as well as Kleinian theory, another potential corrective to the dichotomized thinking that befuddles academic discussions of subjectivity is contemporary relational psychoanalysis, to which the remaining discussion is devoted. One of the gifts of relational theory is to offer a vivid picture of the middle ground that lies between congealed and fragmented subjectivity. Relational theorists see a sense of self-continuity as essential for psychological life. Yet they believe this is achieved alongside an ongoing experience of multiplicity and fluidity. In the words of Jody Messler Davies, one of the movement's most brilliant theorists, relational theory "has begun to conceive of self, indeed of mind itself, as a multiply organized, associationally linked network of parallel, coexistent, at times conflictual, systems of meaning attribution and understanding." More simply, what we call "mind" is arguably constituted by "multiple selves." Further, it is ideal if, as individuals, we can hold in tension the centripetal processes that make us feel cohesive – "the primarily memory-based connections that give us a sense of psychic integrity" – and "the dynamic processes that threaten to splinter our internal organization."[39]

Davies suggests, for example, that within an analytic session, the analyst might say a few words that quietly invite into the dialogue an aspect of the analysand that embodies the analysand's childhood self-experience. The thoughts and feelings that then come forward can be so dissonant that they seem to belong to a separate self, one that has been dissociated in favor of "the rational, adult self" the analysand has "so carefully constructed." Davies writes of the delicate, often risky processes through which she helps analysands to bring the various jarring aspects of their self-experience into conversation with one another, so that the different personae can come to share "memories, overwhelming affect states, and seemingly irresolvable interpersonal conflicts."[40] It might sound as if I here describe an analyst's work with people with dissociative identity disorder. But the point is precisely that a certain amount of dissociation is ubiquitous in psychological life, and that at the same time it is fruitful to bring the various aspects of one's self-experience into a kind of shared awareness.

For readers new to relational theory, an excellent point of entry is *Relational Psychoanalysis: The Emergence of a Tradition*, an anthology of 1999 in which Stephen Mitchell and Lewis Aron gathered essays by many of the founding figures of this school.[41] Within the present space, I can continue to offer a glimpse of the potential stakes for our own discipline by describing, first, some ideas of the relational theorist Philip Bromberg, and then the uses to which the literary scholar Max Cavitch puts some of his ideas.

LISA RUDDICK

Like Davies, Bromberg thinks of human self-experience in terms not of a singular self but of multiple "self-states." Citing findings from infant observation studies and psychiatric research, he remarks that

> There is now abundant evidence that the psyche does not start as an integrated whole but is nonunitary in origin – a mental structure that begins and continues as a multiplicity of self-states that maturationally attain a feeling of coherence which overrides the awareness of discontinuity. This leads to the experience of a cohesive sense of personal identity and the necessary illusion of being "one self."[42]

Working with Bromberg's ideas, Cavitch writes of the need to conceive of self-experience in terms of a "relation between identity and multiplicity."[43] This dynamic, like the tension Davies describes between centripetal and centrifugal processes, represents precisely the middle ground that our own discipline occludes when it pits a "sovereign" subjectivity against a "fragmented" subjectivity. Just one of the implications for literary studies is that to the extent that our profession engages in social critique – something it often does very well – we might rethink our assumptions as to what it takes for a person to break free of the scripted sense of identity that follows from compliance with social norms.[44]

I would argue in fact that relational psychoanalysis offers more powerful models than academic antihumanism does for the kind of personal transformation that can disencumber an individual from the weight of societal roles and expectations. Cavitch notes, for example, that the therapeutic work of psychoanalysis can be radical, in helping the analysand to relax the "disabling self-protectiveness" that has led him or her to dissociate whatever forms of self-experience might be subject to social "shaming." Through the therapeutic dialogue, formerly dissociated parts of the self can be heard that from the perspective of the social mainstream actually look like "maladjustment." Further, Cavitch remarks of Bromberg that "although he is well known for his work on affect *regulation,* it would clearly be an error to identify his work with the normative emphasis some of his fellow clinicians place on adjustment to the world as it is." In reality, "socioaffective life is risky at best, and to live our lives in a way that *feels* like living requires feats of maladjustment as well as adjustment." Cavitch movingly describes the role an analyst can play as a trusted other who provides a setting – "safe but not too safe," in Bromberg's phrase – in which nonnormative aspects of self-experience can be greeted.[45]

Without for a moment discounting the value of therapeutic conversations that grapple explicitly with forms of social oppression, Cavitch recognizes a "social radicalism" in "all of the best psychoanalytic writing, even where there is little or no reference to economics, history, institutional life, or the state's oppressive and marginalizing disposition toward the vast majority of persons."[46] Nor does Bromberg, or Cavitch in turn, suggest that the analyst's office is the only place in which a person can find interpersonal resources for moving past a socially adaptive self-narrative, nor again that collective experiences are not often crucial for this work.

Cavitch is not the only theorist to draw on relational psychoanalysis in such a way as to suggest an alternative to the strict antihumanism of the theoretical past. Lauren Berlant's work, wonderfully eclectic in its range of psychoanalytic reference, draws on relational psychoanalysis as well as object relations theory.[47] Though Berlant's work has already profoundly influenced the conversation in our field, much could be learned if colleagues were to mine more fully Berlant's psychoanalytic bibliography, as well as follow Berlant's example in reading widely in the theories that are in fact most interesting to practicing psychoanalysts today.

The relational school altogether offers a variety of models that have the potential to enrich our own discipline's approaches both to intersubjectivity and to literary experience, in the wake of years of academic conversation that assumes the decentered nature of subjectivity. The kind of sensitive, difficult therapeutic work Cavitch describes is in fact a more practicable route to political and ethical self-transformation than the experiences of self-dissolution unrealistically posited by Marshall, or the identification with the death drive that Edelman, with comparable hyperbole, has advocated.[48]

This discussion has focused on theorists of the middle ground, those interested in the expanse of life that is lived in between a fragmented experience of subjectivity and the illusion of entirely unified selfhood. Why, though, has literary studies gravitated toward a form of reasoning that occludes this middle ground? To repeat, this is a logic that presents us with a false choice between a congealed, static selfhood and (supposedly preferable) the abolishment of all inwardness and coherence. Who or what is served?

In an earlier essay, I attributed our discipline's revulsion against inwardness to the imperatives of the profession itself. Particularly in a time of circle-the-wagons institutional embattlement, our discipline behaves like a "greedy institution," one that thrives to the extent that it can coopt members' investment in their private worlds.[49] In the small space that remains, I consider a related possibility. If we academics are to be asked to renounce our affinity for the inner world, it is possible not just to shame but also to entice us into doing so.

The shaming is something I have touched on above; it occurs whenever the label "conservative" is applied to a scholar who affirms there is some value in private selfhood or self-integration. A carrot, however, complements this stick. Scholars who align themselves with a school of thought that makes human inwardness look retrograde are surely assuming a bleak vision of life; but they are rewarded with the prospect of seeming inhumanly edgy and bold. Donald Carveth, whom I have mentioned above as an important contemporary theorist in a Kleinan vein, writes of the appeal of Lacan's ideas for readers who may find themselves in a state of narcissistic depletion. "In privileging lack as ultimately more real than plenitude," Carveth argues, Lacan offers the reader an experience of "narcissistic gratification," which can ward off "a deeper narcissistic depression." There is a certain thrill in taking "a view of oneself as possessing sufficient courage and realism to embrace, stoically, the 'tragic sense of life.'"[50]

Something like "narcissistic depression" has chronically afflicted our own profession as a collective since the 1980s. The country's swerve to the right in that decade damaged the discipline's sense of connection to a wider society, at the same time that employment within the profession became precarious because of declining resources. This situation has only intensified in the era of adjunctification, when institutional policies create a vast underclass of instructors who take care of students' needs without the benefit of adequate wages, health insurance, or job security. In a word, our profession has been humiliatingly feminized, within the university and within the culture as a whole.

It is possible, then, that we have compensated by embracing theories that impart a fantasized masculinity in creating the impression that it is we in literature departments, among all intellectual communities, who have the grit to stare into the abyss. Our preferred theories appear to strip away all notions of a human need for "safe but not too safe" places – places where, in the presence of a trusted other, a person can let some of the disparate parts of his or her self-experience be seen, held, and known.[51] It is only within what I have been calling the middle ground, between sovereign subjectivity and shattered subjectivity, that such places exist. Differently put, the middle ground is a relational space. It thus codes as a conventionally feminine space.[52] It takes on a degraded status in the defensive posture of a profession attempting to assert its place in an institutional environment that cares less and less for what we do.

As it happens, this gender codification informs some remarks Edelman makes in the course of an extended dialogue with Berlant on the differences between the two theorists' understandings of the nature of subjective life. Edelman, who opposes the concept of self-cohesion, writes that when readers appraise his thinking alongside Berlant's, he is "likely to be cast," though "falsely (at least from my point of view)," as "theory's equivalent of Darth

Vader." In contrast, he says, Berlant, because their version of affect theory may be taken to assert the value of "the subject's being held (hence neither abandoned nor allowed to drop)," may be associated by readers, again too easily, with the "sustaining maternal hold" of the "good enough ... mother," a concept Edelman draws from Winnicott's theories.[53] Though Edelman denies that the analogy with Darth Vader is apt, there is probably something exciting in seeing oneself as theory's avatar of the dark side. Next to this image, the role of "mother" looks tame, even trivial within what is ultimately an adolescent economy of cool, as Susan Fraiman notes in a profound analysis of the same scholarly posturing.[54] Yet for purposes of actual living, how many academics believe, deep down, that it is not a good thing to find places in life where one can be "held" – "neither abandoned nor allowed to drop"?

To the extent that members of our profession use theory in the compensatory way I have just described, we are not helping ourselves at all. In fact, the profession's fantasies about its own superhuman mettle weaken us as a collective, in creating the conditions for a culture of mutual shaming and fear. A place to start, then, in bringing new resources to literature and psychoanalysis is to ask, along with various colleagues I have mentioned in these pages, what our literary objects can tell us about the ways in which, for individuals in a particular social category or at a particular cultural moment, experience unfolds within the middle ground, where human beings live. Our discipline has been fraught with intellectual intimidation for so long that we can hardly predict where that new conversation might take us, once it gathers momentum.

We can also bring new theoretical resources to the question how literature itself can serve as an agent for psychological transformation. I earlier mentioned the pandemic of 2020, which has abruptly altered the conditions of life for human beings on this planet. During these months, I have noticed that colleagues in literary studies have turned often to works of social critique as we try to grasp the implications of the crisis for the political future of our country, as well as for global health. But many of us are turning with passionate interest to literary works as well. On social media, we share poems that move us; the poems seem to catalyze complex experiences of fellowship. What are these poems giving us, during these stressful weeks, that expository genres such as journalism, however crucial in their own right, do not?[55]

As Cavitch notes, Bromberg thinks of literary experience as offering the potential for "an authentically relational experience of intersubjectivity between author and reader."[56] This relational experience is enabled as well as sometimes strategically disabled by literature, and by art more generally. But from a conventional antihumanist perspective, the very idea that the author's subjectivity meets our own through the text looks misguided, having settled almost into the status of an academic taboo. On the other hand, Freud himself, in the course of discovering truths within the matrix of literary and cultural contexts, could articulate his findings only by violating many of the taboos of his intellectual milieu. Surely it is one of the ironies of our own day that the revival of questions long relegated to the "humanist" past now offers openings for disciplinary renewal.

Notes

1. Marianne Noble, *Rethinking Sympathy and Human Contact in Nineteenth-Century American Literature: Hawthorne, Douglass, Stowe, Dickinson* (Cambridge: Cambridge University Press, 2019), 14–15, 103.
2. Katherine Ding, "The Legible Face and the Illegible Body: Face-Work in Lichtenberg, Haywood, and Garrick," *ELH* 85, no. 3 (Fall 2018): 721, 718, 720. Ding's article has a somewhat "postcritical" tenor: like the work, for example, of Heather Love, it draws on the sociology of Erving Goffman, rather than on disciplines such as psychoanalysis that are associated with what, after Paul Ricoeur, is often called the hermeneutics of suspicion. But later in this chapter I speak of conceptual principles that prevail across a wide variety of critical approaches.
3. For those unfamiliar with the contours of antihumanism and posthumanism, a concise and accessible account appears in Rosi Braidotti, *The Posthuman* (Malden, MA: Polity Press, 2013), 13–54. Briefly, both paradigms include an idea that the human experience of cohesive selfhood is peculiar to modern Western societies, and is bound up with the ideology of bourgeois individualism. A further shared understanding is that the "self" or "ego" we experience in these societies is a pernicious illusion, which masks the fact that human subjectivity (in all eras) is nonunitary and incoherent – "decentered," "fragmented," "split," or, within a posthumanist lexicon, "distributed" or "assembled." Among the continental theorists whose antihumanist perspectives profoundly influenced the American academy in the last quarter of the twentieth century were Jacques Derrida, Michel Foucault, and, within psychoanalysis, Jacques Lacan. When I speak, in these pages, of *poststructuralism*, my reference is to the theorists of this founding generation and to disciples within the academy who share(d) their views. The term *high theory*, used later in this chapter, refers to an array of literary-critical perspectives that were heavily influenced by poststructuralism, and that flourished in the 1980s and the early 1990s. Academic antihumanism persists to the present time, but poststructuralist theory is no longer its commanding element. Since about the turn of the millennium, the decline in the relative status of poststructuralism has commonly been referred to as the "death of theory." See, for example, Terry Eagleton, *After Theory* (New York: Penguin, 2003).
4. Tara Brach, Facebook, March 17, 2020.

5. See for example the influential contributions of the psychoanalytic theorists Peter Fonagy, Jody Messler Davies, and Lewis Aron.

6. Eve Kosofsky Sedgwick, "Paranoid Reading, Reparative Reading, Or, You're So Paranoid, You Probably Think This Introduction Is About You," in E. K. Sedgwick ed., *Novel Gazing: Queer Readings in Fiction* (Durham, NC: Duke University Press, 1997), 1–37.

7. For *high theory*, see note 3.

8. For *poststructuralism*, see note 3.

9. For *decentered*, see note 3.

10. For a groundbreaking essay that covers this theoretical terrain as well as providing some historical review, see Lewis Aron, "Self-Reflexivity and the Therapeutic Action of Psychoanalysis," *Psychoanalytic Psychology* 17 (2000): 667–89.

11. This last assumption, widespread in literary studies, goes back to Lacan's attack on midcentury American ego psychology, a psychoanalytic school that arguably did overemphasize the analysand's adaptation to existing social roles.

12. D. W. *Winnicott*, "Ego Distortion in Terms of True and False Self," *in The Maturational Processes and the Facilitating Environment: Studies in the Theory of Emotional Development* (New York: International Universities Press, Inc., 1965), 140–57. As a rough and ready measure of the incidence that here concerns me, a search on JSTOR for "Winnicott" alongside "true self," for the discipline "Language and Literature" from 2000 to 2019, yields only sixteen items. But alongside this datum, I'd note that the recent book of Eng and Han, discussed in note 44, makes innovative use of the concepts of the true and false selves.

13. Fredric Jameson, "The End of Temporality," *Critical Inquiry* 29, no. 4 (2003): 710.

14. Vera J. Camden, "'The Language of Tenderness and of Passion,' or the Place of Sex in Paradise: A Response to Gavin Miller," *New Literary History* 38, no. 4 (2007): 684–85. Camden here paraphrases and expands on a point made by Gavin Miller in the excellent essay to which she formally responds.

15. For a sensitive summary of developments within relational psychoanalysis that are relevant to this point, see Bruce Reis, "The Self Is Alive and Well and Living in Relational Psychoanalysis," *Psychoanalytic Psychology* 22 (2005): 86–95. "Within relational theory the concept of the self continues to occupy a central role. It has survived the premature reports of its demise through a supposed postmodern dissolution" (86).

16. Susan Fairfield, "Analyzing Multiplicity: A Postmodern Perspective on Some Current Psychoanalytic Theories of Subjectivity," *Psychoanalytic Dialogues* 11, no. 2 (2001): 227. The phrases Fairfield here quotes, from Benjamin's *Shadow of the Other: Intersubjectivity and Gender in Psychoanalysis* (New York: Routledge, 1998), are in turn, as Fairfield notes, Benjamin's quotation from Margo Rivera, "Linking the Psychological and the Social: Feminism, Poststructuralism, and Multiple Personality," *Dissociation* 2 (1989): 28. The bracketed phrase is Benjamin's.

17. Fairfield, "Analyzing Multiplicity," 223.

18. Raul Moncayo, *Evolving Lacanian Perspectives for Clinical Psychoanalysis: On Narcissism, Sexuation, and the Phases of Analysis in Contemporary Culture* (London: Karnac, 2008), 264–65. See also Bruce Fink, *A Clinical Introduction*

to Lacanian Psychoanalysis: Theory and Technique (Cambridge, MA: Harvard University Press, 1997), for example, the discussion on p. 89.

19. Cynthia Marshall, "Psychoanalyzing the Prepsychoanalytic Subject," *PMLA* 117, no. 5 (2002): 1208, 1211.

20. For readers unfamiliar with the Lacanian concept of the Imaginary, a good introductory account appears in the entry "Symbolic/Real/Imaginary" on the website "The Chicago School of Media Theory," from the University of Chicago. https://lucian.uchicago.edu/blogs/mediatheory/keywords/symbolicrealimaginary/

21. For a concise presentation of this critique, see Philip Cushman, *Constructing The Self, Constructing America: A Cultural History Of Psychotherapy* (Boston: Addison-Wesley, 1995), 186–88.

22. For a fuller account of the persistence of this idea, see Lisa Ruddick, "When Nothing Is Cool," *The Point Magazine*, December 15, 2015, https://thepointmag.com/criticism/when-nothing-is-cool/

23. Among other issues, the antihumanist depreciation of the "autonomous individual" has dire implications for questions of human rights. For a penetrating account of the stakes, see John Brenkman, "Extreme Criticism," *Critical Inquiry* 26, no. 1 (1999): 109–27. Brenkman presents, for example, what I see as an unanswerable criticism of Judith Butler's articulation, in *Excitable Speech*, of "a politics of the performative" that "does not affirm the principle of individual liberty." Rather, Butler "seeks to justify her stand" on free speech "via an ostensibly anti-individualist theory of the subject, language, and power" (125–26). Though Brenkman's article is now two decades old, and the moment of Butler's *Excitable Speech* has come and gone, the impasse Brenkman identifies in "post-Enlightenment, postmodern" approaches to questions of "rights and freedoms" remains a problem (118). Within the domain of literature and psychoanalysis, a stunning article by Kay Torney Souter, also from the turn of the millennium, describes how our profession's critique of the "bounded individual," indebted above all to Lacan, can simplify and even occlude certain "questions of … human suffering." Souter, "The Products of the Imagination: Psychoanalytic Theory and Postmodern Literary Criticism," *The American Journal of Psychoanalysis* 60, no. 4 (2000): 348, 343. Souter's essay is capacious in its range of psychoanalytic reference, making particularly sensitive use of the theories of Winnicott, Benjamin, Wilfred Bion, Klein, and Fonagy.

24. Lee Edelman, *No Future: Queer Theory and the Death Drive* (Durham, NC: Duke University Press, 2004), 51.

25. Michael D. Snediker, *Queer Optimism: Lyric Personhood and Other Felicitous Persuasions* (Minneapolis: University of Minnesota Press, 2009).

26. Amber J. Musser, "Surface-Becoming: Lyle Ashton Harris and Brown Jouissance," *Women and Performance: A Journal of Feminist Theory* 28, no. 1 (2018): 37.

27. For *death of theory*, see note 3.

28. Andrew Rose, "The Unknowable Now: Passionate Science and Transformative Politics in Kim Stanley Robinson's *Science in the Capital* Trilogy," *Science Fiction Studies* 43, no. 2 (2016): 264, 268, 276.

29. The book-length work is Cynthia Marshall, *The Shattering of the Self: Violence, Subjectivity, and Early Modern Texts* (Baltimore, MD: Johns Hopkins University Press, 2002).

30. For example, see Peter Fonagy, "Thinking about Thinking: Some Clinical and Theoretical Considerations in the Treatment of a Borderline Patient," *International Journal of Psycho-Analysis* 73, no. 4 (1991): 653.

31. Charles Brenner and Ralph Greenson are two of the most notable of these "ego psychologists." See, for example, Charles Brenner, *An Elementary Textbook of Psychoanalysis* (New York: Anchor Books, 1973) or Ralph R. Greenson, *Explorations in Psychoanalysis* (New York: International Universities Press, 1978). Psychoanalysts have since revised the ego psychologists' vision of a "one-person psychology." See for example, Stephen A. Mitchell, *Relational Concepts in Psychoanalysis* (Cambridge, MA: Harvard University Press, 1998).

32. Marshall, *Shattering*, 2, 13.

33. Shakespeare, *Hamlet*, III.ii. 257.

34. Rita Felski, *The Limits of Critique* (Chicago: University of Chicago Press, 2015), 73.

35. Mari Ruti, *The Ethics of Opting Out: Queer Theory's Defiant Subjects* (New York: Columbia University Press, 2017), 28, 37. A fine analysis of the same false binary is that of the philosopher and psychoanalyst Joel Whitebook. *Perversion and Utopia: A Study in Psychoanalysis and Critical Theory* (Cambridge, MA: MIT Press, 1995). As Whitebook writes, "Critics of the ego, like Adorno and Lacan, ... tend to hypostatize pathological, rigidified forms of ego formation into the ego as such. As a result, they are left only with a choice between two poisons, namely, violent unification or no unification at all" (p. 14). Whitebook's work, altogether illuminating, has hardly been recognized by literary scholars. An exception is Lauren Berlant, "Intimacy: A Special Issue," *Critical Inquiry* 24, no. 2 (1998): 284.

36. Amy Allen and Mari Ruti, *Critical Theory Between Klein and Lacan: A Dialogue* (New York: Bloomsbury, 2019), xi.

37. Allen and Ruti, *Critical Theory*, 20. The quoted words are Allen's.

38. See especially D. L. Carveth, *The Still Small Voice: Psychoanalytic Reflections on Guilt and Conscience* (London: Karnac, 2013).

39. Jody Messler Davies, "Multiple Perspectives on Multiplicity," *Psychoanalytic Dialogues* 8, no. 2 (1998): 195. For a work within literary studies that makes powerful use of Davies' theories, see Dawn M. Skorczewski, *An Accident of Hope: The Therapy Tapes of Anne Sexton* (New York: Routledge, 2012), especially 27–35.

40. Davies, "Multiple Perspectives," 201, 205.

41. Stephen A. Mitchell et al. (eds.), *Relational Psychoanalysis: The Emergence of a Tradition* (New York: Routledge, 1999).

42. Philip Bromberg, "'Speak! That I May See You': Some Reflections on Dissociation, Reality, and Psychoanalytic Listening," *Psychoanalytic Dialogues* 4, no. 4 (1994): 541. The article was written in 1994, but subsequent works in relational psychoanalysis do not, to my knowledge, contradict the generalizations Bromberg here makes as to the salient scientific understandings.

43. Max Cavitch, "Dissociative Reading – Philip Bromberg and Emily Dickinson," *Contemporary Psychoanalysis* 43, no. 4 (2007): 683.

44. In remarking that critique is something our profession excels in, I am not referring to those forms of critique that hinge on the theory of decentered subjectivity. My objections to the latter should be clear from the foregoing discussion. But literary studies abounds in modes of social critique that do not rely on that

theoretical tradition. For a somewhat fuller discussion of the distinction I here draw, see Ruddick, "When Nothing." For an outstanding example of specifically psychoanalytic inquiry that contributes to social critique but without positing an altogether decentered subjectivity, see David L. Eng and Shinhee Han, *Racial Melancholia, Racial Dissociation: On the Social and Psychic Lives of Asian Americans* (Durham, NC: Duke University Press, 2019). Working at an intersection of clinical practice and literary criticism, Eng and Han draw particularly on the theories of Klein and Winnicott, alongside Freud. They also occasionally cite contemporary relational theorists.

45. Max Cavitch, "Irregulars," *Contemporary Psychoanalysis* 49, no. 3 (2013): 414. Italics in the original.

46. Cavitch, "Irregulars," 411.

47. See for example Lauren Berlant, *Cruel Optimism* (Durham, NC: Duke University Press, 2011).

48. Edelman, *No Future*, 9.

49. Ruddick, "When Nothing." In that essay I borrow the phrase "greedy institution" from the sociologist Lewis Coser.

50. Donald L. Carveth, "Some Reflections on Lacanian Theory in Relation to Other Currents in Contemporary Psychoanalysis," unpublished paper presented to the Toronto Psychoanalytic Society (March 1987): 28–29.

51. For a related argument, see the rich analysis in Camden, "Language of Tenderness."

52. For a psychoanalytic account of the ways in which "patriarchal culture has historically given different contents" to the categories of masculinity and femininity, see Benjamin, *Shadow of the Other*, xvi, 35–78.

53. Lauren Berlant and Lee Edelman, *Sex, or the Unbearable* (Durham, NC: Duke University Press, 2014), 58. Edelman's comment regarding the ways in which readers may read or misread Berlant's theories is mediated through the figure of Eve Sedgwick, who according to Edelman offers a version of affect theory that is in fact more invested in the "maternal hold" than Berlant's is. But I refer readers to Edelman's commentary itself, so that amid his sometimes obscure formulations they can decide where they think he takes the overlap between Sedgwick's ideas and Berlant's to begin and end.

54. Fraiman anatomizes the ethos of "cool masculinity" as it expresses itself within popular culture as well as within scholarly thought. Susan Fraiman, *Cool Men and the Second Sex* (New York: Columbia University Press, 2003). Fraiman compares academic cool to the mentality of "the modern adolescent boy in his anxious, self-conscious, and theatricalized will to separate from the mother." As she adds, "it goes without saying that within this paradigm the place occupied by the mother is by definition uncool" (xii).

55. Rita Felski inquires into the "uses of literature" in a series of works that challenge the maxims of the critical past. See, along with the extremely influential *The Limits of Critique*, her earlier *Uses of Literature* (Malden, MA; Oxford: Blackwell, 2008), and the recent *Hooked: Art and Attachment* (Chicago: University of Chicago Press, 2020). Felski's work has been crucial in inaugurating a "postcritical" turn in literary studies. The subfield of literature and psychoanalysis is poised to make interesting contributions to this postcritical conversation.

56. Cavitch, "Dissociative Reading," 687–88.

15

MARI RUTI

Queering Melancholia
Bad Feelings in Giovanni's Room

Psychoanalysis has been so central to queer theory, and queer literature is so full of themes that can be interpreted through a psychoanalytic lens, that it would be impossible to provide a comprehensive overview of the crosspollination of these fields without producing a multi-volume treatise. I consequently limit my discussion to one psychoanalytic concept – melancholia – in its relationship to queer theory and literature. My decision to focus on melancholia is motivated by the fact that both theoretical and literary renditions of queerness connect it to melancholia with such regularity that it is tempting to view melancholia as intrinsic to queer subjectivity, queer relationality, and queer modes of dwelling in the world. Even other negative feelings that queer theory and literature customarily align with queerness – such as shame, abjection, longing, despair, desolation, loneliness, mortification, and disillusionment – carry a melancholy hue. Although there are certainly times when less melancholy affects – including anger, defiance, delight, and ecstasy – emerge in theoretical and literary depictions of queerness, it is difficult to avoid the impression that queerness is inextricable from the kind of melancholia that characterizes wounded subjectivity, psychosocial injury, and failed intimacy. It is moreover significant that the assumption that melancholia haunts queerness is not merely produced by an unenlightened heteronormative society; rather, it permeates the history of queer literature – consider the iconic status of forlorn novels such as Radclyffe Hall's *The Well of Loneliness*, Djuna Barnes's *Nightwood*, and Leslie Feinberg's *Stone Butch Blues* – as well as large segments of contemporary queer theory.

During recent decades, queer theory's emphasis on negative feelings – including melancholia – has functioned as a counterpoint to queer activist assurances that "it gets better."[1] Where queer activists have spoken a language of hope, pride, and progress, queer theorists have asserted that this language conceals, and therefore silences, personal and collective histories of suffering, isolation, humiliation, and degradation. Queer theorists have noted that although the political impulse to turn gay shame into gay pride is understandable, it can generate an invisible melancholy residue that persists all the more stubbornly because it remains unacknowledged.[2] That is, even though queer individuals appear to have attained greater degrees of cultural acceptance and sociopolitical equality, they can remain psychologically entangled in histories of traumatization that continue to damage the quality of their lives. This can lead to situations in which even queers who in principle lead rewarding lives feel inexplicably despondent: the ravages of a painful collective past can pull them toward melancholia and other bad feelings in ways that they do not fully comprehend, causing both confusion about why they feel bad and shame about feeling that way; queers, in short, can feel bad about feeling bad. This situation can be especially perplexing for young queers who do not feel that they have personally been the targets of homophobic cruelty but who nevertheless feel encumbered by a violent queer history.[3]

This chapter uses James Baldwin's 1956 *Giovanni's Room* as a literary case study of what one might call *queer melancholia*. However, before proceeding, it is necessary to acknowledge two complications to this approach. First, queer theory's relationship to psychoanalysis is notoriously fraught. On the one hand, queer theory – which emerged within the Anglo-American academy during the 1990s heyday of "high" theory – was initially steeped in psychoanalysis. Groundbreaking texts within queer theory by Judith Butler, Leo Bersani, Teresa de Lauretis, and Eve Sedgwick could not have been written without psychoanalysis.[4] More recently, prominent scholars in the field – including Tim Dean, Lee Edelman, David Eng, Madhavi Menon, Amber Jamilla Musser, Ann Pellegrini, and Darieck Scott – have continued to rely on psychoanalytic models in their theorization of queer subjectivity, relationality, pleasure, and desire.[5] On the other hand, David Halperin and Lynne Huffer have staged vehement critiques of psycho-analysis at the same time as other influential queer theorists – such as Elizabeth Freeman, Gayatri Gopinath, Heather Love, Jack Halberstam, José Esteban Muñoz, Hiram Pérez, Jasbir Puar, Juana María Rodríguez, C. Riley Snorton, Rinaldo Walcott, Michael Warner, among many others – have remained noncommittal (neither hostile nor enthusiastic).[6] In sum, psychoanalysis has been instrumental to queer theory at the same time as it, in part due to its history of pathologizing homosexuality, has understand-ably elicited resistance and skepticism among key thinkers in the field.

It would be pointless to deny that psychoanalysis – like most theoretical schools developed during the nineteenth century – is tainted by legacies of racism, sexism, and homophobia. As forward-thinking as Freud was – for instance rejecting the assumptions of his time about the weakness of the female libido – he was unable to transcend all the prejudices of his historical context, with the result that psychoanalysis has at times aligned homosexuality with perversion, narcissism, and infantilism, even suggesting that it is due to stunted psychosexual development. It is therefore no wonder that Michel Foucault, who is one of the most important precursors of modern queer theory and whose personal experience with clinical psychoanalysis during the 1950s amounted to an attempt to exorcise his homosexuality, launched a scathing critique of psychoanalysis in his 1961 *History of Madness*.[7] What is less known is that in his 1981–1982 Collège de France lectures, *The Hermeneutics of the Subject*, Foucault qualified his stance by admitting that there are varieties of psychoanalysis, particularly the antinormative genre developed by Jacques Lacan, that accord with his own theoretical commitments.[8] Foucauldian queer theorists tend to overlook this latter moment in Foucault's thought, which means that they remain resistant to psychoanalysis even in instances, such as the analysis of melancholia, where psychoanalysis provides a richly sophisticated toolbox.

The second complication to relying on psychoanalysis in the context of queer theory and literature is that during the last two decades queer theory's attempts to comprehend bad feelings such as melancholia have generated a powerful alternative to psychoanalysis: affect theory. Affect theory begins from the premise that bad feelings such as anxiety, depression, and melancholia are generated by structural inequalities such as poverty, racism, sexism, and homophobia. That is, affect theory draws a connection between oppressive social forces and wounding emotional experiences. One of its strengths has been to reveal how toxic group or interpersonal dynamics cause suffering among those who are on the receiving end of such dynamics. It has brilliantly illustrated how damaging affects, including covert homophobic messages, are transmitted from one group to another, or from one person to another, in invisible yet tangible ways, poisoning the very air we breathe. As a result, affect theory appears to offer an antidote to the tendency of psychoanalysis to individualize – and hence to depoliticize – trauma due to its penchant for tracing trauma's causes to childhood experiences. Affect theory, in sum, comes across as a politically attuned, queer-friendly alternative to psychoanalysis. Although it is the case 1) that there is a great deal of astute contemporary psychoanalytic work being done at the intersection of the psychic and the social, 2) that some of the most important predecessors of affect theory – including Teresa Brennan and Anne Cheng – are psychoanalytic scholars, and 3) that many of the most celebrated queer affect theorists – such as Sara Ahmed, Lauren Berlant, and Ann Cvetkovich – used to, and sometimes still do, work with psychoanalytic models,[9] there is no doubt that, within queer theory, affect theory has during the twenty-first century to a large extent replaced psychoanalysis as a theoretical repertoire for analyzing negative affects.

One of the greatest contributions of affect theory – and besides the names I have already provided, readers are invited to consult the work of Sianne Ngai and Kathleen Stewart[10] – has been to illustrate that even when the bad feelings associated with disenfranchised subjectivity are politically generated, they can seem politically useless because they cannot easily be translated into collective action. Melancholia, for instance, is more likely to cause a paralyzing sense of inertia – even the inability to get out of bed – than it is to encourage people to agitate for social justice. From this perspective, melancholia is associated with defeatism rather than agency. In other words, affect theory has showcased the impasses of marginalized subjectivity by revealing that bad feelings can bruise and stifle subjects in ways that severely compromise their ability to act. This explains why those who have the most to gain from rebelling against the normative social order frequently fail to do so.

At the end of this chapter, I show that a psychoanalytic understanding of melancholia opens toward important themes that affect theory sidelines, such as the constitutive role of melancholia in human subjectivity, the connection between melancholia and creativity, the ethical potential of melancholia, and the utopian promises of melancholia. However, it is worth noting right away that Freud does not contradict affect theory's assessment of melancholia's paralyzing tendencies, for in "Mourning and Melancholia" he emphasizes the life-arresting impact of melancholia when he defines it as the kind of pathological mourning that does not come to an end.[11]

Freud explains that, under normal circumstances, the loss of a beloved object – for example, the loss of one's lover, ideal, or country – gives rise to mourning. Mourning in turn extinguishes desire so that a person who is mourning a significant loss finds it impossible to replace the lost object (lover, ideal, or country) with a new one. However, as time passes, mourning gradually subsides, with the consequence that desire is reignited and finds new objects. For instance, although those who have lost a lover may at first find it inconceivable that they could ever love someone else, after sufficient time has passed they frequently find a new lover. Likewise, those who lose their ideal or country may over time come to embrace a new ideal or country. In other words, people who manage to mourn their losses eventually get over these losses; they move on. Melancholia, in contrast, prohibits such a transfer of affections: simply put, melancholics remain fixated on, and faithful to, their lost objects in ways that make it impossible for them to desire new objects.

278

In "healthy" mourning, the subject gradually untethers itself from what it has lost. The melancholic, in contrast, fails to do so. Furthermore, Freud specifies that melancholia is particularly likely to occur when the nature of the loss that we have experienced remains ambiguous. For example, after the loss of a lover, we know *whom* we have lost – we know the identity of the person we have lost – but not *what* we have lost in losing this person: we do not know the details of the future that we might have had with our lover; we do not know what we might have discovered about our lover during years of intimacy; and we do not know what we ourselves might have been like – or how we might have evolved – if we had been able to sustain the relationship. In such instances, melancholia is not merely a matter of grieving the loss of a beloved person but also of grieving the practical, psychological, and emotional promises that this person represented; it is a matter of grieving a life that could have been lived but now never will. It is therefore no wonder that melancholics have trouble moving on: having lost the future that they anticipated, they remain wary of the future altogether, preferring to remain entombed in their crypt of sorrow.

Baldwin's *Giovanni's Room* provides a poignant portrayal of this type of lingering melancholia. Even though the novel's protagonist, David – an American expatriate in Paris – falls in love with Giovanni early in the novel, thereby seemingly transcending his failed relationship with his boy-hood crush, Joey, the melancholy trace of Joey persists so tenaciously that it cannot be disentangled from David's relationship with Giovanni – or, more specifically, from David's inability to embrace his relationship with Giovanni. In a scene that both opens and concludes the novel, David sits in a house that he has rented in the south of France contemplating the manner in which he has rejected both Joey and Giovanni. The situation is dire because David knows that Giovanni is about to be executed for having killed their mutual acquaintance, Guillaume. He is understandably overwhelmed by vivid images of Giovanni waiting for his death in prison. Yet he also recalls the night he spent with Joey as a teenager, admitting that he has "never for an instant truly forgotten it":

> I feel in myself now a faint, a dreadful stirring of what so overwhelmingly stirred in me then, great thirsty heat, and trembling, and tenderness so painful I thought my heart would burst. ... We gave each other joy that night. It seemed, then, that a lifetime would not be long enough for me to act with Joey the act of love.[12]

Unfortunately, this lifetime of love never materialized, for panic about their homosexual experience quickly drove the boys apart. David admits that after his night with Joey, he decided to allow no room in his life for "something which shamed and frightened me."[13] Years later, this flight from homosexuality causes David to abandon Giovanni, thereby initiating the chain of events that leads Giovanni to murder Guillaume. Sadly contemplating his image in the window of his rental, David declares that the dilemma of his homosexuality "is somewhere before me, locked in that reflection I am watching . . . It is trapped in the room with me, always has been, and always will be, and it is yet more foreign to me than those foreign hills outside."[14]

The dilemma of David's homosexuality is "foreign" to him in the sense that he has never been able to fully live out its implications, to find out how things might have gone if he had been able to accept it, starting with Joey. According to the formulation that I borrowed from Freud a moment ago, in losing Joey, and later Giovanni, David knows whom he has lost but not what he has lost; he does not know what a sustained homosexual life might have been like. At the same time, his gayness is locked inside his reflection, inside the room he is sitting in: it is – always has been and always will be – an inescapable part of who he is.

In the course of the novel, David's behavior epitomizes what Freud called *the repetition compulsion*: our tendency to reenact painful patterns of behavior due to our unconscious conviction that if we continue to place ourselves in the kinds of situations that have hurt us in the past, eventually we might learn to master such situations, in this manner protecting ourselves from more pain. This explains why many of us are prone to recreate intimate scenarios that cause us suffering. It is not that we repeat the past exactly: there are always variations to the theme. Yet somehow we frequently inexplicably get wounded in ways that feel all too familiar to us. This is what happens to David: even though he is deeply in love with Giovanni, he flees from Giovanni in exactly the same ways as he once fled from Joey.

David's tumultuous relationship with Giovanni unfolds as follows. He meets Giovanni at Guillaume's gay bar, where Giovanni – who has moved to Paris from an Italian village after having lost his son at childbirth – works as a bartender. David – who is ostensibly straight in the sense that he is waiting for the return of his American girlfriend, Hella, from a trip to Spain – has come to the bar with a wealthy older gay man, Jacques. Jacques, like everyone else at the bar – including the lecherous Guillaume – immediately has his eyes on the handsome and vivacious Giovanni. But it is David whom Giovanni chooses.

The morning after they meet, the two men end up in Giovanni's decrepit room, a room that serves as an apt metaphor for the melancholia associated with the impossibility of queer love. The windows of the room are tightly shut and painted white in order to protect the dangerous secret of same-sex love. One of its walls has been messily stripped of wallpaper whereas the other portrays a pastoral scene of "a lady in a hoop skirt and a man in knee breeches perpetually walking together, hemmed in by roses" – a sentimental heteronormative scene that acts as a constant reminder of the social obstacles to queer love.[15] The room is tiny, dirty, dusty, and desolate, so that even though the men's relationship brings them the same kind of joy as David experienced with Joey, it is from the start enveloped in a melancholy atmosphere of looming tragedy.

The relationship burns brightly for several months, during which David lives in Giovanni's room. However, David feels conflicted about it: "I was in a terrible confusion. Sometimes I thought, but this *is* your life. Stop fighting it. Stop fighting. Or I thought, but I am happy. And he loves me. I am safe. Sometimes, when he was not near me, I thought, I will never let him touch me again."[16] In the end, due to his doubts, his guilt, and Hella's return, David calls off the relationship, shattering Giovanni. The scene of David's last visit to Giovanni's room is heartrending and filled with clashing emotions. Giovanni both accuses David of having ruined his life and begs him to stay, telling him that he will not survive the separation. David, in turn, recognizes the intensity of his longing for Giovanni at the same time as he feels a combination of alarm and numbness: "I felt nothing for Giovanni. I felt terror and pity and a rising lust ... I looked at the room, thinking: I cannot bear it."[17] Despite his desire to comfort Giovanni, the more Giovanni sobs and pleads, the more detached David feels. Desperate to get out of Giovanni's room, he asks, "What kind of life can we have in this room? – this filthy little room. What kind of life can two men have together, anyway?"[18]

David meets Giovanni's pain with indifference even as he recognizes his own anguish: "Something had broken in me to make me so cold and so perfectly still and far away."[19] During the final moments, when David is struggling to leave the room, he expresses his mixture of desire and terror as follows:

> I wanted to beg him to forgive me. But this would have been too great a confession; any yielding at that moment would have locked me forever in that room with him. And in a way this was exactly what I wanted. I felt a tremor go through me, like the beginning of an earthquake, and felt, for an instant, that I was drowning in his eyes. . . . I had to get out of there for my face showed too much, the war in my body was dragging me down.[20]

The scene ends with David admitting, "it was as though my mind had become one enormous, anaesthetized wound. I thought only, *One day I'll weep for this. One of these days I'll start to cry.*"[21]

Like the Freudian melancholic, David is not able to enter the process of mourning: he is not yet able to cry. Instead, he attempts to conceal his devastation by throwing himself into his relationship with Hella. But his enthusiasm for Hella functions as a manic, unconvincing defense against a melancholia that hovers over him "like the shadow of some vast, some predatory, waiting bird."[22] In the meantime, Giovanni loses his job at Guillaume's bar and, out of financial necessity, ends up in a sexual relationship with Jacques, whose desperation for young men's companionship he had formerly ridiculed. Indeed, when David runs into Giovanni after their breakup, Giovanni has become the kind of "kept man" that they both had earlier despised. As David states:

> I could not endure something at once abject and vicious which I began to see in his eyes, nor the way he giggled at Jacques' jokes, nor the mannerisms, a fairy's mannerisms, which he was beginning, sometimes, to affect. ... [he] was really amazingly giddy and girlish, and very drunk – it was as though he were forcing me to taste the cup of his humiliation. And I hated him for this.[23]

The homophobic stereotypes in this description reveal the depth of David's ambivalence about his homosexuality, including his fear that one day he might become like Jacques and Guillaume: "Would I ... like all the others, find myself turning and following all kinds of boys down God knows what dark avenues, into what dark places?"[24] Giovanni, in turn, sinks so far into financial hardship that he is forced to join "the street boys of the quarter" who exchange sexual favors for money and whom he had previously described as "lamentable."[25] It is in fact his abhorrence at having to cater to the sexual predilections of older, wealthier men that causes him to kill Guillaume after Guillaume pressures him into a sexual encounter.

Feeling responsible for Giovanni's fate and recognizing the truth of his passion for Giovanni – the truth of love that Giovanni had demanded him to admit when he was leaving Giovanni's room – David loses interest in Hella. If David flees same-sex love because he deems it to be impossible, heterosexual love also turns out to be impossible for him because it can only function as a pale substitute for the homosexual love that he cannot allow himself to have. Through Hella, David strives to burn out the "image of Giovanni and the reality of his touch," "to drive out fire with fire."[26] But this strategy fails. Furthermore, it is noteworthy that even though David's love for Giovanni is deeper than his affection for Hella, his breakup with her resembles his breakup with Giovanni in the sense that the more Hella cries and demands "the truth," the colder David feels; as was the case with Giovanni, David's rejection of Hella renders her so desperate – so repugnant to him – that he detaches himself from her in disgust.[27] We thus once again witness the repetition compulsion in action.

The scene of David staring at his frozen image in the window of his rental – a scene that frames the novel as a whole – symbolizes the kind of sadness that has congealed into an enduring melancholia. In addition, even when David finally walks out of the house, tears into pieces the note that Jacques has sent him to update him about Giovanni's trial, and throws the pieces into the wind, the wind blows some of them back at him. The reader thus knows that he will forever carry a piece of Giovanni within himself, that he will never fully get over the homosexual love that he has rejected. In this sense, David represents the epitome of queer melancholia.

Queer melancholia in fact permeates *Giovanni's Room* as a whole. All of the novel's queer characters exude prolonged sadness: Giovanni's vitality conceals a depression that borders on self-hatred; Jacques's desolate demeanor embodies the lonely resignation of an aging gay man; Guillaume's bravado hides a more belligerent resentment regarding the fading of youth and beauty; and the street boys that Giovanni loathes – yet is later forced to join – put on exaggerated airs purely out of financial necessity. This sense of pragmatism lurking beneath displays of sparkling dynamism is especially palpable at the restaurant in Les Halles where David and Giovanni accompany Jacques and Guillaume for breakfast the morning after they have met at Guillaume's bar (and right before David first visits Giovanni's room). The novel describes the abject attempts of Jacques and Guillaume to raise the erotic interest of the younger male patrons of the establishment by buying them champagne and oysters. The surface-level conviviality of this courting ritual cannot conceal its thoroughly utilitarian, dispiriting tenor. The novel's portrayal of the melancholia that hangs over this early scene arguably sets the affective tone for the rest of the novel.

Yet even though *Giovanni's Room* offers an evocative portrait of queer melancholia, it simultaneously universalizes the affect. On the one hand, the novel is bathed in an atmosphere of queer melancholia; on the other, it also reveals the desolation of its straight characters. David's father's womanizing life is eclipsed by a photo of his dead wife on his mantelpiece. David's aunt hides her anguish with excessive makeup and clanging jewelry. Hella, initially glowing and confident, gradually grows sad, wary, and insecure. Even Sue, a young woman with whom David has an embarrassing sexual encounter – an encounter during which he wants "only to get out of there"[28] – uses perkiness to conceal her despondency. In other words, as much as *Giovanni's Room* functions as a tragic account of the impossibility of queer love and the melancholia that this impossibility generates, it also highlights the ubiquity of melancholia in human life. It reminds us that a degree of dejection is an unavoidable component of the human condition, so that in the end no one is spared: *one day all of us will weep.*

Giovanni's Room demonstrates that when it comes to bad feelings, such as melancholia, it might be helpful to consider two levels of experience: the context-specific (circumstantial) and the constitutive (foundational). The novel's queer melancholia is context-specific in the sense that it arises from a homophobic culture that produces guilt, shame, and panic. At the same time, the ubiquity of the novel's melancholia gestures toward the constitutive role of melancholia in human life. Although it is true that every one of the novel's characters – gay or straight – has context-specific reasons to feel sad, the fact that the affect nibbles at the edges of almost every scene in the novel speaks to Baldwin's attempt to display the connection between melancholia and the general human condition. His queer characters are not exceptions to this condition but rather bring into greater focus something fundamental about this condition, namely that there is no human subjectivity without melancholia. This is the conclusion of much of psychoanalytic theory as well. For instance, at the core of Lacanian theory is the idea that there is no subject without the kind of loss that engenders melancholia.

According to Lacan, melancholia is the price that human beings pay for their social intelligibility, for their capacity to communicate with each other. Lacan speculates that the moment a child begins to speak – the moment it is inserted into the sociosymbolic (cultural) order that surrounds it – it is "split" by the signifier, by language. Although the child does not in reality lose anything through this encounter with language, it retroactively generates a fantasy of having lost something irrevocably precious, with the result that it comes to experience itself as lacking and alienated. For this reason, the Lacanian subject is intrinsically a subject-of-lack, a subject that suffers from the kind of foundational melancholia that nothing can conjure away.

Affect theory has sometimes criticized Lacanian theory for being so focused on the subject's constitutive lack-in-being that it ignores more context-specific forms of loss. This is in some ways a fair criticism. Yet in principle there is no reason to force a theoretical choice between context-specific and constitutive levels of loss. Likewise with context-specific and constitutive levels of melancholia, both are a part of human experience and can commingle in complex ways. For example, people with a melancholy constitution may be acutely sensitive to context-specific forms of loss, lack, and melancholia. Vice versa, individuals who have had to endure a great deal of context-specific loss, lack, and melancholia may be more in touch with their constitutive melancholia than others. In other words, there is no good reason for queer theory to choose between affect-theoretical and psychoanalytic models: combining their contributions can only deepen our understanding of human subjectivity, including the specific burdens that complicate the lives of many queer subjects.

Although affect theory is right to call attention to the oppressive social origins of bad feelings, its tendency to push aside the constitutive link between subjectivity and melancholia makes it impossible for it to find anything redeemable about melancholia. In contrast, inasmuch as psychoanalysis universalizes melancholia, it – like some other Western intellectual traditions, such as German and British Romanticism – is able to see the creative potential of melancholia. For instance, from a Lacanian perspective it is only insofar as the subject experiences itself as lacking that it turns outside of itself in search of ideals, objects, and people that it hopes will fill its lack and ease its melancholia. Likewise, it is only insofar as the subject experiences itself as lacking that it is motivated to create things – poems, novels, songs, paintings, and so on – in order to compensate for its melancholia (or existential malaise). This is why Julia Kristeva – whose theory shares many of Lacan's basic insights – proposes that there is no imagination without melancholia, that melancholia constitutes the invisible lining of every creative endeavor.[29]

I want to end by noting that psychoanalysis allows us to consider three other affirmative interpretations of melancholia that affect theory tends to ignore. First, it is possible to argue that melancholia contributes to the deepening of a person's character. Freud takes a step toward this reading when he admits that the melancholic – and one could propose that in *Giovanni's Room*, David is such a melancholic – possesses an acutely realistic assessment of the general plight of human beings. Freud recognizes that the melancholic has "a keener eye for the truth than other people."[30] That is, unlike more sanguine individuals, the melancholic comprehends that loss is constitutive of human life. At the same time, the only way that the melancholic is able to cope with the loss of its objects is by internalizing them, by absorbing them into its ego, so that they are never entirely lost – as Joey was never entirely lost to David and as Giovanni, presumably, will never be entirely lost to him either. In Freud's words, "by taking flight into the ego love escapes extinction."[31] Through this process of sheltering beloved objects – Joey, Giovanni – that originate in the outside world, the ego augments and enriches the subject's character, which over time becomes a layered depository of its past losses. From this perspective, it may even be that the more the subject has lost, the more complex its character.[32]

Second, it is possible to argue that there is something ethical about the melancholic's refusal to relinquish its lost objects. This ethical component clicks into view when we compare melancholia with mourning. Mourning, though obviously necessary, is a violent undertaking in the sense that it entails the metaphorical killing of lost objects. Sometimes, especially in the aftermath of love, this is done by devaluing and disparaging the object that was once cherished; other times, it is done simply by forgetting about this object over time. The point is that, through mourning, the subject ensures its own survival at the expense of the object, which is banished from its psychic life.[33] In contrast, the melancholic obstinately holds onto its object, valuing this object more than its own wellbeing. This is why David Eng, among others, has proposed that there is an ethical value to melancholia: it remains loyal to its objects even when this faithfulness is inconvenient or damaging.[34] In *Giovanni's Room*, David's inability to banish the memory of Giovanni will not make his life easier. Yet this inability represents an enormous gesture of love. It is arguably even an ethical gesture of rebellion against our society's demand to overcome our losses.

Third – and along closely related lines – one could argue that melancholia represents a utopian rejection of our society's reigning reality principle, of our society's portraiture of what constitutes a reasonable life. In refusing to enter the process of mourning, the melancholic defies the pragmatic imperatives of our society, which, precisely, ask that we conquer our losses as expediently as we can so that we remain capable of high performance, constant productivity, and relentless cheerfulness. Against this backdrop, the melancholic insists on the possibility of an alternative way of life – on a different reality principle, if you will – which is the very definition of utopianism. As Julia Cooper proposes, the melancholic, like the utopian thinker, is concerned with how things could be rather than with how they in reality are.[35] That is, the melancholic may be realistic about the human condition as a condition of lack, but this is not the same thing as accepting the reality principle of the hegemonic social order. For example, the melancholic does not concede that what no longer exists – or what is deemed incapable of existing – in reality must therefore be *affectively* discarded.

In *Giovanni's Room*, this type of utopianism is most obvious in Giovanni's disregard for heteronormative society's insistence on the impossibility of queer love: Giovanni may be sad but he is also a utopian in the sense that he believes that his love for David could prosper inside his crumbling room, that the two of them could elude the limiting dictates of their social world. It is David's loss of faith in this vision that destroys their relationship. That is, even though David is capable of an ethical gesture of love that preserves the memory of Giovanni, he does not share Giovanni's conviction that queer love is viable. That Giovanni kills Guillaume makes it difficult to read him as a heroic character. Yet he is undeniably driven by a voracious hunger for an alternative world in which queer love would be not only possible but also one of the foundations of queer flourishing. Even his tragic death at the end of the novel cannot fully extinguish this utopian spark, for it is in the nature of utopianism to dream of things that are not possible – until they are.

Notes

1. The "It Gets Better Project" was founded in 2010 by Dan Savage and Terry Miller.
2. See, for instance, Heather Love, *Feeling Backward: Loss and the Politics of Queer History* (Cambridge, MA: Harvard University Press, 2007).
3. See D. A. Miller, *Place for Us: Essays on the Broadway Musical* (Cambridge, MA: Harvard University Press, 1998).
4. Judith Butler, *Gender Trouble: Feminism and the Subversion of Identity* (New York: Routledge, 1989); Leo Bersani, *Homos* (Cambridge, MA: Harvard University Press, 1995); Teresa de Lauretis, *The Practice of Love: Lesbian Sexuality and Perverse Desire* (Bloomington: Indiana University Press, 1994); Eve Sedgwick's groundbreaking 1995 essay on paranoid and reparative reading, reprinted in her *Touching Feeling: Affect, Pedagogy, Performativity* (Durham, NC: Duke University Press, 2003).
5. Tim Dean, *Unlimited Intimacy: Reflections on the Subculture of Barebacking* (Chicago: University of Chicago Press, 2009); Lee Edelman, *No Future* (Durham, NC: Duke University Press, 2004); David Eng, *The Feeling of Kinship: Queer Liberalism and the Racialization of Intimacy* (Durham, NC: Duke University Press, 2010); Mahdavi Menon, *Indifference to Difference: On Queer Universalism* (Minneapolis: University of Minnesota Press, 2015); Amber Jamilla Musser, *Sensational Flesh: Race, Power, and Masochism* (New York: New York University Press, 2014); Ann Pellegrini, *Performance Anxieties: Staging Psychoanalysis, Staging Race* (New York: Routledge, 1996); Darieck Scott, *Extravagant Abjection: Blackness, Power, and Sexuality in the African American Literary Imagination* (New York: New York University Press, 2010).
6. David Halperin, *What Do Gay Men Want? An Essay on Sex, Risk, and Subjectivity* (Ann Arbor: University of Michigan Press, 2007); Lynne Huffer, *Mad for Foucault: Rethinking the Foundations of Queer Theory* (New York: Columbia University Press, 2010); Elizabeth Freeman, *Time Binds: Queer Temporalities, Queer Histories* (Durham, NC: Duke University Press, 2010); Gayatri Gopinath, *Impossible Subjects: Queer Diasporas and South Asian Public Cultures* (Durham, NC: Duke University Press, 2005); Love, *Feeling Backward*; Jack Halberstam, *The Queer Art of Failure* (Durham, NC: Duke University Press, 2011); José Esteban Muñoz, *Cruising Utopia: The Then and There of Queer Futurity* (New York: New York University Press, 2009); Hiram Pérez, *A Taste for Brown Bodies: Gay Modernity and Cosmopolitan Desire* (New York: New York University Press, 2015); Jasbir Puar, *Terrorist Assemblages: Homonationalism in Queer Times* (Durham, NC: Duke University Press, 2007); Juana María Rodríguez, *Sexual Futures, Queer Gestures, and Other Latina Longings* (New York: New York University Press, 2014); C. Riley Snorton, *Black on Both Sides: A Racial History of Trans Identity* (Minneapolis: University of Minnesota Press, 2017); Rinaldo Walcott, *Queer Returns: Essays on Multiculturalism, Diaspora, and Black Studies* (Toronto: Insomniac Press, 2016); Michael Warner, *The Trouble with Normal: Sex, Politics, and the Ethics of Queer Life* (New York: Free Press, 1999).

7. Michel Foucault, *History of Madness*, trans. Jonathan Murphy and Jean Khalfa (London: Routledge, 2006).

8. Foucault, *The Hermeneutics of the Subject: Lectures at the Collège de France, 1981–1982*, trans. Graham Burchell (New York: Palgrave Macmillan, 2005).

9. Psychoanalytic scholars who work at the intersection of the psychic and the social include – but are by no means limited to – Amy Allen, Margaret Crastnopol, Jennifer Friedlander, Sheldon George, Lynne Layton, Noëlle McAfee, Todd McGowan, Hilary Neroni, Jamieson Webster, and Slavoj Žižek. The journal *Psychoanalysis, Culture & Society* is devoted to this intersection. Teresa Brennan's *The Transmission of Affect* (Ithaca, NY: Cornell University Press, 2004) and Anne Cheng's *The Melancholy of Race* (New York: Oxford University Press, 2001) represent important precursors to affect theory. Among the numerous texts by queer affect theorists, I will merely name Sara Ahmed, *The Promise of Happiness* (Durham, NC: Duke University Press, 2010); Lauren Berlant, *Cruel Optimism* (Durham, NC: Duke University Press, 2011); and Ann Cvetkovich, *Depression: A Public Feeling* (Durham, NC: Duke University Press, 2012).

10. See Sianne Ngai, *Ugly Feelings* (Cambridge, MA: Harvard University Press, 2005) and Kathleen Stewart, *Ordinary Affects* (Durham, NC: Duke University Press, 2007).

11. Sigmund Freud, "Mourning and Melancholia" (1917), *SE* 14: 239–58.

12. James Baldwin, *Giovanni's Room* (New York: Vintage, 1956), 8.

13. Ibid., 20.

14. Ibid., 10.

15. Ibid., 86.

16. Ibid., 88.

17. Ibid., 138–39.

18. Ibid., 142.

19. Ibid., 140.

20. Ibid., 144.

21. Ibid., 145.

22. Ibid., 146–47.

23. Ibid., 147.

24. Ibid., 84.

25. Ibid., 147.

26. Ibid., 122.

27. Ibid., 161.

28. Ibid., 100.

29. See Julia Kristeva, *Black Sun: Depression and Melancholia*, trans. Leon S. Roudiez (New York: Columbia University Press, 1987).

30. Freud, "Mourning and Melancholia," 246.

31. Ibid., 257

32. Freud argues along these lines in "The Ego and the Id" (1923), *SE* 19: 12–66.

33. Freud, "Mourning and Melancholia, 267.

34. See Eng, *The Feeling of Kinship*.

35. See Julia Cooper, "Melancholy Utopias: The Ethics of Vulnerability in Contemporary American Literature and Film" (PhD thesis, University of Toronto, 2016).

16

CARLA FRECCERO

Animal Figures

Literature has long deployed the figure of the (non-human) animal in a variety of ways: as symbol, allegory, and metaphor, to name some of the most prominent. It was, for example, a favorite practice of the middle ages to assign symbolic meaning to animals and likewise to "use" them to represent qualities of the human. So, lions symbolize courage, bees a well-functioning social order, wolves the savagery of tyrants. As allegory, animals have often served to soften social and political messages that, were the protagonists human, might be too risky for their authors to articulate. Among these, novels such as *Black Beauty* or *Animal Farm* immediately come to mind. As metaphor, non-human animals, like nature more generally, make up the material from which the poetics of language are fashioned. Indeed, as with other forms of human technology, language can be seen to take its figural cue from the non-human world.[1] Animals have also constituted a far more literal material substrate, in the West, insofar as parchment – and thus the skin of animals – was the inscribed surface of European manuscript culture.[2]

Psychoanalysis has made use of the non-human animal in both similar and different ways. Psychoanalysis is one of the few analytics of the human that does not take the human for granted but that, rather, starts from the premise that humans are mammalian beings who learn to be human, with psychoanalysis being the materialist account of the theoretical implications of empirical observations about the vicissitudes of that process, both its successes and its failures. As Althusser put it in "Freud and Lacan": "Psychoanalysis … is concerned with … a war that, at every instant, is waged in each of its offspring, who, projected, deformed, rejected, each for himself, in solitude and against death, have to undertake the long forced march that turns mammalian larvae into human children, that is, *subjects*."[3] However, as Althusser's remarks also demonstrate, psychoanalysis and most psychoanalytic theorists have, at least historically, been invested in theorizing what makes humans different or other than other animal being, and draw a line at some point that serves irrevocably to divide human from animal even as they maintain the material continuity of being between them. This is most often located in the human property of linguistic signifying. Insofar as psychoanalysis has been understood to be the story of how an infant mammal becomes, developmentally, human, and lives in society, it has relied on the animal kingdom to forge both evolutionary continuities and discontinuities and, like philosophy, has often set itself up as the discipline that articulates the distinction, or the border, between these orders of being. To the extent that it explores the involvement of non-human animals in the life of humans, psychoanalysis also deploys literary techniques of interpretation to understand animal figures in human fantasy. Several of Sigmund Freud's case histories prominently feature animals – The Rat Man, The Wolf Man, Little Hans, for example – and inevitably they come to stand for something about the human.[4] Freud, and Jacques Lacan after him, engage animality on a centuries-old continuum, where animality represents what is most primitive about the human, or even the human's precursor, along the lines of Haeckel's "ontogeny recapitulates phylogeny."[5] On the one hand, then, animality is the infancy of humanity (and human infants are, it is argued, therefore closer to animals); on the other, they live on a continuum rather than belonging to a wholly different order of being. Here too, animality can be thought of as a material substrate for the emergence of the human, both literally and figuratively.

In an important intervention into the question of narrative literature and the animal, Susan McHugh proposes the theory that, rather than "giv[ing] voice to the individual subject of representation," the success of narrative form for the animal is, rather, "its usefulness for experiments with multiple perspectives and processes that support models centered on agency rather than subjectivity."[6] Through the course of her argument, it seems the case that agency and subjectivity are not as distinguishable as she argues here, and her call for a narrative ethology proposes a kind of "inter-subjectivity" and "inter-corporality"[7] for aspects of sometimes-popular narrative and popularizing ethology that, she argues, help both science and the humanities rethink the relations of the living beyond anthropocentrism. If psychoanalysis has an object, it can be said to be the unconscious and, therefore, the psyche and its corresponding "expression," subjectivity. To the extent that literature (or in its expanded definition, textuality) can be said to be worldmaking as or through subjectivity, it is a privileged medium for the representation of subjectivity, as McHugh points out.

There are obvious problems with representing animal subjectivity beyond or other than the human. At the turn of the century, McHugh notes, there was a proliferation of such narratives, and they occasioned heated debates about anthropomorphism, insofar as talking, thinking nonhumans seemed to be mostly humans in other kinds of bodies.[8] Akira Lippit argues that humanism itself is an anthropomorphism[9] in that it projects on to the living a restricted concept of an idealized, rational human. This is another way psychoanalysis affords the possibility of rethinking the humanist human and thus the other than human: it is anti-Cartesian, focusing not only on the cognitive dimensions of consciousness, but also on the embodied affective aspects of the always ongoing and partly unconscious process of "becoming human."

On the other hand, without anthropomorphism, one could argue that it would be impossible to engage in relationality at all, given that identificatory gestures establish relationship and, ultimately, the ego itself, and given that no human (or non-human) emerges apart from sociality. Anthropomorphism permits humans not only to relate to the other than human, but also to other humans, insofar as remaking the other in the image of the self is one of the technologies for recognizing an other.[10] To the extent that the biological sciences (and now many of the imaging techniques for observing their actions in the body and brain) affirm intimate continuities among mammals, at least, one could also argue that resemblance, even if unidirectional, is not a fabrication, but founded in the deep material likenesses of mammalian being. Anthropomorphism would not be, in this case, a relation imposed on animals alone, but a gesture performed by and on all the living to bring it into a circle of resemblance.

Lacan, at least early on, was interested in these continuities across the living, and his essay on the mirror stage relies extensively on studies of nonhumans to understand aspects of prelinguistic infantile identity formation, which he does in part through theories of mimicry, particularly those, among others, of Henry Wallon, Wolfgang Kohler, and Roger Callois.[11] He argues that visual mimicry performs a fundamental role in shaping identity through a creature's identification with an image, its own or another of its species, and that this mimetic effect amounts to an entire gestalt. This observation finds echoes in current neuroscientific theories of embodied simulation and the existence of mirror neurons that help infants learn by seeing and doing. Lacan extends this well beyond mammals, as did Callois, whose study of the phenomenon of mimicry in insects argued against the adaptive theories of his day and in favor of a kind of figure/ground perceptual confusion akin to something like the death drive, the tendency of insects to merge with their surrounds.[12] Lacan's animal psychoanalysis in "The mirror stage" relies, however, almost exclusively on regimes of the visual in a way that could be said to perform the anthropomorphization that is philosophical humanism, by privileging speculation as formative of the (cognizing) human.[13] Thus he remains vulnerable to Jacques Derrida's critique, elsewhere, that Lacan and a host of other philosophers in the Western tradition over rely on a kind of certainty about what the human is in order to argue its distinctiveness from the animal. The issue, Derrida remarks, is not so much the assertion that animals do not possess this or that quality, but rather the confident assumption that the human does:

> It is *not just* a matter of asking whether one has the right to refuse the animal such and such a power ... It *also* means asking whether what calls itself human has the right rigorously to attribute to man, which means therefore to attribute to himself, what he refuses the animal, and whether he can ever possess the *pure, rigorous, indivisible* concept, as such, of that attribution.[14]

Another problem is the privileging of the visual in the formation of subjectivity and the elision of a rich and varied sensorium. Jacob von Uexküll, in arguing for the specificities of animalian *umwelten* or lifeworlds, makes an effort to account for subjectivities other than those formed by vision, while also (at least potentially) challenging the prelinguistic primacy of the visual in the formation of subjectivity, whether human or other.[15] His development of biosemiosis – meaning-making tailored to the biological constitution of a being, something Freud also made an effort to do for the human – suggests pathways other than language for thinking psychic formation, or rather makes of the linguistic a singular and specific modality adapted to human meaning-making.

More recently, evolutionary biology, through the Gaia hypothesis and Lynn Margulis's work on symbiosis and symbiogenesis – the merging of more than one life form into a complex organism – as the origin of "higher" orders of being, confirms this de-anthropomorphizing of the human; it is a de-subjectivation of the human subject in favor of a multiplicity of organisms participating in the material life of the being called human.[16] This is what Donna Haraway means when she affirms that "we have never been human."[17] The material conceptualization of the human as a teeming collectivity of life forms thus expands both Darwinian and Freudian decenterings of human subjectivity as distinct, exceptional, conscious, and intentional.

These ways of thinking about psyche, subjectivity, and even the unconscious might permit a more non-anthropocentric psychoanalysis, even for the human, that would also be more attentive to the variations of humanity that are now designated as differently abled. If the human subject is decentered away from philosophical traditions of the unique, exceptional, conscious subject; if the dominant sensorium is no longer assumed to be vision, and if language is no longer the sole or most critical technology upon which so much of psychoanalytic theory and its philosophical underpinnings are built, then psychoanalysis, which already has the capacity, unlike many forms of philosophical/critical thinking, to analyze the full spectrum of relationships between living creatures and the social formations within which they/we develop that are not confined to the conscious deliberative self, could become a critical tool for situating humanities within a broader ecological community. Finally, this would also permit an analysis of language that treats it in greater specificity, as the figural and privative, restricted medium through which humans communicate their sensorium in symbolic exchanges.[18] It is this privative understanding of language – how it does its material-semiotic work through figuration – that Freud analyzed in dreams and that impelled him to use interpretive and rhetorical techniques proper to the figural – repetition, condensation, and displacement, among others – to understand meaning in registers more literary than philosophical and "scientific."

In an effort to examine the place of the other-than-human animal so crucial to the formation of the human but also to the humanist human-animal divide in a way that would not reduce the animal to symbol, or strip animal materiality from the signifying work it does, Derrida proposes the term "animot," a singular/plural word (in French, *animot* sounds like the plural of animals, *animaux*) that merges the word (*mot*) with the animation of the living. As Matthew Senior explains,

> The neologism suggests, very broadly, that the animal, the figural, and the discursive have something important and generative in common. The encounter with the animal produces language from the human side, but also signs, traces, and *responses* from the animal side. Animot thus means granting a kind of language to animals and developing subtle, poetic expressions that capture the proximity yet separateness of humans and animal, arising in moments when animal movements, paths, and sounds intersect with human displacements and language.[19]

Derrida has long claimed that what he refers to as the trace – a kind of ur-writing – is not confined to humans alone, and that inscription, in its many forms, is not a property of the human and does not set humanity aside as exceptional in the leaving of signifying marks; in invoking "animot" he finds the point of convergence between human figurality and animal trace. His concept of the trace – the substitution of inscription and trace for language and the signifier – crosses, as he puts it, "the frontiers of anthropocentrism": "mark, gramma, trace, and différance refer differentially to all living things, all the relations between living and nonliving."[20]

The living thus participate in a material semiosis, the expression Haraway uses to think figurality with and through animality.[21] Lippit further argues that Freud himself makes this observation when, in *The Interpretation of Dreams*, the unconscious expression of wishes in the dreamwork is the point of convergence between animal and human.[22] In deploying the term "animetaphor," Lippit likewise brings together animality and figuration, conferring upon the former the status of originary metaphor:

> One finds a fantastic transversality at work between the animal and the meta-phor – the animal is already a metaphor, the metaphor an animal. Together they transport to language, breathe into language, the vitality of another life, another expression: animal and metaphor, a metaphor made flesh, a living metaphor that is by definition not a metaphor, antimetaphor – "animetaphor." The animetaphor may also be seen as the unconscious of language, of *logos* ... The animal brings to language something that is not part of language and remains within language as a foreign presence.[23]

The relationship between language, animality, and figurality outlined here suggests ways the literary might participate in decentering philosophical and scientific categories that serve neither what has been called the human nor what has been called the animal, through narrative – as in McHugh's notion of "narrative ethology" or Erica Fudge's "poetics of narrative" – and the figural operations of language that bring into being altered forms of subject-ivity that cannot be accounted for through taxonomic categories of thought.[24]

Whereas McHugh and Fudge focus on the way narrative enables agencies beyond or other than the so-called human, I want to focus on a text that, while narrativizing human-animal relating, performs its categorical estrange-ment through language's figural capacities and in this way potentially enables new ways of thinking about intertwined species subjectivities. The text demonstrates how the literary opposes the philosophical precisely through the tropological or figural dimension that philosophy generally tries to expunge. And, while it meets "the" animal in figural terms, it also re-animates catachrestic figures, restoring animal breath to dead metaphors.

Emmanuel Levinas was a French Jewish philosopher of Lithuanian birth whose essay collection, *Difficile liberté: essais sur le judaïsme* [Difficult Freedom: Essays on Judaism], contains "Nom d'un chien, ou droit nat-urel" ["Name of a Dog, or Natural Right]," a hybrid essay, short story, philosophical, and religious meditation that references the time he spent as a prisoner of war in a German camp (he was spared the fate of many other Jews because he was a prisoner of war), when he and his fellow prisoners met and were befriended by a dog. In today's generic categorizations, one might call this auto-fiction or perhaps auto-theory, since it combines theology, philosophy, autobiography and creative non-fiction. The essay appears in the section titled "Polemics," and its logics, its connective tissue, follows the associative pattern of dream narratives more than that of a philosophical argument.[25]

Levinas is generally known as a philosopher of the ethics of the other, that is a philosopher who thought that the encounter with the alterity of the other was "first philosophy," preceding the attempt by metaphysics to make of self – or other – the object of knowledge. For him, the other is not knowable and cannot be made into an object; rather, the face-to-face encounter with the other makes a demand and engenders responsibility. Late in life, in an interview conducted by graduate students from Essex and Warwick Universities, Levinas responds in a conflicted way to questions about this ethics of the other around, precisely, the face and the ethical demand it makes from the place of (what kind of) other:

> One cannot entirely refuse the face of an animal. It is via the face that one understands, for example, a dog. Yet the priority here is not found in the animal, but in the human face ... I cannot say at what moment you have the right to be called "face." The human face is completely different and only afterwards do we discover the face of an animal. I don't know if a snake has a face.[26]

Although Levinas agrees that "the ethical extends to all living beings" he does so in the mode of Jeremy Bentham,[27] out of a concern for the shared suffering of which mortal beings are capable. He refuses the notion that the ethical is biological (and he places what he calls the animal on the side of the biological) because, for him, the biological is the Darwinian "struggle for life," whereas the human is a break from that, a break that makes of the human a being for whom the life of the other is more important.[28]

But "Name of a Dog," which includes a meditation on doggish-ness and a story about a particular dog (named Bobby), suggests to readers that Levinas has more to say about the ethical and figural relations of humanity and animality than philosophers, and even Levinas himself, give him credit for.[29] As Peter Hulme reminds us, psychoanalytic theory "offers the one model of reading we have that can claim to make a text speak more than it knows," and in this chapter it is the literary and figural dimension of the text that offers a glimpse of a non-anthropocentric psychoanalytics of the living.[30]

In *The Animal that Therefore I Am*, Derrida offers a brief reading of the essay, thinking to "catch" Levinas in a philosophical "denegation" resembling the one Derrida grapples with in his own text: the impossibility of a narrative ethology that does not allegorize or otherwise completely dematerialize animal being in the struggle to encounter what Derrida calls the "actual" animal. Derrida demonstrates in his own work that the articulation of a relation to the other in language, however much it is a grappling with – and for Derrida it is most certainly a grappling with – cannot avoid a generalizing whose agent may very well not be human at all. In introducing his cat, an "actual" cat, Derrida insists that it is not any of the other literary or philosophical cats, not Hoffman's, Kofman's, Montaigne's, Baudelaire's, Rilke's, Büber's, Alice's (Lewis Carroll's), not La Fontaine's or Tieck's.[31] The repeated negations suggest the difficulty of ever "representing" a "real" cat and pose the conundrum of reference in an essay where precisely the problem of the category, and categorization, of "the" animal is at stake, and where the singularity of the other is an ethical matter.

This is the symptom – negation/denial/disavowal – that Derrida identifies in Levinas's story. Seeing no fewer than eleven exclamation marks in the space of the eight pages of Levinas's text, Derrida detects the work of negation: "Moreover, two of them follow the utterance 'But no! But no!' which in truth attests to the truth of a 'But yes! But yes!' when it comes to a dog that recognizes the other and thus responds to the other."[32] Derrida concludes that although Levinas insists – as Derrida does for his cat – on the literality of the dog, its specificity, this singular dog with a name (Derrida's cat remains nameless), "Levinas's text is at once metaphorical, allegorical, and theological, anthropotheological, hence anthropomorphic . . . at the very moment when Levinas proclaims, claims, *prétend*, by exclaiming, the opposite."[33] He reminds us elsewhere that "every animal . . . is essentially fantastic, phantasmatic, fabulous, of a fable that speaks to us and speaks to us of ourselves."[34] Thus Derrida persists in reading Levinas's "Name of a Dog," only within the terms of its explicitly allegorical philosophico-ethical framing – "natural rights," "transcendence in the animal,"[35] and "the last Kantian in Nazi Germany."[36]

The essay begins with an exegesis of two chapters in Exodus that feature dogs: the first is Exodus 22.31 ("And ye shall be holy men unto me: neither shall ye eat any flesh that is torn of beasts in the field; ye shall cast it to the dogs"), where God enjoins humans to leave the torn flesh of the animal in the fields for dogs to devour; and the second, Exodus 11.7, where the dogs do not bark on the night of the slaughter of the first-born, thus ratifying the righteousness of the Jews and protecting them ("But against any children of Israel shall not a dog move his tongue, against man or beast: that ye may know how the Lord doth put a difference between the Egyptians and Israel"). The first allows Levinas to invite us to think about our disavowal of the killing and devouring of flesh as an act of war; the second marvels at the role played by the animal – who has no ethics, who has no *logos* – in conferring dignity on the human ("with neither ethics nor logos, the dog will attest to the dignity of its [the] person"),[37] and is the occasion for Levinas to remind us that, in this, there is a debt owed, a debt that is always open.

The essay then describes Levinas's internment in Camp 1492, where he was one of a group of French soldiers held as prisoners of war by the Nazis. There, he says, they were stripped of their human skin:

> We were subhuman, a gang of apes. A small inner murmur ... reminded us of our essence as thinking creatures, but we were no longer part of the world ... We were beings trapped in their species; despite all their vocabulary, beings without language.[38]

Bobby is a dog who arrives in the camp, a dog they name, a "wandering" dog. The dog recognizes the prisoners as human, as men: "He would appear at morning assembly and was waiting for us as we returned, jumping up and down and barking in delight. For him, there was no doubt that we were men."[39] And the essay concludes, "This dog was the last Kantian in Nazi Germany, without the brain needed to universalize maxims and drives. He was a descendant of the dogs of Egypt. And his friendly growling, his animal faith, was born from the silence of his forefathers on the banks of the Nile."[40]

David L. Clark, reading this essay thematically from the point of view of Levinas's possible investment in the ethics of human-animal relating, argues that Levinas succeeds in juxtaposing – rather than analogizing – the infamous comparison that Heidegger made (between the animal industrial complex and the Holocaust) and that has been taken up, first and foremost perhaps by Isaac Bashevis Singer ("eternal Treblinka"), then by more unfortunate and less well-credentialed analogizers, PETA among others ("Holocaust on Your Plate") – the casual killing and eating of animal flesh and the animalization – and mass murder – of Jews in the camps.[41] Levinas does not, Clark notes, directly compare; in fact, it's difficult to understand the connection that's being made between the meditation on meat eating and the anecdote about Bobby. But he does put both there together in this essay and suggest a relation. This is not a relation that simply reverses the terms and thus remains within their lethal circuit. As the Jewish poet Stern in J. M. Coetzee's *The Lives of Animals* points out, to say "the Jews died like cattle," does not allow one simply to say, "therefore cattle die like Jews."[42] Rather, Clark notes, it "creates a rhetorical neighborhood in which animals and humans dwell and summon each other into responsibility."[43] The passage that effects the hinge in this (non-)comparison is the sentence: "There is, at least, enough there to make us want to limit, through various interdictions, the butchery that every day claims our 'consecrated' mouths!,"[44] with its homophonic resonances between *boucherie* (butchery) and *bouche* (mouth). As Clark puts it, "'we' live in a culture that failed catastrophically to grasp the injustice of killing Jews; but 'we' also live in a culture for which the justness of putting animals to death is simply not an intelligible consideration."[45] Here in this essay and in the neighborhood of the everyday "butchery" of the "familial," Levinas suggests that reason sublimates the mutual devouring of animals into "hunting games" and erects in the place of bloody inter-species battles the spectacle of intra-species war.

> The flesh torn by beasts in the field, and the remains of bloody struggles between wild animals that half-devour [*s'entre-dévorent*] one another, from the strong species to the weak, will be sublimated by intelligence into hunting games. This spectacle suggesting the horrors of war, this devouring within species, will provide men with the artistic emotions of the *Kriegspiel*. Such ideas make one lose one's appetite! In fact, they can also come to you at the family table, as you plunge your fork into your roast.[46]

Even as species difference (a theme of the essay) marks the struggle of strong against weak, these wild animals (*fauves*) are brought together as a community by the "entre" of *s'entre-dévore*, mutual devouring, as does war within the human "species." The connections Levinas forges fashion a continuum among species, a community where hunting, war, and meat eating are all connected.

Clark's mention of the rhetorical alerts the reader to the figural dimensions of this astonishing essay, which has mostly been read by philosophers as philosophy, even when those readers are looking for a Levinasian ethics of the animal. What is so rarely attended to is of a different order, not the order of ethics, except insofar as something about the figure may be said to do the work of coming face-to-face with the animal other, not philosophically so much as literarily. This is what Derrida fails to read: the *animot* of Levinas's text that does its animetaphorical work, not through the discourse of philosophy, but in a literary register whose resemblance to psychoanalytic thinking implicitly critiques philosophy's humanism. The word Levinas uses for "face" is "visage," but the invocation of "face" in Levinas's philosophy also recalls another French word for face, "figure." It is thus the figure of the face, and the face of the figure, the *figure* of the figure, that Levinas's writing performs.

And what better place to invoke the figure than in the prosopopeia of the name – the name that is *not* named in the title of the essay, "Nom d'un chien."[47] This "name of a dog" is, in French, the polite imprecatory substitute for a curse, "Nom de dieu!" (the equivalent of the exclamation, "Jesus Christ!"). From the beginning, "dog" substitutes for God in what would be called, were this in English, a heteropalindrome, a lovely name for the condensed transpecies encounter the reversal invokes. And "dog" continues to substitute, thematically as well, obeying the divine injunction to silence on

Passover and recognizing the human in the second scene of captivity, the prisoner of war camp.

Lippit discusses the animal in language as at the limits of figurality, the place where metaphor is haunted by its end, by death, by the literal that, as in Nicolas Abraham and Maria Torok's theory of melancholic incorporation, turns figures into literal things, and metaphors into metonymies, things that can be – literally – eaten, taken in, ingested into the self as secret crypts.[48] "When the metaphoricity of the metaphor collapses, the concept becomes a metonymic thing that can be eaten."[49] The "animetaphor," as he and Derrida call it, is "never absorbed, sublated, or introjected into world, but rather incorporated as a limit … the animetaphoric figure is consumed literally rather than figuratively … The animal returns like a meal that cannot be digested, a dream that cannot be forgotten, an other that cannot be sublated."[50]

In Levinas's text, then, metaphor and allegory reach their limit at the mouth, at the eating of flesh, and what is incorporated is, we could say, that encrypted and indigestible trauma of the loss of speech "beings without language"), the loss of the human ("we were subhuman, a gang of apes," 153), the becoming-animal through the loss of language in the thematics of the narrative itself ("How can we deliver a message about our humanity which, from behind the bars of quotation marks, will come across as anything but monkey-talk?").[51]

But the figure of the dog does not end with God and mouth, with the literal consumption of flesh that is sublimated, metaphorized in the human species as hunting or war games. As Eva Hayward remarks, "literal animals are always part of figural animals; animals cannot be displaced by words, rather words carry the nervous circuitries, the rhythms, the tempos of the literal."[52]

So who is this dog at the end of the verse? Someone who disrupts society's games (or Society itself) and is consequently given a cold reception *[que l'on reçoit, dès lors, comme un chien dans un jeu de quilles]*?

Someone whom we accuse of being rabid *[que l'on accuse de rage]* when we are trying to drown him? *[quand on se prépare à le noyer?]* Someone who is given the dirtiest work – a dog's life – *[le métier de chien]* and whom we leave outside in all weathers, when it is raining cats and dogs *[temps de chien]* even during those awful periods when you would not put a dog out in it? But all these, in spite of their misery, reject the affront of a repulsive prey.

So does it concern [is it about] the beast that has lost the last noble vestiges of its wild nature, the crouching, servile, contemptible dog? *[du chien couchant, d'un méprisable chien servile?]* Or, in the twilight *[entre chien et loup]* (and what light in the world is not already this dusk?), does it concern [is it about] the one who is a wolf under his dogged faithfulness, [*loup sous sa fidélité de chien*] and thirsts after blood, be it coagulated or fresh?

But enough of allegories! We have read too many fables and we are still taking the name of a dog in the figurative sense. So, in the terms of a venerable hermeneutics, more ancient than La Fontaine, orally transmitted from early antiquity – the hermeneutics of the talmudic Doctors – this biblical text, troubled by parables, here challenges the metaphor: in Exodus 22:31, the dog is a dog. Literally a dog![53]

Even as meat enters the mouth, what issues forth is a bounty of figures, a bounty that – ironically enough – degrades or abjects the animal in question (except for one of them, the expression for twilight), a dog, that very animal that in this French discourse seems to signal a domestically degraded condition of animality. Levinas emphasizes Lippit's observation that "the animal brings to language something that is not part of language and remains within language as a foreign presence,"[54] for by listing the expressions in rapid succession he underscores the strangeness of the dog's figural and degraded appearance in everyday language. At the same time, the rapid-fire list carries those "nervous circuitries, the rhythms, the tempos" Hayward attributes to what is literal about these figural dogs. At the end of this dizzying series of French idioms reanimating those doggish dead metaphors, the very lively if abject figure of the dog emerges as literal, as non-allegorical, in Exodus. And finally, in a remarkable slippage of pronouns, available by virtue of French being a gendered language that confounds the English translation, Levinas brings dogs and humans together in their servitude.

> La liberté de l'homme est celle d'un affranchi se souvenant de sa servitude et solidaire de tous les asservis ... A l'heure suprême de son instauration – et sans éthique et sans logos–, le chien va attester la dignité de la personne. L'ami de l'homme – c'est cela. (201)
>
> Man's [sic] freedom is that of an emancipated man [*un affranchi*] remembering his servitude and feeling solidarity for all enslaved people [*solidaire de tous les asservis*; in solidarity with all who are enslaved] ... At the supreme hour of his [its] institution [establishment], [and] with neither ethics nor logos, the dog will attest to the dignity of its [the] person [*le chien va attester la dignité de la personne*]. This is what the friend of man means [*L'ami de l'homme – c'est cela*].[55]

"Affranchi" – emancipated slave – is a colonial marker designating here the condition of Jews after Egyptian captivity. Levinas says that this is the kind of freedom (a difficult freedom) of man [sic], the freedom of an emancipated slave remembering his slavery and in solidarity with all those who are enslaved. The next sentence, "at the supreme hour of its establishment," seems to refer to that freedom, where the dog in Exodus has a role to play: the dog bears witness to the dignity of the person. Juxtaposed with the string of expressions yoking degradation or contempt with all things dog, this moment forges an intimate identification: dogs too are "asservi," enslaved, like "men," like the Jews. And dogs remember their servitude, unlike men, and attest to the dignity of other emancipated "persons." The passage prefigures, tropologically, the story that Levinas goes on to recount about Bobby recognizing the prisoners in the POW camp as "men": "halfway through our long captivity ... a wandering dog entered our lives ... For him, there was no doubt that we were men."[56]

As the essay comes to a conclusion, Levinas declares, "This dog was the last Kantian in Nazi Germany, without the brain needed to universalize maxims and drives," seeming, here, to return to the anthropocentrism (and, indeed, the anthropomorphism) of which his philosophical orientation has been accused. But his final gesture suggests, rather, a different way to think animalian being than as a philosophical question: "He was a descendant of the dogs of Egypt. And his friendly growling, his animal faith, was born from the silence of his forefathers on the banks of the Nile."[57] What I have elsewhere called "figural historiography" – a writing of history that attends to the affective resonances and hauntings of the past as they appear in, and make demands upon, the present – operates here to effect a genealogy of "dog" who, like his palindromic other, returns to confer upon the present a sacralized destiny.[58] Dog and Jew do not belong to separate domains in this figural nexus, but rather both participate in divine history. While the recognition conferred in the encounter is not, thematically at least, mutual for the Kantian human in the scene, God and dog, Levinas implies, are in dialogue in Jewish history. There is a link, an intimacy between "man" and "friend," conferred by the hermeneutics of storytelling, which, like dreams, juxtaposes, condenses, and prefigures according to an affective logic of association, both figuratively *and* literally.

"Name of a Dog" thus performs, in its figural extravagance, another "narrative ethology," another poetics of narrative, in the place where animal being and language meet. In so doing, it follows logics other than those of philosophical humanism, logics more proximate to Talmudic interpretation, literary hermeneutics and psychoanalysis, figural logics that reanimate the place where language and "animal," or language and the living being, meet.

Notes

1. Susan Crane, *Animal Encounters: Contacts and Concepts in Medieval Britain* (Philadelphia: University of Pennsylvania Press, 2012); Akira Lippit, *Electric*

Animal: Toward a Rhetoric of Wildlife (Minneapolis: University of Minnesota Press, 2000).

2. Bruce Holsinger, "Of Pigs and Parchment: Medieval Studies and the Coming of the Animal," *PMLA* 124, no. 2 (2009): 616–23.

3. Louis Althusser, *Writings on Psychoanalysis: Freud and Lacan*, ed. Olivier Corpet and François Matheron, trans. Jeffrey Mehlamn (New York: Columbia University Press, 1996), 23.

4. See Katie Gentile, "Animals as the Symptom of Psychoanalysis Or, the Potential for Interspecies Co-Emergence in Psychoanalysis," *Studies in Gender and Sexuality* 19, no. 1 (2018): 7–13; also Maud Ellman, "Psychoanalytic Animal," in *A Concise Companion to Psychoanalysis, Literature and Culture*, ed. Laura Marcus and Ankhi Mukherjee (Oxford: Wiley Blackwell, 2014), 328–50.

5. See Waldo Shumway, "The Recapitulation Theory," *The Quarterly Review of Biology* 7, no. 1 (1932): 93–99.

6. Susan McHugh, *Animal Stories: Narrating Across Species Lines* (Minneapolis: University of Minnesota Press, 2011), 1.

7. Ibid., 217.

8. Ibid., 212.

9. Lippit, *Electric Animal*, 78–80.

10. James Serpell, "Anthropomorphism and Anthropomorphic Selection – Beyond the 'Cute Response,'" *Society & Animals* 11, no. 1 (2003): 83–100. See also Lippit, *Electric Animal*, 78–80.

11. Jacques Lacan, *Écrits: A Selection*, trans. Bruce Fink (New York: Norton, 2002). For a more extended examination of Lacan's use of animal studies, see, among others, Freccero, "Mirrors of Culture," *California Italian Studies* 2, no. 1 (2011), https://escholarship.org/uc/item/8c91sock. For an essay that puzzles over the appearance of animals in Lacan's later work, see Peter Buse, "The Dog and the Parakeet: Lacan Among the Animals," *Angelaki* 22, no.4 (2017): 133–45.

12. Roger Callois, "Mimicry and Legendary Psychasthenia," in *The Edge of Surrealism: A Roger Callois Reader*, ed. and trans. Claudine Frank (Durham, NC: Duke University Press, 2003), 91–103.

13. Jacques Lacan, *Écrits: A Selection*. trans. Bruce Fink (New York: Norton, 2002), 3–9.

14. Jacques Derrida, *The Animal That Therefore I Am*, ed. Marie-Louise Mallet, trans. David Willis (New York: Fordham University Press, 2008), 135.

15. Jakob von Uexküll, *A Foray into the Worlds of Animals and Humans: With a Theory of Meaning*, trans. Joseph D. O'Neill (Minneapolis: University of Minnesota Press, 2010).

16. See McHugh's discussion on 216–17; also Donna Haraway, *When Species Meet* (Minneapolis: University of Minnesota Press, 2008), 30–32.

17. Donna Haraway, *When Species Meet*, 3–4. See also her discussion of material-semiotic figures, 4.

18. "Language, as trope, is always privative," in Paul de Man, "Autobiography as De-facement," *MLN* 94, no. 5 (1979): 930. I understand him to mean that linguistic figuration is deprived of the full human sensorium (smell, sight, touch, sound) in its efforts – often successful – to convey the whole gamut of the senses.

19. Matthew Senior, David L. Clark, Carla Freccero, "Editors' Preface: Ecce Animot: Postanimality from Cave to Screen," *Yale French Studies* 127 (2015): 2.
20. Derrida, *The Animal*, 104.
21. Haraway, *When Species Meet*, 4.
22. See Lippit, *Electric Animal*, 163; he is referring to Sigmund Freud, *The Interpretation of Dreams* (1900), *SE* 4: 131 ff., Chapter 3.
23. Lippit, *Electric Animal*, 165–66.
24. Erica Fudge, *Animal* (London: Reaktion Books, 2002), 12, 16; see also McHugh, *Animal Stories*, 218.
25. Emmanuel Levinas, *Difficile liberté: Essais sur le judaïsme* (Paris: Albin Michel, 1963, repr. 1976), 199–202; " Name of a Dog," in *Difficult Freedom: Essays on Judaism*, trans. Seán Hand (Baltimore: Johns Hopkins University Press, 1990), 151–53.
26. Emmanuel Levinas, "The Paradox of Morality," in *Animal Philosophy: Essential Readings in Continental Philosophy*, ed. Matthew Calarco and Peter Atterton (London: Continuum, repr. 2005), 49. The interview is originally published in *The Provocation of Levinas: Rethinking the Other*, ed. Robert Bernasconi and David Wood (London: Routledge, 1988), 169.
27. Bentham is a philosopher known as the founder of utilitarianism.
28. Levinas, "The Paradox of Morality," 50.
29. For several attuned, philosophically focused, readings of this essay, see John Llewelyn, "Am I Obsessed by Bobby? (Humanism of the Other Animal)," in *Re-Reading Levinas*, ed. Robert Bernasconi and Simon Critchley (Bloomington: Indiana University Press, 1991), 234–45; and Peter Atterton, "Ethical Cynicism," in *Animal Philosophy*, 51–61.
30. Peter Hulme, *Colonial Encounters: Europe and the Native Caribbean, 1492–1797* (London: Routledge, 1986, repr. 1992), 11–12.
31. Derrida writes, "No, no, my cat, the cat that looks at me in my bedroom or bathroom, this cat that is perhaps not 'my cat' or 'my pussycat,' does not appear here to represent, like an ambassador, the immense symbolic responsibility with which our culture has always charged the feline race … " (*The Animal*, 9).
32. Derrida, *The Animal*, 115.
33. Ibid., 116.
34. Ibid., 66.
35. Levinas, "Name of a Dog," 152.
36. Ibid., 153.
37. Ibid., 152.
38. Ibid., 153.
39. Ibid., 153.
40. Ibid., 153.
41. David L. Clark, "On Being 'The Last Kantian in Nazi Germany': Dwelling with Animals after Levinas," in *Animal Acts: Configuring the Human in Western History*, ed. Jennifer Ham and Matthew Senior (New York: Routledge, 1997), 165–98.
42. J. M. Coetzee, *The Lives of Animals*, ed. Amy Gutman (Princeton: Princeton University Press, 2017), 49.
43. Clark, "On Being," 178.
44. Levinas, "Name of a Dog," 151.

45. Clark, "On Being," 178.

46. Levinas, "Name of a Dog," 151.

47. Prosopopeia is the rhetorical figure that consists in giving a face to a name, or personification; it is also used as the figure of speech to describe animals or objects being ascribed human characteristics. Here the name is not explicitly mentioned, but it is referred to by the expression, and the "personification" or face-giving works in two directions, toward dog and toward God.

48. Nicolas Abraham and Maria Torok, *The Shell and the Kernel: Renewals of Psychoanalysis, Volume I*, ed. and trans. Nicholas Rand (Chicago: University of Chicago Press, 1994); see also *The Wolfman's Magic Word: A Cryptonomy*, trans. Nicholas Rand (Minneapolis: University of Minnesota Press, 1986).

49. Akira Lippit, "Magnetic Animal: Derrida, Wildlife, Animetaphor," *MLN* 113, no. 5 (1998): 1121.

50. Ibid., 1121.

51. Levinas, "Name of a Dog," 153.

52. Eva Hayward, "Lessons from a Starfish," in *Queering the Non/Human*, ed. Noreen Giffney and Myra Hird (Farnham: Ashgate, 2008), 257–58.

53. Levinas, "Name of a Dog," 151–52.

54. Lippitt, *Electric Animal*, 166.

55. Levinas, "Name of a Dog," 152.

56. Ibid., 153. Throughout, I have been using the term "tropologically" in its secularized sense, as figurative language. Here, however, tropology returns to its roots in Biblical hermeneutics as a question of interpretation: is the Biblical text to be read literally or figuratively? This is the question Levinas is asking regarding the dog in Exodus, and he answers it – after mentioning hermeneutics several times – by saying that Exodus is about a literal dog (or dogs, as is the case), that is, it is literally, in that episode, about dogs qua dogs. But by "illustrating" his point about the dogs in Exodus through the story of Bobby, he makes Exodus prefigure the scene in the POW camp, when the dog attests to the humanity of the captives by recognizing their humanity as men. This is borne out by the penultimate sentence of the essay, "He was a descendant of the dogs of Egypt" (153).

57. Levinas, "Name of a Dog," 153.

58. Freccero, "Figural Historiography: Dogs, Humans, and Cynanthropic Becomings," in *Comparatively Queer*, ed. Jarrod Hayes, Margaret Higonnet, and William J. Spurlin (Basingstoke: Palgrave, 2010): 45–67.

FURTHER READING

Abel, Elizabeth. *Virginia Woolf and the Fictions of Psychoanalysis*. Chicago: University of Chicago Press, 1989.

Ahmed, Sara. *The Promise of Happiness*. Durham, NC: Duke University Press, 2010.

Allen, Thomas E. "A Psychoanalytic Look at Herman Melville from His Use of Source Materials for *Moby-Dick*." *Psychoanalytic Review* 96, no. 5 (2009): 743–67.

Armstrong, Philip. *Shakespeare in Psychoanalysis*. London: Routledge, 2001.

Bartolovich, Crystal, Jean E. Howard, David Hilman, and Adrian Poole, eds. *Marx and Freud: Great Shakespeareans Volume X*. New York: Continuum, 2012.

Berlant, Lauren. *Cruel Optimism*. Durham, NC: Duke University Press, 2011.

Berman, Emanuel. *Essential Papers on Literature and Psychoanalysis*. New York: New York University Press, 1993.

Bernstein, J. M. "Self-Knowledge as Praxis: Narrative and Narration in Psychoanalysis" in *Narrative in Culture: Uses of Storytelling in the Sciences, Philosophy and Literature*, 53–80. Edited by Cristopher Nash. New York: Routledge, 1990.

Billington, Josie. *Is Literature Healthy?* Oxford: Oxford University Press, 2016.

Bion, W. R. *Learning from Experience*. London: Maresfield, 1962.

Second Thoughts. London: Maresfield, 1967.

Attention and Interpretation. London: Maresfield, 1970.

Bollas, Christopher. *Cracking Up: The Work of Unconscious Experience*. New York: Routledge, 1995.

The Mystery of Things. London: Routledge, 1999.

Brivic, Sheldon. *Joyce Through Lacan and Žižek: Explorations*. Basingstoke: Palgrave Macmillan, 2008.

Brooks, Peter. *Reading for the Plot*. New York: Vintage Books, 1984.

"The Idea of a Psychoanalytic Literary Criticism." *Critical Inquiry*, 13 (1987): 334–48.

Brown, Carolyn. *Shakespeare and Psychoanalytic Theory*. London: Bloomsbury Arden Shakespeare, 2015.

Butler, Judith. *Gender Trouble: Feminism and the Subversion of Identity*. New York: Routledge, 1990.

Precarious Life: The Powers of Mourning. London: Verso, 2004.

Camden, Vera J., ed. *Compromise Formations: Current Directions in Psychoanalytic Criticism*. Kent, OH: Kent State University Press, 1989.

Caruth, Cathy. *Unclaimed Experience: Trauma, Narrative and History*. Baltimore, MD: Johns Hopkins University Press, 1996.

Literature in the Ashes of History. Baltimore, MD: Johns Hopkins University, 2013.

Charles, Marilyn. *Psychoanalysis and Literature: The Stories We Live*. New York: Rowman and Littlefield, 2015.

Cheng, Anne. *The Melancholy of Race: Psychoanalysis, Assimilation, and Hidden Grief*. Oxford: Oxford University Press, 2001.

Christoff, Alicia M. *Novel Relations: Victorian Fiction and British Psychoanalysis*. Princeton: Princeton University Press, 2019.

Critchley, Simon, and Jamieson Webster. *Stay Illusion! The Hamlet Doctrine*. New York: Pantheon Books, 2013.

Dalsimer, Katherine. *Virginia Woolf: Becoming a Writer*. New Haven: Yale University Press, 2001.

Dalton, Elizabeth. *Unconscious Structure in "The Idiot": A Study in Literature and Psychoanalysis*. Princeton: Princeton University Press, 1979.

Davis, Philip. *Reading for Life*. Oxford: Oxford University Press, 2020.

Dean, Tim. *Unlimited Intimacy: Reflections on the Subculture of Barebacking*. Chicago: University of Chicago Press, 2009.

Derrida, Jacques. *Positions*. Chicago: University of Chicago Press, 1981.

Echevarría, Roberto González, and Enrique Pupo-Walker, eds. *The Cambridge History of Latin American Literature*. Vol. 3. Cambridge: Cambridge University Press, 1996.

Edelman, Lee. *No Future: Queer Theory and the Death Drive*. Durham, NC: Duke University Press, 2004.

Elliot, Anthony. *Psychoanalytic Theory. An Introduction*. Durham, NC: Duke University Press, 2002.

Ellman, Maud, ed. *Psychoanalytic Literary Criticism*. London: Longman, 1982.

Eng, David L. *The Feeling of Kinship: Queer Liberalism and the Racialization of Intimacy*. Durham, NC: Duke University Press, 2010.

Fanon, Frantz. *Black Skin, White Masks*. New York: Grove Press, 2008.

Felman, Shoshana. (ed.), *Literature and Psychoanalysis – The Question of Reading: Otherwise*. Baltimore: Johns Hopkins University Press, 1982.

Felman, Shoshana, and Dori Laub. *Testimony: Crises of Witnessing in Literature, Psychoanalysis, and History*. New York: Routledge, 1992.

Ferro, Antonino. *Psychoanalysis as Therapy and Story Telling*. London, New York: Routledge, 2001.

Fineman, Joel. *Shakespeare's Perjured Eye: The Invention of Poetic Subjectivity in the Sonnets*. Berkeley: University of California Press, 1986.

Fonagy, Peter. *Attachment Theory and Psychoanalysis*. New York: Other Press, 2001.

Foxe, Gladys. "'And Nobody Knows What's Going to Happen to Anybody': Fear and Futility in Jack Kerouac's *On the Road* and Why It Is Important." *Psychoanalytic Review* 95, no. 1 (2008): 45–60.

Frosh, Stephen. *Hauntings: Psychoanalysis and Ghostly Transmissions*. New York: Palgrave Macmillan, 2013.

Gallop, Jane. *The Daughter's Seduction: Feminism and Psychoanalysis*. London: Macmillan, 1982.

———. *Reading Lacan*. Ithaca, NY: Cornell University Press, 1985.

Garber, Marjorie. *Shakespeare's Ghost Writers: Literature as Uncanny Causality*, 2nd ed. New York: Routledge, 2010.

Gay, Volney P. *Joy and the Objects of Psychoanalysis: Literature, Belief and Neurosis*. New York: State University of New York Press, 2001.

George, Sheldon. *Trauma and Race: A Lacanian Study of African American Racial Identity*. Waco, TX: Baylor University Press, 2016.

Giddens, Anthony. *Modernity and Self-Identity*. Palo Alto, CA: Stanford University Press, 1991.

Goldstein, Jan. "The Woolfs' Response to Freud." *Psychoanalytic Quarterly* 43, no. 3 (1974): 438–76.

Goulimari, Pelagia. *Literary Criticism and Theory: From Plato to Postcolonialism*. London: Routledge, 2015. (See section on "Psychoanalytic Literary Criticism.")

Green, André. *The Tragic Effect: The Oedipus Complex in Tragedy*. Translated by Alan Sheridan. Cambridge: Cambridge University Press, 1979.

Green, Kelda L. *Reading Aid: Investigating the Therapeutic Potential of Literature*. New York: Anthem Press, 2020.

Grosz, Elizabeth. *Jacques Lacan: A Feminist Introduction*. New York: Routledge, 2015.

Groves, James E. *Hamlet on the Couch: What Shakespeare Taught Freud*. London: Routledge, 2017.

Gunn, Daniel. *Psychoanalysis and Fiction*. Cambridge: Cambridge University Press, 1988.

Hanly, Margaret Ann Fitzpatrick. *Essential Papers on Masochism*. New York: New York University Press, 1995.

Hirsch, Marianne. *The Mother/Daughter Plot: Narrative, Psychoanalysis, Feminism*. Bloomington: Indiana University Press, 1989.

Hogan, Patrick C. *On Interpretation: Meaning and Inference in Law, Psychoanalysis, and Literature*. Athens: University of Georgia Press, 2008.

Homans, Peter. *The Ability to Mourn: Disillusionment and the Social Origin of Psychoanalysis*. Chicago: Chicago University Press, 1989.

Jacobs, Amber. *On Matricide: Myth, Psychoanalysis, and the Law of the Mother*. New York: Columbia University Press, 2007.

Jameson, Fredric. *The Political Unconscious: Narrative as a Socially Symbolic Act*. New York: Cornell University, 1981.

Johnson, Barbara. *The Feminist Difference: Literature, Psychoanalysis, Race, and Gender*. Cambridge, MA: Harvard University Press, 1998.

Khanna, Ranjana. *Dark Continents: Psychoanalysis and Colonialism*. Durham, NC: Duke University Press, 2003.

Klein, Melanie. *The Psycho-Analysis of Children*. London: Hogarth Press and the Institute of Psychoanalysis, 1949.

Kris, Anton. "Unlearning and Learning Psychoanalysis." *American Imago* 70, no. 3 (2013): 341–55.

Laplanche, Jean. *Problématiques III: La Sublimation*. Paris: Presses Universitaires de France, 1980.

de Lauretis, Teresa. *The Practice of Love: Lesbian Sexuality and Perverse Desire*. Bloomington: Indiana University Press, 1994.
Freud's Drive: Psychoanalysis, Literature and Film. New York: Palgrave Macmillan, 2008.
Lee, Hermione. *Virginia Woolf*. New York: Knopf, 1997.
"On Being Ill" in *Body Parts: Essays on Life-Writing*, 86–99 London: Pimlico, 2008.
Levinas, Emmanuel. *Basic Philosophical Writings*. Edited by Adriaan T. Peperzak, Simon Critchley, and Robert Bernasconi. Bloomington: Indiana University Press, 1996.
Loewald, Hans. "On the Therapeutic Action of Psychoanalysis." *International Journal of Psychoanalysis* 4 (1960): 16–33.
Lupton, Julia R., and Kenneth Reinhard. *After Oedipus: Shakespeare in Psychoanalysis*. Ithaca, NY: Cornell University Press, 1993.
Malcolm, Janet. "A House of One's Own" in *Forty-One False Starts: Essays on Artists and Writers*. New York: Farrar, Straus Giroux, 2013.
Marcus, Laura, and Ankhi Mukherjee, eds. *A Concise Companion to Psychoanalysis, Literature and Culture*. Chichester: John Wiley and Sons, 2014.
Marcus, Laura. *Dreams of Modernity: Psychoanalysis, Literature, Cinema*. New York: Cambridge University Press, 2014.
Meisel, Perry, and Walter Kendrick, eds. *Bloomsbury/Freud: The Letters of James and Alix Strachey 1924–1925*. New York: W. W. Norton, 1990.
Menon, Mahdavi. *Indifference to Difference*. Minneapolis: University of Minnesota Press, 2015.
Mitchell, Juliet. *Women: The Longest Revolution: Essays on Feminism, Literature, and Psychoanalysis*. London: Virago, 1984.
Morgenstern, Naomi. *Wild Child: Intensive Parenting and Posthumanist Ethics*. Minneapolis: Minnesota University Press, 2018.
Muller, John, ed. *The Purloined Poe: Lacan, Derrida, and Psychoanalytic Writing*. Baltimore, MD: Johns Hopkins University Press, 1987.
Phillips, Adam. *Promises, Promises: Essays on Literature and Psychoanalysis*. New York: Basic Books, 2002.
Going Sane. London: Penguin, 2006.
ed. *The Penguin Freud Reader*. London: Penguin, 2006.
Side Effects. London: Hamish Hamilton, 2006.
In Writing: Essays on Literature. London: Random House, 2016.
Rabaté, Jean-Michel. *The Cambridge Introduction to Literature and Psychoanalysis*. New York: Cambridge University Press, 2014.
Razinsky, Liran. *Freud, Psychoanalysis and Death*. Cambridge: Cambridge University Press, 2013.
Ricouer, Paul. *On Psychoanalysis*. Cambridge: Polity, 2012.
Rose, Jacqueline. *The Case of Peter Pan or the Impossibility of Children's Fiction*. Philadelphia: Philadelphia Press, 1984.
On Not Being Able to Sleep: Psychoanalysis and the Modern World. London: Vintage, 2004.
Rose, Phyllis. *Woman of Letters: A Life of Virginia Woolf*. New York: Harcourt Brace Jovanovich, 1978,

Roth, Merav. *A Psychoanalytic Perspective on Reading Literature (Art, Creativity and Psychoanalysis)*. London and New York: Routledge, 2019.

Schorske, C. *Fin-de-Siècle Vienna: Politics and Culture*. New York: Vintage/Random House, 1981.

Scott, Darieck. *Extravagant Abjection: Blackness, Power, and Sexuality in the African American Literature Imagination*. New York: New York University Press, 2010.

Silverman, Kaja. *Male Subjectivity at the Margins*. New York: Routledge, 1992.

Spillers, Hortense. "Interstices: A Small Drama of Words" in *Black, White, and in Color: Essays on American Literature and Culture*. Chicago: University of Chicago Press, 2003.

"Mama's Baby, Papa's Maybe: An American Grammar Book" in *Black, White, and in Color: Essays on American Literature and Culture*. Chicago: University of Chicago Press, 2003.

Symington, Joan, and Neville Symington. *The Clinical Thinking of Wilfred Bion*. New York: Routledge, 1996.

Svolos, Thomas. *Twenty-First Century Psychoanalysis*. London: Karnac, 2017.

Tangerås, Thor M. *Literature and Transformation: A Narrative Study of Life-Changing Reading Experiences*. New York: Anthem Press, 2020.

Tutter, Adele. "*Set This House on Fire*: The Self-Analysis of Raymond Carver." *Psychoanalytic Quarterly* 80, no. 4 (2011): 915–59.

"Text as Muse, Muse as Text: Janáček, Kamila, and the Role of Fantasy in Musical Creativity." *American Imago* 72, no. 4 (2015): 407–50.

"A Veritable Murder: Émile Zola, His Friend Paul Cézanne, and His Book *L'Œuvre*." *American Imago* 75, no. 1 (2018): 67–103.

"Sex, Text, Ur-Text: Freud's Dora and the Suggestive Text." *International Journal of Psychoanalysis* 100, no. 3 (2020): 523–48.

Walton, Jean. *Fair Sex, Savage Dreams: Race, Psychoanalysis, Sexual Difference*. Durham, NC: Duke University Press, 2001.

Whitebook, Joel. *Freud: An Intellectual Biography*. New York: Cambridge University Press, 2017.

Winnicott, D. W. *Playing and Reality*. London: Tavistock Publications, 1971.

Wyatt, Jean. *Reconstructing Desire: The Role of the Unconscious in Women's Reading and Writing*. Chapel Hill: University of North Carolina Press, 1990.

INDEX